Evelyn M. Monahan and Rosemary Neidel-Greenlee

A Few Good Women

Evelyn M. Monahan, a retired psychologist, served in the Women's Army Corps from 1961 until 1967. She subsequently earned her M.Ed. and Ph.D. at Georgia State University and her M.Div. in theology and ethics at Emory University. She worked at the Department of Veterans Affairs from 1980 to 1996.

Rosemary Neidel-Greenlee served in the U.S. Navy Nurse Corps on active duty from 1962 until 1965 and on reserve duty between 1989 and 1991. She has a master's degree in nursing from Emory University and worked at the U.S. Veterans Affairs Medical Center in Atlanta from 1981 to 2002.

ALSO BY

EVELYN M. MONAHAN AND ROSEMARY NEIDEL-GREENLEE

And If I Perish:
Frontline U.S. Army Nurses in World War II

All This Hell:
U.S. Nurses Imprisoned by the Japanese

Albanian Escape:
The True Story of U.S. Army Nurses Behind Enemy Lines

A FEW GOOD WOMEN

A FEW GOOD WOMEN

★

AMERICA'S MILITARY WOMEN FROM WORLD WAR I TO THE WARS IN IRAQ AND AFGHANISTAN

Evelyn M. Monahan
and
Rosemary Neidel-Greenlee

ANCHOR BOOKS

A DIVISION OF RANDOM HOUSE, INC.

NEW YORK

FIRST ANCHOR BOOKS EDITION, MARCH 2011

Copyright © 2010 by Evelyn M. Monahan and Rosemary Neidel-Greenlee

All rights reserved. Published in the United States by Anchor Books, a division of Random House, Inc., New York, and in Canada by Random House of Canada Limited, Toronto. Originally published in hardcover in the United States by Alfred A. Knopf, a division of Random House, Inc., New York, in 2010.

Anchor Books and colophon are registered trademarks of Random House, Inc.

The Library of Congress has cataloged the Knopf edition as follows:
Monahan, Evelyn.
A few good women : America's military women from World War I to the wars in Iraq and Afghanistan / Evelyn M. Monahan and Rosemary Neidel-Greenlee.
p. cm.
Includes bibliographical references and index.
1. United States—Armed Forces—Women—History—20th century.
2. United States—Armed Forces—Women—History—21st century.
3. Women and war—United States—History. I. Neidel-Greenlee, Rosemary, 1941–
II. Title.
UB418.W65M66 2010
355.0082'0973—dc22
2009038529

Anchor ISBN: 978-1-4000-9560-5

Author photographs © Herbert Kuper

www.anchorbooks.com

Printed in the United States of America
10 9 8 7 6 5 4 3 2 1

To Nancy A. Hardesty, Ph.D.
With deep appreciation for introducing me
to the importance of women's history

EVELYN MONAHAN

and

To all the U.S. military women who have lived this history

ROSEMARY NEIDEL-GREENLEE

Until lions have their own historians, tales of the hunt shall always glorify the hunter.

—Kenyan Proverb

CONTENTS

ILLUSTRATIONS

INTRODUCTION

Feelings of patriotism have never been an exclusive attribute of the male heart. Throughout recorded history, women have defied the cultural conventions of gender roles that barred them not only from combat but from the military in general. Despite those cultural conventions, women around the world have always included themselves in the defense of their homelands and even in combat itself. In biblical times, Deborah led soldiers during the occupation of Canaan, and Esther risked her life to plead before an enemy king for mercy for her people.

In the mid-ninth century BC in southern Iraq, two women, Queens Zabibi and Samsi, merged their armies and led them into battle against the Assyrians, who planned to add their lands to the possessions of the Assyrian king, Tiglath-Pileser IV. At the time, the Assyrian army was considered one of the most powerful in the world. Zabibi and Samsi rode at the head of their armies and put up a significant battle.

Hundreds of years later, another queen, Bat Zabbai, accompanied her husband, Odainat, on hunting trips and in the wars he fought. When Odainat died in AD 266, Zabbai became regent for her young son and led her armies to acquire new lands. In 269, she conquered all of Egypt and claimed what land remained for Syria. Eventually, Zabbai's kingdom stretched from "Egypt to the Bosphorus, and from the Mediterranean to India." She then ruled over the Eastern Roman Empire and declared herself to be completely independent from Rome.[1]

If we add to these women warriors Queen Boudicea of Britain, who led her troops in battles where thousands of Roman soldiers and civilians were killed; Queen Thyra of Denmark; Joan of Arc; and Catherine the Great, Empress of Russia, we have a strong but limited sampling of the patriotism and military prowess that have been no strangers to women despite the fact that their lives and deeds are not well known in twenty-first-century America.

We do not have to look far into history to discover that patriotism and courage in the face of war have never been absent from the female heart. American women have always been a volunteer force in the defense of their nation. During the Revolutionary War, women volunteered and followed colonial troops to the front lines as laundresses, cooks, and nurses. Some accompanied their husbands, and others disguised themselves as men, enlisted, and served as soldiers. Margaret Corbin, whom some historians credit as the source of the Molly Pitcher legends, took over her husband's cannon when he was killed during the Battle of Fort Washington in 1776. She fired on British troops until she was wounded. Two years later, Mary Hayes did the same at the Battle of Monmouth in New Jersey. Margaret Corbin's grave and monument can be found today in the cemetery of the U.S. Military Academy at West Point, while Mary Hayes's statue stands near her gravesite in Carlisle, Pennsylvania, home of the U.S. Army's Institute of Military History and the U.S. Army War College.

Not all women who felt an irresistible urge to enlist in their nation's military chose the army as their preferred branch of service. For some women, the sea exerted a greater attraction than cavalry posts or cities, and for them, the navy or marines was the military service of choice. One such woman was Hannah Snell, who in the 1700s left her home to go in search of her missing husband. For safety reasons, Hannah dressed as a man, believing the disguise would afford her more protection as she walked the roads and streets in pursuit of her quest. As time passed and neither her husband nor a job was in sight, Hannah enlisted as a marine in Adm. Edward Boscawen's fleet as they recruited sailors and marines in the town of Portsmouth, England. Within days, she sailed as a marine to the East Indies. Despite the fact that she was wounded several times during combat at Pondicherry, she was able to keep her gender hidden from superiors, crew, and fellow marines. Eventually, Hannah served aboard the frigate *Eltham,* and for many months passed as a man despite the fact that the crew nicknamed her "Molly" because of her smooth and whisker-free skin. When her secret finally did come out, she was mustered out of the service with a pension of one shilling a day. Hannah supplemented that pension by joining a circus and theatrical group, where she exhibited herself in her marine uniform at county fairs throughout England. In 1789, at age seventy, she died, still sad that she had never found the husband who had deserted her years ago.

Another woman drawn to military service at sea was Lucy Brewster. In 1812, Lucy disguised herself as a man and, under the assumed name of

George Baker, enlisted in the marines. Lucy, alias "George," was assigned to the frigate *Constitution,* where she became an excellent rifleman and fought alongside other crew members off the coast of Brazil when the *Constitution* engaged the frigate *Java* in a long and intense sea battle. While the *Constitution*'s forty-four shipboard guns blasted away at the *Java,* "George" perched in the top mast and fired on the enemy with her musket. After several additional sea battles and a successful career as a marine, George Baker retired, reclaimed her identity, and married.

A Few Good Women is the story of how the U.S. women's military corps came into being. It tells of the women who fought for the right to defend their country and its Constitution by serving in America's armed forces as enlisted members and officers with full military rank and benefits, and of the fight and issues still being fought and addressed by the military women of today for the right to serve in combat units as well as in combat support positions. This right has been earned by the blood, sweat, and tears of the more than one million women who have volunteered to serve this nation. These women have lived a proud history that is too little known by the American people, too little addressed by American historians, too little appreciated by the American government, and still to be rewarded by granting all women the full rights of citizenship granted specifically to men by the U.S. Constitution.

A FEW GOOD WOMEN

PROLOGUE

⭐

Those who live in memory are really never dead.
                              —Kate Morton, *The Shifting Fog*

Falluja, Iraq: 23 June 2005, 1920 hours (7:20 p.m.). Cpl. Sally J. Saalman finished roll call of the women marines in her charge, climbed onboard the old truck, and seated herself on one of the parallel benches that ran along both sides of the cargo area. Her eyes took in the deserted streets as the three-vehicle convoy began the fifteen-minute trip back to Camp Falluja and the Women's Marine Corps barracks. Corporal Saalman and the other nineteen female Leathernecks in the Women's Search Force had been making this trip twice a day since the inception of the special unit in February 2005. The routine of the Women's Search Force was as predictable as sunrise and sunset. Day in and day out, the members of this platoon awakened at 0500 hours, ate breakfast, loaded onto a cargo truck, and were transported along the identical route to the staging area in "downtown" Falluja.

From this central point, the Women's Search Force was dispersed to various checkpoints throughout the city and began their daily mission of stopping and searching Iraqi women for contraband items or messages they might be carrying to, or on behalf of, an insurgent group.

Now, in the 120-degree evening heat, the women marines were glad to be finished with work for the day and headed home. The improvised armored paneling on both sides of the old cargo truck extended only as high as the women's shoulders and left them with an unobstructed view of either side of the road and backward and forward on the road itself. Looking in the direction from which they had come, it was clear that the second Humvee, whose mission was to protect the convoy from the rear, was nowhere in sight. In compliance with standing orders, the rear guard was keeping a prescribed distance as part of the security plan to protect escorted vehicles. The truck slowed slightly, and the women looked toward the lead Humvee to see if they could determine what was causing the slowdown. The marines in the lead were signaling to the only car in sight to pull to the side of the road and stop. The car's driver obeyed immediately, and the convoy continued on its way. As the Humvee moved forward and cleared the car, the driver pushed down on the accelerator and aimed the car at the cargo truck carrying the women marines.

In a matter of seconds, the car struck its target just behind the cab on the passenger side. The sound of the explosion rolled outward as thick fingers of orange and yellow flames reached upward, then closed around the truck like an angry fist determined to destroy its enemy. The heat was so intense that two male marines in the cab and two women in the cargo area were killed instantly. For those still alive, the horror was just beginning. Despite their own wounds, women marines crawled back to the truck to drag their more severely wounded sisters from the still burning truck. Women's voices were calling for water, while another badly burned female asked over and over again how she looked. The extreme heat that had fused one woman's goggles to her cheeks also exploded the ammunition the women carried. In less than a minute, enemy snipers began firing at the wounded and dead marines scattered in the road.[1]

1

★

No army can withstand the strength of an idea whose time has come.
—Victor Hugo

The entrance of American women into the U. S. military was not an easy one. Its conception was analogous to parthenogenesis, and few men in the military, Congress, or the street saw the product of that conception as anything that would affect mankind, America, or the American culture in a positive manner. The population as a whole and particularly those in power saw the very idea as a threat to America and an abomination to the "natural order" that was the foundation of American society. That ingrained belief was supported by every major institution that held power to keep the status quo or to effect change: America's laws, religious denominations, educational systems, labor markets, military, manufacturing, and marketing all stood in some part on the belief in support of the God-given natural law that prescribed and enforced gender roles that had been handed down from one generation to the next and were the molds in which the lives of Americans were shaped and encouraged to grow. There had always been a fringe element of women who felt they should be allowed equal rights with men, in citizenship and opportunity, but society had always known and willingly supported the fact that these women and their ideas were, to say the least, "unnatural" and made sure they would pay a high price for straying outside the natural boundaries inherent in men and women by their very nature.

True, there were times, as in times of war or national emergency, when men had to set these natural limits aside for the good of society, but those same men called for a return to "normalcy" once the emergency was past.

When the United States entered World War I on 6 April 1917, there were approximately 2,000 women volunteers serving as enlisted members of the U.S. Navy (USN). By 1918, that number had increased to 11,000, and yeomen (F) (for "female"), as they were designated by the U.S. Navy, were serving in U.S. Naval Districts throughout the continental United States. In a society that strongly believed that "a woman's place is in the home," women between the ages of eighteen and thirty-five headed for recruiting stations to sign up and "Free a Man to Fight."

Not all Americans, including men serving in the navy, were happy about the service of women in a previously all-male bastion. Accepting women as enlisted navy personnel was a gigantic change, and in the minds of many, it was a drastic mistake. Newspapers ran articles on the subject, and letters from readers flooded in, expressing a majority of negative responses to the Navy Department action. Many of the American people, and particularly active-duty and retired navy personnel, wanted to know how such a horrible mistake could have been made. The "mistake" originated with Secretary of the Navy Josephus Daniels.

Like many Americans, Secretary Daniels could see the day when America would enter the fray of World War I as an active combatant. The United States had managed to stay out of the war raging in Europe since Germany had declared war on Russia and France within the first three days of August 1914, and Great Britain had declared war on Germany on 4 August. In 1916, a native-born Washington, D.C., resident and graduate of Washington Business High School, Charlotte L. Barry, called on the navy secretary to inquire about women being allowed to serve in the U.S. Navy. She did not receive an immediate answer but apparently raised a question that would alter the course of the history of women in the U.S. military.[1]

By the beginning of 1917, Secretary Daniels began asking his advisers if Department of the Navy regulations under the Naval Act of 1916 specified that U.S. citizens joining the navy had to be males. Those advisers confirmed Daniels's belief that there was no such regulation. The word "male" did not precede "U.S. citizen" in the regulations, and therefore there was an open avenue for Daniels to enact his idea of enlisting American women as a noncombatant force that would free otherwise land-locked and deskbound sailors and marines to become direct combatants against Germany, if and when America entered World War I.

In March 1917, the navy announced its decision to enlist women between the ages of eighteen and thirty-five as yeomen who would "free a man to fight" by taking over clerical duties and other positions that would be designated as the program grew. Hundreds and then thousands

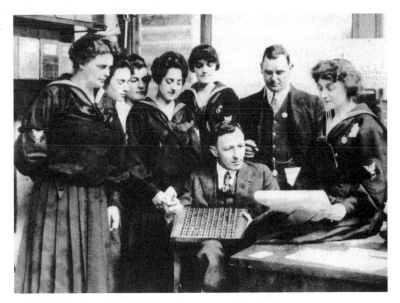

World War I Yeomen (F) at the munitions factory in Bloomfield, New Jersey.

of women responded by making their way to recruiting stations to enlist and take the oath of military service.

One of the first women to join the yeomen (F), Gertrude Edna Murray, signed up with the U.S. Naval Coast Reserve on 18 April 1917. "She was working at a company called Globe Wernicke Co. across the street from the Fleet Supply Base in South Brooklyn. Someone from the Navy called up and asked if they had someone who could set up a filing system and they recommended [her]." Soon Chief Yeoman Murray had a unit of forty women yeomen (F) to supervise. The Naval Reserve Force asked Chief Murray to assist with the design of the uniforms for a growing number of enlistees.[2]

In 1917, Barry, who, a year earlier, had first raised the question of gender with Secretary Daniels, joined the navy with her sister Sophie Bean, both as yeomen third class (F). Throughout the war, Charlotte was a typist at the Washington Navy Gun Factory or Washington Navy Yard. Following her discharge in 1919, Yeoman (F) Second Class Barry stayed on at the Navy Yard in a civilian capacity, doing her old active duty job until after the Korean War, when she retired in 1953.[3]

It is doubtful that Josephus Daniels foresaw the effect his decision would have from that day forward, not only for American women but for the U.S. Armed Forces and American society in general. Secretary Daniels had crossed the Rubicon, and he had taken the nation's future with him. The military service of American women in World War I would change the lives of all Americans living then and the lives of the tens of millions who would come after them.

Those changes would affect America's future in uneven steps and in lasting ways. The pattern that surfaces for women in time of war or emergencies can be seen in the development of the American West. Women pioneers faced all the dangers of travel by wagon train and of establishing homesteads and towns when their destination was reached. Not only did these women help establish family homesteads, farms, ranches, and towns in new territories; they helped defend those gains by fighting alongside men and fighting alone when those men were absent. As the west was tamed and towns grew, women were expected to step back into their former roles of homemakers and mothers. Nor did these "part-time citizens-for-emergencies" have the right to vote in national elections or in most state elections, save for a right given in some states for women to vote for school board members. Even this right was capriciously granted, as was evidenced by several cities in Kentucky in 1894 when they gave women the right to vote in school board elections, repealed the right in 1902, and then granted it again in 1912. As the plight of Blanche DuBois in *A Streetcar Named Desire* evidenced, "depending on the kindness of strangers" does not always turn out well. Women's suffrage, championed by Elizabeth Cady Stanton and Susan B. Anthony at the Seneca Falls Conference in 1848, was seventy years into a tough political fight against injustice and still more than two years of hard work away from a constitutional amendment.

In August 1918, with these arguments swirling around them, the U.S. Marine Corps, faced with heavy losses in France during the spring and summer of 1918, decided to enlist women. American women responded immediately, yet, by then, in addition to the U.S. Navy, which had peaked at 11,000 women sailors, there were other women's groups, the Red Cross, the YWCA, and the Salvation Army, who were requesting women volunteers for their organizations. Add to this fact that the end of the war was less than four months away; only 305 women became Marinettes before the armistice was signed on 11 November 1918.

Yeomen (F) and Marinettes were mainly assigned to clerical jobs, but a few found themselves assigned to more unorthodox billets for women such as radio operator or supervisor for naval shipments by rail. The Yeomanettes, as they were known, were referred to in the press of the day as "useful 'handymen.'"[4] Yeomen (F) served in Washington, D.C., in the Navy Department, at shipyards, and in many naval districts. It did not take base commanders and the Navy Department long to realize that women in military uniforms marching in parades and attending bond drives were a powerful statement for patriotism and increased the purchasing of bonds. To their credit, the Department of the Navy paid yeomen (F) and Marinettes the same pay received by sailors and marines of the same rank.

In November 1917, U.S. Gen. John J. Pershing placed a request with the U.S. War Department for one hundred U.S. telephone operators who spoke fluent French. At that time in America, all telephone operators were female, a fact that could not have escaped General Pershing's notice. It was very clear that the general intended to turn over U.S. Army switchboards in France to American women. Pershing had seen with his own

World War I contract telephone workers known as the "Hello Girls."

eyes the excellent work done by British women running switchboards and performing other duties in war zones and did not see why American women would not do just as well.

Unfortunately, the War Department's first efforts at filling General Pershing's request were doomed from the start. The War Department decided to advertise in Louisiana and Canada for women who spoke fluent French. Out of almost 300 applicants, only six possessed all the prerequisites of the job. Faced with this dismal failure, the U.S. Signal Corps decided to place ads in newspapers for telephone operators who spoke fluent French. By spring of 1918, more than 7,500 applications had been received, and the Signal Corps chose approximately 600 women. About 150 of these women were sent for further training in what the army expected from them while serving as telephone operators in France. The remaining 450 women were placed in a reserve for future training as the military situation dictated.

Despite the fact that these "Hello Girls," as U.S. Army Signal Corps operators were called, received the same pay as male soldiers in comparable jobs or with comparable responsibilities, the army would not supply the uniforms each woman was required to wear. Each telephone operator was expected to provide between $300 and $500 for the complete set of uniforms needed for various weather conditions and seasonal changes.

One important condition of service for these women that the U.S. Army did not make clear or expand upon was the essential fact that unlike the women serving in the U.S. Navy, women telephone operators with the army did not have military rank and were considered by the army to be contract civilian workers. Not only did this mean that Hello Girls were not considered veterans after their service and were not entitled to armed forces discharges, service ribbons, or medals, it also meant that should they be wounded or killed or captured overseas, they had no military standing for collective bargaining and could find themselves interned in a prisoner of war camp or an internment camp without the official protection of the United States under the rules of war.

It was arguably unconscionable to put these women into such danger without informed consent, and just as arguably unconscionable not to make clear to them that they were not considered members of the U.S. Armed Forces and would have no veterans' benefits when they left the service for any reason whatsoever. For the 223 Hello Girls who served in war zones overseas during World War I, there would undoubtedly have been questions and second thoughts if the U.S. Army and War Department had made their status with the military clear. When military and veterans' status was granted to these women in 1979, only a handful remained alive to know of their final victory.

Until the U.S. Army Nurse Corps was established in 1901, nurses working with the U.S. Army were contract employees. That contract relationship existed throughout the Spanish-American War of 1898. More than 1,500 nurses signed contracts with the army, and by September 1898 more than 1,000 were on duty, caring for U.S. Army personnel. Although the Spanish-American War ended officially on 12 August 1898, contract nurses were kept on active duty to care for the thousands of soldiers suffering from an epidemic of typhoid that had claimed thousands of lives. When the epidemic was brought under control in the United States, the army released all but seven hundred contract nurses, who remained on active duty. The number of contract nurses dropped to slightly more than two hundred in June 1900. During and following the Spanish-American War, twelve contract nurses died from typhoid fever, including Clara Louise Moss, who had volunteered as a subject to help Dr. Walter Reed, MC, determine the transmission vectors for the disease yellow fever. The efforts against yellow fever and the care of those stricken while on active duty with the army took a step forward when, on 20 June 1899, the surgeon general of the army established a Nurse Corps Division in his office that was tasked with coordinating the efforts of individual civilian groups such as the Daughters of the American Revolution and the Red Cross that were active in providing military nursing care to the U.S. Army.

In 1899, Surgeon General George M. Sternberg, who had previously not seen a need for a permanent Army Nurse Corps, asked the vice president of the National Society of the Daughters of the American Revolution (DAR), Dr. Anita Newcomb McGee, to write a federal bill for the establishment of a permanent, exclusively female U.S. Army Nurse Corps.

That bill went before Congress in 1901 and was passed on 2 February 1901, creating the U.S. Army Nurse Corps as a permanent corps of the Medical Department under the Army Reorganization Act (31 Stat. 753). The law also directed the surgeon general to keep a list of nurses with at least six months of satisfactory service with the army or on reserve status. This was the first reserve corps established within the Army Medical Department, and each reserve army nurse signed an agreement to report by letter every six months to the surgeon general and to report for active duty whenever required. It should be noted that the Army Medical Reserve Corps for medical officers was not established by Congress until 23 April 1908. Two hundred twenty members of the U.S. Army Nurse Corps were on active duty at the end of February 1901, approximately eighteen of whom were in their home states awaiting discharge from the corps.[5]

When America entered World War I on 6 April 1917, 403 army nurses, including 170 reserve nurses who had been ordered to active status, were on duty. By June 1918, 12,186 army nurses were on active duty, including 10,186 reserve nurses called to active duty, taking care of wounded and ill military personnel. Of 12,186 army nurses, 5,350 were serving overseas.[6]

On 9 July 1918, the Army Nurse Corps was redesignated the U.S. Army Nurse Corps by the Army Reorganization Act of 1918. The act also restricted appointments to women nurses and raised the base pay to sixty dollars a month. Despite this raise in pay, women nurses serving in the Army Nurse Corps were paid half the pay of male soldiers of equivalent military rank with equivalent responsibility.[7]

When the war ended with an armistice on 11 November 1918, 21,480 army nurses were on active duty and more than ten thousand of them were

U.S. Army Nurses wearing gas masks in France, World War I.

13

serving overseas in France, England, Belgium, Italy, Serbia, the Philippines, Hawaii, and Puerto Rico. The influenza epidemic, raging in the United States and throughout the world in 1918, claimed the lives of two hundred army nurses. On 13 November 1918, eighteen of the first "Negro" army nurses of the Army Nurse Corps were assigned to work with ailing black soldiers, nine at Camp Grant, Illinois, and nine at Camp Sherman, Ohio.[8]

The U.S. Navy Nurse Corps was established by an act of Congress on 13 May 1908. Former U.S. Army Nurse Esther Voorhees Hasson was appointed superintendent of the first group of navy nurses who later became known as "the sacred twenty."[9]

Since the navy had no hospitals in Europe when war broke out in August 1914, the Navy Nurse Corps released two of its nurses to sail aboard the SS *Red Cross* and work alongside medical relief units sent to aid the victims of war. They sailed from the United States in September 1914 and worked until the medical relief units were withdrawn in 1915 because of lack of funds.[10]

Thanks again to Navy Secretary Josephus Daniels and the foresight of the Department of the Navy, the U.S. Navy Reserve, created in 1916, provided for the enrollment of navy nurses into the force. There were 160 navy nurses when America entered World War I, and fifteen months later that number had grown to 1,082. In addition to establishing naval units at several civilian hospitals within the United States, approximately forty navy nurses served overseas in Great Britain and France, including several who were loaned to the U.S. Army surgical teams working near the front in France.

Of the more than three hundred navy nurses who served outside the continental United States between 1917 and 1919, a small number served on troop ships. Of those nurses, a small minority served on troop transport ships between 1917 and 1919, and they were the vanguard for the thousands of navy nurses who would serve on navy hospital ships in the future. The majority of those nurses served in navy hospitals in the Philippine Islands and on Guam.

No navy nurses were killed as a result of enemy action; however, thirty-six died while serving on active duty. Of those, twenty-five died as a result of the influenza epidemic that killed more than twenty-five million people during 1918.

With the end of World War I, American women were again expected to return to the status quo that existed before war compelled women to leave their traditionally assigned roles in society. American women had worked not only as army or navy nurses but also in factories such as munitions plants to fill jobs left vacant by men called to service in the military. Others had enlisted as newly created yeomen (F), Marinettes, and in the Army Signal Corps as Hello Girls. But the emergency was over, and the U.S. military and industry no longer needed the help of women in those areas. Like the women who helped settle the Old West and the women who had helped win the victories in the Spanish-American War, these women were expected to leave their nontraditional jobs and take their place again in the home, leaving the military and industry to men.

Perhaps one of the most lasting effects of the military service of American women in World War I was the emphasis it added to the arguments for an amendment for national women's suffrage. Women had been working for such an amendment since Elizabeth Cady Stanton and Susan B. Anthony attended the Seneca Falls Conference in 1848. Finally, after 133 years of living in an America and under a constitution that did not give women citizens the right to vote in national or state elections, and after seventy-two years of fighting without success to get that right granted by a constitutional amendment, American women saw the Nineteenth Amendment granting them suffrage added to the Constitution in 1920.

It is reasonable to argue that the service of American women in and with the U.S. military in World War I and in American industry working for the war effort provided the tipping point to get the amendment for women's suffrage passed by Congress and ratified by the requisite number of states. When Tennessee cast the final vote needed for ratification, opponents of women's suffrage attempted to have the Tennessee legislature change its vote. When that effort failed and the Nineteenth Amendment was adopted, opponents took their fight further. Maryland prevented two women from registering to vote in Baltimore and argued that since Maryland's state constitution excluded women from voting, and since the votes cast by Tennessee and West Virginia also violated their states' constitutions, the Nineteenth Amendment was not a part of the U.S. Constitution. Men of Maryland further argued that the electorate of a state could not have an excluded group added to it by the federal government without the consent of the state.

On 27 February 1922, the unanimous decision of the U.S. Supreme

Court upheld the validity of the Nineteenth Amendment. In his statement for the Court, Justice Louis D. Brandeis pointed out that not only did federal law supersede state law but that Connecticut and Vermont had also voted to ratify women's suffrage and that the Nineteenth Amendment was indeed part of the U.S. Constitution.[11]

Women had won a significant battle, but their struggle for equal treatment and rights as American citizens was a long way from over. Just two years after the Nineteenth Amendment was upheld, women who had served in the military in World War I found themselves in another battle with Congress when Rep. John McKenzie of Illinois introduced a bill that excluded all women except military nurses from collecting the bonus ($1.00 a day for each day served in the United States, $1.25 for each day served overseas) awarded to veterans of World War I. The bill Representative McKenzie was trying to replace awarded that bonus to all veterans of World War I, while McKenzie's bill inserted the word "male" before the word "veteran," thereby denying the bonus to yeomen (F) and women marines. McKenzie actually argued that since women had made more money in the military than they had ever made in their lives, they were not entitled to the veterans' bonus.

It was clear to anyone who looked at the situation with unbiased eyes that despite the fact that women had won the battle for national suffrage and had contributed significantly to the American victory in World War I, the war to grant women the rights of full citizenship was far from over. A new cadre of women's rights pioneers was about to step forward and would find the battles yet to be fought as serious and as bloody as those that had brought them to this point.

2

★

Congresswoman Edith Nourse Rogers has been determined for some time to introduce a bill to provide a women's organization in the Army. We have succeeded in stopping her on the promise that we are studying the same thing, and will permit her to introduce a bill which will meet with War Department approval. Mrs. Roosevelt also seems to have a plan. The sole purpose of this study is to permit the organization of a women's force along the lines that meet with War Department approval so that when it is forced upon us, as it undoubtedly will be, we shall be able to run it our way.
— Brig. Gen. Wade H. Harslip, memorandum, 29 April 1941

When Rep. Edith Nourse Rogers, Republican of Massachusetts, informed Chief of Staff Gen. George C. Marshall in March 1941 that she intended to introduce a bill to establish a Women's Army Corps, Marshall asked for a week to consider the bill. The week stretched into a month while the War Department and the United States Army decided how best to respond to Rogers's stated intentions.

On 28 May 1941, Representative Rogers rose on the floor of the U.S. House to introduce a bill to establish a Women's Army Auxiliary Corps (WAAC). It was not the bill she wanted but the one she felt had a chance of becoming law. Rogers wanted a Women's Army Corps *in* the U.S. Army, not a Women's Army Auxiliary Corps to serve *with* the army without receiving the protection of military status. The fact that the War Department and the U.S. Army were not willing to grant women full military status led Representative Rogers to introduce a bill that she hoped could be succeeded by a bill that would give women military status, equal pay, and equal veterans' benefits. It had been a dream and a goal for more than a decade.

Without a doubt, and by her own admission, Edith Nourse Rogers's interests in establishing a women's corps within the U.S. Army that would give women who served full military status began with her volunteer work for the Women's Overseas Service League in France during World War I. Her whole life proved to be an excellent preparation for her career in Congress and her interest in the welfare of women in the U.S. military.

Edith Frances Nourse was born in Saco, Maine, on 19 March 1881 and moved with her family to Lowell, Massachusetts, in 1895. Edith's wealthy parents provided their daughter with a privileged education consisting of private tutors, boarding school, and finishing school at Madame Julien's outside of Paris. Upon graduation, she returned to Lowell where, in 1907, she married John Jacob Rogers, a young attorney who opened his practice in the city of Lowell. In 1912, her husband was

Edith Nourse Rogers, representative from Massachusetts, 1925 to 1960.

elected to Congress as the representative of Massachusetts's Fifth District and the couple moved to Washington, D.C. When John Rogers was appointed to the Foreign Affairs Committee and sent to France in 1917, Edith accompanied him and worked for the Women's Overseas Service League inspecting field hospitals where wounded and ill American military personnel were treated. During this time, the future representative was very impressed by the military service of British women who worked on loan to the U.S. Army and Navy. These British women enjoyed full military status and protection, while American women who were not members of the U.S. Navy, the U.S. Army, or the U.S. Navy Nurse Corps had no military status or legal protection as military personnel.

When the armistice was signed on 11 November 1919, John and Edith Rogers returned to Washington, where he continued his work as the congressional representative for Massachusetts's Fifth District, and Edith volunteered with the American Red Cross and worked at Walter Reed General Hospital with wounded veterans and active-duty soldiers.

In 1921, Warren G. Harding became president of the United States and offered Edith Nourse Rogers an appointment as a presidential assistant to work with disabled veterans. Her work earned her successive appointments to the same position by succeeding presidents Coolidge and Hoover. Mrs. Rogers's service in this position ended when, on 28 March 1925, following surgery, her husband died.

The Republican Party convinced Edith to run in a special election to succeed her husband. That election was held on 30 June 1925, and Rogers's opponent for the vacant seat was Eugene Noble Foss, a man who had served in Congress in 1910 and who had been governor of Massachusetts for three one-year terms, 1911–13. Rogers won the election with 72 percent of the vote: 23,000-plus for Rogers, 9,000-plus for Foss.

Edith Nourse Rogers was the first woman ever elected to Congress from a New England state and the seventh woman to serve in the U.S. House of Representatives. When *Time* magazine interviewed Representative Rogers about her victory in the 30 June 1925 election, she responded with complete confidence in herself to do the job for which she had been elected. "I intend to continue my husband's work. I know I am equal to the detail of the office, for in fact, I have been continuing the work since my husband died and have managed to keep two secretaries busy."[1] Her self-confidence would prove prophetic as Edith Nourse Rogers was reelected to office eighteen times and to-date holds the record as the woman congressional representative who served the most time in the U.S. House of Representatives.

Representative Rogers not only brought her knowledge and experience as to how women who volunteered to serve with the U.S. military during World War I were treated by the military and the government, she also brought years of experience and knowledge concerning national politics and the politics of Washington, D.C. She brought the dedication and determination of the suffragettes who had fought for decades to get women's suffrage added to the U.S. Constitution. In addition, she had a history of familiarity and good relations with the Business and Professional Women's Organization, which had for many years fought against the right of women to serve in the military. Also, she had an inside track to knowledge concerning the reactions of Congress and the military to the fact that, in 1920, the Nineteenth Amendment gave American women the right to vote. Congress and others in power could no longer afford to ignore with impunity the votes and opinions of millions of American women who recently had gained power through their newly won suffrage. Rogers had witnessed firsthand how important women were in winning the victory in the Great War. She had witnessed the gender discrimination that left most American women serving overseas without protection should they be wounded, killed, or taken prisoner of war. These women had been left without any veterans' benefits, let alone a military discharge recording their service to the country. She had seen it for herself.

Not only had thousands of women volunteered to serve with the army during World War I, the army officers actually put in formal requests for the War Department to allow the recruitment and enlistment of women to serve in auxiliary corps with the army. The Quartermaster General went so far as to request legislation that would allow for the formation of the Women's Auxiliary Quartermaster Corps. The commanding officers of other army corps, including the Surgeon General, Chief of the Engineer Corps, and the Chief of the Ordnance Corps, each requested that he be allowed to recruit and enlist women who could release men for combat. The Chief of the Ordnance Corps suggested a uniform for the proposed women's corps be made from a "soft-silver brown wool material." It would include a tan blouse and a brown Windsor-knotted tie. Further, it was also agreed that no furs were to be worn with the uniform.

It did not take long for Secretary of War Newton D. Baker to deliver a strong and clear response that expressed disagreement with the suggestions and requests to establish a women's service corps within the U.S. Army. In December 1917, Baker's memorandum expressed his disagreement in no uncertain terms, and in May 1918, the War Plans Division sent its reply, which made the War Department's response official. "The enlistment of women in the military forces of the United States has never been seriously contemplated and such enlistment is considered unwise and highly undesirable. . . . The action provided for in this bill is not only unwise, but exceedingly ill-advised."[2]

The War Department also looked with disfavor on the Army Surgeon General's request for the authority to recruit and commission women doctors for the U.S. Army. The federal government's refusal to accept women in the military forces of the United States did not deter approximately five hundred women physicians from forming hospitals and going on their own initiative to combat zones to help treat wounded and ill military and civilians in France, England, and Germany. In a *New York Times* article of 7 October 1917, "Woman's Hospital Unit for France," Dr. Carolyn S. Finley stated, "Although our original offer was not accepted by the Government, as no provision has been made to accept women in the United States Medical Reserve Corps . . . our plan has received the hearty sanction of the [U.S. Army] Surgeon General's office and the Government, so our unit will sail with the approval and moral backing of the United States Army authorities."[3] Other women formed groups and went overseas to drive ambulances and perform other duties to help ensure victory in World War I.

When the war ended on 11 November 1918, the push to get a women's corps within the U.S. Army all but ended. The War Department and the commanding officers of the army considered the idea to establish a women's corps within the army dead and buried. Their attitude changed when the Nineteenth Amendment passed in 1920 and American women were granted the right to vote. Most military and War Department staff agreed that suffrage was extremely dangerous in the hands of women, whom they viewed as natural pacifists. They feared that women might vote the military out of existence, thinking it might ensure the world's best chance for peace. To counter what they considered a real threat, the U.S. military and the War Department took steps to lessen and possibly eliminate such an outcome.[4]

In 1920, Secretary of War Baker established a position of Director of Women's Relations, United States Army, with an office located in the G-1 Division of the General Staff. The director's duties would include acting as a liaison between women and the army in order to win the women's confidence. When the first director resigned after just one year, Anita Phipps was appointed as the second director.

Phipps soon concluded that her two greatest obstacles to success could be found in the fact that she was not granted military status and in the failure of the War Department to support her by backing up the commitments she had made to influential women's organizations interested in seeing women given more influence over the army's and military's future plans. Despite these obstacles, Phipps studied how a U.S. Army women's corps could best be established and used for the country's benefit while still granting women members the protection of military status. More often than not, Phipps's studies and extensive plans were filed with no further action.

In 1929, after approximately ten years of Phipps's work, Secretary of War Dwight F. Davis approved Phipps's plan to bring powerful women's organizations such as the League of Women Voters, the Daughters of the American Revolution, and American War Mothers together to act as civilian advisers to the Secretary of War. On 25 February 1929, Secretary Davis announced this plan to the press. It did not take long for a tide of negative letters to inundate the Department of War.

Just fifteen days later, a new Secretary of War, James W. Good, contacted each women's group to cancel the national meeting at which the organizations' leaders were to nominate the civilian aides who would fill these proposed positions. The actions of the new secretary alienated the women's groups and greatly disillusioned Director Anita Phipps. When

Secretary Good followed his March cancellation of the national meeting with an October letter that stated, "The present is not a propitious time for appointing civilian women aides," Phipps formally requested the Secretary of War to define the responsibilities and authority of her position or to abolish the position.[5] In 1930, Phipps made her request again. The department took no definitive action; in 1931, assailed by ill health and the actions of a new Chief of Staff, Douglas A. MacArthur, Phipps made her appeal yet again. After MacArthur's statement to the Secretary of War that Phipps's position was of no military value, her work was brought to an end and the government abolished the position. Phipps left her position but not without leaving behind studies and plans for establishing a women's corps in the U.S. Army. As the Nazi party in Germany was emerging, the study and plans were filed away and forgotten.

In the intervening years before Representative Rogers's bill became law, Congress, the military, and the American public were engaged in a heated, emotional debate concerning what would be the overall effect of allowing women to serve in or with the American armed forces. The majority of American society still held narrowly defined gender roles and was shocked and outraged at the very idea of "needing" women in or with the military in order to win a war. Arguments ranged from statements by the military, Congress, and the civilian population expressing concern that "No man would take orders from a woman," and that "Women generals would be rushing about giving orders to men." "Who will do the housework?" was another concern voiced. The heated debate on the floor of the U.S. House of Representatives reached a zenith for gender bias when members passionately argued:

> "I think it is a reflection upon the courageous manhood of the country to pass a law inviting women to join the armed forces in order to win a battle.
>
> "Take the women into the armed service, who then will do the cooking, the washing, the mending, the humble homey tasks to which every woman has devoted herself?
>
> "Think of the humiliation! What has become of the manhood of America?"[6]

If an individual from the closing years of the twentieth century or the opening years of the twenty-first century could be transported to the visitors' gallery of the U.S. House in 1941 or early 1942, that visitor might well have been shocked to hear that many of the same arguments used by House members in those years were also used to oppose women's increasing military roles, particularly regarding the question of women in combat, during more recent decades, 1970 through 2000.

Not only were members of Congress and the American people using defensive stereotypes to argue against giving members of a Women's Army Auxiliary Corps military status, they completely ignored what women had done in or with the military in World War I. They had forgotten how civilian American women had voluntarily gone to France, England, and Germany, banding together in women's organizations in order to help America win the victory. Further, they had neglected to mention the voluntary military service of U.S. Army and Navy Nurses who were currently serving in the Philippines and Hawaii even as politicians and the public spoke their arguments in favor of barring women from the U.S. Armed Forces and denied those nurses full military status and benefits. For all their spoken concern for the unfitness of American women for military service, Congress had already allowed American women to serve in the U.S. Army and Navy Nurse Corps and paid them approximately half the salary of male officers of the same rank. Even the Navy Department was determined to argue against the establishment of a Women's Army Auxiliary Corps, despite the fact that women had served with honor in the navy and U.S. Marine Corps during World War I.

When the Japanese attacked Pearl Harbor on 7 December 1941, and days later the Philippines, the American people and Congress knew that scores of American military women nurses were serving in those places and were caring for the wounded despite the fact that they were exposed to the same bombing and strafing as the American servicemen stationed there. Add to these facts that, when the island of Guam fell on 9 December 1941 and five navy nurses, along with male soldiers, became prisoners of the Japanese, the arguments raging in Congress against the establishment of a Women's Army Auxiliary Corps seem even more far-fetched. Women—U.S. Army and Navy Nurses—were acting with dignity and professionalism as they continued to care for the wounded despite the battles raging around them, just as military nurses had carried out their duties in World War I.

The armed forces had made some progress, however, in the recruitment and enrollment of female volunteers for the nursing services. In

World War I, the military sought and accepted a "coalition of the willing" rather than a coalition of the qualified and experienced graduate nurses. Although the War Department and the military had refused to accept women physicians who were graduates of accredited medical schools into the U.S. Army Medical Corps, the government made it clear that these women physicians could, if they liked, join the U.S. Army or Navy Nurse Corps. These women physicians elected instead to band together and go to France, England, and, later, Germany as private organizations of women completely separate from the U.S. military. The War Department and the military did not hesitate to accept and station overseas women who had little or no nursing experience or education.

The Japanese attack on Pearl Harbor and the surrender of Guam and the Philippines did change the attitude of the War Department, the military, and Congress but still did not lead them to grant women in the U.S. Armed Forces full military status. On Christmas Eve 1941, Secretary of War Henry L. Stimson sent word to Congress that the War Department was 100 percent behind the formation of a Women's Army Auxiliary Corps. In addition, Representative Rogers added the suggestions of the War Department to a new bill, HR 6293, establishing the Women's Army Auxiliary Corps and reintroduced it in the House of Representatives.

On 28 January 1942, a House committee approved the bill, which was followed by a Senate committee's approval on 9 February 1942. By this time, newspapers and newscasts were reporting the horrific Battle of Bataan that was raging in the Philippines. More than one hundred U.S. Army and Navy Nurses were serving in military field hospitals on Bataan and Corregidor, and there was no hope of getting reinforcements to the greatly outnumbered American and Filipino troops. These military women were facing the same dangers and making the same sacrifices as the U.S. and Filipino soldiers, yet the War Department and Congress had not objected to their joining the Army and Navy Nurse Corps, nor to their being stationed in Hawaii or the Philippine Islands despite the precarious diplomatic situation that had existed for months between the United States and the Empire of Japan. There had been no arguments based on gender to bar these women from service in the U.S. Army and Navy Nurse Corps.

A national consensus existed concerning the military service of nurses, who at the time were almost exclusively women. In fact, the Army and the

Navy Nurse Corps barred male nurses from these corps. A male nurse could serve as an enlisted medic or corpsman but could not be admitted to either of the nurse corps. The nation seemed to have lulled itself into denial concerning women in military nurse corps by referring to their profession as a "calling" and to the military nurses as "angels of mercy." Through psychological defenses, the War Department, armed forces, Congress, churches, and the American people were able to overlook and not recognize that the U.S. military nurse corps was comprised solely of women. It might be argued that the *need* for nurses in the military outweighed, and even made invisible, the fact that these nurses were, each and every one of them, flesh-and-blood women.

Objections to a Women's Army Auxiliary Corps began to change as the perils presented by World War II grew by the day. The arguments that the "honor" of American men would be diminished by accepting women in the military in order to help win the war were replaced almost overnight by a focus on preventing women from attaining high rank and on not placing women in positions where they could give orders to men.

As Congress and the War Department debated, conditions on Bataan got worse daily. General MacArthur and key staff members were taken off Bataan by submarine and delivered to Australia. Supplies were dwindling so rapidly that the hardworking carabao, or water buffalo, had to be slaughtered for food. The meat was so tough that a recipe for rock soup made its way among American and Filipino soldiers: "Place the carabao meat in a pot of boiling water with a large rock. When the rock melts, the carabao is done."[7]

On 8 April 1942, U.S. Army Nurses, some of the wounded troops, and other military personnel made their way across Manila Bay to the island fortress of Corregidor, where they would make their last stand in Malinta Tunnel, a supposedly impregnable underground headquarters and hospital. On 9 April 1942, Bataan surrendered to the Japanese, and thousands of American and Filipino troops became prisoners of war. Newspapers around the world carried the story on their front pages: "Defense Crushed: Stimson Reveals Defeat Followed Failure to Get in More Food, Corregidor Is Held."[8]

On 27 April 1942, the bill authorizing the establishment of the Women's Army Auxiliary Corps hit a serious setback in the U.S. Senate.

The sudden stop was brought about by the senators' reactions to an attempt to substitute a new bill that would establish the Women's Army Corps as a corps *in* the army rather than as an auxiliary that would work *with* the army. The newly proposed bill would grant women in the corps the same benefits as men of equal rank. Rank would not be relative but would be identical to the system used by the army, thereby granting women in the corps the same pay as men in the army with the same rank. The bill would also place the women under the same discipline as male soldiers. The one exception would be the fact that women would be non-combatants and could not be ordered into combat.

Sen. Elbert Thomas of Utah submitted the new bill and informed his colleagues that the War Department and Gen. George C. Marshall, Army Chief of Staff, had written the new bill, and both were anxious to have it passed as quickly as possible. Several senators, including Democratic senators Francis Maloney and Walter F. George, along with Republican senators Robert La Follette and Albert Austin, demanded that before such an important step could be taken, the new bill would have to be submitted to a Senate committee for further study and would need to be accompanied by a formal request from General Marshall. Senator Austin further stated that the new bill was so different from the original bill that it should be sent to the Military Affairs Committee for consideration. Senator La Follette addressed his fellow senators and stated that he "wanted nothing to do with the bill until the men who had proposed it were willing to come up here and stand behind it." By a voice vote, the senators referred the bill to the Military Affairs Committee.[9]

The debate took place despite the fact that, only two weeks earlier, the House had approved a bill that made the Women Accepted for Voluntary Emergency Service (WAVES) an integral part of the navy, despite the fact that the Senate never required or even discussed sending the navy bill to the Senate Naval Affairs Committee for prior consideration.

On 6 May 1942, Corregidor surrendered, and approximately one hundred U.S. Army and Navy Nurses became prisoners of the Japanese. Parents of these women prisoners of war received postcards from the War Department: "Your daughter stationed in the Philippines is missing in action." The message that followed later read, "Your daughter is a prisoner of war of the Japanese and she is imprisoned in Santo Tomas [Internment Camp]."[10]

Just eight days later, on 14 May 1942, the bill establishing the Women's

Army Auxiliary Corps (WAAC) passed Congress, and the following day it was signed into law by President Franklin D. Roosevelt and became Public Law 77–554. As Congress and the War Department had insisted in order to pass the bill, women in the Women's Army Auxiliary Corps had no military status, nor a system of equivalent ranks.

The next day, Oveta Culp Hobby, the publisher of a large Texas newspaper, the *Houston Post*, and wife of a former governor of Texas, was sworn in as the first director of the WAAC and given the rank of major. She was, in fact, the only major in the WAAC and the highest-ranking woman officer with the Women's Army Auxiliary Corps. Her education, accomplishments, and executive abilities had prepared her for the challenges of the position.

Oveta Culp lived in Killeen, Texas, where as a young child she read portions of the *Congressional Record* to her attorney father, Isaac William Culp. After considering such diverse occupations as the stage or missionary work, she graduated from the University of Texas with a law degree, and at twenty-two authored a parliamentary law book while she was parliamentarian of the state legislature. By the time she was twenty-four, Oveta had run for a seat in that legislative body and lost. In 1931, after marrying William Pettus Hobby, she worked for the *Houston Post*, and by age thirty-two was the *Post*'s executive vice president. Oveta Hobby also served as the executive director of a local radio station and was on the board of directors of the Cleburne National Bank and the board of regents at a Texas college. The Texas League of Women Voters elected Hobby their president, and she chaired a Texas committee of the New York World's Fair.

Well-known for her skills and drive to succeed, Hobby had come to the attention of the military, and, in 1941, the War Department tapped her for the task of leading a newly conceived Women's Army Auxiliary Corps. Within the War Department, and as a civilian, Hobby was titled Chief of Women's Interest Section, Bureau of Public Affairs, 1941–42, and Chief of Pre-Planners for the Women's Army Auxiliary Corps, February to May 1942. Despite the fact that she had two children, William and Jessica, aged nine and six, respectively, in 1941, Hobby plunged into establishing the policies, procedures, and organization of WAAC administration, recruitment, training, assignments, and discipline.[11]

Director Hobby and her staff began immediately to prepare a place at Fort Des Moines, Iowa, for the First WAAC Training Center. Fort Des

Moines had been an old U.S. Cavalry post, and on 20 July 1942, the empty stables, after much renovation, became the barracks for the first 770 women in the WAAC, and the source of the WAAC nickname, "Hobby's Horses."

While renovations and plans took shape, young women from all over the country streamed into recruiting stations to join. For many, if not most, of these women, acceptance in the WAAC would provide their first experience of living any length of time away from their parents' homes and from the towns where they had lived since their birth.

Among the earliest to join the WAAC was an American serving in the Canadian Women's Auxiliary. Mary Warburton Long, the daughter of a well-known Brooklyn, New York, physician, joined on 18 May 1942, reportedly the first woman to join the WAAC. Long had joined the Canadian Women's Auxiliary Air Force in October 1941, and when she heard about the passing of the WAAC bill, she responded to an invitation that was sent out to Americans in foreign militaries to join the U.S. Armed Forces. Long met Maj. Gen. Guy V. Henry, who had been assigned by the army to travel around Canada to facilitate transferring men into the U.S. Armed Forces. General Henry's mobile processing station had arrived in Toronto on 17 May. Henry wrote, "A young woman in Royal Canadian Air Force uniform came to me and stated she was a U.S. citizen and requested transfer to the WAACs. My reply, there are no WAACs. Her, the papers say the President signed the bill yesterday." General Henry contacted the War Department and learned that Mary Long was right, but he was told "it was against the policy to accept any women for some months . . . nevertheless I enrolled her on 18 May 1942 for service with the WAACs."[12]

In an interview for the *Phoenix News-Sun* in 1977, Long recalled, "There were no forms, no papers, nothing ready. The general had a long face because he couldn't get a direct commission for me." Because Long had entered the WAAC so early, she was sent on furlough for two months before being ordered to report to Fort Des Moines, where she graduated with the first WAAC officer training class.[13]

That first graduating class would set a high standard for those following them. With no well-worn roads for them to travel, these women, like the pioneer women who helped settle the west, carved out trails for others to follow. In time, the trails became paths, the paths became roads, and the roads became well-traveled highways leading into a future where

American women would play an ever-increasing part in defending their country. Many of the WAAC officers and enlisted women to graduate in the first and other WAAC classes of 1942 would leave an indelible mark for the later generations to follow.

Betty Bandel was born in Washington, D.C., in 1912, and in 1918, she moved to Tucson, Arizona, with her parents. Since they were well-educated themselves, the Bandels expected Betty to attend and graduate from college. In 1933, Betty graduated from the University of Arizona with a degree in music and then went to work as a newswoman with the *Arizona Daily Sun*. In 1942, Betty graduated in the very first WAAC officer candidate class, ranking second in class honors among 440 newly created officers.

Billie Burk Davis had lived in Charleston, West Virginia, was twenty-six years old, and was running a Comptometer (a state-of-art calculating machine) school and training others when she was sworn in to the WAAC in the spring of 1942. Billie had vivid memories of that time: "[I had] an IQ test, interview, and a character check by the FBI. . . . [My] mother thought the FBI [would be] no problem for me, having grown up in a small, straight-laced town and imbued with the notion that every person's opinion of me was important." The army recruiting office called Davis for her physical exam. "I knew I'd survived the first three hurdles. I had no doubt an elimination process was in motion; indeed, from more than 200,000 applications, 450 were selected for the first OCS [officer candidate school] class. I was the first woman called from West Virginia. I was assigned Serial No. 500,011 and boarded a train for Des Moines with dozens more OCS candidates in civilian finery. They appeared to be leaders and successful. Many were teachers, a few were lawyers, all seemed to me better educated than I was. The administrative experience at the [Comptometer] school must have helped."[14]

When these women were interviewed in the years from 1988 through 2006 and asked why they had joined the WAAC, their answers shared a common thread of patriotism and a spirit of adventure.

For Stella D. Therault, a twenty-one-year-old from Florida, enlisting when the opportunity presented itself did not take a great deal of mental debate. "Patriotism. After Pearl Harbor, I felt that I had to do something to help," Therault said. "I also was looking for adventure and travel. I was curious about my potential." Stella remembered that the reactions of her family and friends were mixed. "[My] parents were proud, but thought I would not be content at home again. [My] boyfriend was angry and said I would be nothing but a camp follower and broke off our relationship. [My] girlfriends were envious, but afraid to join."[15]

For a future general and Director of the WAC, the decision to sign up with the WAAC seemed only natural. Elizabeth P. Hoisington was born in Newton, Kansas, on 3 November 1918. Her family moved around the country as her father, a career army officer and West Point graduate, moved from assignment to assignment. An excellent student, Elizabeth graduated from Notre Dame of Maryland High School in 1936 and in 1940 from the College of Notre Dame of Maryland with a degree in chemistry. In November 1942, she followed in a family tradition and enlisted in the WAAC. Like so many of the earliest members of the WAAC, she attended basic training in the cold and mud of Fort Des Moines, known to the recruits as "Boomtown." Hoisington fit in easily to army life. When asked what surprised her about herself as the result of her service during World War II, she responded, "That I adapted to army life so easily, no doubt due in part to my having been raised in an army family that traveled all over as I was growing up."[16]

For two of the four daughters in the Chiboucas family living in Savannah, Georgia, joining the WAAC did not require much deliberation. On 2 September 1942, twenty-two-year-old Vicky Chiboucas raised her hand and enlisted in the WAAC. "I sincerely wanted to do something for my country," Chiboucas said when asked why she had enlisted. "I was a small-town girl, one of seven children, raised with strict parents, Greek, and I knew I'd never get out of Savannah if I didn't take this step. My friend, Mary Jones, and I were the very first to enlist in Savannah. My older sister also enlisted." Chiboucas said that her family was devastated when she enlisted in the WAAC. "No one could believe that two of the Chiboucas girls joined the military," she said. "After the initial shock, my parents were great and really proud. They remembered the Statue of Liberty when they came to America, and they stood by their children. They proudly watched their three sons and two of their four daughters go into the service."[17]

Vicky Chiboucas remembered her first days and basic training at Fort Des Moines, Iowa. She arrived at the First WAAC Training Center minus her suitcase. "My first day was tragic as I arrived in Des Moines with no bag," she said. "For weeks, I only had the clothes I was wearing, but everyone from everywhere was wonderful. Finally, we were issued army clothes." The weather was cold and wet and the ground a sea of mud. The clothing issued to the WAACs was predominately men's army issue and was grossly oversized for the majority of the young women of the day. "There were men's coats and boots, and here I was five feet, two inches. Nothing fit," Chiboucas remembered. "I marched right out of my shoes and boots and continuously stopped to pick them up; it was terrible. The whole platoon giggled, and the officer, with a straight face, ordered them to stop giggling."[18]

Bette J. Morden enlisted in the WAAC in 1942 at the age of twenty-one and left Michigan by train for Fort Des Moines. Like the majority of women answering their nation's call for women to enlist and free a man for combat, she joined with the intent to do her part and help win the war as quickly as possible. "It was great to feel that we were part of something much larger than any one of us," Morden said. "It was also my first train trip, and that too was very exciting."[19]

The career of a future air force major general and future Director of Women in the U.S. Air Force (WAF) began as a WAAC during World War II. Of all the young women who left their homes and traveled to Fort Des Moines to begin their military service, Jeanne Holm, a twenty-one-year-old WAAC recruit from Portland, Oregon, was among the most determined to do her military job and help win the war as quickly as possible. Holm had been a member of the Oregon Women's Ambulance Corps since she was nineteen. The ambulance corps taught its members not only to drive an ambulance, it also taught them close-order infantry drill, and Holm not only loved the training, she had a real talent for doing it well and teaching others to do likewise.

"Our government issue [uniforms] were few as they were not ready for us WAACs at Fort Des Moines, Iowa, in 1942; there were no uniforms—only GI underwear and men's coats and this rain coat." Laverne Gibnich on right; on left, Auxiliary Hechhant.

On 14 July 1942, three weeks after her twenty-first birthday, Holm and thirteen other women from her area were sworn into the WAAC and boarded a train to Chicago, where they would change trains and travel the final leg of their journey to Fort Des Moines. Holm's memories of that time are strong and full: "I remember that first night at Fort Des Moines. There were two hundred of us sleeping in one huge room. When the lights went out and everything got quiet, what I had done in signing up hit me like an express train. My life would be very different, and it only took me about fifteen minutes to conclude that I had done the right thing and was about to start living a wonderful adventure."[20]

Recruit Holm stood out from the very first day. When the sergeant asked if anyone was familiar with close-order drill, Holm was the only WAAC to raise her hand. The sergeant put her in charge of a platoon with instructions to teach them how to drill and march. "My experience in the Oregon Women's Ambulance Corps paid off," Holm said. "Not only did I know close-order drill, I had a loud command voice. The army was never foreign to me."[21]

During the summer of 1942, the army trained the women of the first WAAC officers' class at Fort Des Moines. Billie Davis recalled a benchmark of that training: the first dress parade. Colonel Hobby, reporters, photographers, and others of importance were in the reviewing stand. "The air was electric with excitement, and tension soared. Company 1, my company, was lined up behind the band, and behind us the other OCS [officer candidate school] companies . . . the WAACs in basic training, the post's servicemen, NCOs and officers, stretching well down the field. When the band started playing and the march began, I felt a greater surge of patriotism and pride in country than I'd ever felt before. The tears rolled down my cheeks, and I wouldn't have traded places with anybody else in this world."[22]

Of the first WAAC officers' class to graduate on 29 August 1942, 40 of the 440 new officers were black. The WAAC decided that 10 percent of the Women's Army Auxiliary Corps would be "Negro," as blacks were called in that time. These black women went to classes with white candidates and ate in the same mess hall; however, they were maintained as a separate all-black platoon and were posted to their first assignment en masse.

Approximately 80 percent of the total of the first WAAC graduating class had at least some college, and many had obtained a college

Lt. Jeanne Holm, WAAC, 1942.

(Left to right) Colonels Morgan and Oveta Culp Hobby and Brig. Gen. Donald Faith, commanding general WAAC Training Command, review the WAACs on parade, Fort Des Moines.

(Left to right) Five of the original WAACs: Billie Davis, Charleston, West Virginia; Ruth Mary Martin, Terre Haute, Indiana; Mrs. W. M. Shuttleworth, Jackson, Mississippi; Mary Armstrong, Cleveland, Ohio; Ruth Reece, Newcastle, Indiana. Shown at Fort Des Moines, Iowa.

degree. The majority of these women had work experience as teachers and/or clerical workers. These first WAACs were trained by male soldiers and gradually replaced the male instructors.

Mary Ellen Rogers had vivid memories of her time at Fort Des Moines. At 5:00 a.m., in ten-below-zero temperatures, amid the ice and sticky mud inevitable in most new army camps, Rogers was on KP and at the rear of the mess hall. "I was cold and I was mad. My patriotic intentions to help shorten the war had not included scrubbing garbage cans. . . . Only the lower half of my body was visible—the other half was hidden in a garbage can. I had been given a large brush, a bar of GI soap and a bucket of steaming hot water and had been ordered to clean the smelly can." That morning, Rogers wore what had been issued to her and other WAACs of her company. A chronic shortage of WAAC clothing forced the issuing of men's clothing that was oversized for the women. The men's overcoats were so large that "the pockets were below our knees and the sleeves rolled above our elbows." A large white WAAC name tag was pinned to the overcoat lapel with "an enormous safety pin." WAAC work clothing was equally unappealing—"ugly cotton stockings, low-heeled matronly shoes, this green and white stripe cotton dress . . . and a silly sloppy hat pulled over our heads."[23]

Kathleen Branson joined the WAAC after, unknown to her, three of her coworkers at the Wright Aeronautical Plant in Ohio gave an army recruiter her name. "A United States Army recruiter called and asked to interview me." Branson, whose father had been in the army in World War I, went with her male cousin to sign up. She wrote, "[I remember] the group discipline, the specialized classes, and the cold Des Moines winter weather. . . . I was very proud of being part of a dress parade to salute WAAC Commander [Director] Oveta Culp Hobby. The [parade ground] was that of a riding or marching area that was oval shaped and the stands rose up to our left as we marched in. We were in our dress winter uniforms, caps, overcoats and yellow silk scarves and gloves."[24]

The Second WAAC Training Center, at Daytona Beach, Florida, opened on 21 November 1942. Director Hobby had no choice regarding this second training center. According to army historian Mattie Tread-well, Daytona was the only site offered since the army did not want "to dispossess the occupants of any established military post." The buildings were leased from the city, and classroom space was provided by the local churches. The barracks for the newly inducted WAACs were not barracks at all but rooms in scattered hotels, inns, villas, and apartment buildings, as well as a camp for six thousand women living in tents. Director Hobby had serious concerns regarding the atmosphere of this new training cen-

"Tent City," Second WAAC Training Center, Daytona Beach, Florida, WAACs in formation, November 1942.

ter since Daytona Beach was a tourist town with resort nightspots and crowds of male military troops from nearby armed forces stations. Instilling the discipline necessary among green recruits under such circumstances would be difficult.[25]

One young WAAC recruit "stunned [her] family beyond belief." Ammora Kelledy had attended a convent school in Washington, D.C., throughout her education. "At first [my family] thought I was outright damned. My father, who had not served in World War I because of poor eyesight, was proud as a peacock." When the FBI showed up for Kelledy's background check, the nuns, who were from a cloistered order, had "the most exciting time most of them ever had." When Kelledy boarded the train for Daytona, her family, standing on the station platform, "were still begging me to stay home." After Kelledy arrived at Daytona, every night she waited late to use the latrine since "we didn't have any walls in the latrines yet." She slept in one of the hundreds of tents in the cantonment area, and the tent "leaked on my bed for the two nights it rained while I was in Tent City." The weather turned cold and rainy, and the army had no raincoats for the new recruits. For the first month, Kelledy said, "I defied authority by wearing a left-over CCC [Civil Conservation Corps] raincoat around Daytona."[26]

Gwendolyn Clymer, whose family and friends thought that she "was very foolish for joining the WAAC," had an all too common issue with the military clothing. At reveille on her first day, standing in formation with other inductees, she not only was wearing an oversized size-42 bra, but "I had on two left shoes . . . that I was issued the day before and I had no idea where to go to rectify the error."[27]

Fort Oglethorpe, the Third WAAC Training Center, opened on 23 December 1942. This new training post was located in the Piedmont of the Appalachian Mountains on the site of a 1902 army post and in the heart of the Chickamauga National Military Park. During the first week in January 1943 and after the renovation of six barracks and construction of new classrooms, 53 WAAC officers, 165 enlisted women, and 32 male army officers opened the doors to the thousands of army women who eventually would move through the reception battalion.

Beverly J. Behr from Marion, Indiana, was the first WAAC to arrive by train at Union Depot in Chattanooga, Tennessee, and, amid the excitement of newsreel cameramen in action, was greeted by the commanding officer, Col. Hobart B. Brown, and administrative officers. One of those staff was 1st Officer Mary Warburton Long, the first woman to enlist in the WAAC, who was by this time assistant to the commandant.

On 17 April 1943, Maj. Oveta Culp Hobby arrived at Fort Oglethorpe and spent the day reviewing troops and inspecting the facility. Rena Lampman, whose younger brother had come home from navy boot camp in time to go with her when she enlisted in the WAAC, was in the first class that graduated from basic at Fort Oglethorpe. She wrote, "One night at retreat, they told us to report to the supply sergeant to get our uniforms. We were told to make them fit as best we could. . . . We were up at 4:30 a.m., went to the drill field to practice marching in review as President Roosevelt was due that morning to inspect the WAAC. It was the only time he did so. I was so thrilled and awed at the twenty-one-gun salute."[28]

Lynn Ashley remembered, "At Fort Oglethorpe we slept on cots and the sheets were cold and wet, the humidity was so high. I thought I'd nearly freeze on cold nights."[29]

Fort Devens, outside of Boston, the Fourth WAAC Training Center, opened 1 March 1943. Army commanders throughout the United States

Visit of Franklin D. Roosevelt to Fort Oglethorpe. Col. Oveta Culp Hobby is seated next to President Roosevelt.

were requesting WAACs, and several areas of training and assignments opened to WAACs at that time.

During the early days of the WAAC, women were further trained in one of five major areas and then assigned to work in that job or a Military Occupational Specialty (MOS). The first WAAC units to be sent into the field were stationed with the Aircraft Warning Service (AWS) units along the east coast of the United States. As more WAACs graduated from basic training and then specialist schools as baker/cooks, motor transporters, and clerks, they were stationed at posts where the commanding officers had requested WAACs. WAACs gradually filled positions with the Army Air Force, Army Ground Forces, and Service of Supply, later renamed Army Service Forces. It did not take long for male commanding officers to discover that women could be trained as parachute riggers, bombsite maintenance specialists, control tower operators, aerial photography analysts, weather forecasters and observers, link trainer instructors who taught pilots how to fly on instruments, and ordnance specialists who worked with munitions and explosives, including mixing gunpowder and loading shells. WAACs were also trained and assigned as electricians, automobile and airplane mechanics, radio operators, and cryptographers.

WAACs had made a solid beginning, and that foundation would lead to growth in numbers and depth in the coming months.

3

⭐

The present conflict is not only a war of nations, it is also a war of men and women. Because of its total character, every element of our population must be mobilized in winning the war. The women of America now have the unprecedented opportunity to serve their country and back up their men in the most effective manner.

—Pvt. Harry Mann

On 9 December 1941, just two days after the Japanese attacked Pearl Harbor and the Philippines, Rep. Edith Nourse Rogers met with ADM Chester A. Nimitz, Chief of the U.S. Navy's Bureau of Navigation, and asked if he would be interested in sponsoring a bill, similar to the WAAC bill, establishing a women's organization within the navy. A politically savvy Admiral Nimitz sidestepped the congresswoman's question by telling her that although there were most likely jobs in the navy that could be performed by women, the navy had no need for an organization of women at the present time. What the admiral did next belied his assurances to Representative Rogers.

In just three days, Nimitz sent an order to all bureau chiefs within the U.S. Navy, asking them to send their opinions, pro and con, to the Chief of the Bureau of Personnel concerning the need and desirability of establishing a women's organization within the navy so the navy would be prepared to speak on the issue before Congress. It would be nice if one could honestly say that Admiral Nimitz's questions concerning the establishment of a women's organization within the U.S. Navy were prompted by his concern for the fair treatment of women within the U.S. Armed Forces, but the facts do not lend themselves to that conclusion.

What appears to have been at the root of the admiral's offer was a strong desire, stoked by a strong fear, to avoid a women's organization that was not established along lines drawn up and laid down by the navy itself rather than mirror the WAAC bill proposed by Edith Nourse Rogers. Joy

Virginia Gildersleeve, dean of Barnard College and chair of the Women's Advisory Council who acted as advisers to the U.S. Navy during World War II.

Bright Hancock, a woman who had served in the U.S. Navy during World War I, categorized the actions of Nimitz and the Navy Department clearly when she wrote, "The actions of Mrs. Rogers really started a fire. The creation of a women's reserve was taken up by the Navy because its leaders feared that if they did not move, Mrs. Rogers and others on the Hill would, and the Navy would be entangled in legislation of a character it could not administer. This fear, rather than any firm conviction as to the need of women, moved them to action, reluctant though it was."[1]

The only positive responses to the question of women in the navy came from the Chief of Naval Operations and the Chief of the Bureau of Aeronautics, where someone knew the history of the women who had served in the navy during World War I. The navy appointed Hancock to determine which positions women could fill and the number of women the navy needed to fill them.

Opposition to creating a women's organization within the U.S. Navy did not go gently into the night. Virginia Gildersleeve, Dean of Barnard College, summed up the logic of those opposing women in the navy very well: "Now if the Navy could possibly have used dogs or ducks or monkeys, certain of the older admirals would probably have greatly preferred them to women."[2]

The needs of a nation involved in a two-front war raised the status of pragmatism above that of tradition and the fragile male ego, and on 2 January 1942, the Bureau of Personnel recommended that a women's organization be established within the navy. When the process of putting the necessary bill into writing and submitting it to Congress seemed to have reached an impasse, the Bureau of Aeronautics called on an influential friend, Dr. Margaret Chung of San Francisco, a staunch supporter of Naval Aviation and Submariners, for help. Dr. Chung was well-known for the hospitality she had extended to Naval Aviators and Submariners over many years. It was this warm relationship that caused Dr. Chung to refer to these navy men as her "sons," and that led to the creation of a group of U.S. Navy men who called themselves "Sons of Mom Chung."

Drawing on this longtime relationship, Dr. Chung called on Rep. Melvin Maas of Minnesota and asked for his help to get the bill through Congress. Representative Maas requested a copy of the pending legislation and, just two days after receiving it, introduced his own bill, HR 6807, creating a Women's Auxiliary Reserve that would be adjunct to, but not within, the navy. Maas requested that Sen. Raymond E. Willis introduce an identical bill, S 2388, in the U.S. Senate, which he did on 19 March 1942.[3]

> Title V: Women's Auxiliary Reserve: Section 501. A Women's Auxiliary Reserve is hereby established which shall be administered under the same provision in all respects (except as may be necessary to adopt said provisions to the Women's Auxiliary Reserve) as those contained in this Act or which may be hereafter enacted with respect to the Volunteer Reserve. Appointments and enlistments in the Women's Auxiliary Reserve shall be made only in time of war and for periods to expire not later than six months after termination of the war.[4]

When S 2388 reached the Senate Naval Affairs Committee, several senators argued that if the bill were passed and signed into law and allowed women to actually become members of the armed forces, "it would destroy their femininity and future standings as 'good mothers.'"[5]

One might well question the validity of this argument in light of the fact that no concerns were expressed in regard to the work itself, other than to exclude women from taking part in combat. If one subscribes to this logic, one must subscribe as well to the argument that it was not the work the women would do in the armed forces but, rather, awarding them military status itself that was bound to have deleterious effects on women and the nation in general. One must also ignore the fact that American women had proved their abilities and commitment as military nurses in every war in which America had fought: had not the majority of these women who served in previous wars married and raised children?

The senators' argument was proven unsound by the U.S. Marine Corps when it decided to locate women who had served as Marinettes in World War I. The Marine Corps published photos of women marines from World War I in newspapers and asked that the women contact the corps or that anyone recognizing the women who knew where they were now, and what their married names were, contact the marines. The response was gratifying. One of the World War I women marines was now Mrs.

Frank B. Zeller and had been enlisted as Ruth Spike. Ruth was now the mother of two.

A second woman in the photos was Mrs. Hurley, formerly Miss O'Keefe and best friend of Ruth Spike. Both women remembered former Marinette Mary Kelly, now Mrs. Howard, but neither knew what had happened to Mary Kelly Howard. It was a fourth woman marine who supplied information as to Mary Kelly Howard's whereabouts. Mrs. Hurley's husband was also a marine and their sixteen-year-old son, Lance, was a student in Brooklyn. Mrs. Hurley "was sorry my boy wasn't old enough to join the Marines."[6]

The former Marinettes, who enjoyed full military status in World War I, had not lost their femininity or their ability to be good mothers. The senators' argument to deny women in the military full military status had no basis in truth. Full military status of women serving in the military did not damage a woman's femininity or her ability to be a good mother. The argument, like all the others to keep women out of the military or prevent them from serving with full military status and benefits, was groundless and most likely the product of prejudice, chauvinism, and hostility toward giving women the full rights and privileges of citizenship. Unfortunately, it would not be the last time such arguments would be used to prevent women from sharing the same rights accorded to male citizens or the last time many women would buy into the falsehoods.

With women nurses already serving on or near the front lines, and given the courage shown by U.S. Army and Navy Nurses in the Philippines and Guam, it is difficult to see the logic in the congressional argument that full military rank would damage women. If these women could perform such essential work on and near the front lines, how was full military rank and pay equal to male soldiers' more dangerous to them than the jobs they were already doing with great courage, dedication, and outstanding effectiveness and proficiency?

The U.S. military nurse corps were comprised solely of women, and the War Department was asking tens of thousands of women registered nurses to join up, and yet Congress was still arguing over the question of awarding women full military rank and privileges and pay equal to that of male soldiers of the same or equivalent rank. The same argument used against the WAAC bill was resurrected as an argument against having women *in* the navy and not *with* the navy. The argument was a repeat of the earlier debate that providing full military status and equal pay would threaten the women's femininity and their future ability to be good mothers. Could military equality in rank and pay actually be more dangerous than the military jobs and assignments themselves, or was it an attempt by Congress and the War Department to keep a once all-male institution that way, barring females from pay and benefits awarded to male soldiers?

On 3 July 1942, the Senate passed a revised bill to establish a women's reserve *in* the navy. In order to promote the bill's passage, senators had permitted several amendments to the bill that would necessitate the bill's going back to the House of Representatives for a vote. The amendment stated that women in the naval reserve would not serve outside the United States; women would not serve aboard naval ships or in combat zones; women could not be placed in command of men; women in the naval reserve would replace naval personnel and not civilian personnel; women would receive the same pay as male sailors of the same military rate or rank; and if a woman in the naval reserve were disabled by injury or illness while serving, she would receive disability pay from civil service and not from the navy.[7]

Rep. Carl Vinson of Georgia, chairman of the Naval Affairs Committee, and others hoped to send the bill to the full House for unanimous approval, but their hopes were dashed on 5 July 1942, when Rep. Beverly M. Vincent of Kentucky blocked the attempt of the Naval Affairs Committee to take the revised bill to the House floor. Representative Vincent stated that he opposed the idea of a women's reserve in the navy and refused to allow the bill to be entered on the unanimous consent calendar. This action on the part of Representative Vincent would send the bill into conference for compromise, and final passage of the bill would face a long delay. Vincent also made clear that he objected to the bill in principle and felt that "the non-combatant shore posts that the women reservists are scheduled to fill should be given to veterans of the First World War." He went on to state that for a variety of reasons, including age and mobility, the navy opposed using World War I veterans instead of a women's reserve.[8]

Although the Chief of the Bureau of Naval Personnel, RADM Randall Jacobs, and his legal adviser, CDR Herbert Hopwood, had explained to the Senate and House earlier that the navy needed physically active young people for jobs it envisioned for the naval reserve, Mr. Vincent did not relent. At this point, Representative Vinson of Georgia went the extra mile and explained to Mr. Vincent that for jobs such as cryptographer and photoanalyst, along with many others demanding strict attention to detail and intense concentration, the navy had already determined that it needed a reserve of young, physically fit, and bright women. Vinson went on to point out that the navy could not pay veterans of the previous war salaries high enough or award rates and ranks commensurate with their experience or age. The explanations and arguments of his fellow senators had little or no effect on Representative Vincent, who rose on 7 July 1942 on the House floor to say that he felt "girls were more experienced with lipstick and looking in mirrors than anything else."[9]

There is no telling how long the establishment of the Women's Naval Reserve would have been delayed if Representative Vincent had been permitted to succeed with his biased opinions concerning the fitness of women to serve in a naval reserve, but actions that took place months earlier were to weigh heavily in favor of a women's reserve that placed women *in* the navy and not *with* the navy as an auxiliary.

Joy Bright Hancock, second Director of the WAVES, revealed years later the behind-the-scenes actions that put the Women's Naval Reserve bill over the top and saw it signed into law. Hancock reported that on 30 May 1942 Dean Harriet Elliot of the University of North Carolina wrote a letter to Eleanor Roosevelt asking her help in getting the Women's Naval

Lieutenant Commander Joy Bright Hancock, USNR (left) and Lieutenant Eunice Whyte, USNR. Both had served in the First World War as Yeomen (F) and were the only World War I WAVES eligible to wear the World War I Victory Ribbon.

Reserve bill passed and signed into law as the U.S. Navy had planned and proposed. In her letter of response to Dean Elliot's request, Mrs. Roosevelt assured her that she "had shown the dean's letter to the President."[10]

On 16 June 1942, Secretary of the Navy Frank Knox informed the Chief of the Bureau of Naval Personnel that President Roosevelt "has given me *carte blanche* to go ahead and organize the Women's Reserve along the lines I think best." The president also suggested "that we now press this matter to as swift an enactment as we can."[11]

Representative Vincent's comment on the House floor seemed to recognize that he knew his objections would not stop the bill establishing a Women's Naval Reserve from becoming law: "I think the whole thing is ridiculous," Vincent said. "I know that technically we've already agreed to the bill and it is just the same as passed, but my conscience wouldn't let me see it go through without voicing my objections."[12]

Despite his statement, Representative Vincent criticized the bill even though it was likely to pass. Vincent rose in the House on 21 July 1942 and decried the bill's passage, saying that "the Navy did not want the reserve" and that it would only create ten thousand more "sit-down jobs." Vincent closed by stating that "given the serious attacks of German submarines along the Atlantic coast, it is irresponsible to take time to put butterflies in the Navy" and pointed out that "women working in war industries wear no bars on their shoulders."[13]

At one point during Representative Vincent's statements that the navy itself was opposed to the establishment of a Women's Naval Reserve, Rep. Edith Nourse Rogers of Massachusetts, the author of the bill creating the Women's Army Auxiliary Corps, rose to dispute Mr. Vincent's assertions and his statement that "the passage of the bill to establish the Women's Naval Reserve would humiliate the Navy."[14]

The bill received final congressional approval in the House on 21 July 1942 and was sent to the president for his signature. Franklin D. Roosevelt, who had served as Secretary of the Navy during World War I, signed the bill on 30 July 1942 and Public Law 689 officially established the Women's Naval Reserve, guaranteeing that the women who volunteered to serve in it, and who were accepted, would serve their country *in* the navy and not as auxiliary members *with* the navy.

The bill establishing the Navy Women's Reserve, which became known as the WAVES (Women Accepted for Voluntary Emergency Service), also covered the U.S. Marine Women's Reserve and the U.S. Coast Guard

Women's Reserve, known as the SPARS, an acronym derived from the Coast Guard motto, "Semper paratus" (Always ready).[15]

Even before President Roosevelt signed the bill establishing the Women's Naval Reserve into law, and while the debate in Congress was hot and furious as to whether the women in the naval reserve would serve *in* the navy or *with* the navy, the Office of Navy Personnel and their civilian advisers were laying the plans the navy would have to have in place for the organization to get off to an immediate and successful start. In June, the nation's newspapers carried stories on the sites being considered as training centers for the women who volunteered to serve in the corps. The heart of the plan was to set up training centers on select college campuses and to appoint women deans and professors to take the leading administrative roles in planning, recruiting, training, and managing the thousands of women who would be accepted in the reserve. From the beginning, Vassar, in Poughkeepsie, New York, and Smith College, in Northampton, Massachusetts, were considered to be among the top choices.

Among the navy's top civilian advisers were Dr. Mildred McAfee, President of Wellesley College, and Dr. Virginia C. Gildersleeve, Dean of Barnard College. The planners appointed a council of civilian educators to act as advisers and were looking closely at Vassar and Smith as prospective sites for the midshipmen's school where officers would be trained, as well as at several midwestern universities as training centers for enlisted women.

ADM Randall Jacobs, Chief of Naval Personnel, told the press that the navy had already identified more than nine thousand jobs the women in the Women's Naval Reserve could fill, thereby releasing male sailors for sea and combat duty wherever they were needed.

The women appointed to the council were highly educated and outstanding in their fields and accomplishments. In a time when few Americans—and even fewer women—attended college, the women on the council were nationally recognized leaders and included:

1. Virginia C. Gildersleeve, chairwoman, was the president of Barnard College, the undergraduate women's college of Columbia University. She was born in New York City on 3 October 1877, and following her graduation from the Brearley School in that city in 1895, attended Barnard, where she earned her B.A. in 1899, graduating first in her class in addi-

tion to being class president. Gildersleeve remained at Columbia University and earned an M.A. in medieval history and began work on a Ph.D. in English literature. In 1904, she accepted a teaching job at Barnard. After receiving her Ph.D. in English literature in 1908, Gildersleeve accepted a teaching position in the English Department of Columbia University. Three years later, she was asked by the president of Columbia, Nicholas Murray Butler, to accept the position of dean of Barnard. In 1911, at the age of thirty-three, Gildersleeve accepted that position. When America entered World War I in 1918, Gildersleeve coordinated the organization of several women's groups, including the Women's Land Army, which dedicated its efforts to agricultural work. In 1919, Gildersleeve, along with M. Carey Thomas, president of Bryn Mawr, was the leading light in the formation of the International Federation of University Women.

In February 1945, President Roosevelt would appoint Dr. Gildersleeve as one of the six American delegates—the only woman—to the United Nations Conference charged with drafting the United Nations charter. Through her efforts on the committee, the Universal Declaration of Human Rights became an important part of the work of the UN Conference.

2. Ada Louise Comstock was a Smith College graduate and former dean of Smith College. In 1922, Comstock was offered the position of president at Radcliffe College in Cambridge, Massachusetts. The faculty and students of Smith were saddened at losing Comstock to Radcliffe and sent her off with a warm and heartfelt tribute. In a ceremony held in the Smith College Chapel, President William Allan Neilson lauded Miss Comstock and in his closing words said, "Her mind as I have conceived it is the mind of an admirable judge. In a different world, Miss Comstock would have sat on the supreme bench of the United States."[16] Comstock was also a past president of the American Association of University Women and held honorary degrees conferred by Boston University, Mount Holyoke College, Brown University, the University of Michigan, the University of Rochester, the University of Minnesota, the University of Maine, Goucher College, Case Western Reserve, and Williams College.

3. Mildred H. McAfee was a forty-two-year-old native of Parkville, Missouri, and president of Wellesley College. McAfee received her B.A. degree from Vassar as a Phi Beta Kappa and member of the graduating class of 1920. Following her graduation, McAfee taught eighth grade and did vol-

unteer church work in Chicago. Among the subjects she taught were French, economics, and sociology. In 1927, McAfee accepted the position of dean of women at Centre College in Danville, Kentucky, where she remained until 1932. She was later appointed dean of women at Oberlin College in Ohio, where she remained until 1936. At Oberlin, returning to campus after a trip to Cleveland, "Miss Mac," as she was called by students, spotted three male students and three female students "hitchhiking on the outskirts of town in an attempt to catch a ride back to their dorms." Mindful of the Oberlin rule that prohibited female students from hitchhiking, Miss Mac pulled up alongside the road and called out, "Hop in boys. I'm sorry I can't take you girls along, too—but you know the college rules."[17]

In 1936, McAfee became the second-youngest woman appointed as president of Wellesley. On 31 July 1942, the *Christian Science Monitor* carried an article in which the reporter wagered that Mildred H. McAfee was a good bet to be appointed the Director of the Women's Naval Reserve and closed with the words "Miss McAfee—whose colonial ancestors crossed the Alleghenies to Kentucky, 'a Bible in one hand, a rifle in the other'—is eminently fitted for the task."[18]

4. Mrs. Thomas S. Gates, Emma Barton Brewster-Waller-Gates, was the wife of the president of the University of Pennsylvania.

5. Meta Glass was the president of Sweet Briar College in Lynchburg, Virginia. She was a native of Petersburg, Virginia, and earned a bachelor's degree from Randolph-Macon Women's College in 1899. Glass earned her Ph.D. from Columbia University. During World War I, Glass served as a YWCA secretary in France and was dean of the Training School for European Women in Paris in 1919. For her work during this time, she was awarded the Reconnaissance Française medal by the French government.

Glass became the president of Sweet Briar College in 1925 and retired from that position in 1946. During her tenure at Sweet Briar, she introduced interdepartmental majors and the honors program. Under Glass's watch, the library grew from eleven thousand volumes to sixty-two thousand volumes.

During 1943 when the school's employees were serving in the U.S. military, President Glass and other faculty members served as soda jerks during evenings at the College Inn. Once a male student at a nearby college addressed a letter to PO Box 408 at Sweet Briar College and stated that he was wondering what the holder of his box number at Sweet Briar looked like. He described himself as tall and dark, the driver of a Ford V-8, and stated that he was a freshman. "What class are you in?" he wrote. Dr. Glass wrote back and stated, "I am tall too, and not as thin as I once was. My hair is white and I drive a Buick. I was a freshman in 1896. You asked what 408 at Sweet Briar looks like. From the recent picture of me in the public press at the time we established the Carter-Glass Chair of Government, I think I look like nothing human." She closed by inviting the freshman to visit her if he ever got up that way.[19] (As far as our research could ascertain, President Meta Glass never heard from this young student again.)

6. Alice C. Lloyd had been dean of women at the University of Michigan since 1930. Lloyd was born in Ann Arbor, Michigan, and was the daughter of a dean of the university's graduate school. For seven months in 1925, her father, Alfred H. Lloyd, served as acting president of the University of Michigan. Alice Lloyd graduated from the university with a B.A. degree in 1916. In 1918, she entered St. Luke's Hospital Training School of Nurses in New York and graduated in 1921. Lloyd worked as a probation officer for the Wayne County Probate Court in Detroit until 1926, when she accepted a position as adviser to women at the University of Michigan. Four years later, her title was changed to dean of women. She was a member of the National Association of Deans of Women and served as the association's president from 1941 to 1943. Lloyd was also a member of the American Association of University Women and Phi Beta Kappa.

7. Alice M. Baldwin was the dean of the Women's College of Duke University. She was born in Lewiston, Maine, in 1879. She earned bachelor's and master's degrees from Cornell University in Ithaca, New York. In 1906, she accepted an appointment as a history instructor at the Baldwin School of Bryn Mawr in Bryn Mawr, Pennsylvania. She remained at Baldwin School for fifteen years and left to pursue a Ph.D. in history at the University of Chicago in 1921. A summer position as dean of women at Trinity College in 1923 changed her career plans. When her summer job ended, Trinity's president, William Preston Few, convinced her to leave the doctoral program at Chicago and accept a permanent position as dean of women. Trinity College became Duke University in 1924, and in 1930, Miss Baldwin was appointed dean of the newly created Women's College of Duke University.

Baldwin worked to bring about improvements in women's educational opportunities and quality of academic life from her earliest days at Trinity College. As early as 1925, decades before Title IX, Baldwin requested that President Few provide a basketball court, soccer field, hockey field, and golf course for women's use.

Baldwin retired as dean of the Women's College of Duke University in 1947.

8. Mrs. Malbone Graham, Ethel Murphy Graham, was the president of the American Association of University Women, an author, and a lecturer. She worked in the office of the director of Naval Officer Procurement in Los Angeles during World War II.

Less than two weeks after the establishment of the WAVES, the navy announced that all naval districts in the United States had been "swamped" by letters from women requesting application forms for commissions in the WAVES. The first Officer Candidate School for WAVE officers would begin in October 1942 at Smith College in Northampton, Massachusetts. By 12 August 1942, the navy received twenty-seven applicants for each of the nine hundred WAVE officer billets. The navy also informed the public that applications for enlisted women in the WAVES would not be accepted until 10 September 1942.

On 31 August 1942, the *Daily Hampshire Gazette* announced to its readers, "Smith College Chosen as Training Place for Women's Naval Auxiliary." A subhead under those words announced, "Hotel Northampton to Be Used as Part of Quarters in City." The article went on to say that Smith College had arranged for five hundred WAVE officer candidates to be quartered in the hotel, four hundred would be quartered in the Capen, Northrop, and Gillett Houses, all dorms at Smith, and would take their meals at the Hotel Northampton along with their peers quartered there. WAVES would march between the hotel and the Smith campus as dictated by the necessities of the program to train officers of the first Women's Naval Reserve in the nation's history. The owners of the hotel made it clear that the historic Wiggins Tavern, a popular meeting and eating place for the residents of Northampton and its surrounding towns, would not be part of the WAVES' quarters and would remain open to the public as usual.[20]

Since the number of regular students at Smith would not be reduced to accommodate the Women's Naval Reserve, it was clear that arrangements would need to be made to realign the Smith students' living quarters. Women displaced from Capen, Northrup, and Gillett Houses would be moved into other dorms on the campus by replacing the traditional sleeping arrangements with double-decker beds provided by the navy in order to accommodate twice as many Smith students in the sleeping space available.

Smith alumnae relinquished the northern part of the Alumnae House for the use of the Women's Naval Reserve Headquarters on campus. In addition, the WAVE training unit was given the full use of the Alumnae Gymnasium and Faunce Hall, with its large lecture hall, as well as six classrooms. John M. Greene Hall was used by the WAVES for evening lectures and large assemblies, and athletic fields were turned over to the officer candidates for drilling, physical education, and parades. When other space was needed by the navy, it was made available in other buildings at specified hours as needed.

It is clear that the residents of Northampton and the faculty and staff of Smith College took extraordinary steps to provide for and welcome the Women's Naval Reserve Midshipmen School and its WAVE officer candidates to the area and the Smith College campus.

The commitment of Smith College to do its part in World War II was not the first time Smith's faculty, students, and alumnae had dedicated themselves to aid the United States in achieving victory over a national enemy who threatened Western democracies and, ultimately, America's freedom and entire way of life. Even before America's entrance into the First World War, Smith College initiated organized programs to aid civilians living in European cities impacted by the war. Smith students collected and shipped clothing to the people of France and Belgium, assembled and shipped kits for American and Allied armed forces, and collected and contributed money to assist organizations formed to aid those suffering from the horrors of war in their own nations. When the United States entered World War I, Smith College established a branch of the American Red Cross that later became a part of the Northampton branch of the American Red Cross. Students pledged $1,331 a month to purchase Red Cross supplies, and nine-tenths of the student body volunteered their time on a weekly basis to work in the Smith Red Cross room, assembling Red Cross packages to be shipped overseas.

In the fall of 1917, Smith alumnae took a gigantic step when they formed, financed, and volunteered for the Smith College Relief Unit, which sailed for France that year, set up in the Somme area, and aided in rehabilitation efforts to help restore people and cities devastated by war. At the same time, Smith College organized "war courses" that were open to the community. The program consisted of a large number of courses including, but not limited to, home nursing, first aid, nutrition, automobile mechanics, and gardening and farming to establish "victory gardens" to aid in providing food for individuals and the community.

When a German offensive overran the Somme in 1918, the Smith College unit aided civilians by evacuating them to safer places behind the battle line. When the war ended in 1919, the Smith unit remained in Europe to aid the people in reestablishing their lives, homes, and cities and remained overseas until April 1922.

This same dedicated and patriotic spirit and commitment infused Smith and the community, even before the first WAVES reported to the Smith campus to be trained and commissioned as Women's Naval Reserve Officers. The first groups of women who volunteered for the first Women's Naval Reserve in our nation's history arrived and worked for weeks in civilian clothes, looking forward to the day when their uniforms would arrive and they could reflect on the outside the patriotism and commitment they felt inside.

Plans for creating and distributing the first WAVE uniforms began, as did other planning, months before the Women's Naval Reserve was legislated and signed in to existence. The newly appointed first director of the WAVES, Mildred H. McAfee, was quick to point out, "One thing we have kept in mind is that there should be no effort to dress the women to look like men. Their uniforms will be becoming and functional."[21] Unlike the uniform for the members of the Women's Army Auxiliary Corps, which was selected by men of the army's Quartermaster Corps, the WAVE uniform was the product of a world-recognized designer who volunteered his time and work to aid the war effort.

When Mainbocher (born Main Rousseau Bocher), a former editor of *Vogue* magazine and favorite designer of wealthy European women, became aware of the creation of the Women's Naval Reserve, he volunteered his time and talent, at no cost to the Department of the Navy, to design the uniform that would be worn by members of the Women's Naval Reserve. The work took two full months of one of the world's top fashion designers, and when it was completed, Mainbocher stated in an interview with reporter Sally Dee of the *New York Times*, "I've put everything I've learned about dress making into designing that uniform." The navy's Admiral King and LCDR Mildred McAfee, Director of the WAVES, agreed that Mainbocher's design, and the uniform that resulted, "was a credit to Uncle Sam."[22]

WAVES would wear navy blue in the winter and white in the summer and would be considered by fashion designers and the American public to be among the best-dressed women in the world. The Department of the Navy and the Civilian Advisory Council appointed by President Roosevelt had distinguished themselves by continuing their drive for excellence, not only in the standards and educational caliber of the women they selected as their officers, and the sites they selected for their training centers, but in the design and style of the WAVES' uniforms themselves.

Newspaper reporters peppered Lieutenant Commander McAfee with questions for a description of the first uniforms for the WAVES, and, beginning in August 1942, newspapers carried articles describing what the members of the Women's Naval Reserve would be wearing. McAfee described the uniform as a "snappy navy blue of tropical worsted." The shirt would be a medium blue and have a "lady's collar" and would be "fastened with a square black bow." The stripes on officers' uniforms would match the blue color of the shirt, since, according to Miss McAfee, "the supply of gold braid is running out!" The director of the WAVES went on to say that there would be one small left upper pocket on the shirt and two small pockets in the skirt. The skirt would be slightly flared. As for the WAVE uniform hat, it would be navy blue and have a small brim "which rolls on the side, but is straight on the front and back." The hat was fashioned after those worn by eighteenth-century seamen such as John Paul Jones. The WAVES insignia, consisting of "a crossed pillar" and an anchor "will be displayed on both the hat and the coat." Stockings would be lisle rather than rayon, in order to avoid shortages. The color of the stockings had not yet been decided. There would be an evening dress uniform for officers, which would be identical to the regular officer's uniform, except for a white shirt and a slightly higher heel.

McAfee also stated that the white summer uniforms would not be ready for that summer's wear and that the navy blue uniforms would be available in the coming days or weeks. A large black purse would be part of the uniform and would be worn over one shoulder. WAVES would wear black "sensible shoes" of an approved design that would be purchased out of a $200 uniform allowance for enlisted women and $250 allowance for officers.

One aspect of the uniforms that generated many questions from newspaper reporters was in regard to WAVES undergarments. In contrast to the army-issued khaki underwear of the WAACs, navy women were to purchase their own undergarments, since the navy only issued clothes that could be seen as outer garments. Girdles were optional. Makeup would be permitted for all WAVES but, according to McAfee, "WAVES will wear enough make-up to be human."[23]

McAfee's academic background as dean of women at Oberlin College and president of Wellesley College had a direct effect on how the navy would train its female officers. The first WAVE officers would be trained at Smith College in Northampton beginning in October 1942. While 900 WAVE officers trained at Smith, an additional 300 would be trained in the first officer classes at nearby Mount Holyoke College. They would then act as procurement officers for the recruitment of women into the Women's Coast Guard Reserve. Since the same bill signed into law by President Roosevelt on 30 July 1942 authorized the WAVES, the SPARS, and the Women Marines, the process of getting them all up and running happened over an extended period of time ranging from two to seven months. The Women's Marine Corps Reserve marked its birthday on 13 February 1943.

On 7 October 1942, WAVE officer candidates began arriving in Northampton to begin the first WAVE officer training classes for the U.S. Women's Navy Reserve and the first of many such classes that would be held at Smith College. The instructors for these first nine hundred WAVE officer candidates would be experienced male navy training instructors, who would be replaced over time by newly commissioned WAVE officers who had completed that first training class. In just three months, the new WAVE officers began replacing the training staff of fifty-two navy men. Since those original fifty-two male navy trainers also taught three hundred WAVE officer candidates at nearby Mount Holyoke College, the new WAVE officers would eventually take over training at that institution too. Male drill instructors made it clear that the WAVE officer candidates caught on fast and were outstanding in close-order drill.

On that same day at 6:00 p.m., ninety enlisted WAVES left Northampton for the Oklahoma Agricultural and Mechanical College in Stillwell, Oklahoma, for yeoman training or for the University of Wisconsin at Madison to be trained as radio operators. Others traveled to the Naval Training School for storekeepers at Indiana University. These enlisted women received concentrated courses on the rating requirements of each specialty and little navy indoctrination or discipline. This was done to prepare the women for work assignments as soon as possible so that they could relieve a man for sea duty. The navy had learned quickly, and requests for WAVES as aviation mechanics and for any other fields where small hands and small frames proved an unexpected asset increased tremendously. The WAVES were off to a great start and grew to a corps of more than eighty-six thousand women before World War II ended.

The first full-time indoctrination program—boot camp—for enlisted WAVES opened on 14 December 1942 at Iowa State Teachers College at Cedar Falls. CAPT Ransom K. Davis, USN, was the Commanding Officer, and LT Margaret Criswell Disert, the former dean of Wilson College at Chambersburg, Pennsylvania, was Officer-in-Charge of Seaman Recruits. In addition to aptitude testing, physical examinations, and fittings for navy uniforms, the six-week indoctrination included classes in naval history, law, and organization; ships, aircraft, and weapons; ratings and promotions; naval nomenclature; and physical education.[24]

Elinor Johnson was among the first recruits headed for Naval Training Station, Iowa State Teachers College. "In December, seventy of us [from California] received orders to report to boot camp . . . in Cedar Falls, Iowa. Our departure was such a momentous occasion that Mildred McAfee who was visiting in L.A. at the time . . . came to the railroad station to see us off." These women were so early in the navy program that the only uniforms they saw were "pictures and drawings." However, beige cotton stockings and black lace-up shoes called "old ladies' shoes" were available and mandatory wear. Johnson wrote, "On rare occasions, we were allowed liberty to go into town and once when I was in a store wearing my civilian clothes plus the Navy shoes and stockings, I heard one shopper say to another, 'You can tell they're WAVES by their shoes.' " Johnson graduated in mid-January 1943 and left for specialty training at the Navy Link Trainer School in Atlanta, Georgia.[25] WAVE graduates of this school were assigned to use link trainers to teach naval pilots how to fly on instruments.

Sylvia Bergstrom, a classmate of Johnson's in boot camp, went to Aviation Machinist Mate Training for six months at Norman, Oklahoma.[26] The one thousand WAVES who graduated with Johnson and Bergstrom

*WAVE Joyce Courtney, Cedar
Falls boot camp.*

soon relieved navy men for sea duty. One
member of their class, Joyce Courtney, formerly a teacher, transferred to the coast guard
following boot camp and was stationed in
Washington, D.C., at the coast guard headquarters.[27]

One of the five WAVES in that first training class of WAVE officers who volunteered
for the SPARS was Dorothy C. Stratton, the
former dean of women at Purdue University in
Lafayette, Indiana, and a former psychology
professor at that institution. Stratton was promoted to lieutenant commander and sworn in
as the first director of the SPARS on 26 November 1942.

On 28 December 1942, the first SPARS entered the Coast Guard
Academy in New London, Connecticut. They were the first women to be
admitted to classes in a U.S. military academy, but they would not be the
last. True, attending classes at the U.S. Coast Guard Academy did not
lead to automatic acceptance as a cadet, and graduation was a long way
away, but it was a beginning. The men in the coast guard were nervous
about women invading what they had historically considered an all-male
domain. However, they did treat the women with respect and cordiality,
and requests for SPARS to fill coast guard billets began to come in immediately. At the Coast Guard Academy, SPARS would study administra-

*WAVES director Mildred McAfee and LCDR Dorothy
Stratton, director of SPARS.*

tion, organization and duties, military etiquette, and history and communications.

The SPARS had already received requests for two thousand cadets who would work at various coast guard stations throughout the United States. Of those, 1,300 were billets for storekeepers; 200 for pharmacists' mates; 250 for radio operators; 200 for mess attendants; 122 for coxswains (drivers for a variety of light vehicles); 150 for telephone operators; 125 for file clerks; 75 for punch operators; 60 for Teletype operators; 35 for financial assistants; 15 for legal assistants; an unspecified number for electrician mates; and several were to be welfare and reception assistants.

The U.S. Marine Corps Women's Reserve was the last women's reserve branch established during World War II. Ironically, the marine corps was the most reluctant to accept women into the corps in order to free a man to fight. After the Battle of Guadalcanal in August 1942, it became clear to the marines that they would need many more men before the war was brought to an end in the Pacific. In November 1942, the marine corps began seriously making plans and preparations for the U.S. Marine Corps Women's Reserve (USMCWR) to begin its first training classes on 13 February 1943. The Women Marines followed the lead of the SPARS and asked WAVE officers to volunteer to transfer into the Marine Corps Women's Reserve to act as the nucleus for the newest women's corps.

Nineteen WAVE officers stepped forward, and Ruth Cheney Streeter was appointed the Marine Corps Women's Reserve's first director. Streeter, from Morristown, New Jersey, was a graduate of Bryn Mawr College and married to Thomas W. Streeter, a retired banker. They had a daughter, who was in school, and three sons, all of whom were in the U.S. military—two ensigns in the navy and one son in the army. Mr. Streeter was supporting the war effort by raising money for the American National Red Cross. When asked by a reporter what her husband had to say about this, her first paying job, Mrs. Streeter stated, "He thinks it's fine."[28]

Streeter was given the rank of major, and her energetic approach to life proved an asset to the latest women's corps. Major Streeter, forty-seven years old, had earned both private and commercial pilot's licenses. She had applied for the WASP (Women's Auxiliary Service Pilots) five times and had been turned down on each application. Streeter then applied to the navy and asked to be assigned as a flight instructor. When she was informed that she would be permitted to teach flying only on the ground, she withdrew her application. As fate would have it, Maj. Ruth C. Streeter would lead the Marine Corps Women's Reserve, 40 percent of whose members were trained and worked in the field of aviation. The first classes for the Marine Corps Women's Reserve were held at Smith and Mount Holyoke colleges. In a matter of months, the marine corps decided that it would do all of its training at Cherry Point, North Carolina, and Camp Lejeune, North Carolina.

Capt. Charlotte D. Gower applied for the Marine Corps Women's Reserve as soon as its creation was announced. Gower was the second woman marine to receive a direct commission and was placed in charge of training the members of the corps. Gower had graduated from Smith College in 1922 and the University of Chicago in 1928, having earned her Ph.D. in anthropology. In 1938, Gower traveled to Canton, China, to teach at Lingnan University. Not long after she arrived in Canton, Japan attacked the city. Gower acted as a pharmacist in a refugee camp for three months before escaping to Hong Kong, where the faculty of Lingnan University had established the school and taught courses. During the seventeen-day Japanese attack on the British base at Hong Kong, Gower set up first-aid stations to care for the wounded, helped rescue the injured, and transported supplies to those fighting the Japanese. She was captured by the Japanese and interned in a prison camp where she taught Chinese to other internees and experienced starvation firsthand. Gower, along with hundreds of other civilian prisoners of the Japanese, was repatriated aboard the Swedish ocean liner *Gripsholm,* which docked in New York on 24 August 1942.[29]

Katherine A. Towle was one of six women to receive a direct commission to the USMCWR and was appointed as the representative for Recruiting for Women Marines. Before she was commissioned in the USMCWR, Towle had been dean of women at the University of California at Berkeley.

The requirements for both officer candidates and enlisted women were the same in several categories. To be accepted in the USMCWR, a woman had to be a U.S. citizen; could not be married to a marine; had to be single or married with no children under eighteen years of age; be no shorter than five feet tall and weigh no less that ninety-five pounds. Applicants were also required to have good vision and good teeth.

The requirements for officer candidates closely matched those for officers of the WAVES and SPARS: aged between twenty and forty-nine years and either a college graduate or with two years of college combined with two years of work experience. Unlike the other women's services, however, the women of the marine corps were to be called "Marines" and not labeled with an acronym. When asked by a reporter about the name for the Marine Corps Women's Reserve, Major Streeter, who was on a cross-country recruiting campaign, said, "We're straight marines. The Marine Corps command wanted it that way, and we are very happy to be asked to share the name of which they are so proud. It is the final proof that they wanted us."[30]

Although there was no regulation specifically requiring that USM-CWR applicants had to be white, black women were not knowingly recruited. The first black women marines officially accepted in the USM-CWR arrived at Parris Island, South Carolina, on 10 September 1949 to begin boot camp. Rumors made the rounds that some black women who could and did pass for white were accepted and served in World War II, the scuttlebutt for many a whispered conversation.

Despite the fact that the thousands of women now applying for the USMCWR took a toll on the recruitment numbers for the WAAC/WAC, WAVES, and SPARS, the directors of the various corps got together and worked out a recruiting policy that would apply to all the women's branches. This general policy was helped along by the fact that each individual director wanted to secure the best candidates possible for her particular branch of the armed forces. In fact, this spirit of cooperation was the source of several meetings that were more like seminars with all four directors of the women's branches. Each was aware that she led a pioneer group of military women and that how these women performed would affect the future relationships of American women and the U.S. military from that time forward. Each also realized that the future of American women and the opportunities presented to them would be forever changed.

Thousands of women had demonstrated to themselves and to the country that the "weaker sex" was capable in so many more areas of life and in so many more ways than society and individual women had thought possible. Women had left homes and hometowns in massive numbers in order to help their nation win the final victory in World War II; their eyes had been opened as to their own abilities as women and to the possibilities that made their lives more satisfying and personally productive in fields they thought were exclusively the domain of men. Their gaze might narrow in coming years, but their eyes would never completely close again.

The first group of officer candidates for the USMCWR began officer's training on 13 March 1943 at the U.S. Naval Reserve Midshipmen's

Women Marines at Hunter College, New York City, 1943.

School, South Hadley, Massachusetts. On 23 March 1943, the first class of enlisted personnel began at Hunter College in New York City.

The requirements for acceptance into the enlisted ranks of the USM-CWR were to be between twenty and thirty-five years of age and have at least two years of high school. Many questioned why males aged eighteen could enlist or be drafted and sent into combat, while women had to be age twenty or older to apply. In the 3rd Naval District, where recruitment had opened with a rush of applications on 15 February, Elizabeth Louise Morris, one of the youngest enlistees, who recently had turned twenty, proudly stated that she was descended from Revolutionary War patriot Gouverneur Morris and that her twin brother, Langdon E. Morris, a marine, was in training at Parris Island. In the same group, Frances Ann Fortune, who had been a secretary in a war plant, was the daughter of marine corps Lieutenant Colonel Harry G. Fortune, who was stationed in Washington, D.C. Morris and Fortune would be proud to wear the recently designed uniform of the U.S. Marine Corps Women's Reserve.[31]

Capt. Anne A. Lentz, who had been employed by a large department store in the school uniform section, designed the Marine Corps Women's Reserve uniform. It looked very much like the WAAC uniform except that it was marine green and made from a slightly lighter fabric. The uniform hat for women marines had a visor/peak that slanted downward at a sharp angle, distinguishing it from the WAAC Hobby hat, whose brim protruded straight out with no downward angle. The uniform was to be produced by the marine corps, and sold, as was the navy uniform, by retail stores. The first class of officers and enlisted women to graduate did so in civilian clothes since uniforms were not available in adequate quantities for many weeks. The women of the marine corps were also issued a dress blue uniform that resembled the male marines' dress blues.

Like the WAVES of the navy, Women Marines received a uniform allowance, $250 for officers and $200 for enlisted women. With her uniform allowance, a woman marine purchased two winter uniforms, hats, shoes, summer uniforms, a handbag, a wool-lined raincoat—the most expensive item in her uniform wardrobe at $41—and various other items required to complete the uniform. Although an officer had the option of wearing a white or dark green shirt, she was required to buy both. An offi-

Josette Dermody, WAVE on liberty,
New York City, September 1944.

cer wore her rank insignia on her jacket shoulders and on the collar of her shirts. A distinctive red cord on the dress hats of Women Marines replaced the brown chin strap on the dress hats worn by marine corps men.[32]

The reasons women enlisted or joined the women's sea services were very much the same as those given by young women joining the WAAC. Martha Jane Williams Hylton joined the WAVES because "my brother was missing overseas. Also, most of our class went into the service." Hylton went on, "I followed my mother's footsteps. She had been a Red Cross nurse in World War I and served overseas during the influenza epidemic."[33]

Mary Simons Winters enlisted in the WAVES "because my younger brother enlisted, and I wanted to do my bit also."[34]

Dorothy Adams White was twenty-one when she joined the WAVES. It was Pearl Harbor and the enlistment of her only brother in the navy that led her to join up. "I was hoping to help in some way," she wrote. "I was very patriotic." Boot camp for her was at Hunter College in New York City. One of her strongest memories from those days was marching on the large parade ground for two distinguished visitors. "I will never forget Eleanor Roosevelt and Madame Chiang Kai-shek reviewing our companies as we marched on Hunter's large parade ground."[35]

Josette Dermody was one of the first enlisted WAVES to be stationed at Hunter College for boot camp. She and her sister WAVE "boots" arrived at Grand Central Terminal and took the subway to the Bronx. She remembered the large brass sign attached to the brick gatepost. The first lines read, "U.S. Naval Training School [WR]"; the second line announced: "NO Visitors." Hunter College became the "USS *Hunter*" for all the WAVES who would attend boot camp on its campus. Josette Dermody marched with her sister WAVES through the gate and along the sand-colored flagstones, walkways that stretched across the wide lawns of the Hunter campus. They reached their destination, a large stone building that looked very much like a fort. Before it became the receiving station for the U.S. Navy Women's Reserve at Hunter College, the fortlike building had been used as a National Guard armory. "On the wall near where I was shifting from one foot to the other was a large poster," Dermody wrote. "Across the top large letters proclaimed, 'Through These Doors Pass the Most Essential Women in the World.' I felt at least two inches taller."[36]

For Elizabeth Hundley Clark, who enlisted in the WAVES at age twenty-one, her strongest memory of boot camp at Hunter College was unusual. In response to the question, "What do you remember most about your first days/weeks in the military?" Clark responded, "Getting a small pox vaccination at Hunter College for the first time in my life. My mother had not been in favor of having me vaccinated as a baby, so you can imagine the reaction I had. I was miserable."[37]

After just three months of having Women Marines train at Mount Holyoke and Hunter colleges, the marine corps concluded that, given the numbers of women applying for entrance into the USMCWR, it would be advantageous to train all future women marine reservists at a marine corps base. In July 1943, all women marine boots at Mount Holyoke and Hunter colleges were transferred to Camp Lejeune in New River, North Carolina. Camp Lejeune was one of the largest marine bases in the world, and a large section of it was given over to train all future USMCWRs during World War II.

In addition, the marine corps announced that, beginning on 15 September 1943, all USMCWR officers would be selected—except for the few who would come from civilian life with scarce and needed specialties—from the ranks. This proved to be a good boost for the over-

Regina R. Slattery at Camp Lejeune,
North Carolina, 1943.

all morale of Women Marines. The only requirements limiting admission to the officer candidate program were that the Women Marines had to have at least three months of service following graduation from boot camp and the recommendation of their direct supervisor.

Camp Lejeune was also the home of USMCWR special schools. Among the specialties offered were paymaster; motor transport; two quartermaster schools, one for regular quartermaster administration and the other to focus on aviation supplies and equipment; and the cooks and bakers school.

One question that troubled some members of Congress was whether women in the sea services should be permitted to serve outside the continental United States. Despite the fact that army and navy nurses and women in the WAAC were serving overseas, Congress continued to deny WAVES, SPARS, and Women Marines the right to serve outside the United States. The old arguments that said women would lose their femininity if exposed to overseas service or service aboard combat ships of the navy still held sway and continued to keep these women firmly stationed in the forty-eight contiguous states. This in spite of the fact that newspapers, including the *New York Times,* printed articles about army and navy nurses who were currently serving in combat zones around the world. One article that appeared in the *New York Times* on 15 August 1943, "The Most Rewarding Work," told the story of army flight nurses who flew into forward bases to evacuate the wounded to rear area hospitals.[38]

Nurses knew they were in great danger, yet they put their patients first. Thousands of American GIs were alive after the war because these army nurses volunteered for the Army Nurse Corps, volunteered again for flight nurse duty, and yet again for frontline service in order to save the lives of wounded American GIs. No one in America, including members of Congress, argued that these women would lose their "femininity or ability to be good mothers" when the war ended. Magazines of the day carried hundreds of ads that sought to persuade more American nurses to join the military nurse corps and "go where they are needed most, in order to save the lives of wounded GIs."[39]

Another *New York Times* article carried the story of army nurses' escaping with their lives when a German plane bombed a hospital ship off the coast of Salerno, Italy, on 13 September 1943. The article went on to quote one of the chief nurses aboard the British hospital ship *Newfoundland.* The reporter could not have known that less than five months later,

Lt. Blanche Sigman, Chief Nurse of the 95th Evacuation Hospital, would lie dead on the Anzio beachhead hospital area, killed when another German attack hit a clearly marked tent hospital. There, thousands of wounded American and Allied soldiers were being cared for by hundreds of army nurses; the hospital area was bombed and/or shelled multiple times almost every day.[40]

One might well ask the members of Congress and the military how and why the lives of female military nurses were less important than the lives of members of the WAVES, SPARS, or USMCWRs. And while one is asking the question, it would seem appropriate to ask the same people why WAACs who went overseas did not have the protection of being full members of the U.S. Army, when WAVES, SPARS, and Women Marines were full members of the military, yet barred from serving outside the United States. The authors suggest that this reasoning—or lack of reasoning—was the result of gender roles crashing head-on into the needs of an America at war.

Just as male pioneers in the west used an elastic definition of gender roles in times of Indian attacks, so the U.S. Congress used, and still uses today, an elastic definition of gender roles in a time of crisis. With each decision to apply this elastic definition of "women's roles" and "what is or is not feminine," the return to the former, more strict gender definitions are more difficult to sell to women who have participated as full American citizens in time of war or national emergency. Each new incident of the elastic gender roles' being applied when women are needed to get through war or national emergency makes movement back to old definitions of what is appropriate more difficult and less complete. Each new incident makes it clearer and clearer that assigned gender roles are artificial restrictions imposed by those who are determined to maintain the lopsided status quo of "women's place" in American society. In the United States in the early 1940s, women who stepped forward to join these new military women's corps—like all courageous soldiers—had to be prepared to "take the flack."

When Theresa Karas informed her mother that she had joined the Women Marines, her mother did not take the news well. Mrs. Karas called on her husband to do something to stop their daughter from reporting to the Women Marines for duty. "She'll come home pregnant! Do you hear me? Pregnant! We'll never be able to hold our heads high ever again in Tonawanda [New York]!"[41]

Another young woman, Virginia Shepherd, joined the Women Marines when she was twenty years old, and stated that she joined "to serve my country in time of war. The 'Free a Man to Fight' slogan caught my eye." When asked about the most surprising thing she had learned about herself as a result of her World War II service, she replied, "I lacked confidence, and serving in the Marine Corps taught me self-confidence."[42]

For Barbara Johnson, patriotism summed up many things about why she and other young women flocked to join the USMCWR. Her strongest memory of World War II was "an entire nation, with few exceptions, united in patriotism. Everyone knew there was a war on and wanted to do their part in winning the victory."[43]

When Alice Julian Herman wanted to join the USMCWR at age twenty, her mother refused to sign the papers. Alice decided to wait until she was twenty-one years old and sign up on her own. "I was so bashful that I would get up at 4:00 a.m. just to get to take a shower alone," Herman remembered. "In boot camp, all the girls had to shower in one big room and there were no partitions separating one shower area from another." After basic training at Camp Lejeune, she attended aviation specialty school at the marine base at Cherry Point, North Carolina. When she graduated, she was stationed in San Francisco as a propeller specialist.[44]

Betty Margaret Riekord was a member of the second class of enlisted Women Marines at Hunter College. While at Hunter, Riekord lived in one of the hotels taken over by the Navy Department to serve as barracks for the WAVES. "I remember quite a few of the Bronx residents lining up their chairs outside so they could sit and watch our close-order drill and marching every night," Riekord wrote. "I also remember the black-outs [air raid drills] every night. We had black shades in our building."[45]

Before World War II ended, more than 18,000 American women had joined the U.S. Marine Corps Women's Reserve and had served their country proudly and with honor. They were among the more than 350,000 American women who truly pioneered a new field for American women of the day and for those who would follow them along the path they trod and into the future.

4
★

In the final analysis, the only testament free people can give the quality of freedom is the way in which they resist the forces that imperil freedom. You are the example of free women defending a free way of life, to the exclusion of everything else, until the war against the Axis is won.
—Maj. Oveta Culp Hobby, director, WAAC

On 15 September 1942, G-3 Division, Assistant Chief of Staff for Operations and Training, notified Maj. Oveta Culp Hobby that the WAAC was to be expanded to 1.5 million members. The directive ordered the WAAC to begin immediately with that expansion plan by increasing the number of training centers and the number of WAACS accepted and graduated so that two units of WAACs could be trained and shipped overseas as soon as possible. An addendum to the directive informed Major Hobby that "dozens more overseas units would be wanted shortly." The previously established ceiling of 63,000 WAACs set in June was no longer operative since the Adjutant General's committee had conducted a study of the 628 military jobs listed by the army. The committee found that 406 jobs were suitable for women, and only 222 army jobs were found to be unsuitable for women. Even this result was considered capable of expansion by a committee that clearly stated that in an emergency many of the 222 jobs could be performed by women. Necessity, it seems, is not only the mother of invention but a very effective lens through which long-held prejudices are transformed into untenable positions. Whether the threats were marauding Indians or bandits of the Old West; the German army in World War I; the Axis powers in World War II; or the Taliban in Afghanistan, necessity proves an effective filter through which prejudice passes quickly in favor of the facts that remain in clear view.

The opportunity for women to step forward and show what they were capable of doing was undeniable, and the conditions and challenges they would have to meet and overcome were huge.

Those difficulties and challenges loomed large in the first months and years of the WAAC's existence. If the WAAC were to grow in geometric progressions as the U.S. Army challenged it to do, the first WAAC officers and enlisted women would have to contribute 100 percent of what they were capable of giving, and Major Hobby and her staff would have to show better than average intelligence, extraordinary planning ability, undisputed leadership, and dedication to the assigned mission. Fortunately, the WAAC did not lack for such leaders or enlisted women. With Maj. Oveta Culp Hobby leading, the WAAC would meet and overcome each difficulty presented to it.

On 8 November 1942, the United States, along with its British allies, staged an amphibious invasion of North Africa, America's first invasion outside the South Pacific in World War II. Accompanying the thousands of American soldiers to go ashore on D-Day for Operation Torch were fifty-seven U.S. Army Nurses of the Forty-eighth Surgical Hospital, the

The first members of the WAAC to serve abroad, these five officers flew to England in November 1942 and a month later sailed for North Africa, where they served as secretaries at the Casablanca Conference. Left to right: 2nd Officers (1st Lt.) Alene Drezmal, Louise Anderson, Martha E. Rogers, Ruth Briggs, and Mattie Pinette, 30 November 1942.

first American military women to wade ashore during battle, and the last, for the rest of World War II. Gen. Dwight David Eisenhower, the theater commander, put an end to the short-lived practice because he feared the American people might respond negatively to women landing on invasion beachheads under enemy fire and call for army nurses to be pulled from all combat zones for the duration. Since such a move would have had a disastrous effect on all wounded and ill service troops, Eisenhower chose the course of political caution. He did, however, request that WAACs be sent to his headquarters in Algiers to act as secretaries for him and his senior officers. He further requested that the WAACs sent be fluent in French and act as an advance party to prepare for a full battalion of WAACs that would follow.

The five WAACs, 2nd Officers (relative to the rank of 1st Lieutenant) Louise Anderson, Ruth Briggs, Alene Drezmal, Mattie Pinette, and Martha Rogers, were assigned to fill Eisenhower's request and soon boarded a troopship at Portsmouth, England, for the journey to their new assignment. English troops, nurses, and officers and American officers and nurses were on the ship. These WAAC officers had been selected for pioneering roles based partially on their prior experience before entering the WAAC. Louise Anderson had worked as the chief clerk in the U.S. Bureau of Reclamation in Denver, Colorado, her hometown. Ruth Briggs, thirty-six, from Westerly, Rhode Island, had been a social worker. Martha E. Rogers, twenty-six, from Jackson, Mississippi, had worked as a court reporter with the U.S. Treasury Department in her hometown before joining the WAAC. Second Officer Mattie A. Pinette, thirty-nine, was from Fort Kent, Maine, and spoke fluent French. Alene Drezmal, forty-three, had grown up in St. Paul, Minnesota.

Although travel by air would have been faster, the military felt that sea travel was safer. Unfortunately for these five WAAC officers and the others on board, that did not turn out to be true. One day out of port, the ship was hit by a torpedo fired from a German submarine. The torpedo smashed through the stern of the zigzagging ship while its passengers were sleeping, and the sound awoke them at once. The ship caught fire and began to sink. Three of the WAAC 2nd officers arrived on deck in time to climb aboard a lifeboat and be lowered to the water. Second Officer Briggs took on the job of steering the lifeboat. Rogers started rowing when one crewman onboard the lifeboat became too seasick to continue in that job. Pinette applied herself to helping get five soldiers who were in the water aboard their lifeboat. The three WAACs and six male GIs were adrift in the lifeboat through the night and were overjoyed when a British destroyer rescued them the following morning. That same British destroyer had also rescued men, several British nurses, and the other two remaining WAAC 2nd officers, Anderson and Drezmal, from the burning and sinking ship. With typical hospitality, the ship's crew served their visitors tea, biscuits, and whisky.[1]

On 22 December 1942, six weeks after American and British troops captured Algiers, the five WAAC officers arrived in port to report for duty. The women were met by Gen. Walter Bedell Smith and other senior army officers assigned to General Eisenhower's U.S. Army Headquarters for North Africa. General Smith and others presented the WAAC advance party with men's clothing in small sizes and assorted toiletry items donated by various military personnel to replace the clothing, equipment, and personal items each woman had lost to the German torpedo and the sea that claimed their ship. Gen. George C. Marshall, Army Chief of Staff, was in North Africa to attend the Casablanca Conference and told the five WAAC officers that when he returned to the United States, he would obtain and ship replacements for their lost items to them as quickly as possible. In the meantime, dressed in donated men's clothes, the five women set about their work in Eisenhower's headquarters along with establishing the necessary plans for the arrival of the first WAAC detachment, expected to arrive in a matter of weeks.

Later, upon his return to the United States, General Marshall set about obtaining the clothing and equipment to replace what the five WAAC officers had lost during the sinking of their transport ship. Marshall was quickly informed that since the WAAC had no military standing at all, the U.S. government would not replace the lost articles free of charge. Marshall paid for the replacements out of his own pocket and shipped them to the WAAC officers at Allied headquarters in Algiers. The five women quickly offered to reimburse him for the full price of the replacements, but Marshall refused any payment and said that the women were to consider the items his gift.

At the same time, in the United States on 1 December 1942, WAAC contingents from the first graduating classes at Fort Des Moines were divided into smaller groups and either remained at Fort Des Moines to help train the newest recruits or were assigned to the newly established Second WAAC Training Center in Daytona Beach, Florida. Another group went to Fort Sam Houston, Texas; another to Fort Huachuca, Arizona; or to the newly established Third WAAC Training Center at Fort Oglethorpe, Georgia. Each group would face its own unique challenges.

It was not until 1970 that the American public learned of a secret anti-aircraft artillery (AAA) experiment conducted by the army using WAAC personnel. On 11 December 1942, WAAC 3rd Officer Georgia B. Watson and nine other WAAC officers reported to the office of their director, Oveta Culp Hobby, in the Pentagon. Hobby informed the ten recently commissioned officers that a secret plan had been set into motion to train WAACs for duty with AAA batteries to find out if it were feasible to replace the men currently doing the job of protecting the president of the United States and the Capitol. Colonel Hobby went on to explain that the entire experiment was secret, as was the location of AAA batteries and the 90 mm guns they contained.

The WAACs of "Battery X," as it was named, were quartered in the YWCA located at Seventeenth and K Streets, which would be their home for the six weeks necessary to train and qualify the WAACs to replace the soldiers currently assigned to the gun batteries.

Since the WAACs of Battery X were involved in a secret project, no equipment, not even the special fur-lined pants, boots, and jackets that were worn on night duty and during cold weather, could be ordered directly from their unit. The WAACs would receive all they needed to carry out their training requirements, including special equipment like SCR-268 radar; the height finder and the director would be donated to Battery X from surplus equipment in other AAA batteries in the military district of Washington. The training, which took place on an undisclosed beach, would last for six intensive weeks, and the WAACs would stand different shifts and sleep in dugouts by the 90 mm guns. Water often collected in the bottom of the dugouts, so the assignment of gun crews to night duty was listed as "wet duty."

The men in the gun batteries made it very clear to the WAACs that the targets they would aim at, and the airplanes that towed those targets, were piloted by members of the Women's Auxiliary Service Pilots (WASP), a volunteer group of licensed women pilots who ferried military planes from one post or airfield to another. (See chapter 7.)

The further training and assignment of Battery X personnel took place in or near five cities: Washington, D.C.; Philadelphia, Pennsylvania; Norfolk, Virginia; Boston, Massachusetts; and New York City. A total of fifty-five WAAC officers and 973 enlisted women took part in the Battery X experiment. When Colonel Hobby announced the end of the Battery X experiment in August 1943, she made it very clear to its participants that the project was a complete success. In fact, if circumstances arose that called for larger or replacement crews for the men assigned to the AAA batteries, the army would not hesitate to assign WAACs, knowing that they would do a professional, efficient, and effective job. While many in the WAAC were participating in this secret project, other WAAC units were carrying out their assignments by replacing male soldiers at whatever posts they were assigned.[2]

WAAC arrival: a troop train of WAACs from Fort Des Moines, Iowa, arrive at Fort Huachuca, Arizona, 4 December 1942.

For the first group sent to Fort Huachuca, difficult challenges were certainly not new. The contingent was a group of black WAACs, officers and enlisted, who had graduated with the first WAAC classes from Fort Des Moines. The WAAC agreed from its inception that 10 percent of its members would be black. Rep. Edith Nourse Rogers had fought hard to get her WAAC bill presented on the floor of Congress and to get it passed. The black women who attended the first officer and enlisted classes at Des Moines had fought, since the start of World War II, for the rights already granted their Caucasian sisters, and during training they faced additional harsh conditions in order to travel the road that would take them into military service for the country. Black women wrote hundreds of letters and signed many petitions that they sent to the secretary of war, the president, the first lady, and members of Congress stating in no uncertain terms that they were eager to serve their country. They urged the government to accept black nurses into the military nurse corps and later argued for the admission of black women into all of the women's military branches.

One of the black women who had been trained in the first officer candidate class at the First WAAC Training Center in Des Moines, Iowa, was a twenty-six-year-old graduate of Wilberforce University in Wilberforce, Ohio, who had majored in mathematics and general science. Charity Adams was born in Columbia, South Carolina, on 5 December 1918. Her mother was a teacher, her father a minister. Charity and her three siblings grew up in a home where education and learning were held in high esteem. There were books in the home and Charity needed little encouragement to become an avid reader for the rest of her life.

When Charity Adams graduated from Booker T. Washington High School, it was as valedictorian. Along with honors in education, she also formed deep and lasting friendships with her classmates. One of her friends, Annie Mae Franklin, helped Charity with spelling, while Charity tutored her in mathematics.

One of the advantages of being valedictorian was that Adams had first pick of all available scholarships for the three leading Negro colleges of the day. Out of those three—Fisk University, Howard University, and Wilberforce University—Adams chose Wilberforce and again distinguished herself as a top student. After her graduation, Adams returned to Columbia, where she taught mathematics and general science for the next four years. In 1942, her alma mater was the link that led Adams to join the WAAC.

U.S. Army recruiters for the WAAC contacted all three well-known Negro colleges of the day seeking referrals of women graduates who might make good candidates for the Women's Army Auxiliary Corps. The dean of women at Wilberforce University sent the WAAC information along with an application to Charity Adams and a note saying she might want to consider the opportunities offered to women who joined the WAAC. Adams filled out the application and mailed it to the army, expecting to receive a response very quickly. When weeks passed without a response, Adams decided to attend graduate school at Ohio State University; she put the WAAC out of her mind. Adams boarded the train that would take her from Columbia, South Carolina, to Columbus, Ohio, to begin classes.

When the train stopped in Knoxville, Tennessee, passengers got off for a short rest stop. Adams was surprised to see her aunt waiting for her. She brought a message for Adams to call home on an important matter. When Adams reached her parents, she learned that the army had sent a telegram saying that the WAAC had accepted her application and that she was to report to Atlanta, Georgia, by 8:00 a.m. the next morning. Knowing that would be impossible, given the hour, Adams went on to Columbus, Ohio, and two hours after her arrival, she went to Fort Hayes to ask the army what she should do about her reporting date in Atlanta. After being passed from one person to the next, Adams met a captain who was from Sumter, South Carolina, who had not been in his hometown in seventeen years. The captain was overjoyed to meet someone from his "neck of the woods" and made a number of telephone calls to Atlanta. After several exchanges with army personnel in Atlanta, an agreement was reached to transfer Adams's papers to Fort Hayes and let her complete her processing there. The captain suggested that she take her physical at Fort Hayes that very day, return home, and wait to get a reporting date from army authorities.

Three days after she arrived at home, word came to report to Fort Hayes for final processing and to be sworn in to the WAAC. Adams arrived at Fort Hayes on 13 June 1942, and after she and seven other women were sworn in to the WAAC, reporters from the *Columbus Dispatch* took each woman's photograph and interviewed them. When the photographs appeared on the front page of the paper the following day, Adams's first reaction was the realization that it was the first time she had seen a black person's face on the front page of a white daily for any reason other than having been charged with a crime.[3]

After a long train trip, followed by a ride in the back of an army truck, the group of eight new WAAC officer candidates disembarked at the consolidated mess hall in the WAAC area of Fort Des Moines. The eight women enjoyed their breakfast while reporters and photographers asked questions and snapped photographs. This done, a young second lieutenant stood in front of the group and spoke the jarring words that would echo in Adams's memory for the rest of her life, "Will all the colored girls move over on this side?" and gestured to a group of isolated chairs. There was a moment of stunned silence, followed by the scraping sounds of chairs being pushed back from tables and the footfalls of several black WAACs following the lieutenant's orders. Adams remembered that the lieutenant's words were a shock "because even in the United States of the forties, it did not occur to us that this could happen." The "colored girls" were marched to Barracks 54, which would be the segregated living quarters for all black WAACs. WAACs—officer candidates and enlisted women—would attend racially integrated classes, eat in the consolidated mess hall—at separate tables—but otherwise living and recreational activities were strictly racially segregated.[4]

By the middle of the next week, the all-black Third Platoon, First Company, First WAAC Training Center, had its full complement, minus one, of the 10 percent of the total WAAC first class of officer candidates.

On 29 August 1942, the first class of WAAC officer candidates graduated and became 3rd officers. Third Officer Charity Adams was assigned to the First WAAC Training Center as a company commander charged with turning new black recruits into full-fledged WAACs.

With the pressure exerted by the Department of War and the army to expand the WAAC as quickly as possible, for most of the newly commissioned WAAC officers, including Charity Adams, military leaves following graduation were bypassed.

By the time Adams was granted leave to visit her home in Columbia, South Carolina, it was the second week in December, and Adams had been promoted to second officer, a rank equivalent to first lieutenant, and was looking forward to how pleased she felt her parents and friends would be to see her with her new captain's bars on the shoulders of her uniform. The train taking her home was the Carolina Special, run by the Southern Railway System, and segregated both in seating and in the dining car. When breakfast time drew near, Second Officer Adams joined a long line of passengers waiting to gain admittance to the dining car. The line moved briskly until Adams reached the door, seeking admittance to breakfast. Suddenly the steward controlling the flow of diners put his arm across the doorway and announced that the dining car was filled and asked that all military personnel in uniform come to the front of the line for immediate seating. With his arm blocking Adams from entering the dining car, the steward looked straight at the new WAAC 2nd officer and said, "I said personnel in uniform would go first." Before Adams could open her mouth, she heard a man's voice behind her say, "Well, what in the hell do you think that is that she has on? Get your —— arm down before I break it off for you."[5]

It immediately registered with Adams that the voice was obviously southern, and when she turned around, she saw a tall, blond second lieutenant whose face was red with anger. "What in the world are we fighting this war for?" the young second lieutenant continued. "She's giving her service too and can eat anywhere I can. And, by Jesus, I am going to eat with her in this diner." When Adams turned back to the dining car door, she realized that the steward had taken his arm down and was already leading her to a table for four. She was delighted when the second lieutenant took the chair opposite her. The dining car was full and silent until Adams and the lieutenant had settled in and were talking between themselves. When breakfast was over, the young man escorted Adams back to her seat, bowed, and wished her well. She never saw the man again, "but I still think of him as a southern gentleman," Adams would write more than half a century later.[6]

During that first leave and visit home, the NAACP had its annual meeting and Adams's father, who was a branch president and the state president, led the meeting, which was held at their local church. Before the meeting ended, a man she had known all her life whispered to her to tell her father that the Ku Klux Klan had surrounded their home and were waiting for him and his family to return. Since the minister at the church was home alone while his family was visiting relatives, the minister and Reverend Adams's family drove home together to find cars parked along both sides of the street that ran in front of their house. After going into his home and getting his shotgun and a box of shells, Adams's father walked the minister home and stayed the night, having given his own family instructions not to do anything provocative. Adams and her family sat in the dark, sneaking a peek out the window now and then at the robed and hooded Knights of the Cross. When dawn arrived, the Klan members at the minister's house and at the Adamses' house got in their cars and left. Second Officer Adams said that her family had notified the police immediately on their return home when they saw the cars parked on the street and the Klansmen in robes and hoods in front of their home. Adams reported that the response of the police over the telephone was that they "couldn't do anything about men parking on the street."[7]

With General Eisenhower's request that two WAAC companies be sent to his command in North Africa and after the ship carrying the first five

WAAC officers was torpedoed, the issue of the military status of the WAAC loomed larger than ever in the mind of Director Oveta Culp Hobby, as well as in the minds of many thinking and concerned American citizens. The ordeal of the five WAAC officers following the torpedoing of their ship put at center stage the question of the military standing of the WAAC and how WAACs would be assigned in the future. The cold, hard facts of the military's refusal to replace the clothing and equipment the five WAACs lost because the WAAC had no military standing—they were *with* the army, not *in* the army—brought all the dire consequences of that fact to the forefront for Director Hobby and others. Since the two companies of selected WAACs were stationed at the Second WAAC Training Center in Daytona Beach, Florida, awaiting deployment to Eisenhower's headquarters in North Africa, and since Maj. Oveta Hobby could not in good conscience order them into the North African Theater of Operations without making the circumstances of that deployment clear to each of the women in the two companies, the WAAC director herself traveled to Daytona Beach to speak to the women.

The three hundred WAACs were assembled, and Hobby addressed them. After explaining that their deployment would either need to be canceled or reassigned to another combat zone, Major Hobby explained that she would not order them overseas against their wishes. She went on to point out that they did not have the protection of military status afforded the men serving overseas: hospitalization, life insurance, the protections granted by the Geneva Conventions to all military personnel captured by the enemy, and not even the protection of replacement for clothing or equipment lost or damaged in the line of duty.

Director Hobby then asked if any WAAC, despite these circumstances, would step forward to serve in the units that would soon be shipped out for duty in a combat zone. Of the 300 women present, 298 stepped forward to volunteer for the assignment. When Director Hobby saw this, she was unable to continue speaking and sought privacy out of the sight of her troops. Half of the WAAC volunteers were selected and sent to the staging area, while the remaining half were held back to fill assignment requests from the European Theater of Operations.[8]

The question of military status for the WAACs was far from clear, as was the case for military status for members of the Army Nurse Corps. Since the Army Nurse Corps at the time consisted entirely of women— male nurses would not be admitted until 1955—the question of military status for nurses was basically the question of military status for women.

Relative rank for members of the Army Nurse Corps was granted on 4 June 1920; in the same year, women won the right to vote. To a greater or lesser extent, the granting of these rights was due in part to the military service of women in World War I.

The road of the proposed legislation that would affect the WAAC was not a smooth one. Every inch of progress was hard won, and it was only persistence on the part of the WAAC director, Major Hobby, and Rep. Edith Nourse Rogers that finally won the long-deserved victory. On 23 July 1942, Rogers introduced a bill to give WAACs the benefits of National Service Life Insurance. The bill did not pass. On 8 October 1942, Rogers introduced a bill to grant WAACs hospitalization and domiciliary privileges through the Veterans Administration. This bill went nowhere for five months, and then it finally passed. Bills to grant WAACs free postage, a benefit male soldiers already enjoyed, were introduced in October, November, and January. All failed to become law.

Also in October 1942, Rogers introduced a bill to place the WAAC in the Army Reserve Corps with military status. The bill failed in large part because Gen. George C. Marshall sent word to Congress that he did not want to delay the pay bill with a debate over military status for the WAAC. Marshall stated that he would prefer to keep the WAAC in its current status until more information could be gathered as to how valuable the corps might be to the army.[9]

In early January 1943, General Marshall changed his mind and notified Major Hobby that he felt that the WAAC had proven itself a very valuable organization and that he would support its becoming part of the U.S. Army. Major Hobby called upon Representative Rogers with a draft of a bill she had drawn up, and on 14 January 1943, Rogers introduced a bill changing the name of the WAAC to the Women's Army Auxiliary Corps, Army of the United States; later the name was changed to Women's Army Corps. On 1 February, the secretary of war announced that he supported the bill. Two days later, Gen. Miller G. White of the G-1 Division testified before the Senate that he also supported the passage of the bill but added the caveat that he did not feel that WAACs could replace men on a one-to-one basis; rather, it would, in his opinion, take three WAACs to replace two men.

The War Department's enthusiasm grew considerably when a study done of the WAACs replacing men at Fort Sam Houston reported that three WAACs did not replace two men but, rather, four men. Favorable reports were also coming in on the work of the WAACs in North Africa and of WAACs taking part in a secret trial of WAACs as antiaircraft teams. Now convinced of the effectiveness and efficiency of WAAC units in replacing men, the War Department ordered that every station receiving 150 WAACs would proceed to release 150 men for duty in combat assignments. Since a number of the WAACs would have to fill the duties of maintaining the WAAC units, the ratio of WAACs to male replacements was actually better than one to one.[10]

The Senate passed Rogers's WAAC legislation on 15 February 1943, but the House of Representatives had more than a few arguments to offer against passage of the bill. During the House Committee on Military Affairs hearing on the subject, a representative from Indiana argued that "draftees should receive soldiers' benefits," but that WAACs and men who volunteered should not get soldiers' benefits because they were not "forced into the Army." The congressman argued that, in addition, WAACs should not get soldiers' benefits because they did not go to the front lines.

WAACs, North Africa, 1943.

This statement ignited an argument as to whether the soldiers at General Eisenhower's headquarters, which was in a combat zone, should get military status even though they were not literally on the front lines.[11]

At the same time these arguments were being presented by representatives in Congress, American and world media were filled with news about American and Allied forces fighting in Tunisia. The same U.S. Army Nurses of the Forty-eighth Surgical Hospital who had waded ashore in Algiers on 8 November 1942 were with the combat troops in Tunisia. On 14 February 1943, all hell broke loose as German forces launched an attack at Faid Pass, heading for Kasserine Pass. The Forty-eighth Surgical Hospital, which had been treating the wounded only miles from the front lines since the Allies' landing in North Africa, continued to care for patients as hundreds of American and Allied soldiers, along with displaced local families, retreated as quickly as possible while the German army drew closer and closer to the hospital's location. U.S. Army Nurses were among the last to be loaded onto army trucks and evacuated to join the army pullback in the face of the German advance. "Our orders were to evacuate casualties and follow the retreat as fast as we could move. Just getting ready took hours," 1st Sgt. Loren Butts reported.[12]

On 17 February, two MPs riding on motorcycles showed up at the First Unit of the Forty-eighth Surgical Hospital set up at Thala to treat the casualties from Faid Pass and Kasserine Pass, in what would come to be known collectively as the Battle of Kasserine Pass. One of the MPs asked Lt. Helen Molony what she and the others were doing. Molony told him, "We're taking care of casualties; we're the Forty-eighth Surgical Hospital." The MP responded, "Well, you're about to become prisoners of war or get killed. You've got to get out of here fast." Hours later, the nurses of the Forty-eighth Surgical Hospital were loaded aboard two 2.5 ton trucks that joined a long column, including a Sherman tank that was making its way to the rear as fast as possible.[13]

Clearly, U.S. Army Nurses, with the full knowledge of General Eisenhower, the U.S. Army, and Congress, were often on, and sometimes in front of, the front lines of ongoing combat, yet these brave women held only relative rank and were not entitled to pay equal to that of male officers standing only feet or inches from the nurses as they carried out their assigned duties.

Despite these facts, the debate concerning military status for women continued in the House of Representatives for months while American women in the military faced the perils of war every day.

First group of "colored" nurses on foreign soil in Monrovia, Liberia, West Africa, 1943.

In March 1943, the first black army nurses left the United States for their new duty station with the Twenty-fifth Station Hospital at Roberts Field, Liberia. The hospital had been located there to care for the wounded and ill soldiers who would have to stop the German army should it decide to attack in that area. The German attack in or near Liberia failed to materialize, and so American and Allied troops did not need the care of the Twenty-fifth Station Hospital and its nurses. The number of troops in the area was greatly diminished, and those troops that remained were assigned elsewhere for their medical care. This placed the nurses in a difficult position. The Chief Nurse, 1st Lt. Susan Freeman, was left to supervise thirty army nurses in conditions that were less than ideal even for a combat area. The climate was hot and humid, the location extremely isolated, the living quarters far below standards the nurses had been told to expect, and nerve-wracking idleness magnified every unpleasant condition the nurses were facing every day. Lt. Gertrude Margarite Bertram recalled the assignment. "Our hospital was not in the front lines. We received and cared for injured behind the lines . . . burned cases (airmen) returning from the front . . . and patients and nurses combating complications from malaria fever. Most of the soldiers we received at the Twenty-fifth Station Hospital had been felled by an enemy called malaria, rather than wounded by enemy German soldiers." These conditions created increasing dissension among the nurses.[14]

In the early spring of 1943, Lt. Gen. Ira C. Eaker requested that an entire battalion of WAACs be sent to England to work with the Eighth Army Air Force headquartered in London. Along with the request, General Eaker included a shipping priority for the WAACs to sail to England that summer. In April, the WAAC Staff Theater Director, Capt. Anna W. Wilson, arrived in London to make arrangements for the arrival of those women. The preparations for the WAAC battalion included finding housing and laundry facilities and assigning the women to duty stations, along with making sure that the post exchanges carried products the women would need in daily living. These preparations for the arriving WAACs were somewhat easier since England had a long history of women in the military services and was already the duty station for Canadian WAACs and Polish and Norwegian women who were performing military duties that otherwise would need to be filled by military men.

Following the receipt of the priority shipping orders, WAAC headquarters began assembling the women who would comprise the First WAAC Separate Battalion at Fort Devens, Massachusetts, and placed it under the command of Capt. Mary A. Hallaren.

While at Fort Devens, the WAACs were outfitted with winter uniforms, gas masks, field packs, canteens, helmets, first aid kits, and pistol belts minus the holsters and pistols. In addition, the women went through physical conditioning, including hiking with full field packs, judo, gas mask training, and running an obstacle course that, although not required for noncombatants, every woman in the unit chose to do.

Spring and early summer of 1943 were busy times for women in the U.S. military. WAACs at Fort Devens continued with their overseas training for deployment to England, and on 9 June 1943, the House of Representatives passed a bill that would allow WAVES to be stationed in Hawaii, give them allowances equal to those of navy men, and raise the highest rank a WAVE could attain to that of captain (equal to the army rank of colonel). Despite this fact, there were still those in Congress who criticized both aspects of the bill, insisting that the navy had been, and should continue to be, a "masculine organization."

On 28 June 1943, the WAC bill passed Congress, and on 1 July 1943, President Roosevelt signed Public Law 110, officially establishing the Women's Army Corps (WAC) as a component of the U.S. Army and not an auxiliary. On 5 July, Maj. Oveta Culp Hobby, Director of the WAAC, was sworn in as the Director of the Women's Army Corps with the rank of colonel. Colonel Hobby and her staff now took on the assignment of converting members of the WAAC to members of the Women's Army Corps. By law that conversion had to take place by 30 September 1943, and WAACs had the option of being sworn in to the new Women's Army Corps or accepting a discharge and going home. This period of conversion was greatly complicated by a slander campaign against the WAAC that was so vicious that it drastically reduced the number of women applying for membership and the number who converted to the new Women's Army Corps. The persistent rumors and stories denigrating women who served in the WAAC/WAC became so vicious that the FBI was brought in to track down the source and determine if it had been started and fueled by Nazis in order to deprive the U.S. Army of the work being done by its members. (The slander campaign will be discussed fully in chapter 6.)

On 16 July 1943, the members of the First Separate Battalion arrived in England and began what would prove to be a proud and distinguished history of military service in the European Theater of Operations.

5

★

The women who served in the military during World War II were both "garden
variety" from every walk of life and the most creative, self-sufficient risk takers
there were. We were intelligent, learned quickly, and were self-disciplined.
                                                    —Dorothy Mae Harrison, WAVE

By the end of January 1943, the Women's Naval Reserve Midshipmen
Training Schools at Smith College and Mount Holyoke College
were well established, and they were the only two schools in the United
States where women were trained to be commissioned as navy officers
upon their graduation. An article in the *New York Times* on 1 February
1943 informed the public that even the language these new officers used
was different in many ways compared to that which they spoke when they
arrived in Northhampton and South Hadley, Massachusetts. For these
new female navy ensigns "floors" were now "decks," "walls" were "bulk-
heads," "stairs" were "ladders," and a "door" was now referred to as a
"hatch." Their lives had changed dramatically, so dramatically that they
were now changing the lives and categories of those around them.

When the first classes of WAVE officer candidates had arrived, the staff,
which taught at both schools, was all male. That staff now consisted of
twelve male officers and forty-one female officers, concrete evidence that
the WAVES were already achieving their purpose and their mission—to
replace navy men and free them for combat duty. Also, WAVE officers
had taken on the job of helping organize and train women officers for the
U.S. Coast Guard Women's Reserve, and they were preparing to do the
same for the newest women's branch in the military, the U.S. Marine
Corps Women's Reserve (USMCWR). In addition, the WAVES and
SPARS would soon mark the opening of the WAVES' newest WAVE
and SPARS training school at Hunter College's smaller Bronx campus. A
new drive by the WAVES and SPARS was aimed at recruiting twelve
hundred new women into their individual branches by 1 March 1943.

One of the original WAVES who transferred to SPARS was Dorothy

Louise Nims, who, in her letter, recalled those first days and weeks. "There were twenty-one of us, and we had three weeks of intensive training at the Coast Guard Academy in New London, Connecticut." Now Dorothy Nims Kutz, she went on to say that after three weeks, "We were sent either to headquarters or to main recruiting and public relations offices. For six months, we served in naval offices before the Coast Guard opened its own." Former LT Dorothy L. Nims, USCG (WR), went on to say, "Dr. Dorothy Stratton, then Commander Stratton, had WAVE uniforms brought from the WAVES to us. This brings back many memories."[1]

ENS Loraine Cornelisen, the first WAVE officer to be assigned to duty at the Brooklyn Navy Yard in New York, was assigned to work for RADM Edward J. Marquart, commandant of the Navy Yard. "You're the first admiral I've met," she said to Admiral Marquart. "You're the first WAVE I've met," replied the admiral. Ensign Cornelisen was the first woman naval officer to be assigned to work in the 141-year-old Navy Yard. She would not be the last, however.[2]

Just six days later, First Lady Eleanor Roosevelt addressed the Advertising Women of New York at the Belmont Plaza. After being introduced by Mrs. Anne O'Hare McCormick of the *New York Times* editorial staff, Mrs. Roosevelt began her talk by telling the audience, "Civilians do not realize the importance of women's contributions to the war." Continuing, she added, "Very often men in their own families don't appreciate what they [women] are doing." Mrs. Roosevelt then went on to say that even fighting men in the South Pacific "looked extremely amused" when she had told them of the work being done by the WAACs and WAVES to help in the war effort. "They had no real conception of the fact that these services were doing absolutely essential jobs."[3]

The soldiers listening to Mrs. Roosevelt's talk apparently did not know that navy nurses were, even then, stationed and working in the South Pacific. For Mabel Duncan, who joined the Navy Nurse Corps on 2 March 1942, the South Pacific and its battles would be unforgettable. After being stationed at the naval hospital in Portsmouth, Virginia, Ensign Duncan was deployed with other navy nurses to care for wounded marines and sailors fighting the ongoing battle on Guadalcanal and adjacent islands. Duncan and her sister navy nurses staffed Navy Base Hospital No. 3 on the island of Espiritu Santo in the New Hebrides. The navy hospital ship *Relief* picked up wounded GIs from Guadalcanal and other islands and delivered them to Base Hospital No. 3 or to New Zealand.

The navy hospital ship *Solace* with navy nurses stationed onboard had been picking up and delivering wounded sailors and marines to navy base hospitals in the South Pacific since the winter and spring of 1942. It was not unusual for navy hospital ships in the South Pacific to onload as many as four hundred wounded at a time, administer medical and surgical care, and deliver their precious cargo to base hospitals throughout the South Pacific or to station hospitals in New Zealand or Australia.

Former navy nurse Mabel Duncan O'Neill remembered her days caring for wounded and ill GIs from battles and islands scattered around the South Pacific. When asked what her strongest memory of World War II was, she responded, "How emotionally close we were to each other—nurses, doctors, etc. I learned how unimportant material things were." When asked what the most surprising thing she learned about herself during the war was, she answered, "How to overcome burnout and emotional trauma by using my religious faith."[4]

On 9 March 1943, 450 more WAVES were graduated from the Naval Midshipmen's School at Smith College and were commissioned as ensigns in the Navy Women's Reserve. These women made up the first class to be trained and tested to use the gas mask under actual tear gas conditions. Their instructor for this particular training was LT F. Hamilton Whimple. The instruction included teaching the WAVES to take the gas mask from its case, snap it on, and adjust its fit as quickly as possible. WAVES, in groups of thirty, and accompanied by their instructor, entered a shack constructed to permit the release of tear gas inside. The WAVES spent approximately ten minutes inside the shack, being drilled in an actual tear gas situation. Before exiting the shack, each WAVE was required to remove her mask and state her name and service number while face-to-face with Lieutenant Whimple, who kept his mask on throughout the drills. He pointed out that the tear gas did tend to cling to clothes and, after several sessions in the shack in one day, his clothes volunteered their testimony to that fact.[5]

While WAVE officer candidates were being trained at Smith College in Northampton, enlisted WAVES were being trained at Hunter College in the Bronx, New York. In fact, New York City was about to experience a first. For the first time, two thousand enlisted WAVES who were completing their fourth week of training at Hunter were given weekend liberty for a Saturday starting at noon until Sunday at 8:00 p.m. It would be the first time the majority of the group would see and explore New York City, and the first time New Yorkers would see WAVES exploring their

WAVES at Hunter College boot camp, September 1943.

city, eating in their restaurants, taking advantage of seeing the sights, and enjoying plays and movies.

In Washington, D.C., seven WAVE officers who were also physicians were waiting for President Roosevelt to sign a bill into law that would permit women physicians to practice medicine and surgery in the navy and army while serving their country as WAVES or WAACs. This would be a far cry from the way women physicians were treated by the military in World War I. Now, with President Roosevelt's signing of the bill into law, women physicians would serve as military officers and physicians in World War II.[6]

Another big step for the WAVES was a weekly radio program entitled "WAVES on Air" that would make its debut on 21 April 1943. On radio station WHYN, the fifteen-minute weekly program would be broadcast each Wednesday night at 8:15 p.m. The program would include musical selections and information about WAVE life at the Naval Reserve Midshipmen's Schools. The purpose of the weekly program was to attract many more young women to join the WAVES.

In April 1943, a bill that would allow WAVES to serve overseas was making its way through the minefield of Congress. Like WAACs and military nurses, many WAVES wanted to be able to serve their country by serving overseas. The debate on the bill would go on for months. While men argued against the bill, Rep. Edith Nourse Rogers and Rep. Claire Booth Luce argued decisively for the bill's passage.

While the debate concerning overseas duty continued, so did the line of women seeking to join the WAVES. Newspapers covered stories of brothers and sisters serving in the navy, while Congress continued arguing about the fitness of women in the navy to serve overseas. While Representatives Rogers and Luce argued for the bill's passage and pointed out that WAACs and military nurses currently were serving in theaters of war overseas, the majority of men in Congress argued against the bill's passage by stating that, as the *Christian Science Monitor* put it on 24 April 1943, "WAVES Too Delicate to Witness War." The majority of the men agreed that "the stark horror of the things that even try the souls of men" would be too much for WAVES to bear. It did not seem contradictory to these "gentlemen" that WAACs, without the legal protection of military status, were currently serving overseas in London and North Africa and had earned the admiration of Gen. Dwight D. Eisenhower, who wanted more WAACs sent to the theaters of war as quickly as possible.[7]

In May and late spring 1943, more and more WAVES were attending specialty schools before receiving their assignments to permanent duty stations. For Margaret A. Hightower, a quiet, shy twenty-one-year-old who enlisted in the WAVES after hearing a recruitment ad on a local radio program, graduation from Hunter was followed by training as a radio operator at the Naval Training School in Madison, Wisconsin. Upon successful completion of the course, Hightower was assigned to a permanent duty station in the Eighth Naval District Headquarters in New Orleans, Louisiana, where she worked first as a radio operator and later as a desk supervisor. Hightower enjoyed her time in the navy and when asked what she would most like to be remembered for, answered, "For the dedication and hard work I put into my navy job. Hopefully, what I did helped win the war."[8]

Jean K. Deckman, a twenty-one-year-old who enlisted in the WAVES in September 1942, was not the first female in her immediate family to take steps to enlist in the navy in a time of war. Deckman's mother had gone so far as to fill out the necessary papers to enlist in the navy during the First World War. "My mother had sought to join the navy during World War I, but ended up getting married . . . to a then serviceman!"[9]

After completing boot camp, Deckman was sent to the First Naval District in Boston, where she was trained in communications and code breaking. Her first duty assignment to a permanent station was to Washington, D.C., where she worked in the office of the Chief of Naval Operations as a specialist in the British code rooms, breaking messages on British code machines. Later, Deckman's security clearance was raised to top secret and she worked in Top Secret Communications in Washington, D.C. When asked what she would like to be remembered for, she responded, "I have always remained quite proud of the fact that I was able to serve with the United States Navy. To this day, I will tell anyone who will listen about my experiences."[10]

LT Jean K. Deckman, U.S. Navy, October 1945.

Betty McCartney was twenty-two when she enlisted in the WAVES in October 1942. Her mother was so sad about Betty's enlistment that she cried almost all the time before Betty left for boot camp. McCartney went to boot camp in Cedar Falls, Iowa. After graduation from boot camp, McCartney attended aviation mechanics school in Memphis, Tennessee. Upon completing that course, McCartney was stationed as an aviation mechanic in Bunker Hill, Indiana. Later, McCartney was trained and worked as an air traffic controller at Bunker Hill. When asked what important lessons she learned from her time in the WAVES, she responded, "That I could be independent and make choices on my own." When asked what she would like to tell people about women who served in the military during World War II, her response was "that women are as capable as men to serve our country." Her response to the question, What would she like to be remembered for? Betty McCartney Dore answered, "That I did, in my small way, serve my country." McCartney Dore was discharged from the navy on 4 October 1945.[11]

On 4 June 1943, a new bill was introduced in Congress. Not only would the bill allow WAVES and all women's branches of the sea services to be assigned overseas, but it would also grant these

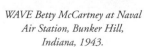

WAVE Betty McCartney at Naval Air Station, Bunker Hill, Indiana, 1943.

women the same benefits enjoyed by male sailors, coast guardsmen, and marines. The bill, known as the Smith bill, passed the House on 9 June 1943 but would drag through Congress for more than a year before it would be signed into law.

On the same day the House passed the Smith bill, New Yorkers witnessed the Chinese flag flying over Hunter College. The flying flag was in recognition of a distinguished visitor, Madame Chiang Kai-shek, first lady of China and graduate of Wellesley College. A special two-deck reviewing stand had been constructed, and a comfortable armchair was put in place for Madame Chiang. For more than twenty minutes, a dress parade of 2,000 WAVES, SPARS, and Women Marines marched in front of the reviewing stand while distinguished guests and 2,500 new "boot" recruits watched the precision marching and listened to the music provided by a forty-piece navy band stationed at Hunter for such occasions.

Following the parade, Madame Chiang requested and received a tour of the mess halls and barracks areas. In a typical recruit's room, the first lady of China lifted the bed covers and inspected the mattress. Madame Chiang smiled at LCDR Mildred McAfee as she remarked that the mattresses were much softer than those in the dorms at Wellesley. Just before the car in which Madame Chiang and Commander McAfee were riding was driven off campus, Madame Chiang commented to CAPT William F. Amsden, commander of the naval school at Hunter, "Tell the WAVES and the Marines and the Coast Guard I think they are grand."[12]

Less than one week after Madame Chiang's praise for the U.S. women's sea services, Sen. David J. Walsh, a Democrat from Massachusetts and chairman of the Senate committee conducting hearings on the subject of overseas assignments for WAVES, the coast guard, and Women Marines, looked directly at LCDR Mildred McAfee, who was seated at the witness table, and said, "The Navy, to my mind, is a male organization." Several members of the Senate criticized the bill for permitting navy women to attain the rank of captain instead of maintaining top rank for women at lieutenant commander.[13]

The battle to keep women serving in the U.S. Armed Forces restricted to lower ranks and lower pay scales was no stranger to the Army Nurse Corps. In March 1942, President Roosevelt appointed Julia O. Flikke, then Superintendent of the Army Nurse Corps, to the rank of colonel and Florence Blanchfield to the rank of lieutenant colonel. The controller general ruled that there could not legally be a female colonel or lieutenant colonel.

In anticipation of the first birthday of the WAVES, Secretary of the Navy John Knox announced that he would ask Congress to allow the navy to assign WAVES wherever they were needed in order to free more navy men for combat duty. He added that the WAVES would be needed in higher numbers, in more navy jobs, and would be promoted to higher ranks in the future. "I can make no promises that these things will come about. However, I do want you to know that the Navy wants them for you and that we're behind you every step of the way."[14]

The WAVES made the news again just a few days later when they celebrated their first birthday on 31 July 1943 with a special church service to be followed by a cake-cutting ceremony and a reception in honor of LCDR Mildred H. McAfee. In her address to the group, McAfee stated that by the end of 1943, there would be 50,000 WAVES on active duty and 91,000 by the end of 1944.[15]

On 27 September 1943, President Roosevelt signed Bill 441 into law, giving all women's sea service branches the authority to deploy women members overseas and opening up higher ranks to women serving in the WAVES, SPARS, and Women Marines. The new law would give an expanded future of possibilities to all women serving in these branches.

The U.S. Coast Guard opened its first training school for enlisted SPARS recruits on 14 June 1943. The training school was located in the Palm Beach Biltmore Hotel in Palm Beach, Florida. Renovations to the "Pink Palace," as the hotel was called by its civilian clientele, had been going on for weeks before the news was announced to the American public.

The Biltmore had lost 430 doors, scores of walls, and most of its luxury appointments like chandeliers and stylish drapes. With walls knocked out and partitions added, the long room that had once held the Biltmore's cocktail lounge was now the office for the training school's personnel officer. It was one of the few, if not the only, coast guard personnel offices that had a completely mirrored ceiling. The former hotel floors that once held hundreds of well-appointed civilian guest rooms had been changed into decks that, although still covered by thick carpeting, now held plain iron bunk beds that would provide sleeping space for more than nine hundred SPARS "boots" and trainees at specialized schools during each basic training indoctrination course that would be held within and without its walls. The playground of the civilian men and women, dressed in the day's latest fashions for dinner, socializing, and dancing, had been replaced by SPARS dressed in the U.S. Coast Guard

SPARS Training Station, Palm Beach, Florida.

Women's Reserve summer uniforms of striped seersucker, and the occasional male coast guardsman assigned to the training school for one purpose or another. More than seven thousand SPARS would receive training at the school between 14 June 1943 and its last class of 16 December 1944.

Although the Biltmore looked much the same on the outside, it was clearly a training ship on the inside. The basement—the quarterdeck in coast guard language—held the classrooms, the clothing locker, the shoe store, regimental offices, the sick bay, and the dentist's office. The first floor—first deck—held captain's quarters, the library, and the mess hall. The second floor—second deck—was the training area for those attending the courses for pay and supply officers. The third and fourth floors, or decks, were areas for training of yeomen, storekeepers, cooks, and bakers. Boots were quartered on decks five and six, ship's company. Training school staff, which numbered seventy-six, were housed on the seventh and eighth decks, and on the ninth deck—topside—SPAR officers were quartered. The most secret specialty for which SPARS were trained and assigned in World War II concerned LORAN.

In the summer of 1943, the U.S. Coast Guard Headquarters decided that SPARS could be trained for and assigned to LORAN monitoring stations within the United States. The LORAN (Long Range Aid to Navigation) system had been developed at the beginning of World War II and consisted of a process "whereby radio signals transmitted from two stations located on the shore are picked up by special receivers installed in ships and planes, enabling them to calculate their exact position."[16] The monitoring station was equipped with the receiver and, since the position of the monitoring station was fixed, the station was able to check the accuracy and other operations of the transmitting stations. The job of the SPARS operating the monitoring station was to maintain a constant watch on the receiver, twenty-four hours a day, taking and recording measurements every two minutes.

The officer chosen to command the first LORAN station to be monitored by SPARS—located at Chatham, Massachusetts—was LTJG Vera Hamerschlag. Lieutenant Hamerschlag had worked previously as an assistant to the naval liaison officer for LORAN at Radiation Lab and was, therefore, somewhat familiar with the LORAN system and the need to treat the entire project as top secret. As required by U.S. law, the coast guard had been transferred from the Treasury Department to the navy when the United States entered the war. The coast guard had many small stations along the coast that had been closed due to the combined effects of the Great Depression and a drawdown in personnel. Two deactivated stations were given to the group headed by the naval liaison officer and that group was tasked with the planning, construction, implementation, operation, maintenance, and security of the LORAN system.

Those first stations were located on Fenwick Island, Delaware, and Montauk Point, New York. At the same time, Canada continued to build LORAN stations in Labrador for the north end of a network that would spread from the United Kingdom, Canada, and the United States across the theaters of war and into the South Pacific. Before the entire system was in place, special units of the coast guard and the army were deployed on secret missions to weave the LORAN system over and through the path U.S. troops would travel in order to defeat Germany and Japan.

Research was aimed at developing a receiver-indicator that was small and light enough to be carried on long-range bombers. As LORAN reached across the North Atlantic, Allied forces were able to markedly decrease the number of their merchant and troop ships sunk by German submarines. In addition, B-29s were now coming off the production lines with a LORAN APN-9 as standard equipment for the plane's navigation. The importance of the LORAN system in bringing an end to World War II cannot be overstated, nor can the decision to assign SPARS to operate the system that was so secret that SPARS were told, "Never even *think* the word LORAN."[17]

As part of their training for this mission, LTJG Vera Hamerschlag and one enlisted SPAR who had volunteered for the mission—a mission too secret to be described to her or any of the enlisted SPARS who would volunteer for it—were sent to Massachusetts Institute of Technology (MIT) to take a two-month course that was misleadingly labeled "Navigation" and was held off the MIT campus. They were the only women at that naval training school. The program was so secret that when ten other enlisted SPARS were chosen to attend a one-week course at MIT Naval Training School, even the training officer was not told what the duties of the SPARS in the program would entail.

In addition to being responsible for the operation and maintenance of the LORAN system and equipment at Chatham, Lieutenant Hamerschlag was also in charge of everything else on the station, including plumbing, the emergency generator, and the 125-foot-high antenna that loomed over the fifty-foot-long and thirty-foot-wide one-story building that functioned as office, work station, and barracks.

The SPARS unit at Chatham, Massachusetts, was officially called Unit 21. When World War II ended, Lieutenant Hamerschlag and her unit received a commendation letter that read, in part, "the operation of Unit 21 under the SPARS has been carried out in a most efficient manner, and the efforts of the SPARS personnel have contributed greatly to the overall efficiency of the LORAN system during World War II."[18]

Not long after the first Women Marines officer candidates arrived at Mount Holyoke College and Smith College, the marine corps decided that the best way to train Women Marines was to do that training at one of the largest marine corps bases on the east coast. Women in the corps were to be called Women Marines and have no acronym-nicknames like WAVES, SPARS, and WAACs. Senior marine corps officers and the director of the U.S. Marine Corps Women's Reserve (USMCWR) thought the best training they could receive would be at Camp Lejeune, at New River, North Carolina. Training at this legendary marine corps base would give the women full immersion in the traditions and history of the corps and would also allow them to learn as much about weapons as women military in other countries such as the United Kingdom and Russia.

The marine corps moved quickly and, by late June 1943, they had a large section of Camp Lejeune set aside for the training of Women Marines. Maj. Ruth Cheney Streeter, Director of the Women Marines, had written a request to her superiors and asked that Women Marines be allowed to attend a weapons demonstration conducted by male marines and male recruits as part of the men's training. She went on to explain that she believed that seeing what kind of training the male marines received would give Women Marines a greater understanding of what the men whom they were replacing would be doing in combat zones.

On 29 June 1943, the third class of Women's Reserve officers graduated from Mount Holyoke, and the members of the fourth class were promoted to officer candidate status. On the same day, the members of the fourth class and the marine corps staff began their permanent move to Camp Lejeune.

At Hunter College in New York, the ninth class of enlisted Women Marines would graduate in a matter of days, and the tenth class would report directly to Camp Lejeune for a class that would begin on 12 July 1943 and graduate on 7 August. They were followed by new classes of 550 women who would enter every two weeks and graduate approximately six weeks later. In each training cycle, three classes were trained simultaneously.

Women Marine recruits and officer candidates traveled to Camp Lejeune on troop trains that would carry approximately five hundred marines at a time. Male marines and Women Marines made the trip on separate troop trains. Each troop movement of women was supervised by a woman lieutenant and two enlisted women. Even before the women boarded the train, they began learning about the marine corps rules, traditions, and discipline that would structure their lives for the duration of

Alice H. Bennett wearing working clothes and shoes called "Boondockers," at Motor Transport School, Camp Lejeune, North Carolina, 1943.

the war plus six months. When their train reached Wilmington, North Carolina, the new recruits detrained and were met by NCOs who immediately began shouting orders at the group and herding them onto crowded non–air conditioned buses for the trip to Camp Lejeune. Once at Lejeune, the women were assigned to the barracks where they would live until basic training ended, approximately six weeks later.

Other women would be stationed at Camp Lejeune and would attend a specialty school to learn a skill the marine corps could and would put to good use in freeing a marine to fight. One other possibility after boot camp was for a Woman Marine to be assigned to a program where she would learn a skill by participating in on-the-job training and would be assigned to a permanent base where that particular skill was needed.

The Women Marines' barracks at Camp Lejeune had large open bays with rows of iron cots lined up in straight rows. One of the first things a Woman Marine learned was to make up a military bunk with square corners and a top sheet and marine corps blanket pulled tight enough to bounce a quarter that was dropped on it from the air.

Showers would be taken in large, open shower rooms, and toilet stalls were lined up against long walls and did not have the benefit of a front door to provide privacy. The buildings had been used previously by male marine recruits and there was a row of urinals along one of the walls in the toilet stall area.

Area 1 also included buildings to be used exclusively for classroom instruction of Women Marines recruits and for instruction in the specialty schools of advanced training of the newly graduated Women Marines recruits.

Once the new recruits were assigned and acquainted with their barracks, they were placed in orientation classes, issued uniforms, and introduced to close-order drill. The next day, the new recruits went through hours of classification tests designed to determine and analyze each recruit's skills and abilities, followed by interviews to assess her education, training, and work experience. Add to this the strict discipline and tight schedules that would fill every minute of their days and nights, and it was only days before most recruits fell into the routine and knew it by heart. Reveille was at 0545 (5:45 a.m.), formation took place at 0630, breakfast at 0645, classes from 0800 to 1130, march to lunch, march back to attend additional classes and/or close order drill until 1600 (4:00 p.m.). March back to the barracks and spend approximately forty-five minutes in personal care and preparing for the next day; formation at 1730 (5:30 p.m.), march to dinner at 1745 (5:45 p.m.); march back to barracks and do laundry, shine shoes, polish brass, and iron clothes for the next day. Lights out at 2130 (9:30 p.m.); sleep until the next day begins at 0545 and they repeat the schedule of the previous day.

Male marines and male recruits conducted a weapons demonstration for one-half day each week during which women recruits could watch as male marines demonstrated the firing of mortars, bazookas, Browning automatic rifles, flame-throwers, hand grenades, and other weapons. Top brass and the director of the USMC Women's Reserve felt that Women Marines would have deeper loyalty and respect for the corps, its traditions, and its men if they knew what the men were trained to do in combat. It was also believed that Women Marines who witnessed a weapons demonstration would have a greater understanding of how important their job of replacing a man to fight was to the national war effort.

Amid the beauty of Area 1 with its trees and manicured landscape, beyond the clean, neat redbrick buildings, was an ugliness that appeared at first to be seen only by the Women Marines and women recruits who had just made Camp Lejeune their new home, and the male marines, mainly drill instructors who were at the heart of its source. The drill instructors at Smith, Mount Holyoke, and Hunter Colleges had made it clear in their attitudes that they were not happy about the marine corps accepting women in the corps and calling them "Marines." Most women at these institutions had not heard specific degrading and prejudiced remarks aimed directly at them, but it became evident that things were different at Camp Lejeune.

On one of the largest marine corps bases in the world, male marines greatly outnumbered Women Marines and recruits. The male marine drill instructors (DI) were greatly outnumbered by women and were working in a college campus atmosphere where highly educated women were in authority both on the civilian campus and in the hierarchy of military rank in the navy and marine corps. Perhaps it was the fact that the drill instructors were not working under the eyes of large numbers of fellow male marines, as they would have to do when instructing the women on the military reservation of Camp Lejeune. Or maybe it was easier to instruct women recruits on soil that was not held sacred by many male marines—that no college campus was held in the same esteem afforded by male marines to Camp Lejeune; Quantico, Virginia; El Toro, California; or Parris Island, South Carolina. Whatever the mix of reasons or emotions, male drill instructors and other male marines at Camp Lejeune became quite verbal concerning their attitudes toward Women Marines and having to instruct them instead of working with the real marines— the men in the corps.

Theresa Karas described her unit's first encounter with a drill instructor at Camp Lejeune. Karas's platoon's first meeting with their DI left a lasting impression on the women recruits. The DI, in his twenties and wearing a dented World War I hat, glowered menacingly at the platoon of women recruits and "his whole body conveyed his utter disgust and boredom with each and every one of us." After minutes of uncomfortable silence while he stared at the group, the DI "lifted his red face with the sunburned nose towards the magnificent blue North Carolina sky and moaned loudly in great pain, 'Holy Mother! First the dogs! Then the niggers! Now the women!' "[19]

At first, most women felt that if they ignored the remarks and worked hard to get the men's respect, things would get better in time. But things did not get better. As time went on, derogatory remarks increased in number and vehemence, and derogatory pranks became more outrageous and frequent. One woman marine recruit put it very plainly when she said that she felt that drill instructors resented women "more than a battalion of Japanese troops."[20]

During the first year or so, male marines and navy men made little or no attempt to hide their feelings about Women Marines. In her book, *Free a Man to Fight*, Mary Stremlow related an incident at Camp Lejeune when a well-known band leader of the day visited the base and performed for the marines. During his address to the marines gathered for the show, Fred Waring referred to the Women Marines by the insulting term "BAMS" (broad ass marines). Many of the Women Marines were so angry that a large group of them got up and left in protest.

Stremlow addressed as well an incident in which a group of Seabees gathered up a large group of stray dogs in the area, shaved their coats in a fashion frequently seen on poodles, painted the letters "BAM" on the animals' sides, and set them free to meander in and out of the ranks of Women Marines during a graduation ceremony to celebrate their successful completion of basic training.[21]

The male marines seemed unable or unwilling to stop their feelings concerning the corps' acceptance of women as marines. Derogatory and hateful remarks became more numerous, and it was not unusual for male marines to remark in the presence of Women Marines and recruits. Several Women Marines were quite angry when male marines expressed their feelings in no uncertain terms. The men expressed outrage at the women and the corps for accepting "niggers, dogs, and women."

When it was no longer possible to ignore the effect this language and attitude was having on morale, Director Ruth Cheney Streeter wrote to the marine commandant asking him to use his authority to stop the verbal abuse and mean pranks that male marines were inflicting on Women Marines. The commandant responded by sending a statement to all commanding officers at marine bases and to the officers in charge of units. The message was clear, left no wiggle room, and stated in no uncertain terms that he would hold unit and base officers totally responsible for any further crude or obscene remarks made by their men to Women Marines. The commandant went on to say, "This conduct indicates a laxity in discipline which will not be tolerated. Commanding officers will be held responsible."[22]

Theresa Karas remarked about Col. K. I. Buse, the commanding officer at Quantico, Virginia, when she was assigned there. "Colonel Buse would tolerate none of this kind of behavior. The word 'BAM' was never even whispered within the perimeter of Casual Barracks. He was a strict commanding officer who ran a tight ship. He was Old Corps."[23]

With the sure knowledge that punishment would follow any infractions of the commandant's orders, the crude and insulting remarks made by male marines concerning their sister marines became almost nonexistent and, with the improvement in the behavior of the men, a definite upswing was also seen in the morale of Women Marines.

In late August, marine headquarters decided that it would take the advice of a marine recruiter in Atlanta who suggested that a good recruiting technique that would secure a large number of women recruits would be the creation of hometown platoons that would be composed entirely of women from a particular city or hometown, who would be sworn in together and go through boot camp together. This made it more likely that friends, classmates, or neighbors could face the first challenges of marine corps life with women they knew from school or perhaps had even grown up with in their neighborhood. The first hometown platoon was formed in Philadelphia, Pennsylvania, and was identified as the Philadelphia Platoon and would be followed in the future by other platoons with big city or hometown names.

The United States Marine Corps Women's Reserve was well on its way to leaving no doubt concerning the patriotism, dedication, or efficiency of its members. In March 1943, Maj. Hunter Hurst was placed in charge of training the new Women Marines at Smith and Mount Holyoke colleges. Major Hurst had a secret weapon to use in making these Women Marines masters of close-order drill that would prove especially beneficial in training the USMCWR "trick" drill team in the coming months and well into the future. That secret weapon was Lt. Phillip McArdle, who had been employed on the torpedo school staff in Newport, Rhode Island, and was formerly responsible for training and instructing the famous Radio City Music Hall Rockettes. The marine corps had released information on several occasions stating the importance of close-order drill and precision in the ranks of Women Marines since they would replace male marines who were assigned to many and various posts where precision was a key component, for example, embassy guard duty, color guards, and ceremonial events. Women Marines would need these skills when they eventually replaced the male marines assigned to those duties. It was a sign of the dedication and willingness of these Women Marines to go the extra mile that when told that anyone who signed up for the "trick" drill team would be expected to practice on their own free time, and would not be excused from their regular duties for that purpose, there was no shortage of volunteers waiting in line to join.[24]

During the same time, Women Marines were receiving more combat skills training than any other women's branch of the U.S. Armed Forces during World War II. This was true despite the fact that Women Marines, like the women serving in all sea services, were still prohibited by law from serving overseas.

The jobs being filled by Women Marines at this time were mainly divided between assignments in the aviation field and clerical work. Forty percent of Women Marines held jobs in aviation including aircraft mechanics, parachute rigging, control tower operations, and link trainer instructors. Approximately 50 percent of the USMCWR was assigned to clerical duties that included secretarial pay clerk and personnel assignments. About 10 percent of the USMCWRs had positions in professional and scientific areas, including drafting, cryptoanalysis, photo analysis, and intelligence, and as language specialists. In fact, one Woman Marine, Maj. Charlotte D. Gower, used her knowledge of the Chinese language and her education and experience gained in obtaining her Ph.D. in anthropology, her four years of work in China, and her experience and knowledge gained as a prisoner of the Japanese until her repatriation on the first trip of the *Gripsholm* in the prisoner of war exchange with Japan in August 1942. Major Gower's knowledge and skills were so extensive that she was assigned to temporary duty with the Office of Strategic Services (OSS), which would evolve into the CIA after World War II, as an instructor in language and intelligence.

The USMC marked the first anniversary of the attack on Guadalcanal by celebrating the opening of a marine corps recruiting station in Times Square. The new center opened to make it even easier for New York City women to join the USMCWR. The center would be open every day except Sundays from 11:00 a.m. until 9:00 p.m. To mark the occasion, a small detachment of Women Marines assembled behind a marine color guard at Sixth Avenue and Forty-third Street. The Women Marines were wearing white dress uniforms with a light green sash and matching shoulder bags. The Women Marines marched from the assembly point to Times Square, where Lt. Col. Frank V. McKinless, officer in charge of recruiting in the area, and other marine corps officers and enlisted men stood at attention to welcome them.[25]

As new recruits were signing up to join the USMCWR in Times Square on 12 August 1943, the first class of Women Marine Reserves, who began their training on 15 July at Camp Lejeune, were graduating from boot camp and were receiving their assignment orders to report to a specific marine base for duty or to report to a special advanced training school for Women Marines located in Area 1 at Camp Lejeune.

Other Women Marines were carrying out their training or work assignments in various fields. Alice H. Bennett, a young woman marine who completed her motor transport training at Camp Lejeune, North Carolina, was carrying out her assigned duties at her permanent duty station

Vera Cooper-Sullivan, aviation machinist mate, works in pretest in the Department of Engine Overhaul at Cherry Point Marine Corps Air Station, North Carolina.

at Parris Island, South Carolina. "I really enjoyed my tour of duty."[26]

Vera Cooper-Sullivan was trained as an aviation machinist mate and stationed at El Toro Marine Base in California. When asked what she would most like to be remembered for, she said, "My devotion to my country and that I did what I could to help win the war."[27]

When Katherine M. McIntyre joined the USMCWR, she was twenty-three years old and driven by a desire to serve her country in time of war. When asked to identify the most surprising thing she learned about herself while serving in the Women Marines, she responded, "I was an exceptionally shy person. I came out of my shell as a result of having to meet and talk with many types of individuals." McIntyre was trained in clerical work at Camp Lejeune and transferred to permanent duty at an arms and ammunition warehouse at Islais Creek, San Francisco. Later, McIntyre was transferred to the Port of Embarkation in San Francisco, where she was the first sergeant in ordnance at a supply depot.[28]

Women serving in the USMCWR and the other women's branches of the military were having an effect on the military draft. On 19 August 1944, the War Manpower Commission announced that "there was a strong possibility that the October 1943 draft would only call pre–Pearl Harbor fathers who were not in defense work."[29]

One of the most far-reaching decisions the marine corps made in the summer of 1943 was to open officer candidate school (OCS) to enlisted marine personnel. The corps was interested in gaining officers who also had had experience as enlisted personnel. It was required that an enlisted marine have six months of experience in the corps before he or she could be recommended for training as an officer candidate. The first OCS at Camp Lejeune to have enlisted personnel as members began in October 1943. Every officer candidate class after that date contained a majority of enlisted personnel. Eventually, the only women who were admitted to

OCS without first serving as enlisted were civilians with what the marine corps considered outstanding leadership ability or special skills that would transfer directly, or with little additional training, into a marine corps military occupational specialty (MOS). The decision proved extremely useful in creating esprit de corps and excellent morale.

One question still being debated in Congress and of great interest to all the women's sea services was whether and when members of those branches would finally be allowed to be stationed overseas. The answers to those questions were still many months away.

6

★

Gosh, how much there is to do! Miss Leis, our nice, hard-boiled, practical statistician-planner, said to me the other day, "My Lord, if private industry talked about expanding from 25,000 to 150,000 before July 1, somebody would lock 'em up!"

—2nd Officer Betty Bandel, letter to her mother

When the bill establishing the Women's Army Auxiliary Corps was signed into law by President Franklin D. Roosevelt, the U.S. Army was of the opinion that WAACs would be able to fill four military jobs and could be assigned only to the Army Service Forces Command. Approximately eight months later, on 14 January 1943, when Rep. Edith Nourse Rogers stood in the well of the House of Representatives and introduced a new bill to establish the Women's Army Corps and grant full military status to its members, the women of the WAAC had reached a level of success that greatly exceeded the army's original expectations.

Women in the WAAC were replacing men in 155 military jobs and were serving in every major army command in forty-four of the forty-eight states as well as in two overseas theaters of war, the North Africa/Mediterranean Theater (MTO) and the European Theater (ETO). Not only were top army officers happy with the discipline, professionalism, and efficiency of the WAACs in their commands, they were asking for more WAACs to be stationed with them and assigning earliest priority transportation orders for the additional personnel they were requesting. General Eisenhower and General Somervell had added their praise to that of commanding officers at army posts throughout the country and overseas. Lt. Gen. Brehon B. Somervell expressed his opinion and approval not only to the military, but to Congress and the American people in general. "The excellent discipline, military courtesy, and appearance of the Women's Army Corps . . . are equaled by few and surpassed by no other groups in the Armed Service."[1]

The WAAC was so successful that its authorized strength was raised from 25,000 to 100,000 and a third WAAC Training Center was planned for Fort Oglethorpe, Georgia. In addition, the navy was now training tens of thousands of WAVES who would fill shore jobs currently held by male sailors, thereby releasing men for combat duty at sea. Women were also being sought by the coast guard and trained to take the place of men to be assigned to sea duty in various theaters of combat. Nor was the marine corps far behind. Faced with tough battles in the Pacific and needing more men to meet the enemy face-to-face, the marine corps would also establish a women's reserve for the purpose of filling shore jobs held by male marines who were needed on the front lines of battle.

The Women's Army Auxiliary Corps had proved itself invaluable in releasing men for combat duty, and the sea services were intent on following the army's example in replacing men assigned to shore duty and adding their numbers to combat forces actually engaging the enemy. To the top military officers at the Pentagon and in the theaters of operations around the world, military women promised to be a strong force multiplier, in addition to actually performing many jobs previously held by male GIs, more efficiently. Newspapers and magazines carried stories of America's military women "doing their part to defend their nation" and

A joint radio recruiting effort by the War Department of the Women Marines, SPARS, WAACs, and WAVES, 1943.

win the victory over the Axis forces of Germany, Japan, and Italy, and to make that victory come much sooner than would be possible without them. It was as if America had discovered a secret weapon that had gone unrecognized previously, a secret weapon that had not only stepped forward of its own volition but one that had actually fought for the right to do more, not less, in helping bring the war to an end.

In January 1943, the army placed ads recruiting women for the WAAC in seven national magazines. At the time, there were several danger signals that recruiters would not have an easy time recruiting an additional hundred thousand women. For one thing, recruiting of WAACs was in the hands of male soldiers, who previously were responsible for recruiting only men and who had little or no knowledge of the psychological factors that were most likely to be successful in recruiting the number of women the army hoped to secure.

One of the danger signals that had begun to make an appearance was the negative attitude of military men concerning any woman who would join the WAAC. With this in mind, Director Oveta Culp Hobby asked the army's Services of Supply to conduct a scientific and formal survey of the attitudes of male active-duty soldiers toward women who joined the army. The survey began almost immediately.

On 15 February 1943, the U.S. Senate passed the bill creating the Women's Army Corps and sent the bill back to the House of Representatives for its concurrence. No one expected entirely smooth sailing for a bill that would grant full military status to army women, but most felt the WAAC had passed every test and deserved to be made part of the U.S. Army. There was even talk of increasing the WAC authorized strength from 100,000 members to 150,000, freeing that many more American soldiers for direct combat duty.

Unlike the army, the navy hired a well-known advertising firm to conduct a recruitment campaign. The recruitment campaigns of the WAVES, SPARS, and Women Marines had a dampening effect on the number of women volunteering to join the WAAC.

During the second week in February 1943, two senators, Warren Austin from Vermont and James Wadsworth from New York, introduced a bill, the National War Service Act of 1943, to authorize President Roosevelt to prescribe regulations under which every man between the ages of eighteen and sixty-five years of age, and every woman between the ages of eighteen and fifty years could be directed to war work by the federal government. Reaction to the Austin-Wadsworth bill was swift and intense. The bill was supported by the American Legion and opposed by the American Federation of Labor.

The idea of conscripting women was not a new one for the Western world. Great Britain had been doing so for years, but it hit the United States with the force of a Category 4 hurricane. Churches that had spoken forcibly against the very idea of allowing, let alone compelling, women to serve in the military once again raised their voices against a proposed law they claimed would damage the home, marriage, and the very foundations of society. In a country that subscribed to the idea that the roles of men and women had been ordained by God, a nation that defined manliness in large part by describing it as the opposite of femaleness, the thought of blurring the boundaries between those preordained role assignments, let alone disregarding or changing them, was a threat to the bedrock assumptions that were critical to defining their own identity and purpose in life.

True, army nurses had taken part in previous wars, and women had served in World War I as telephone operators with General Pershing's troops in France, but that had been a relatively small number, and when the war ended so did their roles in the military. The general argument ran: Anyone with half a brain realized that nurses were not like other women. Nurses were called to their profession in the same way as priests, ministers, and doctors. Everyone knew that military nurses were "angels of mercy" and were more disembodied spirits than ordinary women. Nurses were with the military to take care of wounded and ill GIs and not to take jobs away from soldiers. Women who wanted to go into the military for any other reason were certainly of questionable character. Volunteering to live and work in a man's world, doing what was clearly a man's job, earned women the suspicions that swirled about them. American men were certainly capable of defending the nation against all enemies—and without the help of American women, whose place was clearly in the home and not in a military barracks.

American magazines and newspapers had carried numerous stories about the war work of British women. Most, if not all, Americans had seen in the papers or heard on the radio accounts of the courage of British women who were serving wherever they could replace men and free them for direct combat operations. British women, like British men, were conscripted and served either in the British military or with civilian groups, like the women of the Land Army, who were doing the agricultural work left undone by British men who were serving in the various British military branches.

The leaders of the American women's corps were well aware that women in Britain's military branches were for a time the subjects of rumors and innuendoes, questioning and disparaging the morals of any woman who would choose to serve in the military rather than with a civilian group such as the Land Army or Ambulance Transportation Corps. Princess Elizabeth (later Queen Elizabeth II) volunteered as an ambulance driver during World War II.

The directors of the WAAC/WAC, WAVES, SPARS, and USMCWR considered their military corps fortunate in being spared the rumors and innuendoes that plagued Great Britain's military women in the first years of World War II. Little did they know that their good fortune was about to come to an end with a slander campaign that threatened to put an end to every U.S. military corps for women.

WAAC director Oveta Culp Hobby was busy laying the groundwork to accommodate the growth in strength recently authorized by Congress. Hobby was quick to inform the army that she did not feel that the WAAC could add 50,000 or 100,000 new women to the corps without the aid of a draft law that included women as well as men. If the Austin-Wadsworth bill became law and women between the ages of eighteen and fifty years were drafted, there would be a greater possibility of reaching the goal the army had set for the Women's Army Auxiliary Corps and its soon-to-be created successor, the Women's Army Corps.

Newspapers, radio, and magazines were keeping the public informed on the progress of the Austin-Wadsworth bill and that of the WAC and women's sea services. On 18 March 1943, the *New York Times* carried a story headlined, "Green Denounces War Service Bill; Says Austin-Wadsworth Plan Threatens the Creation of 'Slave-Labor Conditions.' " The American Federation of Labor argued against the Austin-Wadsworth bill. Just weeks later, on 11 April 1943, the *New York Times* announced to its readers, "Draft for Women? National War Service Bill Fails to Win Endorsement of Women in Congress"; six of the seven women members in the House of Representatives failed to support the bill. Rep. Margaret Chase Smith of Maine stated clearly that she favored the registration of women for the draft as well as the registration of men. Despite this, however, Representative Smith refused to commit her backing to the bill. Rep. Edith Nourse Rogers stated that she had full confidence that American women would volunteer for the military even if the Austin-Wadsworth bill failed to become law.[2]

Complaints about the morals of WAACs to this point had been annoying but relatively easy to prove false. On the whole, these rumors were based on misinterpretations and not the kind of viciousness that would characterize the completely fabricated stories that would sweep across the country in the coming weeks and months. As the number of WAACs at WAAC training centers grew, the opportunities for misunderstandings, combined with the inconvenience felt by many of the civilians living in or around towns where WAACs were concentrated, gave rise to stories of WAACs drinking heavily in public, taking men to their hotel rooms, being drunk on trains, and sleeping in berths with male passengers.

When the military investigated these stories, it usually turned out that civilians had misidentified women dressed in WAAC uniforms, or close copies of the uniform, as members of the WAAC engaging in misconduct that elicited questions concerning the moral standards and overall character of the women serving in the military. Upon investigation at the request of Director Hobby, it was discovered that the women in question were not WAACs at all but civilians who had purchased WAAC uniforms or near copies of those uniforms who were wearing them to gain access to bars and other businesses near army posts where WAACs were also stationed as recruits in training, trainees in specialist schools, or permanently serving. Hobby was quick to complain to the army that WAAC uniforms, or close copies of the uniform, were being sold in department stores around the country. The near copies often differed from the originals only in the buttons on the jacket, and/or in the insignia worn with the uniforms.

A typical case involving "WAACs" who were drinking heavily and inviting men to their hotel rooms took place in Shreveport, Louisiana, and at Stockton Ordnance Depot in California. Upon investigation, the army learned that the women whose actions had engendered the complaints and gossip were not WAACs but were civilian employees of the Women's Ordnance Workers known as WOWs. Many WOWs wore WAAC uniforms or close copies and this practice had been authorized by the Army Ordnance Corps. As a result of the investigation, the army ordered the women to remove military insignia from the uniform and allowed those who chose to wear the uniform to continue to do so. This decision was made despite the fact that it was a definite crime for a civilian to wear a male soldier's uniform and those uniforms were not being sold in the nation's department stores.

One might well ask why the army did not enforce the same rules in connection with women's uniforms. We suggest several possible reasons, alone or in combination: the attitude of the army itself to being ordered by Congress to accept women; the fact that the army had many conflicting views in regard to WAACs, for example, it wanted the benefits these volunteers could provide to the army, to the nation, and to the overall war effort, but it fought tooth and nail against granting the WAAC/WAC full military status. These same individuals fought to maintain the exclusion of WAACs/WACs from many military jobs; put a ceiling on the rank to which a WAAC/WAC could be promoted; had different regulations that penalized dependents' benefits for women soldiers; paid the women less than male soldiers; excluded qualified women pilots from the ranks of Army Air Force pilots; and in perhaps the most telling discriminatory act of all, all but excluded army women in general from U.S. Army history. The army that prided itself on giving credit where credit was due created and maintained the delusion that military women served only in safe areas, were excluded from service in combat zones, and did not share the dangers of war on or near the front lines. Few Americans of the day realized that military women had lost their lives in combat situations and had won military decorations, including the Purple Heart, the Bronze Star, the Silver Star, and the Distinguished Service Medal.

Despite the protests lodged by Director Hobby concerning civilians' wearing WAAC/WAC uniforms or close copies, the army continued to allow civilian women to purchase and wear them. In fact, many department stores along the eastern seaboard still advertised "Junior WAAC uniforms" up to size fourteen and boasted that the uniforms were exact copies of the official uniform worn by members of the Women's Army Auxiliary Corps. One manufacturer advertised that salesmen who purchased the uniforms from them would find a number of buyers since there was a vast new market of women who were volunteering for the war effort and "all doing their part and all wanting to dress the part." For the director of the WAAC and her staff, it was even more galling that when the WAACs could not get all the uniforms they needed, manufacturers were able to buy large quantities of material in order to make and sell their "exact copies" of the WAAC uniform. Add to this the fact that civilian women doing war work were not the only civilians purchasing the uniforms.[3]

A large number of organized prostitutes in eastern cities were buying the uniforms in order to get easier access to bars and hotels located near military posts. Some of the prostitutes were so aggressive that they even lined up outside the gate of the Hampton Roads Port of Embarkation to proposition the soldiers as they left the military area. In fact, it became so difficult to distinguish the real WAACs from the prostitutes wearing copies of the uniform that the post commander ordered WAACs to pin their insignia on the collars of their khaki shirts so they might be distinguished from the prostitutes posing as WAACs.[4]

Nor was it helpful to the WAAC/WAC when the army quartermaster sent five thousand WAAC winter uniforms to the French "WAAC" in North Africa. At the time, the French "WAACs" were not organized under military discipline, and it was not long before Director Hobby and her staff were receiving letters from soldiers complaining about the WAACs in the area "wearing earrings and bobby sox" with their uniforms. At the time of the complaints, there were no WAACs in that part of North Africa.

With the arrival of late spring 1943, the quantity and viciousness of the rumors increased exponentially. In mid-May 1943, Director Hobby asked the army to investigate the rumors and ascertain if the slander was not being fueled and spread by Nazi sympathizers who wished to damage the reputation of the WAAC so badly that the women's corps would be discontinued, thereby depriving the military of a large military force that was enabling thousands of GIs to be added to the ranks of regular combat troops. When the rumors began about boatloads of pregnant WAACs being sent back to America from their overseas assignments, the army requested that the FBI get involved in tracking down the source of the rumors and whether there was any truth behind them. Support for the theory of Nazi propaganda grew as the rumors spread to dozens of major cities. One rumor had it that 90 percent of WAACs were prostitutes and 40 percent were pregnant. Another rumor was that military physicians did not approve any women for the armed forces if upon examination the women were found to be virgins. The rumors reached a new low when gossip had it that WAACs were routinely issued prophylactics so that "they could do the job they were recruited for—keeping male soldiers sexually happy." It was this set of rumors that finally brought the slander campaign to the attention of the American public.

On 8 June 1943, the syndicated column "Capitol Stuff" blew the slander campaign to new heights when columnist John O'Donnell stated in his column that "Contraceptives and prophylactic equipment will be furnished to the WAAC according to a super secret agreement reached by high ranking officers of the War Department and the WAAC Chieftain, Mrs. William Pettus Hobby . . . It was a victory for the New Deal Ladies . . . Mrs. Roosevelt wants all the young ladies to have the same overseas rights as their brothers and fathers."[5]

The fact that there was no truth to the rumor seemed to make absolutely no difference to those who were spreading the lies as quickly as they were able. The G-2 Division of the army, Army Intelligence, undertook an extensive investigation and reported that the rumors had no basis in fact. The G-2 Division added the following comments: "It is indicated that these articles are not even generally purchased in Post Exchanges and drug stores by individuals in the WAAC; in all cases of reported sales, the purchases have been married women."[6]

Army Intelligence also issued their opinion on the "super secret" documents. The G-2 Division felt that the statement referred to a War Department pamphlet printed for the WAAC, titled "Sex Hygiene," which offered six lectures to be delivered by WAAC officers and WAAC officer candidates, modest versions of the lectures required for male soldiers, to the women under their charge. The pamphlet contained the same sort of sex hygiene lectures as might be delivered to high school or college students. The topics covered feminine anatomy and physiology, the nature and dangers of venereal diseases, and the facts about menstruation and menopause. The pamphlet said nothing about the issuance or use of contraceptives or prophylactics. The pamphlet had been carefully examined by Director Hobby and the courses could be given only by WAAC officers who had successfully completed a course on its presentation. G-2 Division gave the pamphlet its unqualified approval and clearly stated that the pamphlet did not even mention contraceptives, let alone give instructions for their use.[7]

In view of the scathing remarks in the 8 June 1943 column "Capitol Stuff," Director Hobby, Secretary of War Stimson, President Roosevelt, and Eleanor Roosevelt all made public comments stating that there was no truth to the column, and each asked O'Donnell to retract the story as false.

The remarks of Secretary of War Stimson were the most frequently quoted and widespread comments concerning the rumors and columnist

O'Donnell's accusation: "Sinister rumors aimed at destroying the reputation of the WAACs are absolutely and completely false. Anything which would interfere with their recruiting or destroy the reputation of the Corps, and by so doing interfere with increase in the combat strength of our Army would be of value to the enemy. The repetition of any unfounded rumor . . . is actually an aid to the enemy."[8]

Secretary Stimson made it clear that since the WAAC was drawn from the general population of American womanhood, an attack upon the WAAC was an attack on all American women and harmed the entire nation by decreasing the number of women volunteering for military service with the army, thereby decreasing the strength of combat troops those WAACs would have replaced. Stimson gave a stern warning. "Anyone who repeats these unfounded rumors is giving aid to the enemy."[9]

The FBI gave the army its full permission to investigate all individuals who were felt to have a connection to the origin or dissemination of the rumors. The investigation was exhaustive, and in addition to being nationwide, also extended to overseas theaters of operations. At Fort Des Moines alone, more than 250 interviews were conducted with civilians living near the army post, and rumors were tracked down nationwide in an effort to uncover their origin and means of distribution. For each story, the investigators amassed a separate and massive file, containing notes, records, and interview transcripts, but the damage done and mistrust created would be evident for years.

As part of the investigations, the army had censors at various posts around the country and overseas monitor mail being sent by soldiers or WAACs to count and record any slanderous remarks made against the WAAC. When the censors' report was completed, the results were a surprise. The nature of those remarks is evident in this sample:

1. "You join the WAVES or WAC and you are automatically a prostitute in my opinion."
2. "I think it is best that he and Edith are separating, because after she gets out of the service, she won't be worth a dime. I would not have a girl or wife if she was in the service even if she was made of gold."
3. "Army service woman——WAC, WAVES, SPARS, nurse, Red Cross isn't respected."
4. "It's no damn good, Sis, and I for one would be very unhappy if you joined them . . . Why can't these Gals just stay home and be their own sweet little self, instead of being patriotic?"

5. "The service is no place for a woman. A woman's place is in the home."
6. "Get that damn divorce. I don't want no damn WAC for a wife."[10]

The main conclusions of the investigations were more painful to the WAAC than a finding that Nazi propaganda was at the root of the slander campaign. The place of origin and dissemination of the vicious rumors about the WAAC were officers and enlisted men serving in the U.S. Army. The motive behind their behavior was a simple one—the more WAACs the army accepted, the more soldiers would be sent overseas. The thought of losing a safe job so that they could be sent into combat was not a winning idea for many soldiers. They repeated the rumors to their wives, families, and friends, and those people in turn repeated the rumors to others. Many wives, girlfriends, mothers, sisters, and aunts were not eager to have their men sent into combat because his noncombat job had been taken over by a WAAC. The investigation also revealed that civilians living near a military post did not like to see their town "taken over by WAACs." Many of these civilians resented the fact that their usual soda fountains, diners, or movie theaters were filled with WAACs, making access for locals more difficult.

In a very true sense, the WAAC had become the victim of its own success. The better the job WAACs did, the more women joined and replaced a man for combat. Add to these facts that men were not overjoyed, either in the military or in civilian life, to see their jobs filled by women who not only did the jobs well but in some cases better than the men whose places they were taking.

The slander campaign did indeed deliver a serious wound to the WAAC and the nation. The number of women seeking commissions or joining the army fell off drastically. Even allowing for the fact that the WAAC had competition from the other women's corps, the slander campaign had done terrible damage and its effects would be long-lasting. Many of the WAAC leaders were not keen on seeing that wound transferred to the Women's Army Corps when the bill was signed, and the WAAC were given a choice to enlist in the WAC or accept a discharge from the WAAC and return to civilian life. The war was still far from over, and America needed all the help it could muster to bring about a speedy victory over her enemies. It remained to be seen just how the new Women's Army Corps would fare after the almost lethal blow delivered by male soldiers and civilians.

Two other forces were also impacting the WAAC negatively. In January 1943, the adjutant general of the army decided, over the objections of Director Hobby, to lower the standards for women joining the WAAC. This decision not only threatened the WAAC in the present and the future, it threatened to destroy the good reputation the WAAC had earned both in the United States and overseas. The adjutant general had lowered the standards for applicants seeking to join the organization in order to meet the new ceiling for WAAC strength. Recruiters were permitted to accept candidates even before the individual's blood test results for sexually transmitted diseases were known. If the test results later returned positive, the recruit would be discharged. When appearing for the recruitment process, the applicant no longer was required to present a health certificate from a civilian physician. The rationale for this was that the certificate put the enlistee to unnecessary expense and duplicated the tests the army would perform.

In addition, applicants no longer had to complete an extensive questionnaire or provide information concerning their work experience. Neither were letters of recommendation any longer required from applicants. Further, an aptitude test score of 50 out of a possible 130+ would be considered passing and educational requirements were abolished. The previous requirement for a background investigation conducted by the provost marshal general was eliminated and replaced with a report from the local office of the Retail Credit Corporation, and this was purely optional, depending on the whim of the recruiter.

In January 1943, the goal of 10,000 WAACs was not only met, but surpassed. In July, however, the goal of 18,000 fell short when only 12,127 young women were processed into the WAAC, leaving a shortfall of 5,730. The quota was raised to 27,000 for March and fell below the January numbers with only 11,464 new WAACs. When March ended, approximately a thousand of these women were sitting around various army posts waiting for assignments since, by that time, the army realized that there were no military jobs these women could fill.

Director Hobby was increasingly unhappy with the fact that numbers of WAAC recruits were falling more frequently, and in increasingly higher percentages, into the lowest two groups of applicants. She directed her staff to determine exactly where these unqualified recruits were being admitted to the WAAC. Scores on the army general classification test had increased from 10 percent of the WAACs tested falling into the lowest two group categories of IV and V; 30 percent in group III; and 60 percent in groups I and II. Distributions changed radically in the first three months of 1943. WAACs tested at Fort Des Moines in this time period divided into 70 percent of the WAACs falling into groups IV and V. More than half of the WAACs were falling into groups too low to be trained to perform semi-skilled military jobs. That 70 percent was classified as semi-skilled, unskilled, domestic service, or laborer.

A further survey of the educational level of WAACs in April 1943 revealed that many had an eighth-grade education or less. Attempts were made to train these recruits as cooks and bakers and in transportation as drivers. When the women were unsuccessful in these fields, a final effort was made to train them as ward orderlies. This program was abandoned when it became evident that women could not replace male orderlies because of the heavy lifting required on the job. Medical personnel revealed that this unskilled group had approximately four times the number of disability discharges as WAACs working in skilled jobs.

It also became clear to Director Hobby that the medical standards for WAACs were grossly inadequate. The largest numbers of WAAC disability discharges were for gynecological and neuropsychiatric conditions. Director Hobby contacted training centers and gathered a list of the worst cases. The list included thirty women who were pregnant when accepted, fifty-two cases of psychoneurosis, thirty-nine cases of menopausal syndrome, and numerous other categories, including rheumatic heart disease, chronic cystitis, fibroid uterus, epilepsy, and duodenal ulcers.[11]

Hobby sent a report to the surgeon general along with a list of the induction centers where physicians accepted the women into the WAAC and asked that he address the issues with those physicians. The surgeon general refused the director's request and commented that the women got the same induction physicals as the men. Director Hobby responded that the situation clearly pointed out the need to publish an official circular stating the medical standards that were to be applied to applicants for membership in the WAAC. Hobby pointed out that the problem hinged on the fact that the examinations given to women applying to join the WAAC had been far too lax and that one half of the women discharged before June 1943 had been in the WAAC four months or less while three-quarters had been in the WAAC for five and a half months or less, indicating that the health issues had preexisted before they applied to the WAAC. A surprising 73.7 percent of those discharged for disabilities were diagnosed with either gynecological or psychiatric conditions.

Several WAAC staff directors stated that they felt some examining psychiatrists were actually screening out the most stable applicants due to an absence of guidelines from the surgeon general. Director Hobby highlighted one outrageous case where an examining psychiatrist "maintained that the only way to determine a woman's stability was to require her to walk into his office naked and to sit down and answer his questions in this condition." One of that psychiatrist's first questions was, "How often during the past month have you had intercourse with a soldier or sailor?" A WAAC staff director noted, "We lost a number of nice young prospects who never came back after he interviewed them. I could just imagine what they told their parents about the purpose of the Women's Army Corps."[12]

Charlotte E. Hertle of Fresno, California, was a young woman of twenty-four when she joined the WAAC in October 1942. Hertle was first stationed in Wilmington, North Carolina, as an aircraft plotter before being deployed to High Wycombe Air Field in England in communications. While stationed at High Wycombe, she experienced attacks by German V-1 and V-2 rockets. Hertle was also trained and worked as a cryptographer. After her transfer to Bad Kissingen, Germany, she worked with the Ninth Air Force. WAC Hertle was an intelligent and dedicated soldier who surprised both authors with her reply to the question, "What do you remember most about your first days/weeks in the military?" Hertle replied, "Running through long halls—naked, during physical. We were told they did not have clothing in supply yet. Embarrassing—since enlisted men lined those long halls. Most of us broke all speed records, then, having to squat naked before a male and female officer for a psychological evaluation."[13]

One could certainly ask why any woman would comply with such a request from a psychiatrist or any other male soldier. It would be difficult to find a woman today who would follow such orders, yet presented with the evidence supplied by Director Hobby, her staff, and WAACs themselves, it would be impossible to ignore such facts. Perhaps such accusations are believable in a world where some male soldiers took advantage of the naïveté of young women, many of whom were raised in small towns and were away from home for the first time.

In 2007, several newspaper articles were published concerning the sexual harassment and sexual assault of women by male recruiters, drill sergeants, and soldiers in general. It is beyond sad and outrageous that the U.S. military did not crack down on every male soldier guilty of such actions and is still ignoring such conduct by male soldiers in the United States, Iraq, and Afghanistan.

In 1943 and after the surgeon general of the army had refused to take any measures to correct the gross deficiencies that existed in the medical care provided for WAAC applicants, and for WAACs in general, Director Hobby took the problem and possible solutions to Generals Marshall and Somervell. Both men assured Hobby that the problem would be addressed and a solution would be found and implemented. When the surgeon general proposed the creation of a position of consultant for women's health and welfare, Director Hobby acted immediately and appointed Maj. Margaret D. Craighill, a physician and former dean of the Women's Medical College of Pennsylvania.

Major Craighill's duties would include recommending medical standards and routine care for 60,000 WAACs and 30,000 nurses. Craighill was also tasked with the establishment and publication of medical standards concerning gynecological and psychiatric examination for women joining or serving in the WAAC and Army Nurse Corps, along with medical standards addressing problems seen in women rather than in men. In order to carry out her duties, Major Craighill was to visit WAAC stations in the United States and overseas.

Director Hobby also addressed the lowering of moral standards in accepting WAAC applicants. The Selective Service Board, which collected data on the histories of male inductees and volunteers, refused to extend this practice to females. A second option was to have the provost marshal of the army post near the female applicant's hometown conduct an investigation of the woman's moral character, reputation, and police record. After the provost marshals refused to conduct such investigations of WAAC applicants, Hobby directed her complains and requests for a solution to Gen. George Grunert, Chief of Administrative Services. Making very clear that "the moral standards applied to men to allow for the admission of all but the vicious criminals, chronic offenders, and habitual drunkards" were not high enough for the admission of a volunteer force of women.

The director pointed out that the police department of a small town had declared a woman clear of any police record or moral offenses and the woman was accepted in the WAAC. Only weeks after her induction, the WAAC discovered that the woman was a well-known prostitute and drunkard with a long police record. When the WAAC contacted the police chief who cleared the woman for admission to the WAAC, the chief informed the WAAC that he had been aware of the woman's police record, but felt that the WAAC would be a good place and opportunity for the woman "to straighten herself out." With this new evidence, the adjutant general and Director Hobby went to General Grunert again. The best offer for help they could get from Grunert was that he would order a "spot check" of one in ten WAAC applicants.[14]

On 5 April 1943, Director Hobby presented a detailed plan for WAAC recruiting and a request that approval of those accepted to the WAAC be in the control of the WAAC itself. On 7 April 1943, responsibility for WAAC recruiting was returned to the WAAC, and Director Hobby set out to restore higher standards for WAAC recruits.

Members of the Writers' War Board who were to assist with nationwide recruiting of women for the military. These writers, who arrived by plane at Lovell Field, Chattanooga, Tennessee, were to make an inspection trip of the Third WAAC Training Center, Fort Oglethorpe, Georgia, 16 April 1943. Left to right: Leo Margulies, editorial director of Thrilling Magazines, Inc., and publisher of numerous pulp magazines; 3rd Officer Madeline T. Hawes, public relations officer; Robert T. Colwell, advertising and radio writer; Laura Hobson, novelist and magazine writer; Jack Goodman, Esquire writer and advertising manager of Simon and Schuster; Katherine Brush, renowned novelist (Red Headed Woman and others); Oscar Schisgall, magazine writer, Collier's; Maj. Frank E. Stillman, assistant commandant, Third WAAC Training Center; Margaret Lee Runbeck, magazine writer; Sarah Elizabeth Rodgers, magazine and fiction writer; Alice Hughes, columnist, radio commentator, author of the column "A Woman's New York," which ran in three New York newspapers; Mrs. Sally Kirkland, associate editor, Vogue; 1st Officer Betty Bandel, Colonel Hobby's staff; Capt. Laurence Curtis, supply officer.

Another factor that was having a negative effect on recruiting women for the WAAC was the civilian labor market. The *New York Times* carried a story on 26 April 1943 with the headline, "5,000,000 Workers McNutt's 1943 Goal." The article quoted the response of Paul V. McNutt, chairman of the War Manpower Commission, to the question, "Where will they [workers] all come from?" McNutt answered, "From the ranks of house-wives, students, older workers, handicapped workers, minority groups, and from workers who transfer from less essential activities into war work. There are no other sources." McNutt had pointed out in an earlier inter-view that in his view "manpower is manpower, because jobs are jobs, and whether they are filled by a woman or a man makes no difference."[15]

In December 1942, when the War Manpower Commission had been given jurisdiction over Selective Service, the commission whose mission it was to recruit four million women for wartime work in civilian industry, put a stop to the military recruitment of men of draft age and limited the military to recruiting men to what they could raise through authorized draft quotas. Since the commission did not feel that it had the same authority over women, on 6 February 1943, it ruled that the military could not recruit or accept women working in federal government or industry unless the woman had a written release from her agency or employer or, in the eyes of the commission, could provide a compelling reason for quitting her current job. No agricultural workers would be per-mitted to change or leave their current employment.

One young woman, Hannah Moore, wanted to leave her job as an industrial nurse in order to join the Army Nurse Corps. "They refused to let me leave my job with the Container Corporation in Philadelphia. The company made boxes with a wax waterproof coating that permitted them to be dropped offshore so they would float to shore, carrying supplies for our troops and allies," Hannah Moore said in an interview in 1998.[16]

When Lynn Ashley, a young woman working as a riveter for Douglas Aircraft in Chicago, decided she would join the WAC, she did not have any trouble leaving her job. "Working at Douglas was kind of a revolving door," Ashley said. "Women would leave when their military husbands were transferred. Or some would get married and go to live with their husbands, so people came to work for whatever period of time they could and then moved on. It was a revolving door." Ashley was accepted by the WAC and served from 1944 to 1946.[17]

In addition to granting WACs full military status, the law made several other important changes. It removed the cap of 150,000 on the number of WACs who could serve at one time in the corps, and it changed the age limits from twenty-one to forty-five to twenty to forty-nine. It established the same system of rates and ranks for women as those that applied to male soldiers, but limited the highest rate or rank that could be held by women in the WAC to lieutenant colonel for officers other than the director, who would hold the rank of full colonel. Enlisted women were held to the highest rank of E-7. The law also granted WACs the same pay, allowances, benefits, and privileges as male soldiers, except regarding

Lynn Ashley, WAC, 1944–1946.

dependent pay for a spouse and dependents. Unlike a male soldier, a woman would have to prove that she contributed to at least 50 percent of her husband's financial support to claim him as a dependent. The disciplinary system would be the same for WACs as it was for male soldiers.

The army also held that WACs were noncombatants and could not be assigned to combat areas. That rule for WACs was enforced with the same care and determination as the rules that said army nurses were noncombatants and would not be stationed in a combat area. United States Army nurses and Women's Army Corps personnel continued to be stationed in combat areas regardless of the noncombatant rule on the books. WACs would serve in the Pacific Theater of Operations and some would carry the army-issue Colt .45 revolver at their side. WACs would experience artillery attacks, bombing raids, strafing, and V-1 and V-2 rocket attacks while serving in a combat zone in a theater of war. Army nurses would be survivors of hospital ships sunk by the German Luftwaffe, six army nurses would be killed by enemy fire in 1944 in Italy, and six by a Japanese suicide plane that aimed for and hit their hospital ship, which was treating wounded soldiers in the Southwest Pacific Theater of War. Army flight nurses would be killed while caring for wounded and ill soldiers, sailors, and marines on medical evacuation flights.

The myth that grew out of a public consensus that said American women did not serve in the military in "harm's way" was then, and remains today, a myth encouraged by a military and society that persist in the delusion that only male soldiers are in combat areas, that only male soldiers are wounded and/or killed by enemy action, that only males serve and protect their country in the U.S. military. The myth was never true and is blatantly untrue today.

On 11 July 1943, the *New York Times* carried an article, "Our Manpower Mobilized: Figures for the Armed Forces, the Farms and the Industries of the Country," that stated that as of 30 June 1943, the number of persons mobilized in the military services was estimated to be 9,300,000. The number of men represented was estimated to be 9,122,000; 178,000 were women. On 22 June 1943, the Department of Agriculture estimated that on 1 June 1943, there were 11,659,000 workers in agriculture, including children under fourteen and wives of farmers. It also estimated that 73 percent, or 8,510,000, were male, and 3,149,000 female.[18]

Persons in nonagricultural industry in July 1943 were estimated to be 42,800,000. Of these, approximately 10,000,000 were in munitions industries. The Bureau of Labor Statistics put the April figure at 9,400,000 for persons in munitions industries. One-fourth of these were women (2,350,000); of the nonagricultural industry of 42,800,000, one-fourth (10,700,000) were women.[19]

On 28 July 1943, despite the heightened recruitment campaign for women to join the WAC, there were 5,000 fewer WACs than there had been on 1 July 1943. WAC enrollment as of 28 July 1943 was approximately 60,000.[20]

There is no doubt that the slander campaign had a drastic effect on the number of WAACs who decided to accept a discharge rather than enlist in the WAC. In the *Radio Digest* of 28 July 1943, an article, "WAC Lacks 85,000 in Reaching Goal Set for Enlistments," expressed the fear that up to 30 percent of WAACs would choose to accept a discharge rather than enlist in the Women's Army Corps. The article suggested that despite the denials by top government officials, who stated that the slanderous rumors about the sexual conduct of WAACs were lies and had no foundation in truth, enlistments continued to decline, and parents, family, and friends of a large number of the WAACs put pressure on the women to accept a discharge from the Women's Army Auxiliary Corps rather than enlist in the newly created Women's Army Corps.[21]

In the final tally, five thousand women chose to be discharged and return to civilian life. This number was approximately 25 percent of the

Conversion of WAACs to WACs at Fort Benning, Georgia, August 1943.

WAAC and lower than the 30 percent or more some predicted would leave. The military still had many battles to fight before Germany and Japan would surrender and World War II would come to an end. Those battles would require more civilians to go into war work to help produce the supplies the troops would need to gain the final victory, and more women would be needed in the WAC, the WAVES, the SPARS, and the USMCWR to replace military men for duty on the front lines of combat.

On 3 September 1943, the *New York Times* featured an article, "Women Must Take Million More Jobs," that ended by stating that perhaps one of the reasons women were not taking more jobs was due to the fact that many thought the war was all but won and that women had been turned down for many of the jobs for which they applied, leading them to think that war workers were not needed as badly as the War Manpower Commission would have Americans believe.[22]

The WAC was strongly engaged in recruiting women for the corps, but since the needs in various parts of the nation were uneven, it was difficult to launch and maintain a national recruiting campaign for women war workers or for women to join the U.S. military. Despite these circumstances, WACs would be employed in military jobs in the United

*War Bond drive parade with WAC recruiting in Montgomery, Alabama,
September 1943.*

States and deployed in higher numbers in the theaters of war overseas.
Women were a vital part of the forces that would bring an end to World
War II and victory to America and her allies. The Women's Army Corps,
which some feared could not survive the conversion from the WAAC,
was proving its essential role in the war again and again. To the chagrin
of some, and the joy of many, the Women's Army Corps was alive, well,
and thriving.

7

★

The most satisfying aspect of being a member of the WAFS was that we were equals. . . . Thus we began welding together as a social unit with a common purpose. We wanted to show that equal among ourselves, we were also equal to men. Anything they could do, we could do and we would try to do it better. . . . We had to. Everyone knew that if a woman got a promotion, she had to be twice as good as a man.

—Adela R. Scharr,
Sisters in the Sky—The WAFS

More than a year before America entered World War II, Nancy Harkness Love and Jacqueline Cochran had already envisioned an important role for female pilots in the fight to defeat Germany and the other Axis powers. The two women came from very different backgrounds yet shared the same passion for flying and the same goal of having America's female pilots contribute their flying skills to America's victory should the United States become a combatant in World War II.

Nancy Harkness Love had grown up in a family that encouraged her to follow her dreams and could afford to send her for flying lessons and for a college education. When Nancy Harkness announced at the dinner table, at age sixteen, that she intended to become a pilot, no family member told her that such a goal was impossible for a woman to reach. In 1936, when Nancy decided to marry, it was a young pilot, Robert Love, she would take for her husband.

When Pearl Harbor was bombed on 7 December 1941, and all airports close to the coast were closed, Nancy and Bob opened and operated Inner City Airways, taught flying, conducted air surveys and sightseeing tours, and accepted crop-dusting contracts. When Bob was called up as a member of the Army Air Corps Reserve and stationed in Washington, D.C., Nancy flew the approximately sixty miles to work every day, while Maj. Robert Love helped design a program for the Army Transport Command to ferry planes from factories to army air bases in the United States and to British air bases in England. Major Love's immediate supervisor was Col. William H. Tunner, who was in charge of the Ferrying Command, tasked with ferrying airplanes. Male pilots to ferry planes were becoming more and more scarce as the military sought pilots for combat flying, and male pilots on the whole were not interested in ferrying planes when they could be flying combat missions instead. In short, male pilots thought it was more glamorous to fly fighters and bombers over enemy territory and deliver bombs on enemy targets. Colonel Tunner had approximately 384 planes under his command and not enough ferrying pilots to deliver them where they were needed most.

One day in a chance conversation with Colonel Tunner, Major Love said he hoped his wife had landed safely at work that morning, and Colonel Tunner asked if Love's wife was a pilot. When Love said that she was, Tunner asked if she knew any other female pilots. Then Love suggested that the colonel speak to Nancy directly.

Nancy and Colonel Tunner hit it off immediately and set about designing a ferrying program for women pilots. Tunner sent the program to his immediate supervisor, Gen. Harold L. George, who in April 1942 had replaced Col. Robert Olds as commander of the Army Air Corps Plans Division. As it turned out, Nancy Harkness Love had written to Colonel Olds on 21 May 1940 suggesting that he and the army might do well to consider accepting women pilots to ferry airplanes, if and when America entered World War II. She went on to tell Colonel Olds that she knew at least forty-nine female pilots who she felt sure would be interested in doing that job for the Air Transport Command. Since Olds was not in need of women pilots at the time, and had more male pilots than airplanes, he filed the letter for future reference, should such a need arise.

Colonel George saw the benefit of such a program and transferred Nancy Love to the New Castle Army Air Forces Base in Wilmington, Delaware, to work with Col. Robert Baker, the base commander. One of the main reasons for selecting New Castle as a center for the Women's Army Ferrying Service (WAFS) was its proximity—about 100 air miles— to the Fairchild aircraft factory in Hagerstown, Maryland.

The requirements for female pilots in the WAFS were different from those of male ferrying pilots. Male ferry pilots were required to be between the ages of nineteen and forty-five and have at least three years of high school and two hundred hours of flying time. Men were hired as civilians and after ninety days of training were commissioned as officers in the army. Women, on the other hand, were required to be at least twenty-one years old and no older than thirty-five and have a high school diploma and at least five hundred hours' flying time, as well as a commercial license, 200 horsepower engine rating, and experience flying cross country. The reason for putting a ceiling of thirty-five years on the age of female ferry pilots was "to avoid the irrationality of women when they enter and go through the menopause."[1]

By consensus, the military considered forty the age at which menopause began for women and reasoned that even if the war lasted five years, the oldest women accepted would just be entering her time of debilitating irrationality. The military had no plans to commission the female pilots as officers in the army, no matter how long the war lasted or how quickly it ended. Some thought that perhaps the women could be commissioned in the WAC, should such a step become necessary. Not too much thought seems to have been given to the fact that the WAC had no air officers in their organization nor any money for either the purchase of planes or the necessary maintenance of flying equipment.

On 24 January 1942, the *New York Times* ran a story under the headline "American Women to Ferry Planes," with the subhead, "Jacqueline Cochran Recruiting Groups to Serve in British Isles Until Needed by the US." The article stated that Jacqueline Cochran would be the leader of a group of twenty-five female pilots chosen by her, who would soon go to England to ferry planes from British factories to British military bases where they were needed. These American female pilots would serve with the British Air Transport Auxiliary (ATA) of the Royal Air Force (RAF) and would be commissioned as officers during their time of service. The women would receive a salary of $4,000 a year and would live on British air bases. The article ended by telling women pilots who were interested in ferrying work to contact Cochran at Suite 4826, 30 Rockefeller Plaza, New York City.[2]

It was Gen. H. H. "Hap" Arnold, chief of the U.S. Army Air Forces (AAF), and a recruiter for ferrying pilots for Britain, who suggested to Cochran that she might be able to contribute a lot to the Allied war efforts by working as a ferry pilot for the British. When Cochran reached England in June 1941, she spent a good deal of her time learning how the

ATA of the RAF was organized and operated. Cochran's objective was to form the same kind of group for female pilots in the United States.

Cochran put that information and experience to work when she returned to the United States for a visit on 1 July 1941. She accepted an invitation to have lunch with President Roosevelt and his wife, Eleanor, at Hyde Park, New York. After filling the Roosevelts in on all her activities with the ATA in England, she suggested that the United States might do well to consider such an organization for women pilots. The president gave Cochran a note of introduction to Assistant Secretary of War for Air Robert A. Lovett. The note stated that FDR wanted Jacqueline Cochran to research and propose a plan for the establishment of female pilots in the Army Air Forces.[3]

On 21 July 1941, Cochran completed her proposal to form an organization of women pilots as a division of the Air Corps Ferrying Command. That proposal reached Gen. Hap Arnold, who suggested that Cochran and her group might be of more help ferrying planes in England.

During the first week in September 1942, the Army Air Forces sent telegrams to eighty-three women pilots whose names had been provided by Nancy Harkness Love. Before that week was finished, Nancy Love was at New Castle Army Air Force Base in Wilmington, Delaware, and began processing responses from women pilots who had received the official telegrams.

On 11 September 1942, the *New York Times* ran the story "Women Will Form a Ferry Command: Army Air Forces Set Up a Squadron with Mrs. Love as Commander." When Jacqueline Cochran arrived in the United States from England, one of the first stories to come to her attention was that story of 11 September 1942, and it hit her with the force of an artillery shell. Cochran was furious and convinced that Nancy Harkness Love and the U.S. Army Air Forces had gone behind her back in establishing an organization of women pilots to ferry military planes throughout the United States. Cochran also felt that General Arnold had broken his word that she would be the director of the first female pilots ferrying group established by the Army Air Forces.[4]

At the base of the misunderstanding and lack of communication was the fact that General Arnold had suffered a heart attack and was on medical leave for a prolonged period. During Arnold's absence, the AAF's need for women ferrying pilots became obvious. In Arnold's absence, and without any knowledge of Arnold's communication with Jacqueline Cochran or of the tentative promises exchanged between the two, General George proceeded to establish the Women's Auxiliary Ferrying Service (WAFS). Adding to the overall miscommunication was the fact that Arnold had no knowledge of the correspondence between Nancy Love and the head of the Army Transport Command, General Olds, in May 1940. One might say that the left hand did not know what the right hand was doing, and a set of circumstances resulted, causing a potentially embarrassing situation for the Army Air Forces and General Arnold, in particular.

Gen. Hap Arnold and the Army Air Forces were in an uncomfortable position. Essentially, the president of the United States had made it clear that he was backing Jacqueline Cochran as the director of the first Army Air Forces organization of women pilots. General Arnold had been in the military long enough to know that it would not be a political plus to ignore the expressed wishes of the commander in chief of the U.S. Armed Forces. The fact was, however, that the existence of the WAFS was a reality, and Arnold and his staff needed to come up with a way to unite the two women pilots' groups without establishing two separate organizations, each with its own command structure and different directors. It was imperative that Arnold and his staff find a solution that would have the least possible negative effects on the Army Air Forces.

On 15 September 1942, after a focused and concerted effort to solve the problem, the Army Air Forces announced the formation of a new group, the Women's Ferry Training Detachment (WFTD), under the command of Jacqueline Cochran. The WFTD would work with the WAFS and, in addition to training women pilots to fly the Army Air Forces way, the WFTD would teach them the traditions and regulations of the Army Air Forces and how to march and drill like well-disciplined soldiers.

While Jackie Cochran was busy establishing the WFTD training program in Houston, Texas, Nancy Love was occupied with preparing the WAFS to fly their first official mission. Included in that preparation were classes in navigation, ferrying routes used by the Army Transport Command, and the correct way to fill out Army Air Forces forms needed for each flight flown by WAFS or Army Air Forces ferrying pilots.

A pocket on the wall inside the cockpit held forms needed for every mission flown. One form was to be filled with the takeoff location and the destination of the flight; the reverse side listed the status of the aircraft itself. If any item on that side of the form was marked with a red diagonal line, it meant that the aircraft was not airworthy. Another form, known as a RON (remain over night), was used when any WAFS pilot found she was unable to reach her terminal destination before nightfall. WAFS were not ordinarily permitted to fly after sunset, and they were required to fill out and file a RON whenever they landed a plane for the night and before resuming a flight to the mission's terminal location.

At New Castle Army Air Field, WAFS were assigned to live in Bachelor Officers' Quarters (BOQ) 14 and learn drill and marching on the base. The first instructors for drill were men but were soon replaced by their sister WAFS. Nancy Love found that she did not possess the voice necessary to call commands and drill her company to take part in the parades and reviews. Love's voice was a soft contralto and did not carry far. In giving orders while drilling her women, Love found her voice cracking, necessitating the repetition of commands that, even then, were not sufficiently loud enough to be heard clearly. On several occasions, Love seemed to be thinking of her next command while the company marched off the road and into a field before the next command was given. Finally, Love placed Betty Giles in charge of drilling the company. Giles had learned drill and command techniques at a finishing school and had a technique and command voice much easier for the company of WAFS to follow.

Love, however, was well respected and liked by her pilots, and inspired creativity and ingenuity in them in dealing with problem solving. This process stood out clearly when Nancy Love was speaking to her WAFS about flying in formation. She pointed out that formation flying could be extremely dangerous since planes that strayed from their assigned places could bump into other aircraft, resulting in damage or even an explosion or air crash. The women immediately began suggesting visual signals, such as waving a plane's right wing to indicate that someone is too far to the left and needs to move to the right to improve the safety of the formation.

The first mission the women flew as WAFS took place on 22 October 1942. Six WAFS—Betty Giles, Cornelia Fort, Aline (Pat) Rhonie, Helen Mary Clark, Adela Scharr, and Teresa James—dressed in flight suits and climbed aboard the plane that would carry them to the Piper Cub factory in Lock Haven, Pennsylvania. When their twin-engine Boeing aircraft landed in Lock Haven, the six WAFS carried their parachutes and bags off the plane and walked to the area where the six L4-Bs, Piper Cubs, were parked and waiting for pilots. The WAFS checked out the tail numbers on the planes and claimed the aircraft they had been assigned to as pilots.

After a brief preflight inspection of their planes, the six WAFS climbed onboard and minutes later were cleared for takeoff. Their destination was Mitchell Field on Long Island, an eighty-minute flight and the first official two hundred miles on their journey into history.

On 9 November 1942, the Army Air Forces sent telegrams to a list of women pilots selected by Jacqueline Cochran. The message told the women that if they were interested in joining a program to train women ferrying pilots for the army, they should report to the Rice Hotel in Houston, Texas, on 15 November 1942 at 10:00 a.m. The telegram also stated that the job would be under civil service and would pay $150 a month. It also informed the women that travel to Houston for the meeting would be at their own expense.

Of the thirty women invited to the meeting, twenty-nine showed up in the lobby of the Rice Hotel on 15 November 1942. They milled about the lobby waiting to be gathered up by the Army Air Forces and oriented to the WFTD program. It was not too long before a group of Army Air Forces men entered the lobby and marched toward the group of would-be ferrying pilots. Leading the group was a fashionably dressed woman wearing a large pin in the shape of a propeller.

Jackie Cochran had arrived to take charge of the women who would comprise the first class of students to go through the training program. The designation for the class was 43-W-1, signifying that they would be the first class of the WFTD in 1943. Future classes would be labeled 43-W-2, 43-W-3, etc. The women would train and attend classes on property belonging to Aviation Enterprises at the Houston municipal airport's Howard Hughes Field. Since there were no barracks for women at the field, it was necessary to quarter the students in boardinghouses scattered throughout the city. The WFTD had made arrangements to lease a bus from Aviation Enterprises and to hire a man to drive the bus to pick up students at their quarters and deliver them to Howard Hughes Field for classes and flight training. The same bus would deliver them back to their quarters when they were finished for the day.

The facilities available at Howard Hughes Field left a great deal to be desired. The field lay adjacent to Ellington Field, where the Army Air Forces was training men to become combat pilots. The male trainees had plenty of space and equipment, including the newest planes to fly while learning combat flying techniques. The women of the WFTD would learn on airplanes that had seen better days and bore both visible and invisible scars.

Add to the war-worn planes the WFTD was flying and using for training in Houston and the winter weather that could often be a challenge on the ground and a monster in the air, and each trainee was facing great risk just by training. Add training to fly at night to these conditions, and the risk grew exponentially.

When trainee Margaret Oldenburg, 43-W-4, took off in a PT-19, a cub with an open cockpit, on the night of 7 March 1943, her instructor was to help her practice spins. The weather in the Houston area had been terrible all day and those grounded during the day were eager to make up time when the weather cleared after sunset. The two had put the PT-19s into a spin but were unable to recover from it before their plane crashed into the ground, killing both student and instructor. The WFTD training command ordered that the crash be kept quiet and not released to the news media. The death of Oldenburg made even more clear the unspoken risk faced by all women ferrying pilots in regard to funeral and burial expenses. Because the women were not military personnel, they had no legal right to have those costs covered by the federal government. Jackie Cochran paid the costs for Oldenburg out of her own pocket and sent Mrs. Leni Leoti Deaton, her executive officer, to escort the young woman's body home for burial.[5]

Deaths among fellow WASPs was the strongest memory of WAFS pilot Edna H. Bishop. In 1989 when she was seventy-six years old, Edna wrote on our questionnaire, "The first girl killed while in training was a marching buddy, Margaret Oldenburg. 'Taps' still brings vivid memories of that day and the loss of my friend. We had a Chinese girl, Hazel Ying Lee, in our class. She was a good student and had a marvelous sense of humor. She too was killed in an accident."[6]

Worn-out planes and bad weather were not the only challenges the women ferrying pilots faced. The lack of knowledge and the gender prejudices were responsible for other indignities the women pilots suffered. In Romulus, Michigan, the WAFS were subjected to questions and bad decisions concerning flying and their menstrual cycles. The flight surgeon at the field asked to be informed of the date of each WAFS pilot's menstrual cycle. The women were ordered not to fly during their menses. The logic behind the order was based on a write-up in the Civil Aeronautics Admin-

WTFD graduation, 1943–1944. Left to right, front row: Maj. Robert K. Urban, Jacqueline Cochran, Gen. Gerald C. Brant, Edna H. Bishop, Kittie Leaming King, Marion Bradley; Second row: unknown civilians, Louise Brown, Rosalie Grohman.

istration handbook that stated that women frequently fainted during menses. It was not known by the women pilots that in part the directive was premised on Cornelia Fort's death during a flight, even though the investigation of the accident determined that Fort was in no way responsible for the accident that killed her.[7]

The accident report of the crash, which took place on 21 March 1943, revealed that on a beautiful, clear day, Cornelia Fort by that day had more than 1,100 hours of flying time while the six male pilots in the group were new graduates of a ninety-day training program. The six pilots were ferrying new BT-13s (low-wing, closed-canopy basic trainers) to Love Field in Dallas, Texas. Despite the fact that close-formation flying was not permitted during a ferrying flight, the men decided to fly a portion of the mission in close formation. At some point, most planes withdrew to safer distances to continue the flight. One male pilot, Frank E. Stammes, who had 267 flight hours to his credit, began flying very close to Fort's plane and then pulling up. On one of the passes, the landing gear on Stamme's plane and the tip of Fort's left wing collided. The tip of the wing broke away, taking six feet of leading edge with it. Fort's plane went into a dive and hit the ground in a nose-down vertical position, killing the twenty-four-year-old pilot. The same woman who had been in the air over Hawaii on 7 December 1941 when Japanese planes attacked Pearl Harbor; the same woman nearly shot out of the sky by a Japanese Zero; the same woman who escaped from a second Zero that was shooting at her and landed her plane safely on the ground; the same woman who had escaped death when the field in which she had landed was strafed by a third Zero, had been knocked out of the sky by an American ferrying pilot who was showing off. Fort had fallen to her death, felled by an American man piloting an American aircraft on a clear blue day, with no enemy plane within thousands of miles.[8]

On 5 July 1943, the name of the WAFS was changed to Women Auxiliary Service Pilots (WASPs). Jacqueline Cochran was named director of women pilots with the Army Air Forces. Nancy Love was made WASP executive on the staff of the Ferrying Division. This put Love in charge of all women ferrying pilots and left her under the direct command of Colonel Tunner, head of all domestic ferrying. Love and Cochran could do their jobs with little contact necessary between them.

In mid-July 1943, a new assignment was given to the WASPs, and on 19 July 1943, Jackie Cochran met with twenty-five recent graduates from the training program at Avenger Field in Sweetwater, Texas. Cochran began the meeting by telling the group that the Army Air Forces had been given a top secret assignment. Cochran's next words caught the women by surprise. She asked any women who did not want to take part in the mission to raise their hands. No hands went up, and Jackie filled them in on the mission. Those assigned to the project would be stationed at Camp Davis, North Carolina, an Army Air Forces base on the southeast coast. The base was as large as some American cities and had a population of fifty thousand, most of them men who were learning how to use antiaircraft artillery effectively. It would be the job of the WASPs to aid in this training by towing targets, large sleeves of silk or muslin approximately thirty feet long. The target was fastened to a 1,500-foot steel cable attached to the plane's tail section. Since there was no way of knowing directly which shooters were hitting the target, bullets were dipped in colored wax, and each color was assigned to a particular shooter so that the hits could be counted later and attributed to the correct students.

More than a few planes returned to the field with bullet holes in them, and several women pilots had been shot in the foot before the WASPs' target-towing mission was ended.

During the summer of 1943, Rep. John Costello of California drew up a bill to grant the WASPs military status. On the first of July 1943, the WACs were granted full military status, and many were sure that granting full military status to WASPs would not be long in coming.

The WASPs were still expanding, and it seemed there would be no end to the growth potential of the organization. The women who signed up for the WAFS, the WFTD, and the WASP had several things in common. They shared a love of flying and, in a time when flight lessons were quite expensive, they were subsidized by their well-off or wealthy families or husbands. They were all self-directed enough to ignore people and a society that thought it quite bizarre that any woman would want to leave her "natural" gender-assigned role to pursue a pilot's license, not to mention volunteering to fly military planes for the Army Air Forces. Although the war had made it more acceptable for women to serve their country as ferrying pilots or members of the armed forces, most of society expected them to return to their traditional roles once the war was won. In fact, women were soon to learn that as the war turned more against the Axis powers and victory drew closer for the Allies, women were seen as less essential in the military and in the workforce.

The women ferrying pilots also shared a desire to serve their country in a time of war and a definite sense of adventure. When the authors asked former WASPs why they signed up to become ferrying pilots for the Army Air Forces, their responses were more similar than different.

Marjorie M. Gray, who served as a WASP from 1942 through December 1944, responded to the question, "Jackie Cochran sent me a telegram announcing military flight training for women in Houston, Texas." Gray went on, "Since I had turned down an earlier telegram asking me to go to England and join the Air Transport Auxiliary—the ATA of the Royal Air Force—I felt I did not want to miss out on such a great opportunity." When asked what was her strongest memory of World War II, Gray answered, "The excitement of flying the best airplanes in the world at that time."[9]

In one way or another, most women had similar answers to the question, What was the most surprising thing you learned about yourself as a

Doris B. Tanner prior to checkout in the cockpit of the famous Doolittle Raider B-25 plane, which had two twin-row, 1750-horsepower Wright engines. Douglas, Arizona, 1944.

result of your service during World War II? Gray and the majority of women interviewed spoke of discovering strengths they did not realize they possessed. "That I had much more stamina and strength than I had thought beforehand. I gained a lot of self-confidence," Gray recalled.[10]

Former WASP Dorothy Eppstein, who was twenty-five when she signed up as a WASP in 1943 and served until 10 December 1944, responded to the questions this way: "I had patriotic feelings about helping to win World War II." Eppstein said, "I also felt that I was in a rut at work." The most surprising thing Eppstein learned about herself was "That I was given a lot of respect for being a pilot—something which came so easy for me." When asked what she would like to be remembered for, Eppstein responded: "Being able to handle a military job well."[11]

Lizbeth Ann (Morgan) Hazzard answered the same questions this way, "I wanted to fly for the USA!" Her strongest memory from World War II was "We *could fly* the big planes." When asked what the most surprising thing she learned about herself in World War II was, Hazzard responded: "That I could fly with the men and still remain a lady. I gained much confidence in myself that has served me well all this time." When asked what she would like to be remembered for she said, "That I served my country!"[12]

When Doris Brinker Tanner responded to our inquiries in September 1989, she was the president of the WASP. She offered to help us honor the women of World War II in any way possible. When photos arrived with a note that ended with, "Thanks for including the WASP! We *ARE* pleased," it brought a smile to our faces and reinforced our conviction that it was time for the courageous women who volunteered and served in World War II to receive at least a small part of the gratitude and national recognition they had earned almost half a century ago.[13]

Mabel Virginia Rawlinson of Kalamazoo, Michigan, left her job as a professional secretary with the Kalamazoo Public Library to join the WFTD. Like other women ferrying pilots, she wanted to serve. When Rawlinson finished her training, she was stationed at Camp Davis Army Air Field, near the coast of North Carolina. Rawlinson towed targets in support of antiaircraft artillery trainees. After sundown on 23 August 1943, Rawlinson and her instructor took off in an A-24, better known as a Douglas Dauntless Dive Bomber, to practice nighttime flying. They had been in the air only a short time when the plane began experiencing mechanical problems. The instructor decided that they should return to the airfield immediately. While on the final approach, the landing gear hit the tops of pine trees that encircled the field. In seconds, the plane nosed down and hit the ground. On contact, the plane split in two, throwing the instructor in the backseat, clear of the wreckage, and trapping Rawlinson in the front seat as the plane went up in flames. Rawlinson tried to open the canopy, but the switch that released the lock from inside had been broken for some time. Rawlinson's screams were muffled by the closed canopy as she burned to death and beyond recognition. Rawlinson was twenty-four years old.

The crash report cited two facts: (1) The A-24s used for target towing at Camp Davis were worn out from war duty and, due to a lack of parts, were not adequately maintained; (2) the Army Air Corps was using lower octane fuel, 90 versus 100, than the planes required. Of the thirty-seven accidents involving towing targets, fifteen involved A-24s and fourteen of the thirty-seven occurred at Camp Davis. The first ten accidents at Camp Davis involved A-24s and occurred between 6 August 1943 and 18 November 1943.[14]

By January 1944, Gen. Hap Arnold was convinced of the WASPs' professionalism and flying skills and put his authority and reputation behind the effort to militarize the women pilots and give them full military status. In January 1944, Rep. John Costello introduced HR 4219, authorizing Army Air Forces commissions for women pilots on duty. The resolution would also grant them all the privileges of Army Air Forces officers, including insurance, pay, hospitalization, and funeral expenses. With General Arnold's support, the resolution was expected to pass with little or no problems. However, something new had been added to the mix. Congress had been inundated with letters and telegrams from civilian male pilots who claimed that the Army Air Forces had been giving jobs that rightfully belonged to them to women pilots.

Arnold stated that there was room in the Army Air Forces for both male and female pilots. However, many of the complaints about women pilots came from civilian men who had been instructors charged with training male pilots for military duty. This category had given these men reserve status, and now with so many women pilots available, the reserve status had been lost and the former flight instructors were now eligible for the draft and could be called up for the U.S. Infantry.

Civilian men stepped up their pressure on Congress to return the positions women pilots had usurped to their rightful owners—civilian male pilots who by tradition had always performed military duties when called upon by their country.

The Army Air Forces was deeply involved in research and test flights for a new four-engine plane called the YP-59A. There were many in the military who were convinced that the planes were not reliable and should be scrapped. Engine fires during test flights had claimed the lives of pilots, the most recent being test pilot Eddie Allen and copilot Bob Dansfield, who were flying the YP-59A on a test run. When the number-two engine burst into flames, Allen radioed ahead and requested fire equipment to stand by near the runway. Before he could land the plane, the flames reached the gas tank and the plane exploded in midair.

Doubts about the YP-59A's integrity, design, and ultimate safety increased exponentially, and male trainees were increasingly less willing to fly these planes and some others. Knowing this, General Arnold sent one of his best pilots to find two WASPs who could and would fly a newly minted B-29 that male pilots were reluctant to fly from Elgin Army Air Forces base to Alamogordo, New Mexico, where a heavy bomber base was located. Arnold believed that once male pilots saw two women piloting the B-29 successfully, they would be embarrassed to decline the missions themselves. A tall, slim, no-nonsense Army Air Forces pilot was given the assignment to find two WASPs who would fly the B-29, dubbed Landybird, from Elgin Field, Florida, to the heavy bomber base at Alamogordo, New Mexico. The pilot turned up unannounced at the dayroom of the Army Nurse Corps personnel. A WASP named Dorthea Johnson was seated, reading a magazine. Without a word of introduction, the young officer asked Johnson if she had any time flying four-engine planes. She responded that she had not but knew of one woman who might just be able to handle the job. The woman's name was Dora, and she was on a flight at the moment. The officer said he would take them both for the mission and they should be ready to leave the next morning for training. The officer was Col. Paul Tibbets, the man in charge of training and leading the crews that would drop the atomic bombs on Hiroshima and Nagasaki in 1945.

When the two WASPs landed the B-29 in Alamogordo, there was a small crowd watching. They had to be surprised when the pilots, both women, deplaned through the forward hatch, carrying their parachutes and smiling. From that day on, there was no more grumbling from male pilots assigned to train on and fly the B-29 Super Fortress.

The Costello bill was scheduled to come up for a vote in June, and new pressure was being exerted on Congress to scrap the bill, dismiss women pilots, and return male pilots to their rightful jobs.

New pressure to defeat the Costello bill and deactivate the WASP was being presented in some of the nation's leading magazines and newspapers. *Time*, the New York *Daily News*, and the *Washington Post* said it was time for women pilots to step down and return their jobs to the male pilots who wanted them. The *New York Times*, the *Herald Tribune,* and the *Boston Globe* printed articles and editorials in favor of militarizing the WASP. A very hard blow against the WASP was delivered when journalist Drew Pearson wrote a column in the *Washington Times Herald* questioning whether funding the WASP was legal. Pearson went even further when he accused General Arnold of falling prey to Jacqueline Cochran's "feminine wiles." The column threw new fuel on the fires to disband the WASP, and male civilian pilots redoubled their letter-writing efforts.[15]

On 5 June 1944, a special investigating committee, the Ramspeck Committee, released the findings of their investigation of the funding of the WASP. The WASP program to date had cost $50 million of government funds that, by the rules, required legislation that was never sought. On 21 June 1944, the Costello bill HR 4219 was defeated 188 to 169. Although the committee lacked the authority to deactivate the WASP, they did have the power to keep it a civilian organization under the civil service and that is exactly what they did.

Few people were aware of a new plane being tested by Army Air Forces. Rumor had it that the plane was powered by "jet propulsion" and would revolutionize flying in the military and civilian spheres. In September 1944, WASP pilot Ann Baumgartner flew the new plane on a test flight from Wright Field, Dayton, Ohio. The test was flawless and without one negative incident to mar its success. The record books of the day could, and should, testify to the fact that WASPs had flown every plane the Army Air Forces was using or even thinking about adding to its inventory.

In August 1944, Jacqueline Cochran sent an eleven-page typed report to Gen. Hap Arnold, enumerating the successful achievements of the WASPs to date. To that list, Cochran added "a poker player's big gamble"; she suggested that if the Army Air Forces would not militarize the WASP, then perhaps they should be disbanded.

Perhaps Cochran's gamble was intimately connected with her original desire to have women pilots become part of the AAF, with herself as commanding officer for that particular organization. It is also possible, and likely, that Cochran's "big gamble" also grew out of her complete dislike of the possibility of having the WASP absorbed by, and become part of, the WAAC/WAC. It seems that Cochran had little tolerance for the idea, let alone the reality, of having a woman outrank her in an organization she considered her creation or in which she saw herself as the natural and rightful leader. Given that Cochran was willing for the WASP to become part of the AAF where she would be in charge of everything affecting the women pilots but unwilling to have the WASP gain military status by being absorbed into the Women's Army Corps where she would be outranked by another woman, Oveta Culp Hobby, Cochran's "big gamble" becomes more understandable but not any less selfish. Cochran's gamble seems predicated on the same reasoning used by children in playgrounds as one child stamps a foot and shouts, "If we don't do it my way, I will take my ball and bat and go home." It is no more admirable on Capitol Hill than it is in a playground.

Jacqueline Cochran's "big gamble" proved a gift for General Arnold. The need to cut back on Army Air Forces strength was not one Arnold was looking forward to putting into action. Cochran had just made the decision on where and whom to cut, an easier one to make. The WASP would be deactivated as of 20 December 1944.

During the first week of October, an identical letter went out to each WASP still on active duty. The message was short and to the point. Arnold thanked each WASP for her wartime duty and said the Army Air Forces would miss them. The date of deactivation was given as 20 December 1944, and the letter ended by wishing each WASP a lifetime filled with "Happy Landings."

The WASPs continued to fly ferrying missions right up the date of their deactivation.

WASPs were ferrying P-63s from the factory in New York to Montana, where the P-63s were picked up by Russians. On 23 November 1944 at the end of this trip, Hazel Ying Lee was killed while landing her P-63 at Great Falls, Montana. Left to right on wing: "B.J.," Frances Snyder Tanassy, and unidentified male officers. Standing are Hazel Ying Lee, A. J. May, and an unidentified pilot.

WASPs at Douglas Field, Arizona, December 1944.

The last WASP to die in service was twenty-five-year-old Mary Louise Webster. Mary had graduated and received her silver wings on 16 October 1944. She was assigned to Frederick Army Air Field in Frederick, Oklahoma. Webster was a passenger, along with a Sgt. Melvin Clark, in a UC-78, a twin-engine Cessna T-50, known as a bobcat, flying from Frederick to Tulsa, Oklahoma. The plane encountered a cold front moving across the state. The aircraft was flying at nine thousand feet. When the plane was on the outskirts of Tulsa, the pilot radioed the control tower for permission to descend. The descent came too late for a plane with heavy ice on its wings. It crashed, killing everyone onboard.[16]

The WASPs were deactivated on 20 December 1944 and left the organization without a single veterans' benefit.

On 30 June 1989, the authors received a letter from Elizabeth "Betse" M. Lewis, Ed.D., informing them that she had served in the merchant marine in World War II and would like to be included in the National Salute to Women Veterans of World War II that was to take place at the World

Congress Center in Atlanta, Georgia, on 29 October 1989. In September, Dr. Lewis returned a completed questionnaire along with other documents pertaining to her World War II service and a letter, which read in part: "I look forward to the exciting prospect of perhaps meeting other Merchant Marine veterans. So far I have not found any, but I believe if there are others they will show up for the meeting in Atlanta."[17]

Since that time, the authors have researched the question of women serving in the U.S. Merchant Marine during World War II. To the best of our knowledge, Lewis and possibly one other woman are the only females who served in that branch during World War II.

Contact with "Betse" made it clear to us that even if Elizabeth M. (Sweetman) Lewis is the only woman who served in the merchant marine between 1941 and 1945, she has earned the right to be remembered along with the hundreds of other women who volunteered to serve their country in a time of war.

It took a federal court case against the federal government, *Schumacher v. Aldridge* (1987), to win veterans' status for those who served between 7 December 1941 and 15 December 1945. (A decade later, on 14 October 1998 President Bill Clinton signed a measure, the Ocean Shipping Reform Act [Public Law 105-258], to extend the terminal date to 31 December 1946, which coincides with the terminal date of all World War II veterans.)[18]

The service of the merchant marine in World War II has not been widely known by the American people, but the facts of that history make it clear that the service these American citizens gave to the United States during World War II has earned them the right to be remembered and recognized.

Merchant mariners who volunteered to serve their country in World War II were trained by the U.S. military, were not subject to the draft as long as they were serving on a merchant marine ship, uniformed by the military, subject to Article 110 of the Articles of War—military statutes—could win military awards, and were subject to court-martial during their service. More than seven thousand merchant mariners lost their lives to enemy action in World War II, one thousand of those within sight of America's east coast. It was not unknown for the bodies of merchant mariners to wash up on east coast beaches after a merchant ship was sunk by a German U-boat off America's eastern or southeastern coastline.

When the United States declared war on Japan, Germany, and the Axis

Elizabeth Matthew Lewis, U.S. Merchant Marine, World War II.

powers, the merchant marine was put under the control of the War Shipping Administration.

The military took it upon itself to establish a ninety-day training program for merchant mariners, and military recruiters directed men who did not meet the qualifications of the armed forces to the merchant marine. Most men rejected by the military were gladly accepted in the merchant marine. Between 1941 and 1945, the number of merchant mariners rose from 55,000 to a figure of between 215,000 and 250,000.

Any merchant mariner who had a ship torpedoed or bombed out from under him also lost his pay from the moment his foot went into a lifeboat to abandon ship or he went into the water. Any merchant mariner who found himself stranded in a foreign port after his ship was sunk by a German U-boat was on his own to find and pay for a journey back to the United States. Until he returned to the United States and was assigned to another ship, he did not collect a paycheck.

When Elizabeth "Betse" Huger married Frank Christopher Sweetman in 1941, she decided to share his occupation as well as his life. Sweetman was the captain of a cargo ship and sought, and received, permission from the State Department to include his wife as a member of his crew. Elizabeth was twenty-five years old and took the job of a ship's cook.

Most of the voyages Elizabeth sailed on left from a port in Miami, Florida. Often the ship's cargo was bananas from Haiti and Cuba. Other voyages took them from Brownsville, Texas, to Tampico, Mexico. In 1942, when their ship sank on Frying Pan Shoals off North Carolina, it was bound for Colombia, South America.

On the afternoon of 9 November 1942, the *Mayfair*, a three-masted New York schooner manned by Sweetman and his crew, foundered in high seas off the coast of North Carolina. The weather on that afternoon was extremely rough and it became apparent that the 184-ton schooner was sinking as waves washed over it. Captain Sweetman and another member of the crew built a raft out of six empty oil drums lashed to boards, and each crew member straddled one of the drums on the raft. The raft was approximately twelve feet by five feet and bobbed up and down in the heavy seas. When a Civil Air Patrol plane spotted the raft, the morale of the crew went up considerably. "It was a long time between when we were spotted by the plane and when a coast guard ship turned up on site to rescue us. We talked and joked among ourselves while we waited," Elizabeth said. "We were all wet but very glad that we had been found." One of the crew members had stood on the raft and held the flag upside down—the international sign of distress—until a passing plane spotted them. Food and water were no problem, since the captain had ordered the crew to eat as much food as they could hold and to drink all the water possible before they got on the raft. In addition, each crew member had brought along food and water. "The food and water were put into watertight containers, tied to the raft, and floated in the water behind us," Elizabeth said. "It took about nine hours for the coast guard boat to spot us. We were all very glad when we finally reached dry land." As soon as they found another ship, the Sweetmans and their crew were off to sea again.[19]

When asked what message she would give the world concerning women veterans, Dr. Lewis answered: "I'd like everyone to appreciate the valor and selfless devotion that I see even now in the women veterans of World War II. America was very lucky to have their help during World War II."[20] The authors feel confident in saying that America was also lucky to have women like Elizabeth M. Lewis who volunteered to help their country win the victory.

8

★

Our country's flag with a star in the center brought pride not only to friends and family but to an entire community who saw it hanging in the window. My mother had crocheted her flags, first one with one star, then two stars, three stars, and, finally, four stars. That act depicted her great pride in us. It also brought her the respect and admiration for being the mother of four children in service.

—Wanda Lucus, WAC

The last five months of 1943 and the first six months of 1944 were a pivotal time in the history of women in the U.S. military, and particularly of those in the WAAC/WAC. On 3 July 1943, President Roosevelt signed the bill to establish the Women's Army Corps *in* the Army of the United States. On 5 July 1943, Director Oveta Culp Hobby took the oath of office as a colonel in the Army of the United States and became the first woman admitted to the Women's Army Corps.

A letter to Colonel Hobby from the commander of Hampton Roads Port of Embarkation, Brig. Gen. John R. Kilpatrick, expressed pleasure that the legislation establishing the Women's Army Corps was now law. The letter read in part: "The Port Band at mess time, accompanied by a large part of our headquarters detachment of enlisted men, proceeded to the WAC barracks and serenaded the girls with 'You're in the Army Now,' and 'This Is the Army, Mr. Jones,' and a general jollification ensued."[1]

To be completely accurate, however, the members of the WAAC were not yet members of the Women's Army Corps. Public Law 110 said the army had ninety days to disband the Women's Army Auxiliary Corps. All members of the WAAC had either to be enlisted or commissioned members of the WAC or discharged by 30 September 1943, the day decreed by law as the date on which the WAAC would cease to exist.

In order for a WAAC to become a WAC, she had to complete a new application, have the recommendation of her company commander, and pass a physical examination that would be stricter than the one she received when she applied to become a WAAC. The standards for passing the exam had been raised considerably, including the visual acuity necessary to pass the eye exam. Colonel Hobby was not in agreement with the surgeon general's standards and wanted them changed. Hobby felt strongly that any woman who had passed the physical and was admitted to the WAAC should not be rejected by the WAC over a physical problem that did not keep her out of the WAAC. The army ruled in favor of the surgeon general and, in June, the standards for the new physical for applicants for the WAC were published.

In August 1943, the number of WAACs who had applied to the WAC and had been rejected grew large enough to cause the army to reevaluate its decision to use the standards recommended by the surgeon general and to suspend discharges based on those standards. The army reversed its decision and accepted the standards for physical exams suggested by Colonel Hobby. The reversal of standards did not affect any of the women previously discharged under the standards supplied by the surgeon general. Those already rejected were banned permanently from admission to the Women's Army Corps.

For many of the women who had been left in limbo while the army was redefining and republishing its standards, the wait went against the WAC. Many who had intended to transfer to the WAC were persuaded by boyfriends, family, or friends to accept a discharge from the WAAC and return to civilian life. The army did little to encourage WAACs to transfer to the WAC. In fact, there were numerous supervisors—military officers—who encouraged the women to leave the military and work at the same job as a civilian and for higher pay. The payoff for many of those male officers was that the women would be available for dating and not under any of the army rules against fraternizing. The women could also live in apartments, where their off-duty hours were unsupervised.

In an attempt to stem the losses to the WAC, orders went out that each military station was to swear in their applicants as soon as they had met the requirements for acceptance, rather than wait for the common date for a national swearing-in set for 1 September 1943.

Other interesting facts emerged when investigators looked at who stayed, at which locations, and for what reasons. The results evidenced the fact that WAACs who felt needed and appreciated on their jobs and who felt they were using their talents and making a difference were the ones who transferred to the Women's Army Corps. Most of those who chose to accept a discharge and returned to civilian life listed as one of their reasons for making the decision that they were no longer willing to put up with the hostility directed at them by camp commanders or from other men on the station who followed the commanding officer's lead. Approximately 25 percent of the WAAC decided to accept a discharge. For those who remained and transferred to the WAC, there would be new benefits, new rules, new titles, and new adventures.

WACs now had military status, and therefore military protection was the same for them as for male soldiers, whether stationed in the States or overseas. Also, women would be paid the same as men of equal rank. However, dependency pay for WACs and male soldiers would remain decidedly unequal. Male soldiers were automatically paid for listed dependents without the soldiers having to produce supporting documentation. WACs, on the other hand, would not receive dependency pay without clear and legal documents showing that they contributed more than 50 percent of the support of their husbands and minor children. As with the old law for the WAAC, having dependents under the age of eighteen would be an exclusion factor for the WAC unless it could be shown that the dependent children were properly cared for by relatives or friends.

WACs were also restricted in the highest rank they could attain. The only colonel in the WAC was the WAC director. WACs could not be promoted to any position where the holder of the position would by necessity command male soldiers. The office of the WAC director would be under the commander of G-1, Personnel Division. WACs were classified as noncombatants even though this was *not* stated specifically in the law. Women would not be promoted to, or assigned to, any position or take part in any technical exercise where knowledge and/or use of tactical weapons was a prerequisite.

Women were permitted to carry a sidearm, usually a Colt .45, when assigned by their commander to jobs and locations where security was deemed to require such precautions, for example, work in code rooms, intelligence, military police, and drivers in specific areas overseas. The public relations office was to prevent photos of WACs wearing or using sidearms. (This, however, did not prevent personal photos of WACs wearing or using sidearms.)

For the first time, women in the army could marry without their CO's permission, and single WACs could receive a medical discharge for pregnancy. In addition, if a WAC became pregnant overseas, she was quickly air-evacuated to the United States. Further, if her baby were stillborn, the single WAC was discharged for "the convenience of the Government." Finally, if a WAC had an illegal abortion, she was given a dishonorable discharge for bad conduct.

It should be noted that the pregnancy rate for WAACs/WACs was 1 per 1,000 per month, as compared to 117 per 1,000 per month for the same age group of women in civilian life. For WACs married to men in the armed forces, medical care in army hospitals was permitted up to and through the delivery.

Colonel Hobby argued for, and won, the right for single WACs to receive medical care in army hospitals up to and through the baby's birth. Hobby was a true champion for the rights and benefits of members of the WAAC/WAC, married or single. It can be fairly argued that members of the WAAC/WAC would have had fewer rights and benefits if it had not been for the willingness of Hobby to stand and fight for equal benefits and treatment for single as well as married WAACs/WACs and for female soldiers as well as male soldiers.

Hobby brought a unique combination of intelligence, education, business experience, and integrity to her position as director of both the WAAC and WAC. She did this despite the fact that she was also the wife of a former governor of Texas, William Hobby, and the mother of their two children, William and Jessica. When her husband became quite ill, he and the children moved to Washington, D.C., so the family could be together. During that time, Colonel Hobby would leave her office after a full day of work and return home to care for her husband and children. In the opinion of the authors, Oveta Culp Hobby was a remarkable woman and the WAAC/WAC were indeed fortunate to have her guidance and direction for those formative years.

In January 1943, when the army responded to the concerns of recruiters at drastically reduced numbers of applicants by lowering admission standards for the WAAC, Colonel Hobby complained long and hard to have the former standards reinstated. Instead of requiring women to have a high school education, two letters of recommendation, and a police check, the lower standards admitted women without a floor on education levels, required no letters of recommendation, and no police check. Complaints from communities concerning WAACs went up in conjunction with the number of women accepted under these new and weakened standards for admission to the WAAC, and Colonel Hobby never gave up her fight to have the former and more stringent standards restored. That would have to wait, however, until she could actually present enough evidence to Gen. George C. Marshall to get him to reverse the lower standards that had been put in place.

The women serving in the WAAC never lost sight of the fact that the slander campaign against WAACs/WACs was continuing, with drastic results to individuals and the WAAC/WAC and other women's branches. If average Americans had been unaware of that fact, a news article that appeared in the *Houston Post* on 11 July 1943 would bring the reality home to anyone who chanced to read it. The article also appeared in syndicated form in other national papers throughout the United States. The main headline for the story read: "WAC's Deportment Commendable, Reporter Declares." The subheading read: "Girl Soldiers Hurt by Rumors." The author of the article, Ruth Cowan, accompanied the first WAACs to sail for their new duty assignment in Africa to check out the rumors for herself.

The article begins by explaining that the WAACs on the ship had "stars in their eyes about their patriotic duty" and wanted to do their part to help America win the war. Cowan points out that a sea voyage on a troop ship is not at all like a cruise on a luxury liner. The WAACs slept in double-decker beds, six to fourteen to a small cabin. There was no hot water or bathtub, and fresh water was rationed to one canteenful twice a day. The women were surprised to learn when they disembarked in Africa that the rumors circulating in America had preceded them to their new duty station. The women had enlisted or accepted commissions in the WAAC in order to do their part in helping America win the war. Cowan pointed out that the girls seemed genuinely hurt to learn of rumors saying that the WAACs who went overseas were issued contraceptives in order to do their real job of keeping the men happy by providing them with sex whenever possible. When the WAACs heard that they were thought of as nothing but "playgirls" for the men, they were genuinely hurt and concerned about the pain such rumors would cause their families and friends. Every woman responded to Cowan's question, "Why did you join the WAAC/WAC?" in a very similar manner: "I wanted to do my part," "I have no brothers, so I thought I should go," "It's my duty as an American," "My husband is serving in the South Pacific, and I want to do my part, too."[2]

The WAACs get their first view of the quarters they are to occupy on the troop ship bound for North Africa, 1943.

They reached their North African home, a fairly deserted convent that had seen better days and was in need of a good cleaning. First, however, their quarters needed to be fumigated to get rid of the insects and spiders that had declared the convent home. After that, cleaning began in earnest.

The WAACs would work six days a week and look forward to their one day off. They worked around the clock, and when writing letters back home, tried to convince their families and friends that the rumors were unfounded and not to give them credence.

Curfew in the barracks/convent was 8:30 p.m.—"an hour when folks back home in the USA are just getting ready to go out to play"— for women lucky enough to have a pass to stay downtown. On nights when a dance was arranged for the WAACs/WACs and GIs, the girls traveled to and from the dance as a unit; they returned about 10:00 p.m.[3]

The WAAC/WACs of that first unit were so outstanding that requisitions for WAAC/WACs came pouring in to the army. Colonel Hobby was already aware of the fact that given the army's estimate of 150,000 WAAC/WACs in the corps by July 1943, the corps was approximately 85,000 women short. Hobby was not shy at expressing to the Pentagon her belief that the WAAC/WAC would never meet the goal imposed by the army as long as the WAAC/WAC depended upon volunteers to fill their ranks. She pointed out that not even the army itself had attained

*WAACs of the first company of women soldiers to serve overseas in a
theater of operations during World War II are entertained in an Arab
chieftain's palace in Algiers, 1943. Left to right: Catherine Jeane Strong,
Iron Mountain, Michigan; Ruby Elizabeth Stroup, Cherryville,
North Carolina; host, Zerrouiak Mehoudine, Arab chieftain;
Helen O. Rosen, Detroit, Michigan.*

sufficient numbers of male soldiers without using a draft. Hobby never
expressed this opinion in public or to the media, since she preferred to
work from inside the organization to make the necessary changes needed
to attract more women into the WAAC/WAC.

In August 1943, a second group of sixty WAAC/WACs arrived in
Casablanca, Morocco, and then were transported almost five hundred
miles to Mostaganem, Algeria, where they would work with the U.S. Fifth
Army. Approximately a month later, the Sixtieth WAC Headquarters
Company arrived to reinforce the 149th WAC Company, the first group
of WAACs working in the theater and still doing an excellent job for the
U.S. Army.

One of the first WAACs to serve at the Allied Headquarters (AFHQ)
was Jeanne Davis, who enlisted in the WAAC on 11 September 1942 and
in the WAC on 31 August 1943. Davis was twenty-two years old, with a
strong sense of patriotism and duty. She had been raised in a family that
was proud of the fact that four generations of its men had served their

country with pride. "I volunteered to go overseas when I enlisted," Jeanne Davis Nixon recalled. "My friends went along with my joining. My brother was also pleased. However, my mother and sisters were very angry," she continued. "They said that 'nice girls don't join the military.' They became more accepting as time went on."[4]

Davis served with the Signal Corps Message Center as a specialist in code and cipher. During the two years she spent in Algiers and Caserta, Italy, she experienced "frequent enemy strafing and bombing." When asked what her feelings and thoughts were while she was stationed in these combat zones, she answered, "I was very young. I was not afraid to die. I guess I was a fatalist then and still consider myself one today."[5]

Martha "Marty" McQuan was twenty-four years old when she signed up for the WAAC in 1942. "I joined because I could perhaps help in the war effort," McQuan said. "I was raised in a very patriotic family, and we are also members of the DAR. . . . When I completed officer candidate school, I was assigned as company commander at Fort Adams, Rhode Island." McQuan continued, "I ended my service as theater chief signal officers staff, stationed in Paris, France. In between, I was stationed in Oran, Africa; Algiers, Africa; Caserta, Italy; and Dijon, France."[6]

For all WAAC/WACs who served in North Africa, the stifling heat of summer and the abundance of insects, poisonous spiders, scorpions, and poisonous snakes were a separate hardship added to the stress of war and long work hours.

A large contingent of WACs arrived in England on 20 July 1943 to take up duties with the Eighth Air Force.

Before Gen. Dwight D. Eisenhower left the North Africa Theater to become the new commander of the European Theater of Operations (ETO), he had some very powerful compliments for the WAAC/WACs who served in the theater and in his headquarters. He pointed out that the WAAC/WACs had proven their usefulness to the army and that there were many cases where one WAAC/WAC replaced two enlisted men who had done the job previously.

The efficiency and professionalism of the WAAC/WAC had not escaped the attention of Lt. Gen. Ira C. Eaker, commander of all U.S. Air Forces in the U.K. and, later, the Allied Air Forces in the Mediterranean Theater. Despite the warnings issued to him by his commanding officer

WAC Anna Mazak Palmares.

not to bring WAAC/WACs into the theater, Eaker insisted on requesting a separate WAC battalion to work with the Eighth Air Force. The commanding officer gave in reluctantly and warned Eaker that he would hold the general responsible for all things connected to their presence and their work.

On 16 July 1943, the first separate WAC battalion arrived in England. An advance contingent of WAACs had laid the groundwork for the arrival of the 555 enlisted women and the 19 officers. They arrived in England on 20 July 1943 to take up duties with the Eighth Air Force. Their quarters and other necessities were waiting, as were their predetermined work assignments. Even the *Stars and Stripes* welcomed the WACs on their front page. Sara W. Meenson, a U.S. Army nurse who had been in the ETO for months, remembered that headline many years later. "I recall the headlines of *Stars and Stripes* that read, 'GI Jane Has Arrived in the ETO,' " Meenson said. "They were referring to the WACs. We all laughed because we had been in the ETO over six months and there were other nurses and units there ahead of us."[7]

One of the WACs who served in England for a while before being transferred to Chartres, France, and then to Rheims for six months before being transferred to Namur, Belgium, was Anna Mazak Palmares. In each of these locations, Palmares worked as an instructor in Morse code. Like the overwhelming majority of women who volunteered to serve in the military, Palmares enlisted out of a sense of patriotism. There were no enlistment bonuses being offered, and the great majority of the American people believed that *every* American citizen owed a debt to his or her country. The greatest majority of the men in Congress had served in the military, and most of the women in Congress were fighting for the right of American women to serve in the military, with the same benefits accorded to male soldiers. Palmares summed it up very well when she stated her reasons for joining the WAAC/WAC. "I had brothers serving and I wanted to do what I could to help. Guess I was patriotic. I love my country very, very much." When asked if she had ever served in or near a combat zone, Palmares responded, "In England, Marks Hall was located between London and Germany. We were awakened nightly by the buzz bombs." She continued, "On one night a buzz bomb dropped so close it shook the bunks."[8]

When asked what her strongest memory of World War II was, Palmares answered, "The thing that stands out in my mind is the night missions." She continued, "When the bombers rose to the sky, it looked like a million stars suddenly appeared and moved on in unison. I can still feel the thrill it gave me and hear the prayer that came to my lips, asking God to bring them back safely." Perhaps it is an answer to a silent prayer that in a world and a city replete with bombed-out buildings and ugly fires set by rockets and bombs, Palmares's strongest memory was of beauty and a prayer to protect the American pilots and crews who flew the missions, night after night.[9]

It might be said that some people seem to have the military in their genes. Rita Geibel of Chicora, Pennsylvania, would gladly have taken the pro side of that argument. When Rita was six years old, she announced to her mother, "When I am big, I am going to be a soldier in the army." Her mother never forgot those words but counted them as a child's daydream. Aspiring to be a soldier, instead of a cowgirl or nurse, may have been an unusual choice, but at the time the only women in the army were nurses.[10]

More than a decade later, when World War II was the main topic in most of the world, Geibel announced that she was going to join the WAAC. Despite her mother's protest and even a few tears, Rita signed up and was off to basic training. On a battery of tests given by the army, she scored very high on mechanical aptitude and soon found herself in an army school where she would be trained as a photographer and photo analyst. "I found the subject fascinating," Geibel said. "The more I learned, the more I wanted to know." Geibel had no way of knowing at the time that she would be one of the WAAC/WACs developing the film and laying out the photographs that would be used by the Eighth Army Air Force in planning bombing raids on German targets throughout Europe or that her work would play a prominent part in the plans for the first Allied invasion of Europe. After completing her training, Geibel was stationed in a photo lab at Bolling Air Field, just outside Washington, D.C. When she and many of her workmates received orders for overseas assignments, she could not have been happier.[11]

On the voyage to her new assignment, Geibel got her first real taste of war. "One of the freighters in our convoy got hit by a one-man German submarine. The torpedo damaged the freighter slightly, and the other ships in the convoy went into action to find and sink the German sub." When one of the depth charges hit the submerged sub, there was debris in a large section of the ocean. Geibel continued, "I was belowdecks and got pretty seasick from our ship's zigzagging. The doctor told me to look out the porthole, and that's when I saw the debris from the German sub." All onboard the ship were extremely grateful when they finally reached their destination in England, and WAACs/WACs and other troops headed for their new homes and duty assignments.[12]

"We operated one of the largest photo labs in existence at the time," Geibel said, a definite tone of pride in her voice. "Our CO was Kitty Huling. We worked on multi-prints and we had to be trained to do our jobs because none of us had worked on multiprints before. When we got the hang of it, we could and did put out 128,000 prints in twenty-four hours." The tone of pride was even clearer in her voice. "Over two million prints a month. It took four of us to operate the multiprint machine, and we became so proficient as a team that we were like a group of synchronized dancers. Even back then, in the forties, we worked a lot of three-dimensional photography and had to wear special dark glasses to be able to see what we were developing. It was my job to print the priority photographs and get them out as fast as possible." Geibel went on to explain that the photos were spread out on the floor, as if they were pieces of a puzzle, and, indeed, they were exactly that. Some of the puzzles formed the next targets for the next day's bomber missions. Others snapped into place

WAC Rita Strobel, Eighth Army Air Force Photography Technician stationed at High Wycombe, England, 1944–1945.

showing how successful the previous bombing runs had been and which targets would need to be hit again the next morning. "We worked long hours, sometimes seventeen hours a day, and seven days a week. If you have ever seen the movie *Twelve O'Clock High,* where Gregory Peck is in charge of selecting the target the Eighth Air Force would hit on its next day, daylight mission, you have an idea of just how important our work was to winning the war."[13]

In addition to the stress of work that had to be done quickly and had to be done right, the Germans added regular bombing raids and showers of V-1 and V-2 rockets. When a raid was in progress at High Wycombe, which was forty miles northwest of London, the thirteen people who worked in the lab had to leave an unheated building for a colder, and often rain-soaked, dirt trench outside. "We knew that one hit from a bomb or rocket on our lab would put us out of business for days or even a week. We also knew that a lull in bombing accuracy and most likely an increase in lost planes and pilot and crew deaths would be a gift to the German military," said Geibel. It is a safe bet that none of the military personnel working in the photo lab or elsewhere at High Wycombe Airfield wanted to give even a token gift to Hitler or the German military. Every American took the war personally, and no American more so than the GIs who were being shot at, strafed, or bombed on a regular basis. "Another thing," Geibel said, "we—the WACs—knew that we were kind of an experiment to see if women could hold up under the stresses in a combat zone. We could even go shoot on the rifle range. We had carbines, and I enjoyed shooting. I had to quit after a while because I developed a terrible ringing in my ears from the noise."[14]

Katherine "Kitty" Young-Huling was commanding officer of the WAAC/WACs at High Wycombe. When Young-Huling (Young married in England in 1944 and became Young-Huling) was asked what her strongest memories of World War II were, she answered, "The buzz bombs and the people of London who would head for the subways every night for enhanced security during the nightly air raids. It was amazing to see hundreds of Londoners, men, women and children, walking calmly toward underground entrances and descending the steps to line up and sleep on the platforms and even along the tracks, while bombs fell on their city." Young-Huling went on, "I also have vivid memories of meeting Lady Astor, of working with Gen. Jimmy Doolittle at the Eighth Air Force, and of having the king and queen of England review my company of

WACs."[15] This was the same Jimmy Doolittle who had led the bombing raid on Tokyo on 18 April 1942.

On D-Day, 6 June 1944, the WACs assigned to the Eighth Army Air Force were thrilled to see hundreds of planes heading over England and toward France. "It was wonderful to see all those planes and know that WACS at High Wycombe had actually played an important part in launching the Allied invasion of France," Rita Geibel remembered.[16]

It would not be long before WACs were leaving their current duty stations and taking up their new assignments on the continent of Europe.

While the war on the front lines was demanding more and more personnel to maintain its forward momentum, a new battlefield was forming inside the United States. If the battles on the new field of combat were lost, the result might spread to all women's corps and put an end to the service of women in the U.S. Armed Forces.

The first shot of the new battle arrived at the Office of the Judge Advocate General (JAG) of the army in Washington, D.C., on 12 May 1944, and was postmarked Westby, Wisconsin. In all the letters that had landed on the judge advocate general's commanding officer's desk, this one stood alone in the seriousness of the threat it communicated. The letter was written by the mother of a twenty-year-old WAC who was stationed at Fort Oglethorpe, Georgia. The letter read in part: "I am writing to you to inform you of some of the things at Fort Oglethorpe that are a disgrace to the U.S. Army. It is no wonder women are afraid to enlist. It is full of homosexuals and sex maniacs. Unless this vice is cleaned out, I am going to reveal that scandal to the world."[17]

The letter went on to say that the writer understood that the lieutenant and the sergeant were the ringleaders. She also said that she knew that her "little girl was clean of heart and mind" when she joined the WAC and was sent to Fort Oglethorpe during the previous winter. The young WAC's mother went on to say that she was shocked at some of the letters her daughter received from a thirty-year-old woman, while she was home on furlough. The mother wrote that this thirty-year-old woman was a sergeant, and "she has ruined other girls and will continue to use her spell over other innocent girls who join up with the WAC because of their patriotic spirit." The woman supplied the sergeant's name and her company and regiment. She also said that she had all of the sergeant's letters and could turn them over if he needed them. "Now you have clubs enough to break up some of those rings." She closed her letter with "yours very truly," and signed her name.[18]

The JAG wasted no time in investigating the charges in the letter and, on 14 May 1944, the sergeant was taken into custody and confined to a private room on the psychiatric floor of Fort Oglethorpe Hospital. An opaque curtain of secrecy was drawn over and around the letter and the investigation it triggered. Every effort was made to keep the letter and the investigation out of the media and to restrict information to as few people as possible. On 8 June 1944, a request was made for a physical exam of the thirty-year-old sergeant. The requested examination was conducted on the same date, and in her report the examining physician reported that she found no physical abnormalities in the thirty-year-old mother of two. A psychiatric examination was also requested on the same date.[19]

The psychiatric evaluation request would never have been made during World War I since, at that time, sodomists—as homosexuals were referred to then—were more likely to end up in jail or prison than in a psychiatrist's office or on a psychiatric ward. Medical professionals and the military considered homosexuals criminals and dealt with them in legal terms. The label "sodomist" itself is a legal term, and the remedy was to put the sodomist in jail or prison before giving him a dishonorable discharge. At one point, 40 percent of the prisoners in Portsmouth Naval Prison in Virginia were there for breaking sodomy laws. The behavior, the laws, and the punishments were seen, judged, and prescribed by the law and the courts.

When the attack on Pearl Harbor propelled America into World War II, the military was forced to address the nation's need for a large army and reconcile that need with the sodomy laws and procedures the army used in dealing with, and ridding the army of, "sodomists." A reform movement was under way to refer to those caught in the practice of sodomy with the medical term, "homosexual," rather than the legal term, "sodomist." Reformers, psychiatrists, psychologists, and other medical professionals hoped that the new language would be followed by a change in perception and procedure that would bring about a change in attitude and in the military's dealings with homosexual soldiers. Secretary Stimson and many flag rank officers thought that a sodomist by any other name was still a sodomist and a criminal and that the law and courts-martial were still the best ways to rid the military of "perverts." New regulations were called for to direct commanding officers not to issue administrative discharges to sodomists/homosexuals but to try to convict them as the criminals the law said they were.

There was a rush in 1941–42 to build and organize an army capable of beating Germany and the Axis powers. Faced with this formidable objective, commanding generals did not want to lose time trying individual sodomists and opted for the more efficient way of removing them from the service through administrative discharges. The debate continued concerning which type of administrative discharges homosexuals should receive: "convenience of the military" under honorable conditions or "bad conduct" under "dishonorable" conditions. There was also a special category for offenders who did not use violence or physical threats to force someone to engage in homosexual acts.

Another special category was the "confirmed pervert" who engaged in sodomy and had no intention to change. For the "confirmed pervert," there was first a hearing by a board of officers, who were to determine if the individual was to be discharged under the provisions of Section 8, for a mental illness. Another category allowed the individual who engaged in sodomy but was not a "confirmed pervert" and was salvageable through a military reclamation process to be assigned to duty with the army following treatment. The officer in charge of the court-martial was to consider the advice of a psychiatrist/psychologist in determining whether or not the individual was a "confirmed pervert" and, if not, whether he could have value for the military if reclaimed through a program of military treatment and discipline.

But what if a soldier admitted homosexual tendencies but had never acted on them? If the individual would not accept a "blue discharge," one of the nicknames soldiers had given to undesirable military discharges, then the military would threaten that person with a trial in order to force the soldier into acceptance and discharge from the military. To say that the situation of defining, categorizing, charging, reclaiming, and treating homosexuals was very confusing to most commanding officers is to put it mildly. Just when it seemed that it could not get any more complicated, a new definition, category, and procedure were added.

The number of women in the military had grown considerably, and recruiters were doing all they could to persuade more women to join the women's branches of the U.S. Armed Forces. Policy makers decided that they should make provisions to include military women in the laws and regulations that covered male GIs in regard to sodomy. Since sodomy was defined as anal sex and a penis was involved, the policy makers decided to add oral sex to the definition of sodomy and thereby cover women as well as men under sodomy regulations.

The new regulations concerning sodomy went into effect in early 1944. Again, the center of power as to disposition of cases reverted to the boards and away from the company commanders. For the first time, the U.S. military considered "female homosexuals" to be a problem they would deal with if and when it made an appearance. The WAC's mother's letter to the judge advocate general, dated 12 May 1944, was the first appearance of the issue of homosexuality as a problem among military women. The judge advocate general and the Inspector General's Division were already hard at work at containing information that could prove seriously damaging, even fatal, to the women's branches.

It should be noted that the level of scientific understanding of what causes homosexuality was in its infancy prior to, during, and for decades following World War II. This is not at all surprising when one considers that when the war began, medicine itself was in its infancy compared to where it is in the first decade of the twenty-first century. In the early 1940s, there was no such thing as penicillin and no transfusions of whole blood in the various theaters of war. The Red Cross collected and shipped plasma to military hospitals overseas, but the seriousness of combat wounds was far beyond the trauma resulting from accidents in the United States. Plasma could replace the volume of blood lost but did not have the red cells necessary to carry oxygen to all of the body's cells. Physicians of the day did not understand the need for whole blood to replace blood lost in massive and multiple combat wounds. Even when Col. Edward D. Churchill, MD, a former medical school faculty member at Harvard University and surgical consultant to the Mediterranean Theater of Operations, realized the importance of whole blood to the recovery of wounded GIs, he had a steep uphill fight to get his peers and the American National Red Cross to agree with him.

A key piece of the puzzle of why it was so difficult to convince other physicians in the United States, the army surgeon general, and the Red Cross of the truth of the necessity to have a dependable supply of whole blood was the fact that the civilian medical establishment had accepted the efficacy of plasma as equal to the efficacy of whole blood with trauma victims. The American National Red Cross did not even have the equipment necessary to collect and store whole blood and had even less belief in the necessity to provide whole blood for combat wounded throughout the world. Finally, when there seemed no other way to get the army surgeon general and the Red Cross to accept the importance of whole blood to

America's combat wounded, Colonel Churchill took his argument to the *New York Times.*[20]

With that move and the help of the *New York Times,* people finally began to listen to the reasons whole blood was needed in combat zones and began to understand that the facts as they had known them were not the entire story. Medicine began to accept that it did not have all the facts regarding the efficacy of whole blood versus plasma for patients of severe or massive trauma. That new fact, that new willingness to listen, and to explore beyond what they regarded as absolute truth and to take the new facts and apply them to how wounded soldiers would be treated in order to give them their best chance to survive their combat injuries brought dramatic changes that were destined to save millions of lives in years to come.

The authors find an analogous situation concerning the accepted view of homosexuality during the first eighty years of the twentieth century. Religions, the military, even medicine and science, thought they had all the facts concerning homosexuality and its causes. It was—most religions and militaries of the world believed—a choice one made consciously to embrace a homosexual lifestyle, a lifestyle most religions taught was sinful and against nature. Could it be that looking beyond what "we believe to be the truth" in order to find objective truth might actually lead to a new realization as startling and society-changing as the fact that whole blood can save lives where plasma cannot?

Unfortunately, in 1944 when the judge advocate general and the Inspector General's Division were investigating the accusations in the letter, no one was having much success in getting people to look beyond what they "knew" and many people found even the suggestion that they should look beyond the opinions of the day seriously offensive. The current view prevailed, and the women accused in the investigation were punished accordingly. The investigations and courts-martial reached the following conclusions, recommendations, and subsequent actions:

1. "Three enlisted women have been discharged under the provisions of Section VIII, AR 615-360, at Fort Oglethorpe upon proof of covert homosexual acts."
2. That Lieutenant [report sanitized] be permitted to resign for "the good of the service."
3. That other women involved in the investigation be given an opportunity for reclamation within WAC.
4. Numerous persons named by a witness in the investigations are presumed

to be "oral addicts" and are no longer at Fort Oglethorpe, but stationed throughout the United States.

5. Under testimony by Captain Rost [a psychiatrist], some of these people mentioned are "oral perverts" who are definitely abnormal.

6. "It is believed that the interests of the Services would best be served by a discreet and careful inquiry by the respective commanding officers of the facilities at which these women are now stationed, and by the psychiatric teams at those stations, conducting psychiatric exams and recommending individual treatments or dispositions."

7. Formal testimony during investigation conducted by the Inspector General's Division ran "the attendant danger that such investigations," which would have to be carried out on a nationwide basis, would draw publicity and adversely affect the morale of the WAC organization.

8. "That Fort Oglethorpe is *not* full of homosexuals and sex maniacs."

9. "A more thorough screening of WAC applicants be conducted to filter out oral perverts."

10. That information concerning homosexual activities be included in the regular training schedule of enlisted WACs.

11. That WAC officers be given training concerning homosexual tendencies and practices. That keeping silent on the subject of homosexuality may not be the most efficient or effective way of handling the topic of homosexuality. Past practices of telling WAAC/WAC officers to ignore signs of "abnormal friendships" must be replaced by a knowledge base that includes admonitions against homosexual practices.

12. That WAC officers be given instruction as to the inappropriateness of fraternization with enlisted women and on awareness of the problems such fraternization can cause, along with the disastrous results.[21]

On the Ides of March 1944, the first five WACs ever to be assigned to duty in the Southwest Pacific Area (SWPA) arrived in Brisbane, Australia. They had been assigned the task of getting things prepared for the first large WAC contingent. The following month, two WAC officers arrived in Brisbane to work in the headquarters of the United States Army Forces Far East (USAFFE).

Eight days later, two WAC officers visited Port Moresby, New Guinea, to determine if it would be a good location to establish a WAC base. The first WAC contingent arrived by ship at Sydney, Australia, and boarded a train for the ride to Brisbane.

One might well ask why it took so long for women in the military, other than nurses, to be assigned to SWPA. The reasons can be found in the fact that when the WAAC was being formed and there was inquiry about how many WAACs particular theaters would need, the U.S. Army Headquarters in Brisbane rejected the offer of WAACs for two main reasons. First, General MacArthur wanted to raise his personnel and equipment levels for combat to the maximum allowed, and, to do this, the SWPA would need all the shipping space it could requisition to achieve that objective. Second, there were plenty of civilian Australian women readily available to work for the U.S. Armed Forces, which already had twenty thousand of them on their payrolls.

Also, the U.S. Armed Forces were planning to take these civilian employees with them when they moved from Australia to various islands on their march to Japan and final victory. Unfortunately, they had no firm commitment from the Australian government that it would cooperate with the plans of the U.S. military.

When the Australian government informed the U.S. headquarters that it would not permit Australian women to accompany American forces in their island hopping to Japan, SWPA Headquarters asked that they be sent general-duty soldiers to take the places of the civilian women. The War Department countered by telling the SWPA that they should cull their own forces on hand in order to find men with the skills needed to replace the Australian civilian women presently working for them. The SWPA Headquarters soon learned that there were only 800 enlisted WAAC/WACs and 200 WAAC/WAC officers who had not yet been allotted to any theater.

The commanding general of the Fifth Army Air Force requested 10,000 WACs and, even when the War Department offered to raise his allotment by 1,000 WACs, was not one bit satisfied. Lt. Gen. George C. Kenney, a member of MacArthur's staff, informed Washington that a representative was on his way to Washington with his request and plans. He made it abundantly clear that 1,000 WACs would not put a dent in his requirements.

When Colonel Hobby returned from her European tour of WAAC/WAC facilities, she was informed of the conference and its decision to send at least 10,000 WAAC/WACs to the SWPA Theater. When Lt. Gen. Richard K. Sutherland, MacArthur's chief of staff in Australia, came to Colonel Hobby's office and told her that a minimum of 10,000 WACs would be needed immediately in the SWPA, Hobby was quick to explain that she did not feel the requisition could be filled since the WAC was now part of the U.S. Army and each WAC would count against the theater's approved level of troop strength. Hobby also pointed out that the WAC had not yet recovered from its loss of 25 percent of its WAACs who chose not to be sworn in to the WAC. In addition, the large numbers of WACs assigned in the ETO had taken a large bite out of their numbers available for other assignments.

When Hobby learned that the first three WAC officers in the SWPA were already working on the station and that the women were Australian and British citizens who had been given direct commissions, she did all she could to talk the powers that be into revoking their decisions. The brass in the SWPA refused to budge, so Hobby submitted her written arguments as to why the three women should be decommissioned and returned to civilian status. Among her reasons, she listed the fact that the Congress had limited *enlistment* in the WAC to American citizens and had said nothing about WAC *officers* needing to be American citizens in order to be commissioned. Her argument was that the fact that the three civilian women had been commissioned as two first lieutenants and one captain was an insult to every WAC officer who had started her services as a second lieutenant.

Again her arguments fell on deaf ears, until they reached Maj. Gen. Miller G. White of G-1 Army Personnel Division. When the general could not talk the top brass out of it, he marched to his CO's office and asked him to revoke the commissions. At that point, Lt. Gen. Joseph T. McNarney, White's CO, informed General White that the commissions had been made at the personal request of General MacArthur and could not be overridden. Hobby registered her request, despite being told her request for revocation of the three commissions would not be granted. The ruling came down that the commissions would stand.

Hobby was learning she had less authority as a colonel in the U.S. Army than she had as a lieutenant colonel and director of the Women's Army Auxiliary Corps. Now, as a member of the army, she was a consultant to the army concerning the WAAC/WAC and had to give her opinions to her superiors and abide by their decisions. Hobby's next request was that the army surgeon general reinstate the full physical exam given to WAACs going overseas. The exam for WACs going overseas was now the same cursory exam given to male soldiers who had orders to deploy to a combat zone. Hobby was met with arguments that the WACs were needed "yesterday" and a full exam would take too much time. The women would receive the same physical examination for duty overseas that male soldiers received—no more, no less. Unfortunately, the "no more" meant no gynecological exam and no exam for pregnancy.

The authors believe they are safe in saying that it is most likely Colonel Hobby had a few sleepless nights wondering what new problems would surface in the SWPA in the coming months.

The U.S. transport ship *West Point* docked at Sydney, Australia, on 12 May 1944. It delivered 640 WACs to the theater, and a crowd of GIs had gathered at the dock to welcome them. The women marched off the *West Point* like soldiers who had marched together for at least a decade. Their winter uniforms were pressed, and the WACs had mastered marching so well that they would have made any drill sergeant proud. They climbed into waiting trucks and were soon on their way to Brisbane. This first contingent of female soldiers would leave for New Guinea after a two-week stopover in Brisbane.

It was not long before those in authority in the SWPA realized that cutting corners and standards to get what they wanted did not always work out well. The greatest need the SWPA had was for WACs with clerical and typing skills; what they received was a shipment of 526 women and 114 WAC officers who were trained in job categories that required little or none of the clerical skills the theater needed most. The best clerically and administratively skilled WACs were currently working in the ETO.

There were exceptions, of course, and one of the outstanding exceptions arrived in Sydney by ship and took the train to Brisbane with the more than six hundred other WACs who were her traveling companions. Elizabeth F. Petrarca was twenty-four years old when she left her job as a secretary to the safety director of an aircraft company located within commuting distance of her home in Akron, Ohio, and enlisted in the WAAC. Her reasons for enlisting sounded like those shared by the majority of the tens of thousands who had already raised their right hands and taken the oath to defend the United States against all enemies.

After basic training at Fort Oglethorpe, Georgia, Petrarca was assigned to Fort Campbell, Kentucky, where she was secretary to the Chief of the Military Personnel Branch. The next transfer she received was for Fort Oglethorpe, where she and her unit would receive orientation for overseas duty. This training was followed by advanced training in California. "We had to climb great big things," Petrarca said. "We climbed up and down ropes on the side of a ship. We also walked miles in our combat boots, with full packs on our backs."[22]

When Petrarca and her sister WACs arrived in Brisbane, Queensland, Australia, she was assigned to the Signal Intelligence Office as a secretary. Petrarca was also told that the army had a special job for her and that the job required a top secret clearance. "When I was selected for that job, they [the FBI] wanted to know if my parents had been born in the United States," Petrarca said. "Were my grandparents born in the United States? They came to my home and interviewed my parents, and they also interviewed our neighbors about me."[23]

Several weeks after the WACs arrived in Brisbane, Petrarca's top secret clearance came through, and she was officially attached to the Office of Scientific Research and Development, officially located in Washington, D.C. Petrarca would work as a secretary to this group of civilian men as they traveled and did research in connection with the Manhattan Project (research and development of the atomic bomb) and a physician who was in the Southwest Pacific Area doing research on malaria, dengue fever, and jungle rot. The scientists were Carl Richards, Ph.D., of the California Institute of Technology; Dr. Carl Compkin, Ph.D., of the Massachusetts Institute of Technology; and H. Conet Stevenson, Ph.D. of Argonne Laboratory in Chicago. All three men would later be counted among the "fathers of the atomic bomb."

The rest of the unit was comprised of Elizabeth Petrarca and two other WACs, Sgt. Minni M. Doan and Margaret Glascock Kalweit; one enlisted man; and one male lieutenant. The group traveled in a small plane that would land and take off from any field that would afford it enough space and a relatively flat landscape. The group's first stop was in New Guinea, and the living conditions were far from luxurious. More often than not, they were living in tents. Little did they realize that the living quarters and living conditions would be the nicest they would see in a very long time.

All army personnel in this special unit carried weapons. The WACs, including Petrarca, carried a Colt .45 in a holster at their sides. This was in spite of the fact that the majority of the American public had read, and believed, that military women did not carry sidearms. The media had pointed out on many occasions that WAAC/WACs were issued pistol belts but were not issued sidearms. The majority of American people were also told, and believed, that U.S. military nurses were not issued sidearms

*Elizabeth F. Petrarca, WAC, with her .45 on duty in
the Southwest Pacific, 1944.*

and served only in safe areas behind the lines. The facts do not bear that out. WAAC/WACs assigned to intelligence operations, for example, the Office of Scientific and Research Development, Cryptography, Code Breaking, and Top Secret Projects, were not only issued sidearms but, in many cases, were ordered to wear them at their sides while carrying out their assignments. An interesting fact that was published in the *New York Times* on 4 September 1944 reported that four U.S. Marines—two of them women—finished at the top in a tournament sponsored by the National Rifle Association.[24]

In an interview with Kathryn Pribram, a navy flight nurse who flew into Iwo Jima to pick up wounded marines, revealed that it was not until almost two years later that she learned that the male corpsman aboard her air evacuation plane had flown with a Colt .45 strapped to his leg, under his greens, and with orders that "if the crew was ever captured, shoot the nurse."[25]

On 20 October 1944, American troops under General MacArthur's command landed on Leyte, in the Philippines. Thirty-six days later, on 26 November 1944, WACs arrived on Leyte and set up to live and work in

Tacloban City. Pfc. Elizabeth Petrarca, her unit, and the four scientists in the unit were assigned to duty also and settled in on the island. Petrarca and her unit were quartered in a school, but worked elsewhere. Petrarca worked on a deserted section of beach, using an old typewriter balanced on a small folding table standing in the sand. "The Japanese bombed our quarters all the time," Petrarca said. "When the sirens blew, we went outside and got into a foxhole. The bombing went on for a long time, and we had to just sit there." She continued, "When it rained, water would pool on the bottom of the foxhole and we would have to stand in the water for hours." But the water in the foxholes and the daily bombings were only part of the trying conditions in Tacloban.[26]

There were supply issues that multiplied the effects of all their problems by a force of at least ten. "Food and water were brought in twice a day. If the supplies didn't land, we went hungry, and when the water was not delivered, we were thirsty and dirty. They brought the water in tanker trucks. The water around us was polluted so if the tanker trucks didn't make it, we had no water." Petrarca continued, "The heat was terrible and, even when they delivered our water, we were rationed to two canteensful a day. That was for drinking and washing. Whatever we used for washing ourselves was then reused for washing our clothes. I can remember that on days when deliveries of food and water didn't make it to us, we went to bed hungry and thirsty. I cried myself to sleep on more than a few nights. It was the camaraderie and knowing that we were doing an important job that kept us going."[27]

Julia Harris-Isaac, who also served as a WAC in Tacloban, spent many hours in a foxhole during bombing raids. "It was frightening the first few times," Harris-Isaac said. "After a while, many of us just stopped going to foxholes during the bombing raids. We had become fatalists. If I die, I die." Harris-Isaac also remembered living on the ship *Mactan* for more than a week while waiting for their quarters. "We got to eat in the ship's mess and that was a lot better than the food troops not quartered on the *Mactan* were getting."[28]

It appears fitting to the authors that the *Mactan,* which was used to evacuate wounded POWs from Bataan and Corregidor in the early days of America's entrance into the war, should return to Manila and help in taking the city back from the Japanese, who had treated Manila's people with contempt and cruelty since their invasion in 1941.

On 7 March 1944, a contingent of WACs, including Elizabeth

Petrarca, arrived in Manila. "Dead bodies of Japanese soldiers were still lying in the streets," Petrarca said. "There were also dead Japanese soldiers inside the old walled city." Petrarca did not get to see much of Manila during her first days there. "I was pretty sick with dengue fever and ended up as a patient in the Santo Tomas Hospital for more than a week," Petrarca recalled. "The army wanted to send me home, but I did not want to go. After my many weeks in the South Pacific, I wanted to stay and see the war through to its end."[29]

In the opinion of the authors, service in the SWPA brought with it tensions and challenges not found in the other theaters of operation. At the heart of those adversities was the fact that neither the commanding officers nor the enlisted men were glad to have the WACs in their area. That fact was brought home with a vengeance for WACs assigned to censorship of the GIs' outgoing mail. The sentiments of the majority of male soldiers were as bad as, or worse than, the comments investigated by the army and the FBI during the heyday of the slander campaign in the United States. The army reached the conclusion that WACs assigned to read enlisted men's letters home suffered from poor morale, depression, and anger. It seemed a rare letter written by an enlisted man that did not contain obscene and/or disparaging comments in regard to the WACs. For women who had volunteered in order to shorten the war, and thereby save lives, the words fell like hammer blows. It was obvious to the women who had withstood the adversities of the SWPA in order to bring American men home sooner that the majority of American enlisted men had little or no respect for the military service of women, including the women who would read their vicious comments day in and day out.[30]

Added to these insults was the fact that the U.S. Army in the SWPA was attempting to downgrade the contributions of WACs to winning the war by saying that the monetary costs of having WACs serving in the SWPA far outweighed their usefulness. In fact, the report argued that it took more man-hours to guard and protect the WACs than the total hours the WACs provided in services in any and all areas within the theater of operations.[31]

WACs who served in the SWPA would bear the wounds and scars of ingratitude, jealousy, and outright vicious lies for decades to come.

9

⭐

Everything seemed so temporary, uncertain, yet I felt pride that I had given up a good job in order to serve my country. Friends I made are the best friends I ever had. We shared so much together.

—Mary B. Tate, WAC

The day the free world had hoped for, dreamed of, and prayed for since the war began was less than one week away from becoming a reality. There were only a handful of people who knew the day and the hour the Allied invasion of France would be launched, but if one lived in England, it was just about impossible not to know that the tens of thousands of Allied soldiers who had been pouring into England were there for something big.

If there was one WAC in the European Theater of Operations who knew what that "something big" was, it was twenty-seven-year-old WAC captain Dorothy L. Starbuck. Captain Starbuck was assigned to General Eisenhower's London Headquarters. "I had a top secret clearance, and controlled every document, from every military service that came in to ETUSA [European Theater of Operations, US Army] that included every detail of Operation Overlord," Dorothy Starbuck remembered. "I worked for Thurston Hughes, who was a classmate and good friend of Gen. George C. Patton," Starbuck continued. "Patton stayed in close contact and visited whenever he got the chance. He wanted Colonel Hughes to join his army group. The colonel told me later that he had to say, 'No Georgie, because about the third time you called me a son-of-a-bitch, I'd have to hit you and you outrank me,' " Starbuck said. General Patton was not the only American legend of World War II with whom Starbuck came into frequent contact. "Part of my job was to hand carry 'eyes only' top secret messages to Patton, Gen. Omar Bradley, and any other top commanders who had to be kept informed."[1]

Dorothy Starbuck was born on 17 October 1917, in Denver, Colorado, and was one of eleven children. She attended public schools and received a bachelor's degree in journalism from Loretto Heights College in Denver and did graduate work at the University of Denver. She taught elementary school for two years in Denver before joining the Women's Army Auxiliary Corps in 1942. She was a member of the second officers' class to graduate from Fort Des Moines. Starbuck's next duty station was Lowery Army Air Field in Colorado, where she was commanding officer of a company of photo analysts who were taking and interpreting aerial photographs and who were assigned to the WAAC Photo Detachment Group. Starbuck later went to Fort Devens for orientation and training for overseas.

Starbuck was not the only one of her parents' eleven children to sign up for service in the U.S. Armed Forces. Four siblings also answered their country's call. "Two of my brothers served in the U.S. Army—one in the ETO, and one in the Pacific Theater," Starbuck said. "A third brother served in the navy, while one of my sisters served in the marine corps," she continued. "It kept my mother busy, writing to kids all over the world. My family was lucky; we all got home in one piece."[2]

Getting home in one piece was no small achievement for anyone stationed in London or its suburbs during World War II. Then again, getting to London in one piece was no easy task either. Mary Ellen Rogers was twenty-six years old when she and the other WACs in her company were assigned to the Air Transport Command and boarded the USS *Mariposa* and sailed to England via Greenock, Scotland, the jumping-off place for the final leg of their journey to London. On 1 June 1944, WACs aboard the *Mariposa* were surprised that they were sailing for England without the protection of a convoy or umbrella of fighter planes. "The rationale for sailing without the usual protections was that the *Mariposa* could outrun any German submarine in the Atlantic waters." Mary Ellen Rogers and her sister WACs did not derive much comfort from the explanation and were soon to have reason for further doubts. "On the third day, most of us were beginning to experience seasickness for the first time on the voyage and it was far worse than any of us imagined," Rogers said. "We alternated between groaning in our bunks and dashing to the bathroom, pushing everything and everybody out of our way."[3]

In a few days, a new challenge was added to their voyage. Suddenly, and without any notice, the *Mariposa* executed a series of sharp turns that took the WACs by surprise. "Kuplunk! I landed on the deck along with all the other WACs in our cabin," Rogers remembered. "The air was filled with shoes, clothing, toilet articles, and anything else that was not tied down. The cabin was filled with comments from WACs still sprawled on the deck of the cabin: 'The captain's gone mad,' 'Who's driving this thing?' 'Can't they maneuver this tub better than this?' " All of a sudden the explanation for the sudden and continuing zigzagging dawned on Rogers. "My God! A German sub must be chasing us. So much for this tub being fast enough to outrun German submarines."[4]

Mary Ellen Rogers and 149 sister WACs of the Air Transport Command arrived in London on 12 June 1944. They settled into their quarters, two five-story English houses that were joined together with an inside passage so WACs could move back and forth without going outside. "We were so tired that our cots felt like the best eiderdown. It did not take long to fall off to sleep," Rogers said. "We were awakened by the sounds of large explosions. I wondered if the Germans had resumed their heavy bombing campaign. Then I realized that the sound was different from the bombing raids I had seen and heard back home in newsreels. Something was different about these explosions, but there was no time to mull it over." Rogers and the other WACs started down five flights of stairs to the air raid shelter in the basement. All along the way, the air raid sirens were screaming a warning into the night. The basement had a hard and damp cement floor, and the space itself was not large enough to allow 150 WACs to lie down to sleep. "We huddled together in sitting positions for warmth and comfort. . . . All I could think about was that I didn't want 12 June 1944 to be my last day on earth."[5]

The sound of antiaircraft guns punctuated the scream of the sirens, and loud explosions went off so frequently that they sounded like corn popping over an open fire. The walls of the buildings shook like a frightened dog, while bricks, shaken loose, battered the walls and windows on their way down to the ground. "In the morning, our officers told us that the very loud and frequent popping sounds we heard were Hitler's new vengeance weapon, rockets called V-1s." The WACs of the Air Transport Command would never forget their first night in London or Hitler's first V-1 attack on England. They would, however, be focused on the future as they continued their trek to Berlin and the surrender of Germany.[6]

The next stop on that journey was France. On 14 July 1944, the first WAC regular unit arrived off Normandy and waded ashore on Omaha Beach. All twenty-five WACs were dressed in full battle dress, minus an

M-1 rifle or sidearm. The pistol belts worn by the WACs held a canteen, a flashlight, a first-aid kit, and a small hatchet. Several of the women had been issued short-handled shovels for digging foxholes. "We looked like walking hardware stores, sounded a little like one too," Frances Lillo remembered. "We were also carrying a gas mask, a bedroll, and a back-pack. We had all kidded about going to France to dig foxholes for the army. We never expected to actually be doing that."[7]

The sun had set and the moon kept dodging in and out of a cloudy night sky. When their eyes accommodated to the darkness, the WACs were able to see a fairly large area of the beach that was a resting place for damaged jeeps, burned-out trucks, and several tanks that never made it off Omaha Beach. The beach was also littered with iron stakes that had barbed wire wrapped around them. "Our gaiety was gone. Here on this foreign beach our brothers and classmates had stormed ashore, poured out their youth and blood to destroy forever the myth of a master race, led by a madman. . . . We walked on holy ground. Heads bowed, we crawled quietly into the truck which made its way down the beach and up through a break in the cliffs to the flat land beyond," Lillo wrote later.[8]

"An army truck and driver delivered us to an area that had tents and told us not to go off the cleared path since the uncleared area was heavily mined." The women remained in their tents overnight, and in the morning went looking for someone who could get them transportation to their duty stations. Instead, a young soldier driving a jeep offered to deliver their message to the company commander. Not long after that, a male officer arrived. He jumped out of his jeep and confronted Lillo and another WAC. He wanted to speak with their convoy officer and they pointed him toward the tent. In thirty minutes, he got back in his jeep, but not before telling the group of WACs that he would get their orders straightened out. That night orders arrived telling the WACs to be packed and ready to move out at 8:00 a.m. "We had been given a one-day supply of K-rations." The K-rations contained individual small cans. You would get a small can of cheese or scrambled eggs or potted meat. The package also contained hard crackers that were supposed to be loaded with vitamins, and a large piece of chocolate, hard enough to use to drive nails, and a pack of instant coffee and instant lemonade. The food would keep one alive, but, as U.S. Army nurses had learned many months before, K-rations could also give a soldier a very upset stomach and diarrhea that could continue all day or all night.[9]

Fifteen hours after the truck left Normandy with Lillo and her sister WACs, it pulled to a stop in front of the Majestic Hotel, just off the Champs-Elysées and close to the Arc de Triomphe. The Majestic Hotel had housed soldiers of the German army.

On 4 September 1944, the Twenty-ninth Traffic Regulatory Group of WACs landed on Utah Beach. After camping out in the woods for several days, they were taken to Paris. The WACs were assigned to duty stations around Paris and began their work with a spirit of adventure. Betty Magnuson was a twenty-three-year-old WAC when she was assigned to be the private secretary of Gen. Frank S. Ross, Chief of Transportation in the ETO. One of the best-known units General Ross and his staff supervised was the Red Ball Express. The unit, except for its officers, was made up entirely of black males who performed the dangerous job of delivering supplies of every kind, including fuel and ammunition, to soldiers on the front lines. The convoys were a favorite target of the German Air Force and artillery, and their cargo transformed the trucks into virtual fast-moving explosive devices. "I remember well a remark by General Ross: 'Our country owes much to those black hands on the steering wheels.' "[10]

One of Betty Magnuson's strongest memories of World War II was the German bombing attack that hit and damaged the Gare du Nord in Paris.

WACs on duty in Paris, France, in 1945. Left to right: Katherine Bell, Betty O'Donnal, Ann St. Germaine, Jennie M. Turner (Swails).

Several WACs worked at the Gare du Nord and were fortunate not to be on duty when German bombs hit the railroad station. The main building of the station had been inaugurated in 1846 and just eight years later was considered too small for the amount of traffic moving through it on an average day. After the German Luftwaffe bombed the station, the WACs assigned to work there continued their work, adapting to the new conditions and scarcely missing a beat in carrying out their assignments.

Carrying out their assignments despite any and all obstacles had become an unspoken and well-ingrained tradition for the Women's Army Corps. Capt. Dorothy L. Starbuck, who had worked in top secret operations in London, was now stationed in Paris and involved in top secret plans to get the Allied troops to Berlin as quickly as possible. "We were all praying for the day when Germany would surrender and the war in Europe would be over," Dorothy Starbuck remembered. "We were all anxious to get to Berlin and finally back home to the United States."[11]

Back in the United States, the WAVES were just as anxious to see the end of the war in Europe and the full force of the Allies unleashed in the Pacific. On 27 September 1944, Congress passed the bill authorizing limited overseas assignments for military women serving with the United States sea services. When the president signed the bill, it became Public Law 441 and limited overseas service for the WAVES, SPARS, and Women Marines to Alaska, the West Indies, Panama, and Hawaii. It was not what most women in the sea services had hoped for; however, it was a victory and advancement in the long fight to attain overseas deployment and assignments for WAVES, SPARS, and Women Marines.

In 1944, there were approximately one thousand WAVES involved in secret and top secret work in the navy. One of those women was thirty-five-year-old Mildred Glendenning of Minneapolis, Minnesota. Glendenning joined the WAVES in 1943 and was trained to plot the courses of warships and supply ships around the world. "I found my job fascinating," Glendenning said. "I was allowed to go aboard all kinds of ships, battleships, destroyers, and carriers. It was my job to plot courses for convoys and their escorts." Glendenning continued, "I worked night and day and my work ran from secret to top secret. I always felt that I would like the navy but never realized that I would like it as much as I did."[12]

The U.S. Navy had discovered that women who joined the WAVES could fill many jobs in addition to clerical assignments. Among those "other" jobs was intelligence work in code/cipher, photo analysis, plotting courses for ships and airplanes, and selecting targets for offshore bombardment by naval ships and for navy aircraft flying missions off carriers and from ground-based naval aircraft. "Very few people realize that WAVES stationed in Washington, D.C., and Virginia were actually selecting the targets for the men in the planes and aboard ship," Capt. Anne Grey said. "We, I and my sister WAVES assigned to Intelligence, loaded and pointed the guns; loaded the bombs and decided where they would fall. Navy enlisted men and naval officers just pulled triggers or pushed the buttons to release the bombs."[13]

Anne Grey was the oldest of four children. Her three brothers followed her into the military. Despite the fact that there were no military men in her family prior to World War II, Anne was fascinated with the military and in high school had a collection of miniature soldiers, and, in her younger brothers' sandbox, she enacted various battle strategies and enjoyed the pastime tremendously. "I wasn't old enough to join the WAAC/WAC. I was delighted when the WAVES were organized and had a lower age requirement. I joined right away and loved every minute of my military service."[14]

Even fewer people would have guessed that hundreds of WAVES were engaged in a top secret program that would eventually save hundreds of thousands of American and Allied lives. That program was born from the determination of the navy to find a way to stop the carnage German U-boats were inflicting on merchant shipping within the territorial waters of the United States. In the first three months of 1942, 216 merchant ships had been sent to the bottom of the sea by U-boats operating within sight of America's eastern seaboard. Even before America entered World War II, U.S. military officers visited Bletchley Park to learn how Great Britain was decoding German naval messages. Bletchley Park was the headquarters for Britain's work on decoding Enigma, the German code, and recoding all messages sent or received by the German navy. Bletchley Park and the British government said they would share their knowledge with the United States and encouraged the U.S. military to establish its own version of Bletchley Park within U.S. borders. The offer and encouragement, however, were dampened by the fact that Britain was not eager to share

Enigma information with anyone the British did not consider to be 100 percent committed to keeping the information top secret. The United States continued to press Bletchley Park for more information, and Bletchley Park continued to drag its heels. Finally, the U.S. Navy decided to act on its own and create its own program to break Enigma and use the information gained to pinpoint and sink German U-boats.[15]

In March 1942, the U.S. Navy signed a contract with the National Cash Register Company in Dayton, Ohio, to work together on a machine called the Bombe (named after a French dessert), which would decode the German Enigma machine quickly and provide up-to-date information that would allow the navy to act as soon as possible against German U-boats in America's waters or anywhere else. That contract established the Navy Computing Machine Laboratory (NCML). In April 1943, navy and marine corps personnel began arriving at the National Cash Register Company in Dayton. Building 26 had been set aside to house the research and the Bombes themselves. In time, 200 sailors and 600 WAVES would work in Building 26. None of the naval personnel nor the marine corps had any idea of what the project was or what effect it would have in giving America and her allies a definite advantage in the crucial battle for domination of the Atlantic Ocean. The WAVES were told that if anyone asked what they were doing at the National Cash Register Company in Dayton, Ohio, they were to say that they were there to learn to operate a variety of business machines that would be used by the navy in its fight for victory in World War II.

None of the sailors, WAVES, or marines working in Building 26 was told the purpose of the research or their work. Security was so tight that everyone assigned to work in Building 26 had to wear an ID card while on the job and while on the campus, in addition to reporting to and departing from the job. An extra measure to ensure the top secret security of Building 26 was the posting of a marine guard at every door inside the building as well as outside. In addition, each door had the names of every individual who was permitted to enter that particular room posted clearly. If a person's name was not posted on a particular door, that person would not be permitted to enter that room.

At any one time, up to three hundred WAVES were assigned to the program in Building 26. The WAVES' assignments varied, and shifts worked around the clock. WAVES worked at setting the Bombe's rotors to predetermined positions; others worked soldering twenty-six wires to particular places on individual rotors, one rotor at a time. Even the colors of the wires were changed to make it less likely that anyone could recall the wiring pattern of the rotors. For an added measure, the colors for the wires were chosen from a pool of twenty-eight colors rather than from a pool of twenty-six. The work could be quite monotonous, and more than one WAVE mistakenly believed she had failed her battery of tests and had been assigned to the monotonous work of soldering wires to rotors because it was the one simple thing she could be trained to do. Other WAVES also worked on checking the results printed out by the Bombe. WAVES working inside Building 26 were not permitted to discuss their work with anyone outside their own work area, and work was not to be discussed outside of Building 26.

With the navy's commitment to build a four-rotor Bombe as quickly as possible, additional WAVES, sailors, and marines were stationed at Dayton to aid in the effort. The second floor of Building 26 became the research and work area for the new Bombe. By 1 May 1943, the first two Bombes were complete and ready for inspection by maintenance teams. The new Bombes stood seven feet high, two feet wide, and ten feet long, and weighed more than two thousand pounds each. The machines were nicknamed Adam and Eve for easy reference.[16]

By 28 May 1943, the Bombes had been given a clean bill of health and were ready for the first test run with a newly received undeciphered Enigma message. The message was fed into Adam, and twenty minutes later, the Bombe printed the deciphered results. The original message was then fed into Eve, and twenty minutes later, Eve printed the decoded results. Both decoded messages were then sent over a secure communication line to Navy Intelligence in Washington, D.C., where cryptanalysts, including WAVES, would translate the German into English and compare Adam's results with those of Eve. The report was then sent to CDR Howard T. Engstrom, Chief of the OP-20-GM, the technology section of classified naval communications. Several days passed before a response was sent from Washington to Dayton. The heart of Engstrom's response was, "That one hit paid for the entire project."[17]

Those in Dayton wasted no time in constructing more Bombes. In a matter of weeks, new Bombes lined the hallways and stairwells of Building 26. Four of the Bombes were placed in a large room, and WAVES received training on how best to operate the machines. That operation was based on setting the rotors to positions provided by the cryptanalysts in Washington, D.C.

In a matter of weeks, the remaining machines and personnel in Dayton amounted to a skeleton crew. More and more WAVES moved into their new quarters in the Navy Annex on Nebraska Avenue, and new WAVES arrived several times a week. The first stop for these women was the chapel on the grounds of the Navy Annex, where navy officers would impress upon them the secrecy and the importance of the work they would do. One remark included in the talk to each new group of WAVES was also the one caution most remembered by those in attendance. "If you ever tell what you are doing, you are committing treason. And don't think that just because you are young ladies, you will be treated any differently than the men who commit treason. If you ever tell, we will shoot you."[18]

Black women in the U.S. military during World War II were a unique group. It was not until July 1944 that a telegram arrived at Fort Huachuca, Arizona, announcing a change in the Army Nurse Corps regarding "Negro nurses." Lt. Margaret Bailey recalled that telegram and its message. "The telegram said that black nurses would be accepted in the U.S. Army Nurse Corps without any limits imposed by a quota." Bailey remembered, "The telegram also said that black nurses would be stationed in the U.S. and overseas. That was a big change and very welcomed." On Lieutenant Bailey's first day on duty at Fort Huachuca, she had an experience that has given her a good laugh since. "I was on duty by myself when the inspection team came through," Bailey recalled. "With every gig [demerit] the team announced, I pointed out that it was not my fault since I had only been at Fort Huachuca since the previous afternoon."[19]

2nd Lt. Margaret E. Bailey, 1944.

The first all-black WAC unit to be assigned overseas was the 6888th Central Postal Directory under the command of Maj. Charity Adams. The battalion of eight hundred WACs sailed for Scotland on 1 February 1945. Major Adams and her executive officer, Capt. Abbie Noel Campbell, traveled to England by plane and arrived several days before the 6888th was scheduled to arrive in Glasgow. In the interim, they inspected several duty stations and met with Gen. Benjamin O. Davis, the only black general in the U.S. Army at that time. General

Davis asked when the battalion was scheduled to arrive and said he would be in Birmingham, England, around that time and would be pleased to review the battalion. On 12 February 1945, the *Ile de France* docked in Glasgow, and Major Adams and Captain Campbell were at the dock to greet the WACs. The battalion traveled by train to Birmingham and only days later was taking over the work in the Central Postal Directory. The Postal Directory served approximately seven million military personnel in the European Theater, and over a matter of months had amassed a large backlog of "undeliverable mail." The 6888th had a daunting workload waiting for them and they earned an excellent reputation for efficiency by working through the mountains of backlogged letters and packages.[20]

It was not long before the members of the 6888th learned that prejudice and discrimination did not end on America's shore any more than it ended when the height of the slander campaign had finally passed. Gurthalee Clark was twenty-four when she enlisted in the WAC in October 1943. When asked what she remembered most about her first days and weeks in the military, Clark recalled: "I found out that the military was a segregated organization—something that hadn't crossed my mind. We were at war and that was first, or at least that was what I thought." Clark also remembered the hurtful lies and rumors that circulated during

Unit of the 6888th WAC Company, Birmingham, England, 1945.

the slander campaign. "The discrimination against military women, both black and white," Clark said, "was very damaging. When the slander campaign was investigated, civilian and military investigators discovered that our own American soldiers were to blame for the stories. They wanted women out of the military and lied to get the military to throw them out. In spite of all that, I still wanted to be part of the military, and I felt we had done our part in the war."[21]

When asked what she would like to tell the women currently serving in the military, and women who would serve in the future, Margaret F. Barbour, a member of the 6888th, replied, "Be it known that a more dedicated or disciplined group of individuals cannot be found than those women who braved the onslaught of prejudice and ridicule during World War II and still maintained their dignity."[22]

For army nurse Alice McKoy Ishmael, the prejudice and discrimination in the army were "plain and simple racism." Alice McKoy applied for active duty with the Army Nurse Corps in January 1942 and was put on a waiting list because "there was a quota on the number for Negro nurses," Alice McKoy remembered. "I was not called to active duty until December 1942." Shortly after reporting to Camp Livingston in Louisiana, McKoy was one of ten black nurses sent to Fort Hood, Texas, to help in a hospital emergency. The wards were overflowing with ill soldiers and army nurses were working ten to twelve hours a day. Lieutenant McKoy and the other nurses in her group arrived at Fort Hood at nine in the evening. "The driver of the bus looked at the group and said, 'This is a mistake.' " The next morning, the nurses reported to the hospital for duty. "The charge nurse told us that it was not the policy to let black nurses take care of white patients," McKoy Ishmael said. "We stayed at Fort Hood for ten days until orders could be cut transferring us back to Camp Livingston," McKoy Ishmael continued. "In the meantime, we did no work while the white nurses continued to work ten to twelve hours a day." Food at Fort Hood was served cafeteria style, but Lieutenant McKoy Ishmael and her group were assigned to a separate table in the corner of the mess hall. In addition, their food was served to them as they were not allowed to go through the cafeteria line.[23]

Lieutenant McKoy Ishmael and her unit were deployed to Manchester, England, prior to D-Day and worked in a hospital for German prisoners of war. Only days after D-Day, the German POWs were transferred to another hospital, and combat-wounded Americans and Allies were flown in directly from the battlefield. "For the first time," McKoy Ishmael said, "we worked on black, white, or whatever." For Lieutenant McKoy Ishmael and her unit, D-Day proved a turning point in their duties and their assignments. "We proved," she said, "that when hurt and bleeding, the color of blood is red for all."[24]

On 3 February 1945, American tanks and troops crashed through the gates of Santo Tomas Internment Camp near Manila and freed the thousands of men, women, and children who had been prisoners of the Japanese since 1942. On General MacArthur's orders, troops fought their way through to the camp without securing the areas they traveled through. In addition, and on MacArthur's orders, the troops had carried their wounded with them, and now wounded soldiers as well as wounded and ill POWs had to be cared for if they were to make it out of Santo Tomas alive. Since the soldiers had brought only one doctor and a handful of medics with them, the task of treating the wounded fell on the shoulders of the one prison doctor and the army nurses who had endured the last three years as Japanese prisoners. Weakened by starvation and illness, they pushed themselves to care for the wounded GIs who had fought so hard to free their fellow soldiers, countrymen, and Allies. Nurses and the prison doctor fainted more than once from hunger and exhaustion during the long hours of that first night and early morning, but they returned immediately to caring for their patients.

Six days later, on 9 February 1945, one hundred army nurses and forty army physicians arrived from Leyte to care for the sick and wounded. For the first time in more than three years, the U.S. Army Nurses who had cared for sick and wounded soldiers and civilians during the battles of Manila, Bataan, and Corregidor; the same frail and emaciated army nurses who had shared the hunger and horrors of Japanese imprisonment; the same military women who had never stopped doing all that could be done to care for the health of their fellow internees, could stand down from the duty that had been theirs alone for more than three horror-filled years and entrust themselves to the care of their sister army nurses who had traveled thousands of miles to help set them free and return them to health and home. Two days later, on 12 February 1945, a C-47 made its way down Dewey Boulevard in Manila, lifted into the air, pointed its nose eastward, and began the first leg of the long journey home.

On 19 February 1945, two U.S. Marine Divisions of the Fifth Amphibious Corps landed on Iwo Jima as part of Operation Detachment. The marines were supported by the aircraft of two U.S. carrier groups, two battleships, and several destroyers and cruisers. In the center of a circle formed by the combat ships, the USS *Bountiful* AH-9 stood ready to receive the wounded. Since Iwo Jima was within fighter aircraft range of Tokyo, Japanese resistance was expected to be very strong. The eight square miles of Iwo Jima were dominated by a 600-foot mountain, Mount Suribachi.

Georgia Reynolds was twenty-four years old when she joined the Navy Nurse Corps on 2 February 1942. After duty at the Portsmouth Naval Hospital and Mare Island in California on the amputee ward, Reynolds was assigned to the *Bountiful* as a nurse in the OR and on surgical wards. The *Bountiful* sailed the Pacific taking on and treating casualties from five separate invasions, including D-Day Plus 2 off Saipan, Tinian, Guam, Iwo Jima, Leyte, and Samar. During each of the five invasions in which the *Bountiful* took part, the ship traveled to within a mile offshore to take on wounded. "When we were entering the harbor off Hollandia, New Guinea, the *Bountiful* had two torpedoes fired at her," Reynolds remembered. "One of the torpedoes went fore of the ship, and the other went aft. The one that went aft ran up on the beach and exploded."[25]

When asked to describe the worst casualties she had seen during World War II, Reynolds responded: "The worst were from Iwo Jima. We had more than two hundred belly wounds." Reynolds continued, "The one that really sticks in my mind is a navy fighter pilot whose plane burned on the carrier deck. He had second- and third-degree burns over 90 percent of his body. He lived to be transferred to a navy base hospital about a week later. I have often wondered if he made it through the war and back into civilian life." Reynolds remembered sharing feelings about the casualties with two or three close female friends aboard ship. "The general feelings expressed during those talks were marked by a determination to do one's job no matter how bad the attacks or dangers became." After the war ended, Reynolds was able to discuss her wartime experiences with a close female friend and one or two other female friends. When the war ended, Reynolds left nursing. "I was frustrated by the limits placed on nurses [in civilian hospitals]. Those limits were especially glaring after all nurses were permitted and required to do during World War II. I decided to use my GI Bill to go to medical school. I graduated in 1951 and, after internship and residency, I went into private practice."[26]

On 1 April 1945, American forces began their assault on Okinawa, an island approximately 400 miles off the coast of Japan and 450 miles east of the Chinese mainland. On the day after the first waves of U.S. Marines landed, the USS *Relief* AH-1, a naval hospital ship, arrived offshore to receive the first wounded marines from one of the bloodiest battles in American military history. While the *Relief* loaded wounded onboard, navy warships downloaded supplies and the next wave of marines to be landed on the beaches of Okinawa. Over the heads of marines, landing craft, and scores of long gray warships, hundreds of large-caliber ships' guns were sending a constant rain of steel onto enemy positions dug into the rock of the volcanic island. The *Relief* continued taking on wounded marines until darkness was less than forty minutes away and then headed out to sea, where it would remain fully lighted until daylight, when it would take up an offshore position again and continue receiving battle casualties from Okinawa's bloody beaches. As dictated by The Hague Conventions, the *Relief* was painted white, had a large red cross on each side and on its smokestack, carried no weapons, and sailed fully lighted at night. Every nurse, doctor, and corpsman onboard was well aware that Japan was not signatory to the Geneva or The Hague Conventions. They also were aware that since October 1944, there had been a steady increase in kamikaze attacks on ships, an increase most expected to escalate as U.S. and Allied forces moved closer and closer to Japan's home islands.

One night spent outside the perimeters of U.S. Navy warships proved more than enough for the *Relief.* While the ship sailed fully lighted through that first night, with hundreds of wounded marines on board, Japanese planes flew overhead on their way to bomb and attack the U.S. fleet off Okinawa. LT Beatrice Rivers, a twenty-nine-year-old navy nurse assigned to the *Relief,* recalled that night: "We finally had one Jap plane which had started to make a pass at our ship and was blasted by one of our destroyer escorts that had tracked it on its radar." Rivers said, "After that, it was decided by those in command that our hospital ship would remain with the rest of the fleet at night, blacked out and in artificially created fog and smoke for added concealment." The Japanese planes and kamikaze were overhead so often that the *Relief* was put on alert status many times during the day and night. The ship's crew and medical staff were getting very little uninterrupted sleep. The air raids had gotten worse since the *Relief* first came under enemy attack in March 1945 while anchored at Ulithi Atoll in the Caroline Islands. On 11 March, the *Relief* was anchored within sight of the USS *Randolph.* "It was early evening and some of our nurses were on the *Randolph* watching a movie on their movie deck when the ship got hit in a kamikaze attack," Rivers said. "They evacuated the casualties to our ship." Just eight days later, on 19 March 1945, the USS *Franklin* was attacked by kamikaze bombers. The first missed the ship and fell into the sea. The second crashed into the *Franklin*'s flight deck, killing fifty-six and wounding sixty. The casualties were evacuated to the *Relief.* "We received some of the worst burn cases I had ever seen," Rivers said.[27]

On Saturday, 28 April 1945, at 8:56 p.m. Tokyo time, the brightly lit and clearly marked army hospital ship USS *Comfort* was attacked by a Japanese plane fifty miles south of Okinawa. The kamikaze pilot hit the ship with two bombs before he crashed his plane into the unarmed floating hospital. The attack damaged the upper wardroom and officers' quarters on the bridge deck and completely destroyed the operating room, dental and X-ray clinics, offices, wards, and hallway on the superstructure deck. On the main deck, three wards, the main diet pantry, passageways, elevator shafts, and telephone exchange were demolished. The suicide attack killed twenty-nine people and wounded thirty-three others. One person was missing. The majority of the casualties were army personnel who had been wounded on Okinawa and members of the medical staff, including six army nurses.

Lt. Ruth Lewis was one of the army nurses assigned to the *Comfort.* More than forty years later she still remembered her service on the *Comfort* as if it were yesterday. "The worst battle casualties we ever received on the *Comfort* were from the USS *Franklin* after it was hit by a kamikaze attack." Lewis recalled, "They were the worst burn cases I have ever seen. Patients with mangled or amputated limbs were the second worst. It was very hard to see these young men, for all intents and purposes, healthy and fit, brought to the point of death or facing life as double or triple amputees, day after day. It was not always easy to remain an objective health care person. At times, we were so angry with the Japanese that most of us—at those moments—would have been willing to shoot them ourselves. Fortunately, the intense anger was a fleeting thing."[28]

Not all the female health care givers remained offshore at Okinawa. For Lt. Bella Abramowitz, a physical therapist with the Seventy-sixth Field Hospital, whether to remain on ship or be transported to Okinawa was a question that would be decided by a discussion between the military officers—one the captain of the ship that had brought them to Okinawa and the other the commander of ground forces on the Island of Okinawa.

Abramowitz recalled the exchange between the two men. "The ship's captain signaled to the commander of ground forces on Okinawa, 'Get these women off the ship. It is dangerous here.' The general responded, 'Keep them on the ship. It's dangerous here.' " The ship's captain won out and the women were to be taken to shore to begin work with the field hospital. The ten-minute trip between ship and shore stretched into three hours. "Every time there was another kamikaze attack, they stopped our LCT [landing craft, tank] and surrounded us with a smoke screen to conceal us from the Japanese planes. Then, when it was all clear, we would continue toward the shore, only to be stopped again as the kamikaze attack continued." When asked how she felt and what she did while under kamikaze attack, Abramowitz responded, "I made my peace with death. I accepted that I might very well be killed, then went on with doing the job I was there to perform." She continued, "I put the needs of the wounded above my own, and injured my back in the process. But, I would do it all again if it were necessary."[29]

The American people were kept in the dark regarding kamikaze attacks in the Pacific. Before the USS *Long Island* returned the members of Air Group 4 to the United States in May 1945, pilots and crew were ordered not to mention the word "kamikaze." The United States Navy did not want the American people to know the extent of the damage being done by kamikaze pilots; nor did it want the Japanese to know how effective the attacks were against American ships and troops. The effects of keeping this information from the American people, combined with the effectiveness of these attacks, doubtless played a part in the opinions of future generations who criticized the U.S. government and military for dropping atom bombs on Hiroshima and Nagasaki in August 1945.[30]

When defeat after defeat in Europe had convinced the German High Command that surrender or the total devastation of Germany was inevitable, they sought to arrange surrender with the best possible conditions for Germany and her people. In the hope of avoiding falling into the hands of Soviet Russia, German representatives contacted British Gen. Bernard Law Montgomery and offered to surrender German armies in Holland, northwest Germany, and Denmark, if that surrender could be made to American Expeditionary Forces alone. Montgomery turned them down flat, and on 4 May 1945, in Lüneburg Heath, Germany, surrendered these troops to the Allies, which included Soviet Russia for the purpose of surrender.

On the following day, Gen. Adm. Hans-Georg von Friedeburg arrived at Eisenhower's headquarters in Rheims, France. Gen. Walter Bedell Smith represented General Eisenhower at the meeting and expected to accept the unconditional surrender of Germany on behalf of the Allies. Smith was surprised when General von Friedeburg said that he did not have the authority to agree to such conditions and reiterated that German forces would not agree to surrender to the Soviet High Command. Smith refused the conditions and von Friedeburg contacted Adm. Karl Dönitz, who had succeeded Adolf Hitler as president of the Third Reich, and asked either to be given the authority to accept the Allies' demands or that someone else be sent who would have that authority. Dönitz sent Col. Gen. Alfred Jodl, who flew to Rheims.

The document for the unconditional surrender of all forces under German control on land and sea and in the air was executed at 2:41 a.m. on 7 May 1945, and signed by Colonel General Jodl for the German High Command, Gen. Walter Bedell Smith for the Supreme Commander of the Allied Expeditionary Force, General Ivan Susloparov for the Soviet High Command, and Gen. François Servez of the French Army, who signed as a witness. The surrender document stated that military operations were to end at 11:01 p.m. on 8 May 1945, Central European time. The surrender documents and all necessary papers were prepared by the WACs at Supreme Headquarters, Allied Forces Europe (SHAFE), who took notes, typed, collated, and posted all documents involved in the surrender process.

The surrender agreement was to be ratified in Berlin on 8 May 1945, and members of SHAFE flew to Berlin to attend the ceremony. For thirty-three-year-old WAC Sgt. Ruth Blanton, who had been with the Intelligence Section of SHAFE since its days at Bushy Park in London, duty in Berlin would offer new challenges. "I was assigned to OMGUS— Office of Military Government," Blanton said. "One of my strongest memories of World War II is taking notes while a British officer questioned Adm. Karl Dönitz about Germany's conduct of the war and its treatment of Jews and POWs." Blanton continued, "When I was with SHAFE in Paris, we worked in Versailles, and WACs were quartered in the stables that had been used by Napoleon's troops. Nor will I ever forget attending midnight mass in the chapel of the Versailles Palace on Christmas Eve some months before."[31]

When the unofficial news of the German surrender reached the cities of Europe, the reactions were mixed. In Paris, despite the lack of official confirmation, thousands of people poured into the streets, singing, shouting, and hugging friends and strangers alike. People set off fireworks; a plane flew low over the city and dropped flares; and loudspeakers in the Place de l'Opéra repeatedly broadcast that hostilities in Europe had ended. An article in the *New York Times* described the occasion with the words, "Paris let itself go tonight and acted—like Paris."[32]

Capt. Dorothy Starbuck had a unique view of V-E Day. After the long road she had traveled from officers' candidate school at Fort Des Moines to London, and her participation in D-Day plans, watching hundreds of planes make their way toward the English Channel and on to France, and after continued work in the European Theater of Operations, U.S. Army (ETUSA) in Paris, she would celebrate V-E Day in a way she would never have freely chosen. As the individual responsible for all secret to top secret documents coming into or going out of ETUSA, she was well aware that V-E Day would come in a matter of hours. Unfortunately, when Parisians and Allied military hit the streets to celebrate the surrender of Germany,

U.S. Army WACs, V-E Day Parade, Paris, France, May 1945.

Starbuck was confined to quarters in her room in a Paris hotel. "I was sick in bed with some kind of flu and had to remain there on doctor's orders," Starbuck said. "A group of my friends came by and brought a bottle of Scotch they had been saving to celebrate V-E Day." She continued, "I wasn't sure I could keep it down, but we all had a drink and toasted Germany's surrender and the V-J Day we all hoped would come very soon."[33]

The unofficial news in London brought about 500,000 people to the streets and Piccadilly Circus, while others pointed out that the war was not over and that those who had lost family and friends were most likely not part of the crowd in Piccadilly Circus; while people in Copenhagen, Denmark, clashed with grueling forces, leaving fifty-four Danish patriots dead, 255 wounded, and more than 10,000 collaborators taken into custody. On 8 May 1945, the headlines of the London *Daily Express* read: "This is V-E Day: Yesterday might have been it but Stalin and Truman were not ready."[34]

When the news reached the wounded in American military hospitals in the New York area, they reacted with "quiet acceptance . . . and a glance westward toward the Pacific." Some of the wounded said they would wait for President Harry Truman to make it official before they accepted the news as truth; others pointed out that there was still a terrible fight ahead in the Pacific; and others said that the "white crosses speak more eloquently than any words." Perhaps the most succinct statement, from the *New York Times,* was "It won't be V-E Day until it's all over and all the boys get home."[35]

A *New York Times* headline pointed out that "Wild Crowds Greet News in City While Others Pray." Actually, the crowd in Times Square was small—500,000—in comparison to crowds for other events.[36]

10

Freedom is not free! It came to us by blood, sweat, tears, sacrifice, and loss of life of others. To us and our heirs came the obligation and duty to preserve freedom at all cost for future generations to enjoy.
—Wanda Lucus, WAC

If any Americans thought that V-E Day meant that the armed forces would need fewer women after 8 May 1945, they were mistaken. In the very month in which Germany surrendered, the U.S. Navy raised the recruitment goal for WAVES to 2,000 a month. The *WAVES Newsletter* for July 1945 pointed out that of the 82,000 WAVES on active duty, 13,000 were serving in the Hospital Corps, and thousands more would be needed to help treat and rehabilitate the wounded expected from the Pacific.[1]

Nine WAVES and two male sailors who had been trained at the Naval Medical Center in Bethesda, Maryland, were stationed at various naval hospitals with the unusual duty of painting the delicate colors of the iris on each acrylic eye needed by a specific wounded sailor or marine. If the kamikaze continued its attacks on U.S. naval ships in the Pacific and if the planned invasion of Japan met the predictions estimated for the number of casualties, many more WAVES would be needed for that and other duties with the Navy's Hospital Corps. At the Naval Training School in the Bronx, New York, more than 140 WAVES were already being trained as occupational therapy assistants, and in rehabilitation as instructors for the blind, the deaf, and amputees.[2]

Most men and women serving in the armed forces were very aware that many of them in the European Theater and in the United States stood a very good chance of being deployed to the Pacific for the invasion of Japan. If the invasion of Japan produced more American casualties than had fallen so far in the island hopping that had brought American troops to within reach of the home islands, every medical unit now on duty in

Europe and on various Pacific Islands would be needed to provide medical and surgical treatment for wounded and ill American soldiers, marines, and sailors.

For Lt. Lillie "Pete" Peterson of the Ninety-fifth Evacuation Hospital, the end of the war in Europe was absolutely a reason to celebrate, but the celebration was dimmed considerably by the haunting realization that the Ninety-fifth and the majority of all army hospitals in Europe would have to be redeployed to the Pacific for the invasion of Japan. "Most of us were pretty tired and wondering if our luck would hold out through another campaign."[3]

The Ninety-fifth Evacuation Hospital had arrived in Casablanca, French Morocco, on 24 April 1943 and had supported American and Allied troops all the way along their march to Berlin. The medics had also provided medical and surgical care for wounded enemy troops who had become prisoners of war. Now, after that long, hard journey, which included the German bombing of two of the hospital ships that carried them to Salerno and Anzio, after the death of six of their sister nurses killed by enemy fire on Anzio, after they and other army nurses won Purple Hearts, after they had cared for the inmates in liberated German concentration camps, they and their sister army nurses would more than likely be going along with the invasion force to Japan.

June 1945 brought an end to the Battle of Okinawa but not before the combat death on 18 June 1945 of Lt. Gen. Simon Bolivar Buckner Jr., commander of the U.S. Tenth Army on Okinawa. Buckner was the highest-ranking officer to be killed by enemy fire in World War II. He was killed when a fragment of a Japanese shell pierced his heart.[4]

Three days later, on 21 June 1945, the Battle of Okinawa ended. American troops and planes now had a vital launchpad from which to send increasing numbers of bombers over the Japanese home islands. Okinawa was also to serve as a well-placed radar station for advanced warning to the U.S. invasion force of Japanese planes on their way to attack the fleet. The price paid for that radar station 400 miles from the southernmost of the Japanese home islands, Kyushu, was extremely high for American troops. In early July 1945, the casualties were estimated to be as follows: 6,999 Americans dead or missing (4,417 soldiers, 2,573 marines); 29,573 wounded (17,033 soldiers, 12,565 marines). The losses suffered by navy ships and crews were withheld in an attempt to keep the success of kamikaze attacks from both the American people and the Japanese military.[5]

In April 1945, the U.S. Navy issued a press release mentioning kamikaze attacks against navy ships in the Pacific. The press release coincided with the announcement of the death of President Franklin D. Roosevelt and was overshadowed by the loss of the man who had been the commander in chief of the U.S. Armed Forces since World War II officially began on 3 September 1939. He had stood before Congress on 8 December 1941 and asked it to declare that "since the dastardly and unprovoked attack by sea and air forces of the Empire of Japan on U.S. Forces at Pearl Harbor, Hawaii, on 7 December 1941, a state of war has existed between the United States of America and the Japanese Empire." His leadership had steered the country's armed forces all the way to Germany in the European Theater and to the Ryukyu Islands and Okinawa in the Pacific. His death plunged the country and her armed forces throughout the world into a state of mourning for the only president they had known since 1932. The nation's loss pushed every other news story off the front pages and out of the minds of the American people while the country and her people said goodbye to FDR.[6]

The Japanese did all they could to extol kamikaze pilots who crashed their planes into U.S. Navy or Army ships. Radio Tokyo spent time every day listing the names of successful kamikaze pilots, who were referred to as "hero gods." Japanese news media also broadcast and printed interviews with young boys who hoped to grow up and become kamikaze pilots.

On 12 May 1945, the War Department released information on how the Readjusted Service Rating would be calculated in determining which military personnel would be eligible for discharge and which would be redeployed to the Pacific to play a part in the invasion of Japan. The subject was on the minds of military personnel, their families, and friends. Since the greatest majority of Americans fell into one of those three categories, it is safe to say that the question of military discharge and redeployment was one of the most talked-about questions since Germany surrendered and V-E Day was declared and celebrated just four days earlier.

Newspapers and news broadcasts announced that the magic number of points for army personnel to be eligible for discharge was eighty-five.

The point system was based on a soldier's length of military service after 16 September 1940; the number of months the soldier had served overseas; the number of months a soldier had been in combat; and by the parenthood status of each GI.

All U.S. Army personnel would be processed through separation centers or redeployment stations located in the United States. It soon became clear that amassing eighty-five points or more was not enough to ensure a discharge and a return to civilian life. Many soldiers who had accrued the necessary points found themselves on the way to redistribution stations in the United States or on their way directly to the South West Pacific Area. This was especially true of Army Air Corps pilots and medical personnel, but equally true of individuals who found that their military occupational specialty was deemed essential.

Prior to this ruling, Army Air Corps pilots and air crews who had completed fifty combat missions were rotated back to the United States, where many served as flying instructors, navigation instructors, or as bombardiers or radio instructors. The rationale behind this "fifty missions and home" policy was based on the statistical chances of the air crew to survive yet another mission over enemy territory. After fifty missions, the statistical chances of an air crew's surviving dropped to less than fifty-fifty, with a downward spiral for each additional combat mission flown. It was not uncommon for air crews to feel their luck was running out as they approached the fifty-mission mark.

With the war in the Pacific and the invasion of the Japanese home islands scheduled for November 1945, the Transportation Corps was facing one of the largest and most important missions in the entire war— transporting more than one million military personnel, along with their equipment and supplies, from the European Theater of Operations and the United States to the Pacific.

The expertise that was in great demand at this point in the war was to be provided by the Transportation Corps, Highway Traffic Engineers, the Superintendent of the Water Division, and legal officers with experience in admiralty law, contract negotiation, and property disposal. Civil affairs and military government officers were needed to be assigned to occupied territories, and officers and warrant officers were training others in negotiation skills involving termination of existing contracts and the need for and structuring of new contracts.

The first overall objective of the armed forces personnel in the Pacific was to invade the Japanese home islands and bring about the unconditional surrender of the Empire of Japan. The need for unconditional surrender was based on past and current history.

Germany had agreed to unconditional surrender when her leaders accepted the fact that their nation had been defeated on the battlefield. The United States and her allies knew, given Germany's statements concerning their loss in World War I, that Germans believed they had been beaten not on the battlefield but in the 1919 negotiations between diplomats that resulted in the Treaty of Versailles. The German people were told and believed that Germany's diplomats had betrayed their nation in their negotiations for an honorable peace and that the German nation had not lost the war but had lost the peace treaty negotiations. This belief led a large number of Germans to see themselves as victims justified in claiming the Sudetenland and other territories taken from them by politicians rather than by enemy forces that had outplanned and outfought them in combat. The treaty set the stage for World War II.

Faced with the prospects for a lasting peace with the Japanese Empire, civilian and military leaders of the Allied forces had to accept the fact that not one Japanese military unit had surrendered to American or Allied forces in World War II. Those same American and Allied leaders reasoned that unless it were clear to the people of Japan that their nation's armed forces had been outfought and thoroughly beaten in World War II, militant civilian and military leaders might very well be able to lead the nation into another war of aggression in a relatively short period of time. Given these facts and judgments made by the Allies, it was agreed that unconditional surrender and the demobilization of Japan's armed forces would afford the best prospect for a lasting peace. With these facts in mind, the American military and war department drew up plans for a massive invasion of the Japanese home islands. That plan was given the code name Operation Downfall.

Women serving either in the U.S. Army Nurse Corps or the Women's Army Corps would be held to similar standards regarding the essential character of their Military Occupational Specialty (MOS) and the Readjusted Service Rating applied to them. In addition to no longer being considered to have an essential MOS, women in the Army Nurse Corps, Medical Specialist Corps, and the Women's Army Corps would need to accrue points to be eligible for discharge. Army nurses needed sixty-five points; physical therapists and dietitians, forty-one points, and WAC officers, forty-four points.

Any female or male officer who was eligible for discharge, yet preferred to remain on active duty, was required to sign a short statement that read, "Regardless of any eligibility which I may have now, or in the future, for relief from active duty under Readjustment Regulations, I elect irrevocably to continue on extended active duty for the duration of the emergency and six months, unless sooner relieved."[7]

The army planned to release two million male and female military personnel by 1 July 1946. One million five hundred of this number would be comprised of healthy able-bodied men with a point score of eighty-five on 12 May 1945. The rules for discharge also provided for the release of married WACs, upon their request, whose husbands had been returned to civilian life in the United States. The army estimated that this provision would affect approximately 6,000 WACS before June 1946. Approximately 5,000 WACs were eligible for release from the army under the Readjusted Service Rating System (RSRS); however, as of 31 July 1945, only 1,100 WACs had actually been separated from the military under the point system.

The RSRS staff ran the entire plan by Gen. Douglas MacArthur and his commanders before putting the system into operation. The planners, General MacArthur, and his commanders agreed that the proposed strategy would allow for the maximum number of discharges from the army without causing an increased casualty rate due to the loss of experienced combat leaders. The U.S. Army estimated that if releases under the RSRS program continued at the same pace until 12 May 1946, 1.5 million soldiers would have been returned to civilian life.

Thousands of WACs who would have been eligible for release under the RSRS program were retained in the army because they worked in an MOS declared essential to the army, for example, as clerk-typists or stenographers. The final two sentences in the memo dated 2 August 1945, released by the public relations section of the War Department, summed up the course the army intended to follow: "We shall not let any men go whose going jeopardizes the life of the men who remain to fight. We shall get every man discharged as rapidly as his service under the point system, the vital needs of the war, and complications of transportation and redeployment allow."[8]

The surrender of Germany also brought changes in the army's leave policy for WACs whose husbands were members of the U.S. Armed Forces and were returned to the United States for temporary duty, rest and recuperation, or reassignment. Concurrent leave would be granted to WAC enlisted and officers whenever it was practical for the army. The leave could be granted for up to forty-five days, and extensions could be granted if the husband was a returning POW. Enlisted WACs would receive full pay for leave time, and WAC officers would receive half-pay for any leave that had to be granted as an advance of leave not yet earned. WACs who had joined the army after 12 May 1945 were required to spend a year on active duty before requesting a discharge, unless their husbands were disabled or dependent.[9]

June brought many changes to Fort Oglethorpe, Georgia. The Third WAC Training Center was officially closing and WACs stationed at the post were being transferred in groups to their new assignments in the United States and overseas. As WACs boarded trains at Union Station in Chattanooga, Tennessee, soldiers of the U.S. Army Ground Service Forces Headquarters, previously quartered at Fort Butner, North Carolina, were detraining on another platform and boarding trucks that would take them to their new home at Fort Oglethorpe, South Post, where they would staff and maintain one of the only two redistribution centers to be located on an army post rather than at hotels throughout the country.

The Fort Oglethorpe Redistribution Center would receive the first group of returnees from overseas on 15 July 1945. The center would process four thousand soldiers every two weeks. The first five days were devoted to processing, which would include a complete physical, interviews, standardized tests, and a recommendation for reassignment or discharge. That recommendation would be forwarded to the War Department for approval or reclassification. The soldiers' remaining nine days were on a "vacation" of sorts, filled with tours of Chattanooga, Lookout Mountain, and Civil War battlefields of Chickamauga and Missionary Ridge; relaxation; and activities such as golf, horseback riding, crafts classes, and sitting around talking and swapping stories with other returnees in the "snack shack" over free sandwiches, coffee, and soft drinks. When the two weeks were up and reassignment orders received, the soldiers would be granted furloughs while awaiting their reporting dates or discharge documents.

Capt. Jeanne Holm was the last WAC at the Third WAC Training

Center to leave Fort Oglethorpe. "I went through every record, stored them in eight U.S. Army footlockers, and literally turned out the lights when I left," Jeanne Holm remembered. The young recruit who had enlisted in the WAAC in 1942, who had taught her company close-order drill and marching during her first weeks at Fort Des Moines, had learned and taught a great deal more about the U.S. Army and life in the WAC. It was only one in a long line of adventures that would fill her military career before she retired.[10]

Almost every WAAC/WAC who was assigned to an overseas station in the European or Mediterranean Theater had spent weeks at Fort Oglethorpe attending classes in what to expect at a duty station in Europe or the Mediterranean. Many of them had been overseas for years and had the required points for rotation to the States for reassignment, or for discharge, if not working in an MOS considered essential. WACs stationed on the Continent would be processed through the Sixteenth Reinforcement Depot; WACs assigned in England would be processed through the Seventieth Replacement Depot located in England. WACs on the Continent would be flown to England and join those at the Seventieth Replacement Depot and flown to the States as a group. Once on American soil, the WACs would be sent to one of the five WAC Separation Centers closest to the home address they had listed when they joined the WAAC/WAC. The five WAC Separation Centers were located at Fort Dix, New Jersey; Fort Bragg, North Carolina; Fort Sheridan, Illinois; Camp Beal, California; and Fort Sam Houston, Texas. The first group of fifty returnees was scheduled to return to the United States sometime in July 1945.

WACs with high RSRS scores serving in the European Theater of Operations also had the option of choosing to remain in the military, in the ETO, or to be discharged and remain in the ETO as a civilian government employee. The army and the federal government promised these women federal jobs without the restrictions imposed by the WAC. There was more than a little suspicion among senior WAC officers when WACs were encouraged to be discharged in Europe and to take up their new jobs or continue in their military jobs without military rank. WAC officers suspected that these job offers resulted from desires of male army officers who saw such assignments as the best of all possible worlds for male officers. These military men would remain as part of the occupation force in the ETO, and the women could stay in their current jobs and yet enjoy the freedom accorded to civilian women, including the right to live off post in their own apartments and to date male officers without military restrictions.[11]

On 6 July 1945, the Instruction and Education Branch of the army released a summary of a study titled "Post-War Education Plans of WAC Enlisted Personnel." The summary provided the results of a study the army conducted of 5,000 enlisted WACs stationed in the United States concerning their plans to attend college or vocational schools after the war ended. The figures indicated that the percent of women planning to pursue full-time education after the military was 7.3 percent or approximately 5,000 to 6,000 WACs. Of that number, 3.5 percent planned to attend school full-time whether or not the government helped with expenses through the GI Bill. For the remaining 3.8 percent, their plans included full-time education only if the government helped financially. In a separate survey of WACs, 8.3 percent (6,000 to 7,000) planned to attend school on a part-time basis. Of this group, 1.3 percent planned to attend school with or without government financial support; 5.1 percent could attend school only if the government helped. Approximately 1.9 percent of the remaining WACs were undecided concerning government aid.

All of the above-mentioned figures include women who expressed interest in vocational as well as academic programs. If only academic programs were considered, the women planning to attend full-time were 5 percent and those planning to attend part-time, 4 percent. The memo goes on to conjecture that the part-time percentage who would actually attend an academic program part-time would most likely be less than the 4 percent who responded that they planned to do so. The summary draws the following conclusion in regard to part-time academic education for former WACs: "the figure (4%) for part-time academic school is a far less precise one than that for full-time school, since it probably represents wishful thinking with little or no realization of the difficulties involved in either working full-time or running a home and family full-time and going to school. It is therefore unlikely that many of these women will actually go back to take any formal academic training."[12]

On 16 July 1945, top secret research conducted under the code name Manhattan Project was about to face its moment of truth. In April 1942, the first WAACs had been assigned to the Manhattan District and Los Alamos, New Mexico. The title "Manhattan District" was designed to be misleading since the work of the Manhattan District was to design, build, and deliver the world's first atomic bomb to the U.S. Army Air Forces for use over enemy targets. Not only were the men and women assigned to the Manhattan District to carry out the objectives laid forth, they were to accomplish this feat in record time, and before Germany or Japan developed their own such weapon.

The title of the project was soon to change from the Manhattan District to the Manhattan Project. The code name Silverplate was used for the purpose of acquiring whatever was needed to complete the top secret project. If those involved in the acquisition of needed materials or personnel were to meet with a "no" in response to a request involving either, the mere use of the word "Silverplate" would remove the obstacles and get the project managers what they needed on a top-priority basis and without giving anyone without clearance for the project even the most cursory response to the questions, "What is it for?" "Why do you need this?" "What are you working on?" or "Where are you located?"

The Manhattan Project would be scattered at secret locations throughout the United States according to which part of the total project that location was assigned. Columbia University in New York was charged with the development of the gaseous diffusion process that would separate uranium-235 and amass enough of the element to produce the chain reaction necessary to release the bomb's destructive power. The Chrysler Corporation in Detroit, Michigan, was tasked with the development and production of the diffusers that would make Columbia University's tasks possible. Oak Ridge, Tennessee, would have one of the largest Manhattan Project sites and would use electromagnetic processors to produce the U-235 much of the project would require for their work. The same Oak Ridge site would also work on gaseous diffusion of the U-235. Illinois would also have two sites, one in Chicago where Enrico Fermi would construct the first "pile" for the production of plutonium, and the other in Decatur, where scientists would work on a barrier to control and contain the nuclear chain reaction that some feared could set the earth's atmosphere on fire when the bomb was dropped. Milwaukee, Wisconsin, was designated as the site where pumps designed for cooling the rods in the nuclear pile/reactor produced and refined the nuclear elements. A site in Hanford, Washington, was responsible for production of the needed plutonium, and E. O. Lawrence's team in Berkeley, California, was responsible for the development of an electromagnetic process that would separate U-235.

The last two sites of the Manhattan Project were located in New Mexico. The site at Los Alamos was a secluded boys' school located on the top of an isolated mesa with one road in and out. The second site in New Mexico was at Alamogordo, in a vast expanse of desert where the atomic bomb would be tested. Los Alamos would house Robert Oppenheimer, the director of the scientific end of the Manhattan Project, the top scientists, and military people charged with the design and assembly of the bomb—usually referred to by them as the "Gadget." It was Los Alamos that would be the home of the first WAACs from the hand-selected First Provisional WAAC Detachment.

The first group of WAACs to be assigned to Los Alamos had arrived on 21 April 1943, four days after that unit was activated at Fort Sill, Oklahoma. The members of the unit were the brightest and the best the WAAC could deliver to the Manhattan Project, not only for post operations, but in the scientific and technical fields as well. The first WAACs to set foot in Los Alamos were 3rd Officer Helen E. Mulvihill and six enlisted auxiliaries, Ruth I. Millwright, Frances E. Steele, Florence E. Mallon, Mable B. Wolven, Anna E. Oliver, and Leota T. Germer. They were joined several days later by Mabel Wood and Lee Brickhouse Klein. For this small group, and for all who would follow in a matter of weeks or months, the trip to Los Alamos would be essentially the same and under the same intentionally deceptive orders.

WAC detachment that was assigned to the Manhattan Project at Los Alamos, New Mexico, at Meritorious Service Award Ceremony, August 1945.

None of the WAACs or male soldiers were told they were being assigned to Los Alamos. In fact, the name "Los Alamos" did not appear on any orders directing them to travel to their new duty station. WAACs were simply told that they were under overseas orders and not to tell anyone that they were being transferred or when their trip would begin. Many left their barracks under orders in early morning darkness to board trains they assumed would take them to a port of embarkation for their new overseas duty stations. Some made the trip on Pullman trains so old that there was a potbellied stove at each end of the car for warmth.

Most of the WAACs were surprised when their trip ended in Lamy, New Mexico, and were quick to tell the person meeting them that there must be a mistake since they were on their way overseas. When they were assured that they were in the right place and had a thirty-five-mile drive to Santa Fe ahead of them, most were incredulous. When they arrived at 109 East Palace in Santa Fe, they were not any happier to learn that they still had an hour's drive before they arrived at their new duty station. Dorothy McKibbin, a civilian who had been hired as a "gatekeeper" for the project, wrote, "Of all of the incoming personnel, the WACs and some of the soldiers were at their lowest ebb in this office. They had not been told what was going to happen to them, they had been alerted for overseas duty, and the overseas silence had been flung around the shoulders of their families." McKibbin and other civilian women who had lived in the area and knew it as home grew used to the surprise on the faces of some women and even to the tears shed by a few of the WAACs who were sure Uncle Sam would not do this to them when they thought they were going overseas.[13]

It did not help much when their driver told them to "take a good look at Santa Fe, because this may be the last time you see it for quite a while." Nor was it reassuring to hear the driver say, "I hope we get there before dark, since this road is dangerous enough in daylight." The road made its spiral way up to the top of the mesa, where the town of Los Alamos was now a secret location: the working place for some of the world's top scientists of the day who were developing the weapon that might just win the war, and if developed by Germany or Japan first, that just might lose the war for America and her allies.

Many of the WAACs selected to work on the Manhattan Project had undergraduate degrees; some had experience as teachers, secretaries, chemists, or businesswomen. There were even a few who had earned doctoral degrees and who later would be assigned to the technical side of the work being done in the research labs.

Several U.S. Army Nurses were also stationed on "The Hill," as it was called by the townspeople of Santa Fe and the locals who lived in the areas around Santa Fe. One did not have to be stationed there long before The Hill became a common reference for the new duty station and home. Between 21 April 1943 and 31 December 1945, 192 enlisted women served in the Provisional WAC Detachment at Los Alamos. This number does not include WAAC/WACs who were either transferred to another unit or released to return to civilian life after serving on The Hill. Three of the original group serving there did not reenlist when, in accordance with the new WAC bill, all other WACs at Los Alamos were sworn in to the U.S. Army on 24 August 1943.

Life at Los Alamos demanded strict obedience to the security rules imposed by the army for all military personnel assigned to the facility. In addition to not being informed of their true destination until after their arrival at Los Alamos, military personnel, including the WAAC/WACs, were forbidden to tell anyone of their true duty station, had no address to receive mail for the first few months after their arrival, could not discuss their work with anyone outside their own work situation, had to leave all letters for mailing unsealed in order that censors could check them for security breaches, and could not travel beyond Taos to the north or Albuquerque to the south. As time went on, even Santa Fe was placed off limits.

Being assigned to work at Los Alamos demanded absolute adherence to security rules and any deviation could result in a transfer to an area of work not requiring a top secret clearance. A large group of military women were being trusted to keep America's most sensitive and crucial secrets and, despite the stereotypical idea that women could not keep secrets, the women assigned to the Manhattan Project met every criterion laid down to safeguard the development of the "ultimate weapon." Even WAAC/WACs who worked as file clerks, typists, and librarians had access to top secret material that, if divulged, could have led to America's defeat in the war.

Third Officer Helen E. Mulvihill, who was one of the first WAAC officers to arrive at Los Alamos, observed that the women under her command kept their work and their mission top secret despite rumors circulating among civilians and military enlisted men stationed in or around Santa Fe that Los Alamos was actually an underground research laboratory for work on "a submarine for the Russians." There were more damaging rumors that attacked the character of the WAAC/WACs who were stationed at Los Alamos. "They called Los Alamos a home for pregnant WACs." Rumors that the women of the WAAC/WAC were no better than prostitutes placed at army posts to service men or else were lesbians reached even the remote and secure location of Los Alamos.[14]

When Lt. Myrtle C. Bachelder arrived at Los Alamos, Lt. Helen E. Mulvihill, the commanding officer for the WACs, had a serious and sobering message for her that Bachelder would never forget. "She said Major de Silva [an intelligence officer] told me essentially to button my lip about the place and promised dire consequences if I didn't." Bachelder was assigned to work in the chemical and spectrographic analysis section and worked for Norman H. Nichtrich, Ph.D., professor of chemistry at the University of Chicago.[15]

Lt. Harryette Hunter Emmerson traveled on secret orders from Camp Ritchie, Maryland, and had no idea what would be her destination. Unfortunately, her train to Chicago was two hours late and Emmerson felt sure she would miss her connecting train, the Santa Fe Chief. When her train pulled into Chicago, Emmerson was stunned to learn that the Santa Fe Chief had been held in the station to wait for her arrival. "I didn't believe it, but it is true," Emmerson remembered. Lieutenant Emmerson was assigned as the dietitian for the post's one-hundred-bed hospital before she eventually became the company commander at Los Alamos.[16]

At 5:25 a.m. on Monday, 16 July 1945, the first atomic bomb was tested on the Alamogordo Bombing Range, 210 miles from its birthplace at Los Alamos. The "Gadget," as Los Alamos scientists referred to the bomb, had been raised to the top of a firing tower that was designated ground zero for the test. Three observation bunkers were located approximately 10,000 yards south, north, and west of the firing tower, a precaution to ensure that if the blast were blocked from view at any angle, two other observation posts would have a line of sight on ground zero and its surroundings. Dr. Robert Oppenheimer, the chief scientist of the Manhattan Project, whose mission was to conceive, design, build, test, and deliver the world's first atomic bomb, had given the test bomb the code name Trinity in honor of one of his favorite poems, "Trinity" by English poet John Donne. Oppenheimer and the other scientists who had labored long and hard to make this day possible had two main fears concerning the possible outcomes of the test: (1) that the bomb would not explode at all, and (2) that the explosion of the bomb would start a chain reaction that could not be controlled and would set the earth's atmosphere on fire.

With observers in place, the countdown began, and at 5:30 a.m., Trinity exploded with such force that the 100-foot firing tower on which it sat was vaporized and the sky became brighter than the best sunny day imaginable. Several of the observers experienced temporary blindness, despite the fact that each was wearing goggles with smoked-glass lenses. In a fraction of a second, the blast sent a tremendous shock wave of wind and searing heat across the desert, knocking several of the observers off their feet. The blast was followed immediately by a gigantic orange-yellow fireball that expanded rapidly in height and width until it appeared to fill the sky. In only seconds, a huge mushroom-shaped cloud rose into the sky and hung over the site, announcing the start of a new era that would change the world forever. The Atomic Age was minutes old, and already beyond the point of no return. There was no way to "un-know" the knowledge gained in developing the atomic bomb, no way to close the door the Manhattan Project had thrown open. The observers present at the Trinity test would never forget the moment the Atomic Age was born or the mushroom cloud that would become the world symbol for atomic energy and unimaginable destructive power.

It would be years before the nation and the world learned what WAAC/WACs were doing at Los Alamos, indeed, before even the WACs who slept in the same room and were good buddies learned what the women in the cots next to their own had actually worked on at the top secret and isolated army post at the top of the heavily guarded mesa. One woman, Corp. Vera Lindrey McDaniel, stationed at the army post near Albuquerque as an aircraft dispatcher, remembered, "My strongest memory of World War II is the explosion of the atomic bomb at Alamogordo, New Mexico. We saw it, the bright light, and heard the rumbling all the way at Kirkland. I was on duty."[17]

Halfway around the world in Potsdam, Germany, Secretary of War Henry Stimson received a message from his special consultant, George L. Harrison, in Washington, D.C. The message read: "Operated on this morning, diagnosis not yet complete but results seem satisfactory, and already exceed expectations. Local press release necessary as interest extends a great distance. Doctor Groves pleased. He returns tomorrow. I will keep you posted."[18]

Secretary of War Stimson conveyed to President Truman the contents and meaning of Harrison's message. For a new president who had only learned of the existence and mission of the decoding projects Ultra and Magic five days after being sworn in as president, and of the existence and purpose of the Manhattan Project eight days later, the news of a successful testing of Trinity must have given him a boost in considering his options for combating and conquering Japan in her own home islands.

Truman, who had been an artillery captain in World War I, knew both the horrors of combat and the weight of being responsible for the lives of his men. The practical knowledge gained from his experience in the First World War must have been invaluable and significant in deciding America's next steps in her war against Japan. Truman instructed ADM William Leahy to question his advisers for an estimate of the length of time they thought it would take for the United States to invade and defeat Japan and for an estimate of the number of casualties, killed and wounded, that American troops were likely to suffer.

American Armed Forces had learned through brutal combat that Japanese kamikaze pilots could cause fatal damage to warships, transports, and even hospital ships. Military leaders fully expected kamikaze attacks on the invasion fleet as the more than three thousand ships came within their striking range as they approached the Japanese home islands; however, their intelligence estimates concerning the number of planes and pilots available for suicide attacks was far below the number the Japanese actually had held back to use against an invasion fleet carrying American forces to Japan's home islands and landing them on their home beaches.

Another lesson the U.S. military thought it had learned was the length to which Japanese civilians would go to avoid conquest or surrender. They had faced such civilians on Iwo Jima, Saipan, and Okinawa and expected more of the same when they invaded the Japanese homeland. However, American armed forces were not the only military learning from the past and adjusting for future battles.

The Japanese learned that stealth had been a powerful weapon for them in the past and they were determined to use it to their advantage when an American invasion of the home islands was thought to be imminent. With this goal in sight, the Japanese moved quickly to organize civilians into fighting units. On 23 March 1945, the government ordered the formation of the Patriotic Citizens Fighting Corps throughout Japan. All men between the ages of fifteen and sixty, and all women seventeen to forty, were automatically obliged to serve in the organization. On the following day, the Japanese Imperial Headquarters ordered the formation of Area Special Policing Units and placed them under area commanders. The approximately one million civilians affected who would be under military control and discipline would receive training in the use of various weapons and would report directly to the area commanders, whose jobs were to ensure that the group was molded into an effective and willing homeland defense force.

For all intents and purposes, the military, the government, and the civilian population were one fighting force, which would defend the home islands to the death of each individual. To facilitate the melding together of these separate entities into one, the government and military ordered that all educational classes in schools, except for grades one through six, be suspended from 1 April 1945 through 31 March 1946. Students and teachers would work in various essential production programs, producing food, weapons, and military supplies to be used in defending the homeland against an American invasion. As part of this effort, Japan located as many manufacturing plants and factories as possible underground to protect them from air strikes and artillery fire. The Japanese army and navy also moved most of their aircraft that could be used in kamikaze attacks off the home islands and into Manchuria until they were needed to repel the American invasion they were convinced would take place in the not too distant future. The inclusion of these thousands of kamikaze planes was so essential to the overall plan that the government and military were working day and night to produce synthetic aviation fuel to power their kamikaze aircraft.

Japanese civilians also were formed into groups to reinforce beach defenses and plant mines and other obstacles from one end of Japan to the other end. Civilians would also be trained sufficiently to pilot kamikaze aircraft, kamikaze subs, and to submerge human-directed torpedoes.

Japanese Imperial Headquarters intended to use the kamikaze force around the clock once the U.S. invasion force was within one-way flight range of their planes. The raids on the fleet would involve 2,000 or 3,000 kamikaze aircraft at a time, and the pilots would have more than 3,000

U.S. ships to choose from as targets. Imperial Headquarters had adopted a strategy of wearing the enemy down to a point where they would be willing to agree to surrender terms more advantageous to a Japan that would come back to fight another day.

The Potsdam Declaration released by the United States and her allies on 26 July 1945 demanded the unconditional surrender of Japan and promised total destruction if the Japanese failed to agree to these terms.

On 25 July 1945, after much thought and deliberation with his military and civilian advisers, President Harry S Truman approved the use of the atomic bomb on Japan in order to save millions of American soldiers, marines, and sailors who would be killed or seriously wounded if they had to take part in an amphibious invasion of the Japanese home islands. The projected toll of more than 1.5 million to 2 million Americans killed and wounded with no foreseeable surrender by Japan was more than a former experienced artillery captain from World War I was willing to pay in an invasion and house-to-house combat with no foreseeable end.

On 6 August 1945, the B-29 *Enola Gay,* under the command of Col. Paul W. Tibbets, dropped an atomic bomb on the city of Hiroshima, Japan. Much of the city and its people were vaporized while others succumbed to radiation burns or radiation poisoning. The U.S. government waited for the unconditional surrender of Japan it hoped would come as quickly as possible.

On 6 August 1945 when people throughout the United States looked at the front pages of their newspapers, they learned that the lives of people all over the world had been changed forever.

In New Mexico, WACs working on The Hill in Los Alamos learned for the first time what all their work, all the secrecy, and all the regulations set up to protect the Manhattan Project, which had been under way for two years, was all about. The headline on the *Santa Fe New Mexican* for 6 August 1945 read, "Los Alamos Secret Disclosed by Truman." An even larger message below that read, "Atomic Bomb Dropped on Japan." Very few who read the headlines knew what an atomic bomb was or what power it could unleash.

While Washington, D.C., and the people of the United States waited impatiently for Japan to surrender, Emperor Hirohito and many in the Japanese military were urging Japan to fight on and at least hold out for better surrender terms. These Japanese favored an "honorable death" to the "dishonor of surrender." The U.S. military and President Truman worried that despite the dropping of the atomic bomb on Hiroshima, the Japanese military wanted the people of the home islands to fight the United States and her allies to the death. On 9 August 1945, the United States dropped an atomic bomb on the Japanese city of Nagasaki, and waited expectantly for the word that Japan would accept the terms of the Potsdam Declaration and surrender unconditionally.

In the morning and afternoon hours of 14 August 1945, President Truman met with Ambassador John Balfour of the United Kingdom and admitted that he had had no word concerning Japan's expected surrender and felt he would have to order an atomic bomb dropped on Tokyo. Official word that Japan would accept the terms of the Potsdam Declaration and surrender unconditionally did not reach Truman until 4:05 that afternoon.

The next day, 15 August 1945, newspaper headlines around the world carried the story of Japan's official surrender and the end of World War II. Americans poured into the streets to celebrate the return of peace, the end of World War II, and the future return of American military personnel.

On 2 September 1945, hundreds of U.S. military ships waited outside Tokyo harbor while the battleship USS *Missouri* hosted Gen. Douglas MacArthur, Gen. Jonathan Wainwright, ADM Chester Nimitz, and hun-

Women Marines and other U.S. Armed Forces Personnel stationed in Hawaii hold Honolulu newspapers announcing Japan's surrender, August 15, 1945.

dreds of other American and Allied military personnel in addition to the representatives of the Emperor of Japan who would sign the surrender documents on the emperor's behalf. Thousands of sailors, soldiers, and marines lined the decks and witnessed the official Japanese surrender they had prayed for and dreamed about for years.

With the surrender documents signed and the war officially ended, it was time for U.S. troops to move into Japan in order to liberate and secure the American and Allied troops held as prisoners of war on Japan's home islands. The next few days would be tense as the United States waited to see if all Japanese troops would honor Emperor Hirohito's command for the military to accept the surrender and lay down its arms. Tenuous conditions did not slow down the movement of U.S. health care givers who moved into the country to care for American POWs. One of the first hospitals to move into Tokyo as the ink was still drying on the surrender documents was the Forty-second General Hospital, whose personnel had worked in the Southwest Pacific for more than three years.

The hospital unit, from the University of Maryland, had sailed aboard the U.S. Army troop ship *West Point* from California to Canberra, Aus-

U.S. Army Nurses from Indiana who arrived in Tokyo the same morning the surrender documents were signed. Left to right: Dorothy Clary, Indianapolis; Theresa Randall, Dunkirk; Verona Carson, Noblesville; Ella Cooney, Terre Haute; Martha Copeland, South Bend; Phyllis Zimmer, Pleasant Lake, 2 September 1945.

tralia, in the spring of 1942. The hospital's chief nurse, Grace Dick, a thirty-three-year-old native of Charleston, West Virginia, remembered being seasick for the entire voyage. The hospital unit worked at a temporary location until their permanent hospital in Brisbane was completed and ready to accept hospital staff who would prepare to care for wounded military personnel.

After several years in Australia, the Forty-second General was transferred to Manila. Three months later, the hospital was ordered to Japan and sailed on the USAH *Marigold*. The ship docked in Yokohama, where hospital personnel set up a receiving station on the Yokohama docks and prepared for the arrival of liberated POWs. Grace Dick Gosnell told what happened next. "We were ordered to proceed to the Tokyo train station to triage and care for American and Allied newly released prisoners of war." Trucks were loaded with candy, gum, and cigarettes before

During World War II, First Lady Eleanor Roosevelt visiting patients at the Forty-second General Hospital, Brisbane, Australia, accompanied by Chief Nurse Lt. Grace Dick, 1944.

hospital personnel climbed onboard. "An Army band was playing 'The Yellow Rose of Texas' and the train was rounding the bend and slowing for its arrival at a train platform within the station," Gosnell remembered. "Soldiers were hanging out every window—waving and shouting. We were waving and calling back. It was a happy occasion," Gosnell remembered, "but it was also sad. They looked so starved and injured—legs and arms off. They wanted to know if they could touch us or kiss us. They were taken to the docks where they were fed—some of them put a half-cup of sugar into a single cup of coffee!" The men were triaged and moved out for further treatment. Gosnell continued, "The most critical were taken by plane; others were put on ships for transport to hospitals in the United States or Hawaii."[19]

From the Tokyo train station, the Forty-second General Hospital moved to St. Luke's International Medical Center in Tokyo, where staff would triage, treat, and evacuate liberated POWs for the foreseeable future.

The horrors suffered by American POWs at the hands of the Japanese must have been a shock even to the most hardened military personnel and to doctors, nurses, and medics who had already seen the horrors of war and the obscenities perpetrated by Japanese captors on American and Allied POWs. The medical personnel and crew of the USN hospital ship *Benevolence,* anchored in Tokyo Bay on 1 September 1945, were among the first to have one-on-one contact with the prisoners of war liberated from the Japanese prison camp at Shinagawa, Japan. For more than a day, the *Benevolence* had been the only hospital in the Tokyo area receiving and treating the eight thousand POWs liberated in the Tokyo area. The POWs had been liberated by a special navy evacuation mission led by CDR Harold A. Stassen, the former governor of Minnesota who was serving as ADM William F. Halsey's assistant chief of staff and flag secretary.

Two of the liberated POWs were U.S. Navy officer Mack L. Gottleib, captured by the Japanese when Guam fell in 1941, and army medical officer Harold W. Keschner, taken prisoner when the Philippines fell to the Japanese in 1942. Both men had served with U.S. military nurses also captured by the Japanese when Guam and the Philippines fell. Army and navy nurses had been liberated in February 1945 from Santo Tomas and Los Baños Internment Camps in the Philippines. Five navy nurses captured on Guam and taken to Japan's Zentsuji POW Camp in Tokyo had been repatriated on the *Gripsholm* as part of a prisoner exchange in August 1942.

Gottlieb and Keschner told of the inhuman "experiments" performed on American POWs imprisoned at Shinagawa. The experiments included injecting a mixture of castor oil and sulfur into the veins of POWs suffering from beriberi and neuritis. The injections caused excruciating pain accompanied by long periods of vomiting.

Word of these sadistic experiments had made its way into other Japanese prison camps in the Philippines and caused stress and horror to U.S. Army Nurses imprisoned at Santo Tomas; Lt. Madeline Ullom and other army nurses were forced at the point of a Japanese bayonet to give injections to fellow POWs. The medication was labeled in Japanese and the nurses were horrified by the very real possibility that they were injecting men, women, and children with plague or some other sadistic combination of bacteria and/or acid. Lieutenant Ullom and the other nurses lived in increasing horror while they waited to see what results might befall the Santo Tomas internees in the days and weeks that followed.[20]

The treatment of POWs by their Japanese captors would be an issue for years and years to come. Little did these men and women realize that the surrender documents signed on the USS *Missouri* and the treaty the Allies would later sign with Japan to officially end the war would preclude the former POWs from obtaining reparations from the government of Japan. The United States had effectively signed away the rights of thousands of American men and women who had been brutally treated by a government that saw all POWs as less than human and completely without honor for not choosing death over surrender.

Before Lt. Grace Dick and the other members of the 42nd General Hospital were returned to the United States, they would triage, treat, and evacuate more than twenty-six thousand American POWs.[21]

The American people welcomed the end of World War II but had little or no awareness that the POW veterans—men and women—held by the Japanese would be legally unable to obtain reparations from a government that had treated its prisoners of war much more cruelly and inhumanely than the government of Germany's Third Reich. Germany, unlike Japan, would eventually pay reparations to the POWs it held during the Second World War.

11

★

Many women served with the best in them in spite of circumstances so different from what they were reared under. They were brave, daring, honorable.
—Mary B. Tate, WAC

With the surrender of Japan, U.S. and Allied forces took on the mission they had anticipated and worked toward for years—the arrest, trials, and punishment of Japanese war criminals of World War II. Preparations for this mission had begun years earlier when the army established the Military Intelligence Service Language School (MISLS) at the Presidio in San Francisco, California, in 1941. After Japan attacked Pearl Harbor, MISLS was moved to Camp Savage, Minnesota, in 1943, and to Fort Snelling, Minnesota, in August 1944. In addition to 6,000 nisei (first-generation Japanese-American) men, 48 nisei women, 3 Caucasian women, and 1 Chinese-American woman were assigned to the school at its new home.

In November 1944, the first group of women arrived at Fort Snelling. The women had completed a five-week basic training course at Fort Des Moines, Iowa, or Fort Oglethorpe, Georgia. Depending on their backgrounds in the Japanese language, the women were placed at one of the three levels of instruction and were trained in document translation only, since women were not permitted assignments with direct combat units. It was not until March 1943 that the U.S. Army was authorized to recruit nisei women into the WAAC/WAC, and not until September 1943 that the exclusionary law against them was abolished. Some of the nisei women who volunteered for service in the U.S. military were still living in Japanese relocation centers when they were inducted into the WAC.

The decision to enlist in the WAC brought many personal challenges as well as the challenge to successfully complete a six-month Military Intelligence Service Language program that came wrapped in military discipline and long hours of hard work. Since the nisei women would not be assigned to direct combat units, they were not trained as interrogators of captured Japanese military. It would be the mission of nisei women to translate captured Japanese documents.

One of the first nisei women to enlist in the WAC was Yaiye Furutani, the daughter of Japanese parents living in Oxnard, California. Furutani was born in the United States and was educated in American schools. When she graduated from high school, her parents sent her to Japan to "learn Japanese traditions and enter an arranged marriage contract with a Japanese-born man." While in Japan, Furutani lived with her grandparents and attended courses in the traditional roles of Japanese women before being sent to a Japanese marriage broker. "I wanted to go to college right here in the United States, but my parents would not allow it. They lived by the old traditions and still do," Furutani recalled. "Anyway, I went to Japan but really rebelled against the old traditions. I liked the finer things, the art, the tea ceremony, etc., but did not like how they put women in subservient roles."[1]

In October 1941, Furutani arrived back in the States on her first visit since being sent to Japan. "I came back to America for a visit aboard a ship that arrived in October 1941," Furutani said. "It was one of the last ships to leave Japan before they attacked Pearl Harbor. I had decided to tell my parents that I was not going back to Japan. When Pearl Harbor was bombed and war was declared, going back to Japan was no longer an issue."[2]

When the federal government announced that all Japanese-Americans would be relocated away from the coasts, they allowed a window of time when people who had the money could choose where they wanted to relocate and move themselves. Furutani had a brother who was a physician practicing medicine in El Paso, Texas, and her parents decided to relocate the rest of the family to that west Texas city. "There were only three Japanese families in the whole town," Furutani recalled. "If you weren't a professional, you couldn't get a job. I volunteered for the WAAC, but they weren't taking any Japanese or Orientals at that time. Finally in March of 1943, Japanese-American women were allowed to enlist in the WAAC. In fact, they were actually recruiting Japanese-American women because they had figured out that nisei women could be very helpful in translating captured Japanese documents."[3]

Yaiye Furutani enlisted in the WAC and was sent to Fort Des Moines,

Iowa, for basic training. Furutani's enlistment so infuriated her mother that she disowned her daughter completely. "My mother refused to talk to me again. She is still alive today and still convinced that I joined the enemy army and helped defeat Japan. My father didn't feel that way. He was a maverick like me. He never intended to go back to Japan to live once he arrived in America." Furutani continued, "He went to school and became an engineer." Furutani was in the WAC Transportation Corps when her commanding officer asked her if she would like to take part in the Military Intelligence Service Language program. Furutani volunteered and was transferred to Fort Snelling to begin the six-month program.

"The program was really tough," Furutani said. "We studied Japanese all day and into the night. Between classes, we did a lot of marching. We even went through the same obstacle course the nisei men went through. It wasn't easy." When Furutani graduated from the MISLS, she was assigned to the Washington, D.C., area and worked at an annex. She was later assigned to Camp David, where she translated captured Japanese documents. "Some of the documents I worked on were captured Japanese papers that had been placed onboard the PT-109, John Kennedy's boat," Furutani recalled.

When the war ended, Furutani was asked if she would like to be included in a group of nisei WACs who would be assigned to General MacArthur. Furutani declined and was assigned to Fort Holabird, Maryland, where Allied forces were working with captured Japanese documents. Furutani was assigned to work with an Australian army major whose mission was to create a list of the members of the Black Dragon Society. "The Black Dragon Society was a secret membership group who were responsible for most of the atrocities committed by the Japanese between 1939 and 1945. The coded names listed in the captured documents were intended to hide the true identities of the members of the Black Dragon. Often a Chinese character had been added, along with the meaning of a name, which made the person's true name extremely difficult to find. The military needed the true names in order to track and arrest Black Dragon war criminals. These people were feared even in Japan before the war started. The Black Dragon was a ruthless and cruel society that would stop at nothing in order to achieve the world power they saw as Japan's divine mission. In some cases these men even ate the POWs they tortured and killed. And in many cases, they dissected their victims while they were still alive and fully conscious."[4]

215

*Japanese-American WACs en route to Japan to assist with cultural issues
at the end of World War II.*

Reference to the Black Dragon Society appeared occasionally in U.S. newspapers, mostly in brief articles that told of an agent's arrest in South America or the United States. The article that appeared in the *San Antonio Light* on 11 January 1942 gave information about the Black Dragon Society and how its members were feared in Japan: "Even children in Japan know not to stare at members of the Black Dragon Society." The article pointed out that the Black Dragon Society bragged that they were stronger than the Emperor and could overthrow him whenever they chose to do so.[5]

The following day, 12 January 1942, the *New York Times* published an article, "An Invasion of U.S. Termed Tokyo's Aim," that reported that a member of the Black Dragon had been arrested and a Black Dragon war plan set down in a book the agent was carrying. This article cited the book as listing the climax of World War II to be the invasion of the United States by the military forces of Japan.[6]

On 1 April 1942, the *New York Times* carried an article, "Black Dragon Acts Shown on Coast," that described espionage on the west coast by members of the Black Dragon. In January 1943, the *New York Times* reported that the Black Dragon was soliciting the help of blacks in the United States to assist the Japanese when they invaded the United States.[7]

When Mitsuru Toyama, the ninety-year-old leader of the Black Dragon, died in Tokyo, in 1944, the *New York Times* carried a long article outlining some of the history of Toyama and the Black Dragon. It referred to him as Japan's "unofficial emperor" and as a cold, calculating assassin. The article further described Toyama as one of the chief architects of World War II, the Russo-Japanese War of 1904, and of the 1894 Sino-Japanese War. The article made it clear that the Black Dragon Society was operating around the world and within the United States. The article also pointed out that the Black Dragon and Toyama were so feared in Japan that the Japanese press was reluctant to print his name and frequently printed asterisks in the place of letters spelling his name out. As if this were not enough, the article went on to describe Japanese prime minister Hideki Tojo as one of Toyama's right-hand men and said he had helped plan the 7 December 1941 attack on Pearl Harbor. The same article described Gen. Sadao Araki as one of the planners of the attack on Nanking and Pearl Harbor and included him in the inner circle of the Black Dragon Society.[8]

A 1945 *New York Times* article, "Araki and [Yoshihisa] Kuzuu Put in Tokyo Jail," told of two more members of the Black Dragon Society's inner circle being tracked down, despite coded membership lists, and jailed to await trial as war criminals.[9]

The work being done by WAC Sgt. Yaiye Furutani and other nisei WACs was paying off by stripping the cloak of secrecy away from highly placed and dangerous insider Japanese war criminals. Once again, U.S. military women were proving their worth and love of country by helping to capture and punish America's most dangerous and cruel enemies.

While active-duty military men and women took on the job of identifying and bringing war criminals to justice, former GIs were taking on the task of finding a civilian job and/or attending college or other training programs. Hundreds of thousands of veterans were discovering that finding work or pursuing higher education or training could be as tough as their years spent serving their country. The Selective Training and Service Act of 1940 had assured veterans that the employers they left when they entered the U.S. Armed Forces would be obligated to hire them back for their old jobs or its equivalent when Uncle Sam called them or when they voluntarily joined a branch of U.S. military forces. Readjustment was rough on the majority of veterans and held additional problems for women veterans.

For the first time in U.S. history, hundreds of thousands of women veterans would be returning to the world they had left behind in order to help America win a war and finding that their attitudes and goals had changed significantly compared to Americans who spent the war years as civilians. Employers who had struggled to fill positions during the war's early years were already cutting back on the number of employees working for them and had begun "letting female employees go" in order to rehire returning male veterans. The American society that had grudgingly accepted women into the workforce to replace men called into the military was even more eager to have those women leave the workforce and for Americans to "return to normalcy" of pre–World War II days.

Women were eager for those days too, yet there were many women who wanted the freedoms they had gained in wartime employment, or in a branch of America's armed forces, to continue after the war and into the future. Hundreds of thousands of women had learned that they could do much more than prewar America permitted, could learn and successfully perform work in fields prewar America had considered "men's work" or "not suitable work for a woman." Now with years of successful experience behind them, many women had learned to value an independence not known to them prior to World War II. Putting that genie back into the bottle would not be easy, and tens of thousands of women would fight the effort every step of the way or, with great disappointment and more than a little depression, would walk back into the cages forged for them by a society run by men and into strict gender roles designed to give men the greatest advantage in almost all areas.

That advantage would favor male veterans over female veterans in their efforts to readjust to civilian society, not because of any written law or regulation, but because postwar America—the media, employers, civil organizations, the Congress, many in the armed forces, and the Veterans Administration itself—did all it could to "return normalcy" to the United States, which meant returning women to their prewar gender roles and educational and professional limitations.

One group of women who had already made up their minds about their future was the thousands of military women who had decided earlier they would pursue a career within the armed forces. The individuals planning to follow this path were aware that for them to reach their goals, the military branches would have to get the Congress to agree to pass a law to establish permanent women's branches in each of the armed forces. That group faced a formidable obstacle. Many in Congress and the military wanted women out of the U.S. military without a women's reserve in any of the branches.

The navy made it clear that it wanted to establish a permanent Women's Reserve and keep a number of active-duty women in the navy and on the job. At the same time, the navy set the date for demobilization in accordance with the Selective Service Act of 1940, which set terms for service in World War II to be limited to the duration of the war, plus six months, as of 1 September 1946.

The army also wanted women as a permanent part of the army and was willing to voice its needs and plans before Congress and to the American people. Gen. Dwight David Eisenhower was one of the staunchest supporters of retaining WACs as a permanent part of the regular army. The women who had served their country in uniform during World War II were certainly deserving of such recognition. The record of their service was outstanding. They had flocked to the recruiting stations when the country called; had served wherever their nation needed them; had served overseas in combat theaters; had been decorated for courage, loyalty, and efficiency; and were still taking verbal flak from civilians who had spent the war in civilian clothes and might have visited a military post or base to see a son or husband, but had certainly never called such bases "home."

One well-respected group of civilian women was determined to see that women did not receive the same veterans' benefits earned by male veterans. As early as February 1945, a news article appeared reporting that the League of Women Voters was not in favor of women military veterans receiving Veterans' Preference in hiring in civilian life. Mrs. Robert Gordon, legislative chair of the League, spoke to groups concerning the unfairness Veterans' Preference would cause to those who had not served in the armed forces. "Discrimination against disabled veterans would be one of the possible effects of the Veterans' Preference under the Downey-Sherman Amendment." Mrs. Gordon also stated that Veterans' Preference would discriminate against all working women who had not served in the military—including the wives and mothers of male veterans who might need or want to work in order to help support their families. Finally, Mrs. Gordon stated that Veterans' Preference would allow the federal government to fill positions in police, fire, and social welfare departments, and even in the area of public health. For an added effect, Mrs. Gordon pointed out that Veterans' Preference would also discriminate against all veterans who were not disabled while serving their country.[10] In fact, all veterans received five points for Veterans' Preference, and disabled veterans, ten points.

It is apparent that Mrs. Gordon was not aware of women military veterans who had sustained disabling injuries or illnesses while serving in the armed forces. To many of these women, it seemed that their government and the American people were discounting their contributions to America's final victory over Germany and Japan. This attitude found its way into the fabric of post–World War II America.

Less than one month after the surrender of Germany, the *New York Times* carried an article addressing the return of military women to civilian life and the college experiences that awaited those who chose to seek higher education. The University of North Carolina set up a veterans' education committee with a special emphasis on the needs of women veterans. As part of their plan, the University of North Carolina would accept into a two-year program former army and navy nurses who wished to obtain a college degree. Military experience as an army or navy nurse would count toward a bachelor's degree.[11]

In the third week of September, another well-known group, the National Federation of Business and Professional Women's Clubs, worked through local business and professional women's clubs throughout the country to reach out to women veterans and offer help in becoming members of the local clubs and obtaining employment in civilian life.[12]

During the same month, Lt. Col. Anna Walker Wilson, former WAC director of the European Theater of Operations, currently stationed at headquarters in Washington, D.C., spoke for many women veterans and active-duty female personnel of the armed forces when she said, "We are the medium through which the knowledge and experience gained in the utilization of woman's power during this war can be preserved." Lieutenant Colonel Wilson continued, "We are also a nucleus, a framework, around which total mobilization of woman power can be effected in the next emergency." Lieutenant Colonel Wilson also sent a memo to the new Assistant Chief of Staff for Personnel, Gen. Willard S. Paul, asking that the date of 14 May 1946, the fourth birthday of the WAC, be designated to announce the permanent creation of a Women's Reserve within the U.S. Army and that membership in that reserve be offered to women who had been honorably discharged from the WAC.[13]

Months would pass before Generals Paul and Eisenhower would present this idea to Congress, making it very clear that the military actually wanted a permanent presence of WACs within the U.S. Army. This added another category to the War Department's intentions to make a permanent reserve for military nurses, physical therapists, and dietitians. As fall of 1945 moved on, more than a hundred thousand veterans, men and women, had returned to civilian life and registered in college programs.[14]

On 20 October 1945, Gen. Omar Bradley addressed a Disabled American Veterans' conference and asked that the best possible care, supplies, and equipment be provided to returning veterans. The general pointed out that there were more than 16,000 veterans missing one limb, and 900 of that group were missing more than one limb. Bradley emphasized that there were more than 2,000 blinded veterans in need of special care if they were to live fulfilled lives and continue to give their country 100 percent effort in contributing to the nation's future. The general stated that cutbacks in wartime medical training had left the country with a shortage of physicians, nurses, and health care providers. He made it clear that in order for the Veterans Administration to obtain more medical personnel, Congress had to allot more money to pay medical care providers better salaries as an incentive to transfer to the Veterans Administration Medical Centers. The next speaker at the convention, Sen. Edwin C. Johnson of Colorado, was quick to point out that "the country owed its first obligation to disabled and handicapped veterans."[15]

In late October 1945, Barnard College announced that it would be admitting women veterans beginning in the spring session starting in February 1946. Veterans had until 24 November 1945 to submit their applications.

In November 1945, the military announced that by 1 December 1945, 1,000 WAC officers and 20,000 enlisted women would be eligible for discharge. The navy reported that between 17 August 1945 and 25 November 1945 they had discharged 24,267 WAVES, both officers and enlisted women. As of 27 November 1945, 13,050 enlisted women and 658 female officers had been discharged. By December 1945, newspapers were carrying stories concerning the increase in the number of veterans, men and women, attending colleges. The number of veterans attending colleges in New York State grew by 385 percent during 1945.[16]

The tens of thousands of military women returning to civilian life when World War II ended did not lack for advice as to what they could do to help America "return to normalcy"—that blissful condition when an individual knew exactly what society expected from him or her. The rules were clear and wiggle room was almost nonexistent. In fact, it had taken the Japanese attack on Pearl Harbor on 7 December 1941 to move the nation into an emergency that demanded the contributions of women outside the home in order to achieve victory over the Axis powers of Japan and Germany.

Now, with the war won, it was time for those women and American society to "return to normalcy"—to reinstate and encourage the adoption of pre–World War II standards, gender roles, and mores. Even before they returned to life outside military bases, female soldiers, sailors, marines, and coast guard personnel were required by their branches to attend military classes on what was expected of them after they were discharged. At four separation centers on large military posts, soon-to-be-discharged military women attended classes on what would be expected of them when they transitioned to civilian life. The first thing the military stressed was the absolute necessity of replacing their military bearing with the civilian standards and mores that had governed their pre–World War II lives and established its strict gender roles. World War II had created an anomaly that a consensus of society felt was needed in order to attain victory and preserve Western civilization and culture.

The national consensus was now at a very different place and planned carefully for America's "return to normalcy." An essential part of that plan called for American military and civilian working women to put away the roles and standards that had dictated their lives during the war years and to identify once again with the standards and gender roles of pre–World War II America. Military instructors informed the women that it was time to become "ladies" again and "to clean up their language and mannerisms" that, although okay for life in the armed forces, would never do in a postwar America.

The very nature of a world war had created a strange paradox within American society. America needed its women to work outside the home and inside the U.S. Armed Forces, if America and Western civilization were to be preserved. Again, the situation was much like the one in the settlement of the American West when women fought and worked side by side with men—and on their own when conditions warranted—to establish the towns, farms, and societies that would grow into America's future cities, agribusinesses, and social and financial institutions. Women's roles had always expanded when a situation or emergency demanded their help, and when the situation or emergency was resolved, women's roles had likewise contracted and returned to the standards in place before such an expansion became a necessity.

That "return to normalcy" to the pre–World War II standards and mores that existed before Pearl Harbor was attacked on 7 December 1941 was about to happen again, but this time hundreds of thousands more women had journeyed beyond their prescribed gender roles and had discovered abilities, talents, and strengths they had not known in the "normal" prewar years. Hundreds of thousands of women from all over the country had awakened to the fact that they were more than someone's daughter, wife, mother, or sister. They were, in fact, individuals: intelligent, capable, strong, dedicated persons in their own right who had accomplished work and reached goals they had never dared dream of before America's entrance into the Second World War. Hundreds of thousands of women had discovered that they could make it on their own in life; they could learn, work, dream, and support themselves without being married or depending on the males in their families. That knowledge was a heady wine, and it would take a gigantic effort on society's part to put that genie back into the bottle fashioned by a nation and institutions with a strong paternalistic bent.

One young U.S. Army Nurse returning to America after more than three years of living and working and being bombed and shot at by the enemy was Lt. Frances Miernicke. "Frenchie," as she was called by her friends, was irate when young male soldiers at a relocation center told her and other returning army nurses that they needed to clean up their language and become ladies again. "We had never stopped being ladies," Frenchie said. "The very idea that there was something wrong with us because we had been just behind the front lines caring for our wounded GIs was ridiculous. I was the only woman on my surgical team and the men treated and watched over me as though I were their sister." She rolled her eyes and continued, "The implication was that our military experience made us less than acceptable in the postwar society America wanted to return to."[17]

Without realizing it, Frenchie had identified the thousand-pound gorilla in the room that waited to transport returning U.S. servicewomen "back to the future" so that returning U.S. male servicemen could have the best of all possible worlds. That world would return them to a future where everything old was new again. Women would return to the narrow gender roles and prescribed opportunities the pre–Pearl Harbor world had valued and considered the "normal" state of things that God and Nature had intended.

In this natural state, men would still be the heads of households and would still have a monopoly on running government, business, industry, medicine, higher education, the justice system, the news media, veterans' organizations, the U.S. Armed Forces, and the church. Women had had the right to vote for twenty-five years, yet were without equal opportunity on the playing field of life and had made little or no political progress— only eleven women had been elected to Congress by 1945. The Equal Rights Amendment (ERA) had been drafted in 1923 and subsequently introduced as a constitutional amendment, only to be buried and die year after year in congressional committees. Without a strong political organization and women understanding what was truly at stake, the ERA would continue to be satirized by "real women" who knew what God and Nature had intended for all women and who trusted in the kindness of the male strangers who ran federal, state, and local governments. Like Blanche Dubois in *A Streetcar Named Desire*, the majority of American women had been so conditioned by their environment, school systems, and the narrow band of goals considered appropriate for them that most did not even question the fairness of a society that declared females second-class citizens from the moment the doctor in the delivery room announced, "It's a girl," to the time that girl reached the age at which male children were permitted to become altar boys and was told that girls and women were not permitted to participate as servers in religious services; nor, by virtue of their gender, were they permitted to become priests, deacons, ordained ministers or rabbis, and so on into adulthood.

The "logic" that is still cited for their exclusion was the fact that "God had sent his only *son*, Jesus, as the redeemer of mankind," and he had appointed only male apostles to run his church. This meant that males were better representatives of Christ, since they most resembled the incarnation of Jesus. There were, of course, some girls and women who dared to question this second-class citizenship both in America and in their churches—they were labeled malcontents and "not real women." Later such labels would expand to include "lesbian" and "man-hater." The major premise that supported this kind of reasoning was that no real woman would question the role God had ordained her to fill, and with which secular states heatedly agreed.

The second benefit white males would maintain by the return to pre–World War II standards was that American society would bend over backward in order to help and support male veterans and to help them take advantage of the opportunities available to them because of a benefit granted to them for serving their country in World War II and marked with the invisible words of an ignored paradox: these benefits can be used as legal tender in the pre–World War II society the American future had returned to for normalcy's sake.

Perhaps a question that needed to be asked in 1945 was how can women veterans who have gone back to the future of pre–Pearl Harbor years use a benefit granted to them when, as residents of a parallel world, everything they did in the U.S. Armed Forces helped reach America's victory in World War II; yet, nothing they did while serving their country in the military had any impact on broadening their prescribed gender roles or expanding the breadth of opportunities available to women in the world the "return to normalcy" had assigned as their past, present, and future home. Women had joined the military from a world desperate to do all it could to defeat an enemy intent on destroying their future and vanquishing the history of their past as Americans. They had been sent back to that future and to an America that saw pre–Pearl Harbor America as the natural and God-given norm to live by and that would reach a silent consensus to ignore, to leave undocumented, and to exclude from oral traditions and stories of World War II, the proud and courageous history these women lived in every theater of operations during America's participation in that war.

The effects of this unspoken decision to cast out the history of American military women during World War II had devastating effects on the way women veterans of that war saw themselves and on the perception of all future generations of Americans and how those generations would perceive women for decades to come. The conscious decision of American historians not to include the history of U.S. military women of World War II in the history books on World War II is a travesty of justice and true scholarship that has helped keep women as second-class citizens in their nation's eyes; has made it more difficult for women to attain the civil rights and privileges of U.S. citizens; has helped keep the Equal Rights Amendment from becoming part of the U.S. Constitution; and has robbed countless women military veterans of the gratitude, honor, and place in the national memory they have earned.

It has robbed millions of American girls of women role models who were courageous and dared to be pioneers in a field and at a time when they had to fight every step of the way to serve their country and to win equal benefits and privileges for women in the armed forces. The American people as a whole were also robbed of their history and the weight it might have given to civil rights issues; to questions of military careers for women in the U.S. Armed Forces; and to the disgrace of sexual assault against military women by military men, with little or no due process for the victims or consequences for the aggressors. In short, it is the sincere belief of the authors that knowing the history of U.S. military women of World War II would have made a dramatic difference in debates concerning the need for and ratification of the Equal Rights Amendment and would have changed the percentages of women in the flag ranks of today's military and in the halls of America's Congress.

The battle to return to yesterday and make that yesterday America's future also played out in the nation's newspapers and other news media. It is well to remember that newspapers of the 1940s had much higher readership numbers than newspapers of the late twentieth century and that stories that concerned what was happening to veterans ran almost daily. The *Evening Bulletin* in Philadelphia published an article in November 1945 that discussed some of the problems facing women veterans. The article pointed out that even the absence of a military uniform would have a serious effect on how women veterans saw themselves and how they were viewed by other Americans. The article stated that the majority of women veterans had not made concrete, realistic plans for the lives they would lead after World War II. This lack of postwar planning, the article said, was particularly true for military women who were returning from tours of duty overseas in the European, Mediterranean, and Southwest Pacific Theaters.[18]

Military personnel in those theaters of operations were virtually isolated from the issues being discussed on an almost daily basis by Americans living and working on the home front. Unfortunately, the isolation, combined with America's desire to return to the prewar status quo, did not serve women veterans well if they were thinking about going to or going back to college.

In fact, the return to the "utopia" of pre–World War II America dampened the higher education plans of any American woman, whether a military veteran or a working woman, who helped supply the nation's war efforts and who had helped to keep the home front together for the men fighting the war. Whether the Rosie the Riveters intended or thought the returning male GIs would push almost all women out of their wartime jobs and that the United States, as a whole, would not look favorably on women veterans or factory workers' keeping their jobs is debatable. No matter what these women believed concerning what would change when the "boys" returned home, each was about to witness it for herself. Most of the nation's newspapers and magazines bombarded the public with suggestions/rules by consensus as to what military women would need to do in order to conform to "the return to normalcy."

At that time, there were many articles addressing the question of women veterans readjusting to civilian life. The January issue of *Glamour* magazine carried an article on the "changes women veterans need to make: hair style, clothing, posture." The article suggested that discharged military women use their $300 mustering-out pay to buy a new civilian wardrobe.[19]

On the last day of 1945, the *New York Times* carried an article titled "Crowded Colleges Reject Veterans: Hundreds Turned Away Daily in City." The crisis drew a response from an American Legion post and the city's mayor-elect, William O'Dwyer, who stated that "The United States is headed for the greatest educational log-jam in history."[20]

By 8 May 1946, the federal government actually warned colleges not to bar women from admission and warned that if colleges did not stop the practice, the federal government would pursue the matter through the federal courts.[21]

By the beginning of the fourth week in May, academics and other citizens were coming forward with pros and cons on the subject of barring women from college until veterans could be accommodated. Dr. Charles H. Gray, president of Bard College, decried the practice, stating that "granting the emergency, to make a distinction between students on the basis of sex is to revert back to the ideas of the Victorian Age and is not defensible even in an emergency." The article also referenced a *New York Times* forum entitled "Should Women Stay Away from College to Give Veterans a Chance?"[22]

A former editor of the army weekly *Yank* magazine and a former Army Air Corps sergeant spoke in favor of barring women from colleges and stated that "If limitations must be set, the women should remain away in favor of veterans." Two women on the forum panel stated that women should make the "sacrifice" of staying away from colleges until the veterans were taken care of and use the time to think about what goals and plans they wanted to set for themselves for two or three years down the line.[23]

In a study entitled "The Woman Veteran," dated 31 August 1946 and conducted by the Research Service Office of Coordination and Planning, Veterans Administration, Washington, D.C., the results indicated that "many of the women were experiencing the same readjustment problems as the enlisted men separated around the same time . . . and that, in addition, women veterans had to deal with problems and bias against women in the military and women veterans." Individual women veterans shared many of the same problems in readjustment.[24]

In the midst of all the readjustment problems, and the exclusion from colleges and certain employment, the U.S. Navy decided it wanted a permanent Women's Reserve and asked WAVES to remain in the service if they were in jobs the navy felt needed to remain staffed by WAVES. The U.S. Army was also fighting for a permanent presence of WACs within the army. An all-out push for legislation to establish a permanent place for WACs, WAVES, and Women Marines in the U.S. Armed Forces began on 2 July 1946.

12

★

The issue is simple—either the Armed Services have a permanent need for women officers and enlisted women or they do not. If they do, then the women must be given permanent status. . . . I am further convinced that it is better to have no legislation at all than to have legislation of this type.

—Rep. Margaret Chase Smith

I n January 1946, the *WAVES Newsletter* published by the Bureau of Naval Personnel, Navy Department, in Washington, D.C., carried a story, "Legislation Bill Introduced to Permit WAVES in Post-War Navy." The story informed its WAVE readers that "in his final report to the Secretary of the Navy, Fleet Admiral Ernest J. King, USN Chief of Naval Operations included the statement, 'The Navy is extremely proud of the work done by the Women's Reserve. It is our plan to keep a WAVE component in the Naval Reserve. . . . If Congress approves, we will seek to retain on active duty a reasonable number of WAVES who wish to remain and who may be needed in certain specialties.' " Admiral King went on to point out that the navy knew from experience that these women could be useful in various navy jobs including communications and the Medical Corps.[1]

On 12 February 1946, the U.S. Army asked women to stay in the service. It seems that the navy and the army had learned a valuable lesson concerning the contributions WAVES and WACs could make to the U.S. Armed Forces during war and peace and were anxious to have them on a permanent basis. WACs were already serving with the U.S. Army of Occupation in Germany and Japan, making up, in part, for manpower lost when hundreds of thousands of soldiers were discharged from the military and living as civilians.

The army took steps immediately to form a committee to gather data and design and write legislation that would be presented to Congress for the establishment of a permanent WAC Corps in the army. To expedite these plans, Gen. Willard S. Paul assigned a group of consultants, including two WAC officers, to have the proposed legislation ready to present to Congress within ten days. The WAC officers assigned to this project were Lt. Col. Emily C. Davis, staff director at the Headquarters of the Army Ground Forces, and Lt. Col. Mary A. Hallaren, who was recalled to Washington from Europe to take up her new duties as deputy director of the WAC. Colonel Hallaren would have the collateral duty of overseeing the process of shepherding the plans for a permanent WAC through the major commands in the army, through the Congress, and onto the president's desk to be signed into law.

Col. Mary A. Hallaren, 5 September 1950.

The planned legislation hit its first stumbling block when Col. Westray Battle Boyce, Director of the WAC, added a sentence allowing women who had served in the Women's Army Auxiliary Corps to receive credit for their time spent in that organization and suggesting that that time be counted in commuting service time and experience when looking at candidates for promotion and retirement. Colonel Boyce was not asking for back pay, only that the time spent in the WAAC would count in active-duty computations. This request seemed justified since, two years earlier, army nurses, dietitians, and therapists had been given credit for their time as civilian contract workers, either with the Army Nurse Corps or as reserve nurses with the American National Red Cross.

In preparation for the reentrance of women into the army, General Paul had questionnaires mailed to all army commanders in the continental United States and throughout Europe and the Pacific, asking for their candid opinions and suggestions concerning the usefulness of WACs in peacetime and the inclusion of WACs as a permanent corps in the U.S. Army. The questionnaires returned to Washington with an overall positive endorsement. During this time, army women worked on a separate bill to obtain permanent status for women serving in the WAC.

On 29 March 1946, Rep. Carl Vinson of Georgia "introduced HB 5919 to amend the Naval Reserve Act of 1938, so as to establish the Women's Reserve on a permanent basis." Representative Vinson was particularly displeased with an amendment added by Rep. Margaret Chase Smith of Maine calling for regular as well as reserve status for WAVES,

Senator Margaret Chase Smith
in her Air Force Reserve uniform.

concerned that it would kill the bill entirely. Vinson must have been at least a little surprised at Smith's response: "Either the Navy needs these women or it does not."[2]

It was VADM Louis E. Denfeld who approached Representative Smith and asked for her help in arguing and shepherding HB 5919 through Congress and into law. Representative Smith had already taken a public stand in favor of granting permanent regular and reserve status to WAVES and added that the Women Marines would be added and receive the same benefits as the navy women.

In the meantime, WAVES and Women Marines did not sit idly by waiting. CAPT Joy Bright Hancock, on 26 July 1946, started a campaign to learn all she could on how best to present positive arguments for the passage of the bill and the best ways to respond to arguments against the bill's passage. Armed with the authority conveyed on her by her new position, Hancock sought the aid of CAPT Ira Nunn, USN, and a member of the Judge Advocate General Corps to help her anticipate, analyze, and counter the arguments of the bill's opponents. Add to this the new prestige of being director of the WAVES, and Captain Hancock had new weight to add in favor of the bill's passage.

The Women Marines were no slackers either and set about organizing reunions of the women who had served in World War II. When the various groups met at twenty-two locations across the country, they were asked to compile lists of former Women Marines, their addresses, and, if they had married, the name of their husbands so they could be located quickly when the bill passed and became law. These lists would be important since married women more often than not took their husbands' names, and lost touch with friends and contacts they had made while serving in the armed forces under their maiden names.[3]

For all intents and purposes, married women lost their individual histories when they signed on the dotted line and said, "I do." Future historians and old comrades would find that "individual footprints" of former military women were effectively wiped out or abruptly stopped when a woman veteran became "Mrs. John Jones." In fact, it might be said that a woman veteran left her footprints in two worlds whose link effectively disappeared in city hall or at the altar. When one adds to these facts that neither the armed forces, the Veterans Administration, nor the military service organizations kept or maintained statistics and records concerning military women and/or women veterans, it is easy to understand why women veterans were difficult to identify and locate in the civilian world. Very few women veterans of World War II maintained a link with the armed forces after discharge or even touched base with the Veterans Administration. Society and history said little or nothing concerning women's military service and veterans' status, a fact that hastened their disappearance from our national history and our nation's memory.

The great majority of women veterans found themselves living in a postwar world where prewar values were still the norm for gender roles, where "women veterans" was an oxymoron even within the Veterans Administration and at Veterans Day parades, where women veterans stood on the sidelines and cheered on the male veterans "who had won World War II." In this prewar values–postwar world, the fight for a permanent place for the WACs, WAVES, and Women Marines was joined, and like all good soldiers facing a pivotal battle, they were "staging" in preparation for the combat to come.

As January 1947 dawned, Colonel Boyce was fighting to raise the standards required of WAC applicants and to keep the WAC alive until the pending legislation passed and the women's branches were made a permanent part of the United States Armed Forces. On 9 January 1947, the Women's Reserve of the navy was authorized to form volunteer training units. On 14 February 1947, former Women Marines gathered to celebrate the fourth anniversary of the U.S. Marine Corps Women's Reserve at twenty-two locations around the country. In New York City, former director of the USMCWR, Ruth Cheney Streeter, addressed the group and said that although she hoped the services of the USMCWR were never needed again, if they were, a nucleus of former Women Marines would be the perfect group around which to build and expand the new permanent organization.[4]

On 15 April 1947, the WAC bill, WAC Integration Act of 1947, HR 3054, was introduced by Rep. Walter G. Andrews of New York, chairman of the House Armed Services Committee, and Senate Bill 1103 was introduced by chairman of the Senate Armed Services Committee, J. Chandler Gurney of South Dakota. (Since most congressional committees had been reorganized at the beginning of the Eightieth Congress, these two committees heard bills that affected the entire U.S. military, and not just a specific military branch.)

On the following day, 16 April 1947, the bill drafted by Col. Florence Blanchfield, Chief of the Army Nurse Corps, and Gen. Norman Thomas Kirk, the Surgeon General, An Act to Establish a Permanent Nurse Corps of the Army and Navy and to Establish a Women's Medical Specialists Corps in the Army, passed Congress, was signed by the president, and became Public Law 80-36. The bill's course to the president's desk had not been without obstacles. The bill was originally introduced by Rep. Edith Nourse Rogers on 25 July 1946, together with a companion bill in the Senate. The bill was not acted on and died when Congress adjourned on 2 August.

When the Eightieth Congress convened in January 1947, Margaret Chase Smith introduced a similar bill. Smith's bill called for the same permanent commissions. When the proposed legislation reached the subcommittee hearings, the American Nurses Association recommended that the bill be amended to include eligibility for male nurses to be commissioned in the U.S. Army Nurse Corps. Since both the army and navy brass were against this move, the amendment failed, as did another amendment to combine the Army and Navy Nurse Corps into one corps.

One of the most contentious battles over amendments took place when the subcommittee of the House Armed Services Committee recommended that the age limit for army and navy nurses be raised from the current twenty-six for a first-time applicant and thirty-four for an applicant with previous service in either of the corps. The idea of accepting older women into the two military nurse corps brought a quick reply from Major General Kirk. Kirk argued that the upper age limits should not be raised since women did not last as long as men. He went on to say that operating room nurses were already too old to do the job when they reached thirty-five. Kirk argued that it was better to accept nurses at a young age so that the army would get its money's worth once they retired them at age fifty, when they were no longer effective. General Kirk concluded his argument with the following statement: "We want to have these people young when they come in, so that we can, without costing our Government too much, retire them when they are 50 years old, when they are no longer effective. Under the old program when there was no retirement age for nurses, the Nurses' Home looked like an old women's home. Many of the nurses were unable to do war nursing. Jobs had to be found for them. They had to be kept on the payroll, and they served no useful purpose."[5]

On 28 June 1947, the *New York Times* carried the story "Permanent Status for WAVES Is Asked; Navy Includes Women Marines in Bill." Senate hearings began on the WAC Integration Act on 2 July 1947. Army and navy officials testified in favor of the bill's passage. The following day, the *New York Times* carried a story "War Chiefs Urge Women's Services," subheaded, "Eisenhower and Nimitz Ask Permanent Status for WACS and WAVES, Praise Record."

On 15 July 1947, the subcommittee combined the WAC and WAVES bills, which would grant the women's corps a permanent place in the regular military, into the Women's Armed Services Integration Act of 1947, S 1641. On 16 July 1947, the Senate Armed Forces Committee approved the bill. On 23 July 1947, the full Senate voted unanimous approval and sent it to the House of Representatives.

The next day, Eisenhower sent a hand-carried letter to the chairman of the House Armed Services Committee, urging rapid action to approve the legislation. The House subcommittee took immediate action and convened a hearing on the same day they received the bill from the Senate. Eisenhower's words had a strong effect on members of the subcommittee. If the man who led American troops to victory in Europe said the country needed women in the armed forces, surely the Congress would be hard-pressed not to recognize the need. Eisenhower had written: "The women of America must share the responsibility for the security of this country in a future emergency as the women of England did in World War II."[6]

Colonel Hallaren thought the bill would pass Congress quickly. She was not expecting what happened next: The subcommittee voted to postpone further hearings on the bill until January 1948. The decision caused many WACs to consider leaving the corps and returning to civilian life.

In the July 1947 *WAC Newsletter,* Col. Mary Hallaren challenged WACs currently on active duty to remain in the corps. Of all her words to them, the following stirred their emotions, spoke eloquently, and stayed in their memories: "Breaking the trail has always been harder than following it."[7]

In February 1948, hearings began on the Women's Armed Services Integration Act. New and unexpected opposition to the bill came from a source that had its roots deep in the slander campaign of World War II. Despite the fact that flag-rank officers of World War II not only backed a permanent place for the women's corps within the military but testified that the women's corps were absolutely essential to the security of America, there existed a sub-rosa group of less senior military officers who felt as strongly against the women's corps being given permanent status as Eisenhower, Bradley, Nimitz, and Halsey felt in support of the Integration Act. The opposition became known as "the cloakroom campaign" since its base operated behind the scenes without directly confronting their senior leaders.

The cloakroom set supported the idea that because America was the only nation that possessed atomic weapons and the means of delivering them, war could be prevented without having to create and support a larger standing military. On the opposite side were those who firmly believed that the saber-rattling of the Soviet Union would more than likely require a peacetime draft and the women's corps to free up as many men as possible for direct combat assignments. Convinced that they knew best, the opposition employed a new argument against the passage of the bill.

They argued that before women's corps were granted a permanent place in the regular military, it would be necessary to observe and study the work of these women to make certain that they could perform in a peacetime military force. After all—the twisted logic went—just because these women's corps had proven themselves in the emergency conditions of war did not mean they could operate successfully in the military during peacetime. Therefore, any decision on a permanent place for women's corps in the regular and permanent U.S. military should be postponed until that peacetime study was organized, carried out, analyzed, and the results studied carefully.[8]

This new tactic took Colonel Hallaren and others fighting in favor of permanent status by complete surprise. All of a sudden, the logic used to keep women out of the military in World War II, that women had no place in a wartime military and definitely no place in combat situations, was turned on its ear. It was, the opposition said, the peacetime military in which women's corps had no useful purpose, and women should be considered for inclusion only during military emergencies, when they could replace military men for combat assignments. Clearly, those opposed to women in the military and women's corps being given permanent status in the U.S. Armed Forces could pivot 180 degrees to tailor their opposition arguments to match the threat they perceived. If it were wartime, women should not be exposed to such stress as one experiences in the U.S. military when the very existence of the nation is at stake. And, just as clearly, in the minds of those who opposed the Integration Act, women were of doubtful use to the military during peacetime; before women's corps were made a permanent part of U.S. Armed Forces, observations and studies must be conducted to determine just how useful women could be in a military that was not facing a national emergency.

In short, those in opposition to the Integration Act did not believe that women would be an asset to the military during a national emergency nor in peacetime, and were willing to argue both sides of the fence if it appeared that one stand and not the other would serve them better in the current situation. Surely such Machiavellian flexibility could cause deceased logicians to spin in their graves and living logicians severe cases of indigestion.

When Colonel Hallaren heard the newest stalling technique, she was shocked. In a letter to a colleague, Lt. Col. Mary L. Milligan, Deputy Director of the WAC, Hallaren wrote, "This is a new development, for, you remember, neither the Senate hearing, nor the first hearing in the House gave any such indication. We expected we would have to defend the question, but we did not expect a block."[9]

The overt leaders of the block against the Integration Act were representatives Walter G. Andrews, chairman of the House Armed Services Committee, and Carl Vinson, the ranking minority member of the committee. They offered an alternative for women's service in the military, which they said would satisfy both the men in the military and the women who wanted to serve in the military. Their plan would allow women to sign up for ten, fifteen, or twenty years with the women's reserve and then sign up for active-duty positions. This would keep women out of the regular military and at the same time would not deny "woman power" to the active-duty force. Even better in the eyes of these opponents was that men would not have to compete with women for promotions in the active-duty force.

Colonel Hallaren and General Paul testified and explained to the committee how minor amendments would allow women to have regular permanent status "without jeopardizing men's promotions, retention, and retirement opportunities."[10]

On 3 March 1948 at an open hearing, representatives of the National

Association for the Advancement of Colored People (NAACP) argued for a nondiscrimination amendment to be added to the Integration Act of 1948. Representative Vinson responded, "Discrimination is forbidden by the Constitution and none can be practiced by the Armed Services." Therefore, in the eyes of Vinson, the amendment was unnecessary. Rep. Lyndon B. Johnson testified that a ceiling of 2 percent for women in the integrated U.S. military was too low and suggested that it be raised to 5 percent. Rep. Leroy Johnson of California questioned the idea of giving WACs access to allotments for their dependents and said it would lead to "wholesale support of husbands by servicewomen." Rep. Adam Clayton Powell Jr. of New York asked that the committee reconsider an amendment against discrimination by race. The Retired Military Officers Association recommended flag rank for the directors of the women's corps, while the National Council for Prevention of War opposed the Integration Act on the grounds that it would "militarize women" and in time of war would place them under "the President's excessive wartime powers."[11]

Other arguments included concerns that women might be drafted under the Integration Act. The fact that Congress and the president had planned to draft nurses for the Army and Navy Nurse Corps during World War II had escaped these people's attention. The nurse-draft bill had been passed by the House in March 1945 and sent to the Senate and was dropped only when Germany surrendered in May 1945. Another argument was that passage of the Integration Act might open the nation's military academies to women and turn West Point and Annapolis into co-ed colleges.[12]

On 23 March 1948, the committee, in a closed hearing, rejected the idea of regular status for women in the military and renamed the bill the Women's Armed Services Reserve Act of 1948. The committee passed the newly named bill by a vote of twenty-six to one. That one voice of dissention belonged to Rep. Margaret Chase Smith, one of eleven women in Congress at that time. Smith rose on the floor of the House and spoke her opposition to the gutted and newly named bill. "The issue is simple— either the Armed Services have a permanent need for women officers and enlisted women or they do not. If they do, then the women must be given permanent status. . . . I am further convinced that it is better to have no legislation at all than to have legislation of this type."[13]

When Representative Smith discovered that S 1641 had been placed on a calendar reserved for bills that were considered without controversy and would pass unanimously, she stopped the ramrod legislation. At that point, the executive for the Reserve and Reserve Officers' Training Corps (ROTC) Affairs in the Pentagon prepared a contingency program that would allow women to serve in the reserve and also gave them a way to continue their fight for regular status.[14]

On 29 March 1948, the *New York Times* printed a story, "Congress Prodded on Military Bill," that read in part, "It appeared probable tonight that by the middle of next month, the Senate would have a bill recommended by its Armed Forces Committee to establish a temporary draft to bring the Armed Services up to their authorized strength and to establish universal military training. These are two of the specific measures asked by President Truman in his special message to Congress two weeks ago on the growing threat of Communist Russia to peace and democracies everywhere."[15]

Three weeks later, on 21 April 1948, the bill reached the floor of the House, and was met by a Michigan representative who objected to the bill on the grounds that since officers who had combat experience were not accepted in the regular army, women should not receive commissions in the regular army. Representative Walter G. Andrews from New York expressed his objection to the bill more succinctly. This bill will "dish out Regular commissions to women" but not experienced men.[16]

The arguments continued when Rep. Dewey Short from Missouri rose and told the House that 8 percent of women in the service became pregnant and that women who were sick and developed disabilities associated with menopause caused great expense to the government, while Rep. Edward Rees of Kansas stated that the work done by military women should be done by civil service employees. In the bill's favor, Rep. Harry Sheppard of California argued, "Let the draft fill up the shortages which men alone can fill . . . but let us not take a man away from a farm, home, or school . . . to be a telephone operator. There are, and always will be jobs . . . women can do better." Rep. Lyndon Johnson rose to remind the Congress that every military leader was for this bill.[17]

Margaret Chase Smith lost no time in introducing two new amendments to the bill, the first to restore regular status, which had previously failed by a stand-up vote that did not record the names of the individuals voting "yea" or "nay," and the second to reduce the number of women on active duty at any one time. Both amendments were defeated.

The bill passed the House on 26 April 1948, and was forwarded to the

Senate, where it went to a Conference Committee for compromise. The Conference Committee requested additional information on marriage, pregnancy, dependents' allotments, and other benefits.

On 26 May 1948, the Conference bill passed the Senate unanimously and was sent to the House of Representatives. The House passed the bill on 2 June 1948 by a vote of 206 to 133, and on 12 June 1948, President Truman signed the bill into law. The Women's Armed Services Integration Act became Public Law 625.

The *New York Times* ran a story on 27 June 1948, "Women in Military Service Now Have Regular Status," which read in part: "The startling war-born idea of using women in the military services reached a full cycle last week when the enlistment and commissioning of women in the regular Army, Navy, Air Force and Marine Corps became law. The new law not only makes permanent the temporary reserve status accorded women during the war, but, in a far-reaching move, also gives them fully equal status with men in the regular military forces."[18]

To say that "the new law not only makes permanent the temporary reserve status accorded women during the war, but, in a far-reaching move, also gives them fully equal status with men in the regular military forces" is somewhat misleading if the reader believes that the "fully equal status with men in the regular military forces" means equal benefits and rights to go along with the "equal status." Under the Women's Armed Services Integration Act, women were eligible to serve in the regular active peacetime forces under very specific conditions. Those conditions were imposed only on women by virtue of their gender and continued many of the discriminating practices that would cause any thinking individual to question the use of the words "equal status with men." Those conditions were as follows:

1. Women can constitute no more than 2 percent of the total force.
2. The number of women officers can total no more than 10 percent of the 2 percent.
3. Promotion of women officers is capped above pay grade 0-3 (Captain/Lieutenant). Pay grade 0-5 (Lieutenant Colonel/Commander) is the highest permanent rank women can obtain. Women serving as directors of WACs, WAVES, WAFs, and Women Marines are temporarily promoted to pay grade 0-6 (Colonel/Captain).
4. Women are barred from serving aboard navy vessels (except hospital ships and certain transports) and from duty in combat aircraft engaged in combat missions.

5. Women are denied spousal benefits for their husbands unless they depend on their wives for over 50 percent of their support.
6. By policy, women are precluded from having command authority over men.
7. The coast guard is not included in this legislation, but a few SPARS remain in the Women's Coast Guard Reserve.[19]

In the end, the victory for military women in gaining permanent regular status was not the result of an "aha!" experience on the part of a military and a Congress that finally saw the justice and fairness women deserved as full citizens, but rather, like all the advances military women and women in general had gained throughout their nation's history, it came by necessity and in the face of a looming threat or national emergency, when the military and Congress could no longer deny that women were essential to victory, security, or mission fulfillment. It came because those who opposed it in Congress were not willing to face the anger of men who would be drafted to fill military jobs that women had volunteered for. It had come despite the fact that the nation and Congress appeared to have forgotten that women had already proved themselves in the settling of America, in the Revolutionary War, in the westward expansion, in the Civil War, in World War I, and on an even larger scale in World War II. The most current battle in the long march of American women toward full citizenship had been won—for the women themselves and for the nation as a whole. The nation would be a long time in claiming that victory, but American women were not willing to abandon the fight.

The summer of 1948 was a time of change for former military women in more ways than one. Colleges were out for the summer break and thousands of college students were making their way across the country to their homes, summer jobs, or in hopes of a taste of adventure before the school year started again. One of those students was Jeanne Holm, a former World War II WAC who had made up her mind to investigate what new opportunities would be available to WACs in a women's corps that had permanent and regular status.

In the spring of 1948, Holm and other former WACs had received a letter from the adjutant of the army asking if they were interested in returning to active duty. Holm had followed the instructions in the letter and had driven to Fort Lewis, Washington, for a physical examination that would be a prerequisite for any woman wishing to join the new permanent-status women's branches of the U.S. military. She completed the exam, filled out an application for a place in the new WAC, along with completing a postcard that asked the individual to check the box in front of the women's corps she was interested in joining. Holm checked the box in front of "Air Force–Regular," dropped the card in the mail, and promptly forgot about it.

When summer break was almost upon the colleges of the nation, Holm still had not heard anything from the army regarding an appointment to commissioned service with the Women's Army Corps. After spending the night in the Bachelor Officers Quarters at Fort Lewis at one dollar a night and hearing taps played, Holm was determined to sign up for the WAC Reserve, which she did the next morning before heading back to Lewis and Clark College in Portland, Oregon.

When the summer break started, Holm borrowed $600 from her grandmother and started out in her 1940 Chevy for Fort Lee, Virginia, to see if she could get into the active-duty WAC as soon as possible. Holm stopped along the way and picked up a friend, Evelyn Nicholson, who was also a former WAC training officer. Since money was a problem, the two women slept in the car each night. As they got closer to Fort Lee, both had doubts as to whether the current WAC company commander (CO) at Fort Lee, Lt. Col. Elizabeth C. Smith, would remember either of them from the World War II WAC. "It had been 1942 or 1943 since we had seen her, and we both hoped she'd recognize and remember us," Jeanne Holm said.[20]

When they reached Fort Lee and parked their car near the WAC CO's office, Nicholson decided to wait in the car while Holm went to talk to Colonel Smith. Holm had no more than introduced herself to the WAC sergeant at the desk and asked to speak with Colonel Smith when she heard a voice from the CO's office call out, "Junior! Is that you?" Holm turned to her left and looked into the eyes of her former commanding officer. "Everyone called me 'Junior' during World War II because I was the youngest WAC in our group," Holm said. After telling the colonel that she wanted to get on active duty as quickly as possible and being told that the colonel would make a call immediately and get her stationed right there at Fort Lee, Holm got Nicholson out of the car, and the two sat in front of the colonel's desk while she called the Pentagon.[21]

Several hours later, Holm and Nicholson parked outside the Pentagon and made their way to Col. Mary A. Hallaren's office. Hallaren, the third director of the WAC, swore the two women in to the active-duty WAC, had their orders cut, and sent them back to Fort Lee, where they would begin their new duties.

When six months passed and Holm's name had not shown up on the appointment list for newly commissioned WACs, she asked Colonel Smith if she would check on things for her. The next day, Holm received a message to report to the CO's office, where Smith gave Holm the information she had been told. "You are not going to receive a commission in the army," Colonel Smith told Holm. "You are in the Air Force, and they will not release you." Holm was shocked, and the memory of the postcard she had filled out months before flashed into her mind. "I didn't have the courage to tell her, or anyone else at the time, that I had actually checked the air force as my preference of women's branches when I made out the postcard." In a matter of days, Holm reported to Lackland Air Force Base in San Antonio, Texas, for duty.[22]

Holm had traveled to Lackland with several air force officers who were on their way to the Erding Air Depot in Germany, near Munich. When the sergeant asked her where she would like to be stationed, Holm chose Erding. When the sergeant responded that no one wanted to go to Erding because it was a large depot where supplies of all kinds were dropped off and held until they were needed somewhere, Holm stuck to her guns, and in several days she was on a plane heading for Erding.

"When I got to Erding, a WAF sergeant asked me what assignment I'd like to have," Holm said. "She told me that I could choose among maintenance officer, supply officer, and wing war plans officer." Holm grinned. "I said, 'Oh that sounds nice.' I had no idea what it was, but I knew that the wing was in the 'big show.' " Holm paused briefly. "They put me in this little office that was off the wing commander's office. It was a real dog-and-pony show. I had these classified, top secret documents, and all this stuff. I had to get clearances. They gave me a temporary top secret clearance so I could start my job. Well, here I sat with these top secret war plans, and the Russian blockade of Berlin had started. We were expecting the Russians to just walk in one day and take us all prisoners. We were the most forward base in Europe. It was exciting." Her eyes twinkled with mischief. "I had mentors, but they didn't know any more about war plans than I did. I soon realized that war plans were a matter of logic—sheer logic. I was taking the plans that came down from our higher headquarters and assigning responsibilities to our wing. We were the only air depot in Europe. We were expecting war at any minute."[23]

Holm went on to describe how she carried out her job. "I would get the instructions to our base for supporting all the air force in Europe, take those instructions out, and incorporate them into our plans. I used sheer logic and drafted up the war plans we would use. Our depot was right outside Munich and I had friends who were army there. I found an infantry friend there and told him my problem—that we didn't know how to do base defense. We got together and talked about our best possible path of action. We decided that it was best to get all base personnel to Switzerland as soon as possible." Holm paused. "There weren't many dependents because most of them had been evacuated because of the Berlin Airlift—but there were still some who had remained behind. Anyway, I and a couple of the male officers got into a jeep and explored all the roads in the area and beyond. We got all the old German maps we could find and drove all over the back roads until we found the best escape routes. Then I put them into the war plans. They were going to evacuate all of the WAFs along with the remaining dependents, and I said, 'No, the WAF is military. They need to stay here and do the jobs assigned to them.' The men had no idea what those jobs were, but they knew the WAF wasn't leaving unless the entire base was evacuated."[24]

Captain Holm had begun her air force career in one of the most potentially dangerous areas in the world. The USSR had been rattling its saber in an attempt to intimidate Allied forces to get out of Berlin and out of Germany. Its intention for American troops was to get them to quit Europe entirely. The stage had been set for World War III, and the United States, Britain, and France were as determined to stay as the USSR was determined to force them to pull out entirely. Berlin and Germany had an excellent chance to become ground zero for World War III should it break out.

The USSR had begun its intimidation efforts in 1947, in response to the United States and the United Kingdom combining their zones in Germany and naming the new creation the "Bizone." The Soviets considered the act a bilateral agreement between the two powers and announced that it would no longer allow Allied trains to travel on or through the Soviet Zone. The United States, Britain, and France tried to negotiate with the Soviets in order to lift the rail blockade they had imposed.

On 20 June 1948, the three Allied powers replaced the Reichsmark with the deutsche mark in an effort to wipe out the huge black market. The USSR considered this action on the part of the three powers equivalent to a declaration of war. On 24 June 1948, the Soviets announced that all surface transportation through the Soviet Zone was off-limits.

The next day, 25 June 1948, the British started bringing in supplies by air. One day later, 26 June, the U.S. Air Force launched Operation Vittles and began an around-the-clock airlift to supply citizens and military personnel living, working, or stationed in Berlin. At the time, there were only two Allied airfields in the Allied zones, Tempelhof in the American Zone and Gatow in the British Zone. France began the process of building an airfield in the French Zone. Food and coal were at the top of the list of essential supplies. Coal was the only source of energy available to Berliners. The United States Air Force and Navy Air Transport Squadron Eight (NATSRON 8) brought 4,760 tons of supplies into Berlin every day. Planes landed every three minutes, maintaining a constant stream of supplies by air.

The only U.S. Navy woman stationed in Europe at the time was LT Margaret E. Carver, stationed with Navy Air Transport Squadron Eight at Rhein-Main, Germany, near Frankfurt. Lieutenant Carver was assigned to

LT Margaret Carver, USN, outside VR-8 Squadron headquarters, a Quonset hut at the end of the runway at Rhein-Main Air Base in Germany in 1948, after her first trip to Berlin to see the destruction there.

the base as personnel and administrative officer and coordinated the navy's air transport role for NATSRON 8 with the U.S. Air Force during the Berlin Airlift.[25]

Margaret E. Carver was born in Bonham, Texas, in 1919. She attended Bonham High School and graduated from North Texas State University in Denton. She joined the U.S. Navy on 7 December 1942 and took her officer training course at Smith College in Northampton, Massachusetts. One of her first assignments was as a recruiting officer in Olathe, Kansas.[26]

At the end of August 1948, the French air field became operational and the French joined the United States and Britain in negotiating with the Soviets. Those negotiations were discontinued in September 1948 when the USSR realized that without an all-out war, it could not move the Allied powers out of Berlin. At this point, the Soviets began planning for a Soviet-backed government in East Germany, while the United States, France, and Great Britain realized that a cold war with the Soviet Union had already begun.

The truth of that realization and the fact that America would need a strong and well-equipped military to meet any challenges that might arise from that cold war probably did more to get permanent status for the U.S. Women's Military Corps than all the words of testimony from General Eisenhower, Admiral Nimitz, and other flag-rank officers from World War II combined. The military leaders of World War II—most of them—had learned the value of woman power in keeping America secure from any would-be enemy intent on harm. However, Congress and the American people had come to understand this reality only from seeing the looming threat of the Soviet Union.

The old saying, "Knowledge can be taught, but wisdom comes only through experience" was certainly in play in this instance. It could only be hoped that the lessons learned would transfer to the future. Unfortunately, hope would not prove enough, and the same mistakes made in the past would be made again and again.

13

★

If the country is going to have the proper respect for its women, the women have to take a share of the responsibility.

—Assistant Secretary of Defense Anna M. Rosenberg

It might seem that a nation that had fought a world war less than five years before would be good at picking up clues that signaled the real possibility of an act of war capable of robbing the world of precious peace it had fought so hard to secure. After all, the Allied powers had seen the dangers posed by the Soviet blockade in Berlin and had discerned the larger Soviet goal of pushing all the Allied powers out of Germany, and the United States out of Europe. How could it have failed to see a looming threat facing South Korea, an Asian country only hours away by air, from the defeated Japan that American troops had occupied since Japan had signed the surrender documents on 2 September 1945?

One might even suspect that the Soviet Union, which once signed a nonaggression pact with Japan and which had been kept out of Japan by the use of the first two atomic bombs ever dropped on an enemy nation, might still crave a foothold in the far eastern neighborhood of the Japanese islands. Somehow, however, the United States had missed the threat that would pull the American people and the United Nations (UN) into a prolonged war in a country the majority of Americans had never heard of and could not locate on a map.

One might even have expected a nation that had stood firm in the face of Communist threats in Germany would be aware of the possibility of such a threat in the nations so close to the Communist countries of China and North Korea. The threat, however, was not perceived by an America that had rushed headlong into the security of a pre–World War II value system that had returned women to the gender roles approved of in pre–World War II America. Male World War II veterans and male civilians longed for a return to pre–World War II societal values and institutions such as churches, schools, factories, and businesses.

That desired state of bliss, that thick cocoon blocked the realities of the real world in favor of the hoped-for world of yesterday. That combination of denial, delusion, and wishful thinking had returned America and the American people to a place where they stood in peril of war once again—even if only a very few could see the new storm clouds on the horizon.

The storm broke on 25 June 1950 when 134,000 North Korean troops crossed the thirty-eighth parallel and invaded South Korea. The United States had approximately five hundred military advisers stationed in South Korea to aid the country in rebuilding itself after fifty years of Japanese rule. In addition to the Korean Military Advisory Group of the American military, American dependents numbered approximately 635, of whom 277, nearly half, were children. Along with the military dependents, there were six missionary nurses and one female physician working in the country. The only American military woman stationed in Korea on 25 June 1950 was U.S. Army Nurse Capt. Viola B. McConnell.

It quickly fell to Captain McConnell to arrange for and manage the evacuation of 635 people from Korea to Japan. Complicating the evacuation was the fact that many of the children were suffering from such problems as diarrhea, pneumonia, chicken pox, and one strangulated hernia that required regular nursing care. In addition, there were four pregnant women, each of whom was within days or hours of her delivery date, and two elderly ladies, one of whom was frail and one suffering from advanced arthritis.

Captain McConnell was aided in her nursing duties by a nurse who was the wife of an army man, a United Nations registered nurse, the six missionary nurses, and the missionary physician. The group was loaded aboard the Norwegian freighter *Rheingold,* which had only twelve berths for its passengers. McConnell designated the twelve passenger berths as an infirmary for the most ill who were in need of regular nursing care. The *Rheingold*'s crew of seven men gave up their quarters for use by evacuees. Of the seven, one volunteered help on a regular basis during his off-duty hours. The remaining crew was a disgruntled bunch who complained about the added hardships they faced because of the evacuees' three days and two nights' journey to Japan.

McConnell's only criticism was reserved for several of the dependents, women who complained about the conditions and lack of privacy aboard the *Rheingold*, and the six crew members who grumbled about how inconvenienced they were by the dependents and the unscheduled journey.[1]

The last five days of June 1950 were busy for the UN and the United States, both of which were working to develop plans to stop the North Korean advance into South Korea. Between 27 and 30 June, the UN authorized member nations to send troops under UN command to Korea to stop the invading force and throw the North Koreans back across the thirty-eighth parallel. The UN also designated President Truman as the UN negotiator for peace, and Truman quickly ordered U.S. ground forces to South Korea to engage, stop, and drive the enemy back into North Korea.

On 1 July 1950, Congress extended the recently created draft for an additional year and activated reserve and National Guard units for twenty-one months of service. For the second time in less than five years, the United States had been caught unprepared for the military response required of it.

U.S. Task Force Smith, comprised of approximately 500 combat soldiers, arrived in Pusan, a city at the southern tip of South Korea, and made their way north to meet and engage the more than 100,000 well-armed and prepared North Korean troops. Task Force Smith moved quickly since they were not weighed down with tanks, artillery, or other heavy weapons. Their rapid forward motion was brought to an abrupt halt when they met the tanks, artillery, and other heavy weapons carried and employed by their North Korean opponents. The results were disastrous for Task Force Smith and the U.S. military. North Korean troops stopped, flattened, rolled over, and left behind the dead and wounded U.S. combat troops and continued their advance and capture of Seoul, the South Korean capital.[2]

Between July 1950 and the end of June 1951, 67 WAC officers and 1,526 enlisted WACs volunteered for the WAC active-duty force. Another 176 WAC officers were added through an involuntary recall to active duty. Other women's corps were ordered to increase their numbers by activating their reserves.

The WAC Reserve had grown considerably since 1948, when its total number was zero, to 1950, when its numbers stood at 4,281. The U.S. Army had identified twenty thousand jobs where WACs could be used instead of male soldiers.

Recruiting former WACs to active duty was not going well, and there were multiple reasons why this was so. First, the WAC was trying to recruit from outdated personnel records and incomplete training and qualification records. Some of the WACs had married and their names had changed on public records, census reports, in telephone books, and in church directories, making it very difficult, if not impossible, to locate former WACs who had served under their maiden names. Some married former WACs had one or more children, and either it was impossible for them to qualify for the corps given dependent qualification rules, or they had no desire to devote their time to the army instead of to their families. Some of the unmarried former WACs had moved to a different neighborhood, different city, or even a different state, and locating them was not easy. A number of former WAC officers did not have the yearly physical examination required for WACs to remain current for reentry into the WAC. Annual physical exams for former WAC officers in the Ready Reserve had been discontinued in 1947 because of a lack of willingness on the army's part to spend money for something they might never need.

Finally, Secretary of Defense Gen. George C. Marshall ordered steps be taken to bring the records of former military women up to date, categorize former WAC units, and to simplify and speed up current procedures for making and processing WAC applications. To make all recruiting more effective, the number of WAC recruiters was raised from 90 to 240. By 30 June 1951, WACs on active duty had risen to 60 percent of their 2 percent ceiling of 17,000, and lacked only 6,000 more recruits to reach that goal.[3]

In mid-August 1950, the WAC's and the Army Nurse Corps' need for additional members had grown to the point where the chief of each requested an involuntary call-up for their organizations.

On 25 August 1950, the army suspended the rule that allowed women who married while serving in the WAC to use that marriage as a means of obtaining a discharge from military service.[4]

World War II–era members of the women's corps must have been surprised when they picked up the *New York Times* and read "Army Issues Call for 1,644 Women," and to read further to find that they might well be one of the women the army wanted back on active duty with the WAC. The article explained that for the first time, the U.S. Army had ordered the involuntary call-up of women reservists for active duty with the WAC. The article went on to say that the involuntary call-up would also include women reservists of the U.S. Army Nurse Corps, the Women's

Medical Specialists Corps, and a number of enlisted women who had served as hospital corps WACs. The women called to active duty under this order would serve for twenty-one months on active duty or for whatever period the law authorized.

The article also pointed out that several months earlier, the navy had issued an order for the involuntary call-up of WAVE hospital corps reservists. That order also recalled 1,110 army nurses needed to staff health care facilities at expanding army training centers. The same order provided a deferment for any female reservists enrolled in an academic program at a college or university, but only until the end of the current academic year.

U.S. Army nurses and army medical specialists were ordered to report by 29 November 1950. Nor was the army ignoring physicians. The article explained that there were plans for an involuntary call-up of physicians and that they would be expected to report by December 1950. As of 26 September 1950, the United States Air Force (USAF) had not issued an order for the involuntary call-up of women Air Force Reservists for the Korean Conflict. (Until 1958, the Department of Defense referred to the Korean War as the "Korean Conflict" or as "a policing action." Pressure from veterans' groups led to the official label, "Korean War.")[5]

Martha J. Briley was one of the former World War II WACs called up for active duty during the Korean War. Briley had enlisted in the WAAC in 1942 and transferred to the WAC when it was formed in 1943. During her military service, Briley served as a dental technician assigned to Fort Hancock, New Jersey. She later trained as an automotive mechanic and was stationed in the motor pool at Camp Pine, New York. Her third stateside duty station was at Fort Sam Houston in San Antonio, Texas, as a classification and assignment specialist. Briley also had served overseas in New Guinea and, when discharged at the end of World War II, was awarded two Bronze Stars for outstanding service to her country. When Briley was recalled to active duty in October 1950, she was assigned to Munich, Germany, where she served until the end of the Korean War, when she received her second honorable discharge from the WAC.[6]

Another former WAC who was involuntarily recalled to serve during the Korean War was Ruth Marschall. She was born in Connecticut and joined the WAAC on 18 August 1942. After basic training at Fort Des Moines, Iowa, Marschall was stationed at Fort Custer, Michigan, where on 1 September 1943 she was sworn in to the WAC. After overseas training at Fort Oglethorpe, Georgia, Marschall sailed to Brisbane, Australia, on

25 June 1944. On 31 August 1944, Marschall was transferred to Hollandia, New Guinea, with the U.S. Army Service of Supply. On 26 November 1944, Marschall was transferred to Tacloban City, Leyte, Philippines. In March 1945, Marschall was stationed in Manila, where she remained until 1 August 1945 when she sailed back to the United States and landed in Seattle, Washington, on 17 August 1945. Two days after the surrender of Japan, Marschall transferred to Fort Dix, New Jersey, and was discharged from the WAC on 26 August 1945. She was awarded the Asiatic-Pacific Campaign Medal with three battle stars, the Philippine Liberation Ribbon, and the WAC Service Medal. Marschall joined the Army Reserve and was called up for active duty shortly after North Korea invaded South Korea. She was assigned as cadre at Fort Lee, Virginia, and later served in Information and Education at Fort Kilmer, New Jersey, from 1951 until June 1953, when she was discharged from the WAC for the second time.[7]

For Marie L. D'Elia, born in Pennsylvania on 10 May 1909, enlisting in the WAC seemed like the "right thing to do." She joined the WAC in 1943 and remained on active duty until 1948. D'Elia arrived at various army posts in the States before being sent overseas and serving in Rheims, France, where she worked as secretary to a Catholic army chaplain and an insurance officer. D'Elia was transferred to Yokohama, Japan, where she worked as a classified documents clerk. Her last assignment overseas was as the secretary to the chief of staff at General Patton's Headquarters in Bad Mülheim, Germany. She was discharged in 1948. D'Elia was recalled to active duty with the WAC in 1950. She received her second WAC discharge in 1966.[8]

Among the World War II WAVES who were recalled for active duty during the Korean War were Ruth Margaret Sullivan and Margaret Driscoll. Ruth Margaret Sullivan was born in Massachusetts on 25 November 1913 and joined the WAVES on 22 December 1942. She attended Officer's Training School at Smith College in Northampton, Massachusetts. Sullivan's first duty assignment was as communications officer and manager of the mail sub center and classified correspondence office. Sullivan was later transferred to Washington, D.C., where she worked as the communications officer for the Chief of Naval Operations. She was discharged from the navy on 10 November 1945. She remained on active duty until 1954 when she received her second discharge from the navy and remained in the Ready Reserves until 1966 when she was retired from military service.[9]

For Margaret Driscoll, born on 5 September 1908, World War II would open up truly new horizons. Driscoll joined the WAVES in 1943 and attended Officer's Training School at Smith College. After graduation, Driscoll was assigned to North Island and Moffett Field, both in California, to study and work as an aerologist. Driscoll was part of a blimp crew whose job was obtaining information to allow accurate weather predictions for the U.S. fleet and naval air stations. Driscoll also employed "free ballooning" in her work as a navy aerologist. She was discharged from the navy in 1948 and, as a member of the Ready Reserve, was involuntarily recalled to duty as a naval aerologist in 1950 during the Korean War. Driscoll was ordered to Lakehurst, New Jersey, and later, to Washington, D.C., where she was assigned to the crew of a blimp. The crew's mission was to gather information needed for the accurate prediction of weather impacting the U.S. fleet and naval aviators. Driscoll was discharged for the second time in 1954 and remained in the Ready Reserve until 1968.[10]

If Winifred Parker Ralston thought she had seen the last of active military duty when she married U.S. Army officer Dale Ralston on 6 April 1947, she was wrong. True, at that time, her military career in the WAC ended because of her marriage, but the change in policy by 30 June 1950 removed marriage as a disqualifier for active duty for women with prior military service, and the Ready Reserve included former military women, married or not.[11]

Winifred "Parky" Parker had joined the WAAC in 1942 and graduated with the twentieth officer candidate class at Fort Des Moines. She was stationed in Rochester, New York, as a recruiter, and then transferred to Utica and the entire northern New York Recruiting Command. In between the two recruiting assignments, Parker had a three-month tour of duty on the commanding general's staff at Fort Richardson in Anchorage, Alaska, followed by a three-month tour of duty at Fort Hayes in Columbus, Ohio, where she opened the officers' club.

Seven months after they were married in April 1947, Dale Ralston was transferred to Tokyo, Japan, as adjutant to Colonel Griener for four years, and his wife accompanied him. When the Korean Conflict started on 25 June 1950, Winifred Parker Ralston was recalled to active duty from the Ready Reserve, sworn in by Col. M. Clarke, and assigned to Camp Drake, near Tokyo, where, for the next three years, she processed soldiers on their way to Korea. Parky Ralston's final separation from the army took place at Fort Leavenworth, Kansas, just two years short of a twenty-year retirement because she was overage in grade.

In 1989, Parky pointed out that as a child in England during World

War I, she and her classmates were taken once a week to a Red Cross location where the students helped roll bandages for soldiers at the front and in hospitals. It was a justifiably proud Winifred Parker Ralston who pointed out, "So you see, I can say that I served in every war in this century, except Vietnam."[12]

One of the most pressing needs in the Korean War was for graduate registered nurses to treat wounded and ill soldiers. Army and navy nurses in the Ready Reserve were among the first to be involuntarily recalled to active duty; however, many volunteered for active duty before the recall was ordered. The first group of fifty-seven U.S. Army Nurses arrived in Pusan on 5 July 1950. The nurses set about working with their MASH (Mobile Army Surgical Hospital) units, MASH 8054 and MASH 8055. Both MASH units were composed of all-volunteer army nurses, physicians, and medics. MASH units, which usually consisted of a 100-bed field hospital and an auxiliary surgical team, were enlarged to 200 beds due to the number of casualties suffered in the early months of the Korean War.

On 6 July 1950, the Twenty-fourth Infantry Division landed in Pusan and headed north to engage the enemy. MASH 8055 traveled about 100 miles north to set up and care for patients in Taejon. The MASH worked close to the front lines, and when the infantry retreated, the 8055 followed and set up in any buildings available, including churches, schools, and barns.

Gen. Douglas MacArthur was named commander of the United Nations Forces on 8 July 1950 and selected Maj. Genevieve Smith to become the chief nurse for Korea. Smith was a native of Epworth, Iowa, and had served as an army nurse in the Second World War. She had remained in the U.S. Army Nurse Corps and was currently the chief nurse of the 155th Station Hospital in Yokohama, Japan, with a retirement set for 1951. Like the good soldier and army nurse that she was, Smith accepted the assignment and prepared to leave for Korea with other member of MacArthur's advance party.

In the early morning hours of 27 July 1950, the three-man aircrew, twenty-two male passengers, and one female passenger, Maj. Genevieve Smith, boarded a C-47D for a flight from Haneda, Japan, to Pusan, Korea. At 4:00 a.m., the aircraft taxied approximately 200 yards to the end of runway 15. At 4:05 a.m., the aircraft was cleared for takeoff and became airborne. At 4:16 a.m., Tokyo received the following transmission from flight 6423, "Climbing over point—clouds thin 2,800 feet, 1,000 feet thick." At 4:21 a.m., the aircraft hit two moderate bumps, "the lights got real dim, went out, and then came back on again to dim."[13]

The engineer was standing near the entrance to the front compartment, shining a flashlight on the baggage and then around the passenger, Major Smith, on the right-front seat on the right engine. The lone survivor of the crash, Sgt. Sasaki reported, "The plane gave a violent jerk and the engines were running very loud." The pilot applied more power to the engines and the safety belts of four or five passengers seated on the right side of the plane either came loose or broke. Suddenly, the aircraft seemed to snap sharply to the left and flip onto its back. The tail section of the plane broke off and Sergeant Sasaki of the U.S. Army, who was seated in the last seat on the right side, was sucked out of the aircraft and remained conscious only long enough to pull the ripcord on his parachute. The plane spun or spiraled into the ocean below, killing all twenty-five people still onboard. Both they and the plane were listed as missing.[14]

When Sergeant Sasaki regained consciousness, he was plunging downward through cold, salty water. When he shot upward and broke the surface of the water, his life jacket, or Mae West, as they were called, kept him above the surface while he struggled to get free of his parachute and managed to gain his freedom. Eight hours later, a Japanese fishing boat picked the sergeant up and took him to Oshima. From there, Sasaki was taken to a hospital. His testimony to the military board investigating the crash helped fill in information that would never have been known had Sasaki not survived the accident. The C-47D was one of many old and worn-out planes from World War II and the Berlin Airlift that had been pushed out of retirement by the Korean Conflict.

It would not be the last accident involving World War II–vintage aircraft that had seen their best days before the Second World War ended. Nor would Maj. Genevieve Smith, ANC, be the last nurse to die in a plane crash during the Korean War. Military nurses who served overseas in time of war had never had it easy and had received little credit, if any, in the pages of history or from the branches of the armed forces.

The Pentagon had decided that WACs would not be stationed in Korea. They could be stationed elsewhere in the Pacific, but not in Korea itself.

The USS *Consolation*, a navy hospital ship, arrived in Pusan Harbor on 16 August 1950. Two additional navy hospital ships were being readied in the United States, the USS *Repose* and the USS *Benevolence*, and would be sent to Korea as soon as all restoration work and shakedown trials were completed. Meanwhile, army and navy flight nurses were being trained at Gunter Air Force Base, a satellite field of Maxwell AFB in Alabama. The course, normally nine weeks, would last only six weeks, and graduates had a better than fifty-fifty chance of being sent to evacuate wounded and ill troops from Korea to hospitals in Japan, Hawaii, and the United States.

Navy nurse LT Bobbie Hovis summed up the training and work thoroughly when she said, "We were worked to death just trying to complete the whole course in six weeks, as opposed to nine. We were either studying or flying, or we went to bed to get some sleep if we could. . . . We went through cold-weather, jungle, water, and desert training."[15]

From 25 August 1950, the USS *Benevolence* T-AH13, a veteran of the Pacific Theater, had been reactivated for the Korean Conflict and was returning from a shakedown cruise in pea-soup fog. It was close to 5:00 p.m., and there were 505 civilian crew and passengers, including fif-

U.S. Navy Nurses receive congratulations upon graduation from flight nurse training in 1950; ENS Bobbie Hovis on right.

teen navy nurses returning from the Farallon Islands, just off the coast of northern California. The *Benevolence* AH-13 was rammed midship by the freighter SS *Mary Luckenbach*. She listed and sank in approximately thirty minutes, forcing passengers to abandon ship and wait in the water for rescue. Twenty-three people aboard the *Benevolence* died, including the prospective captain of the hospital ship and one navy nurse, LT Wilma Ledbetter from Chillicothe, Texas.[16]

ENS Ruth Martin was one of the fifteen navy nurses aboard the *Benevolence* on that day, and she recalled the collision, the sinking, and the rescue of the survivors. Ensign Martin described standing on the top deck and looking out over the ship and the ocean. She thought about how beautiful the *Benevolence* was and how upbeat everyone onboard was as the ship headed back to Mare Island and passengers began to get ready for dinner, which would be served at 5:00 p.m. Martin left the top deck and walked toward the nurses' head, or lavatory. She remembered the moment when the *Benevolence* was struck by the freighter. "Suddenly, I heard a loud crashing sound and felt a severe jolt which almost knocked me off the toilet. My first thought was that one of the boilers probably had blown up." Martin went on to say that she and the other nurses in her group had heard that a boiler had blown up on the USS *Repose* during its shakedown cruise.[17]

Martin thought she should get her Mae West, which was one deck below, and ran down the ladder and along the next deck to her cabin. The ship's deck and the cabin were at a forty-five-degree angle, which made pulling her life jacket out of the locker difficult. Martin was putting the life jacket on when the loudspeaker crackled a message telling everyone to get their Mae West and report to their lifeboat stations. Martin and other navy nurses were wearing their life jackets when they arrived at their lifeboat station. The ship had listed so far to the port side that it was now necessary to walk with one leg on the deck and the other on the bulkhead. Crew members grabbed the nurses' hands and pulled them up on deck. As the ship leaned even farther onto its side, people walked upward so they could stand on the starboard side of the ship.

A medical officer and a dental officer had gone into the ship and retrieved two eight-foot rafters and some rope. They tied all the nurses together around the waist and tied the rope to the rafters. "We slid down the ship and into the water."[18]

The life jackets had straps that were supposed to be brought from the back, through the legs, and fastened in the front to help keep the jacket in place. Since all the nurses were wearing uniforms with skirts (not slacks) and pumps, they did not fasten the straps, and consequently the life jackets rode up into the nurses' faces when they hit the water.

When an army tugboat came on the scene, the crew threw a rope to the group of nurses and men holding on to the two rafters, pulled them to the side of the boat, then tried to pull them onboard. Finally, the tugboat crew realized that the nurses were tied together and several men jumped into the water to cut the connecting ropes. This done, they pulled the women on board, one by one. One of the nurses, LT Wilma Ledbetter, died of an apparent heart attack on the deck of the rescue vessel.[19]

On her many flights from Korea to Travis Air Force Base in California, Navy Flight Nurse LT Bobbie Hovis frequently got a look at the USS *Benevolence* lying on her side beneath the water some six miles beyond the Golden Gate Bridge in San Francisco Bay. Hovis remembered, "You could see that beautiful ship lying on her side, with the red cross, the green stripe, and the white hull clearly visible in the sunlight. Seeing her there . . . knowing she was never going to be salvaged was heartbreaking."[20]

In the early morning hours of 15 September 1950, ten UN warships lay off the shore of Wolmido Island at the entrance of Inchon Harbor in South Korea. The battle group consisted of six U.S. destroyers, two U.S. cruisers, and two British cruisers. The battle group carried U.S. Marines who were to go ashore on Wolmido and destroy enemy gun emplacements and other equipment capable of inflicting damage on a 261-ship group that carried thousands of army troops. These troops were to storm ashore at Inchon Harbor, secure the area, march to Seoul, engaging North Korean troops on their way, and cut off the supply line of the North Korean Army.

When Gen. Douglas MacArthur had first announced his plan to invade at Inchon, the majority of U.S. Army and Navy officers who would be charged with carrying the plan out thought it would not be successful and listed their concerns to General MacArthur. Their first concern was the height of the tides inside Inchon Harbor. The tides were the highest on record in the world at twenty feet. The actual high for the Inchon invasion on 15 September 1950 was predicted to reach thirty feet.

Compounding the difficulties of a landing on Inchon was the fact that when the tide started to go out, it did so quickly, at seven miles an hour, and could leave ships and boats stranded on the mudflats at low tide. One ship left on the mudflats during low tide could block every other craft attempting to reach the Inchon shoreline. Troops who landed onshore could find themselves alone and without a supply line to land equipment, supplies, and additional troops.

Those soldiers would be dependent on the Fourth Field Hospital for their first medical care if wounded or ill. The Fourth Field Hospital and the 8055 MASH were supposed to go ashore on the first day of the invasion, and not being able to reach shore because of a stranded ship blocking the harbor could cause casualties and loss of life both in the battle group and onshore.

As if that were not enough, the gun batteries on Wolmido Island could easily reach Inchon Harbor and the city itself. Any stranded ship on the mudflats would be a sitting duck for enemy fire. It would be up to the marines to land on Wolmido, clear the gun batteries, and take control of all enemy facilities on the island. The enemy guns would be particularly deadly to any ship or landing craft at the Flying Fish Channel, the narrow entrance to Inchon Harbor. Another problem was that Inchon was the second largest city in South Korea, and the beachhead, therefore, was in the middle of a sizable city of 250,000 people.

Despite the difficulties of securing Wolmido, the marines completed the mission in less than one hour and raised the American flag over the island. The marines then turned on the beacon in the Wolmido lighthouse, and ships in the battle group used the beacon to enter the Flying Fish Channel. The marines scaled the fifteen-foot seawalls that ringed the harbor, and helped troops land with their equipment and supplies. Among the troops going ashore on the first day were the U.S. Army Nurses, physicians, and medics of the Fourth Field Hospital and the 8055 MASH unit.

One of the nurses with the Fourth Field Hospital was Capt. Anna Mae McCabe, a veteran of the China-Burma-India Theater of Operations in World War II. Brig. Gen. Anna Mae McCabe Hays remembered that landing. "We went in with a thirty-foot tide. I remember climbing down the side of the ship on a rope ladder and then getting into a landing craft," Hays said. "The marines had gone in first and secured the area as far as it could be secured, then the army troops went in, and then we entered." She paused briefly. "That was probably the worst war for me because it was so cold. We had little water and firewood, and few supplies. . . . It was so cold, we wore heavy pile jackets under our scrub dresses in the operating room."[21]

McCabe had experienced an entirely different climate during World

War II. After landing in Bombay, India, taking a train on a narrow-gage railway, traveling by truck, then by a flat-bottom boat up the Brahmaputra River, and finally by truck again, McCabe's unit arrived at Margherita, Assam, India. They got off the truck and onto a road that was deep with mud. "And here we were in the middle of the jungle, wearing heavy woolen uniforms. We had gotten some material in Bhatti, a town where we stopped for several days because the [train] conductor had family there and wanted to visit them."[22]

Another army nurse with the Fourth Field Hospital was Capt. Katherine Jump, the chief nurse of the unit. She recalled her landing and time at Inchon. "We got off the ship and they started putting up tents right away, and we had our hospital up in no time. . . . Talk about women's lib. We in the army were liberated long before they started talking about all this stuff. We carried everything with us. We did everything ourselves that we possibly could." Jump went on to speak about her time with the Fourth Field Hospital. "At night, you could see the fire [tracer bullets] and you could hear it. . . . They put casualties on these makeshift buses with litters, and they were brought to us that way. We'd always get all of these wounded at sundown. The very serious ones were flown in on helicopters . . . flying in and all of us running out there to help get those really critical ones in as fast as we could. We'd triage them and find out who should be moved first . . . that was day in and day out like that for a long time."[23]

On 19 September 1950, a military transport plane carrying eleven navy nurses who had been assigned to the naval hospital in Yokohama, Japan, crashed when taking off from Kwajalein in the Marshall Islands, where it had made a refueling and rest stop. Just one week later, a C-54D carrying Capt. Vera Brown, ANC, and twenty-three passengers and crew were killed when their plane crashed near Ashiya, Kyushu, Japan. Captain Brown was a flight nurse assigned to the 801st Medical Air Evacuation Squadron.[24]

The 121st Evacuation Hospital arrived in Inchon just behind the marines and the Seventh Infantry Division. Lt. Margaret Gibson, a twenty-four-year-old army nurse from Birmingham, Alabama, shivered as she walked up the Inchon beachhead. She and the other army nurses with the 121st Evacuation Hospital had landed in Inchon wearing only the summer uniforms the army had issued them for their tour of duty in the bitter and worsening subfreezing temperatures of Korea.

Gibson had graduated from St. Vincent's Hospital School of Nursing in Birmingham, Alabama, when she was just twenty years old—too young to take state boards for her nursing license. Several nurses in her class belonged to the U.S. Cadet Nurse Corps and Gibson learned that the Army Nurse Corps (ANC) might accept her as a graduate nurse with no postgraduate experience. At that time, the Navy Nurse Corps (NNC) only accepted nurses with at least two years' experience, which made the ANC look like the perfect answer to a military nursing job she could get right now. After talking to army recruiters, Gibson learned that she could be part of a National Army Nurse Corps recruiting campaign by taking the ANC oath on one of the most popular radio programs of the day.

Kate Smith, a nationally recognized singer and radio personality, had a reputation for doing all she could to help the military nurse corps recruit the nurses they needed to care for wounded and ill GIs during World War II. It was difficult to find an American who did not recognize Smith's strong and emotionally packed rendition of "God Bless America." That song had become an "unofficial national anthem" during the Second World War, and the woman most identified with it had become an "unofficial national treasure." Few, if any, Americans did not know Kate Smith's theme song on her radio show, "When the Moon Comes Over the Mountain," and even fewer did not hum along when its rousing notes and patri-

Entertainer Kate Smith.

U.S. Army Nurse Lt. Margaret Gibson, 1949.

otic prayer loomed from the 1940s radios, records, or newsreels shown in movie theaters.

And so Margaret Gibson raised her right hand in unison with hundreds of other nurses being sworn in to the ANC over Kate Smith's national radio program.

"I became a 'Kate Smith Army Nurse,'" Gibson said proudly, sixty years later, the pride just as obvious then as it must have been on that memorable day in 1946.[25]

"General MacArthur had told all of us in Korea that we would be home for Christmas," Col. Margaret Gibson Duckworth remembered, "but that didn't turn out to be true." December and Christmas found the 121st Evacuation Hospital in Wonsan, a town on Korea's east coast. "Not more than ten minutes after we had disembarked in Wonsan, the adjutant announced that there were about five thousand Chinese army troops in the area and gave us instructions on what to do if the Chinese attacked our hospital." Duckworth's eyes seemed a little brighter as she continued. "If the Chinese attacked from the north, we were to do thus and thus; if they attacked from the west, we were to do something else. The one thing we were to do, no matter the direction from which a Chinese attack came, was to defend ourselves and our patients." She leaned forward in her chair. "How we were supposed to do that was never made clear. None of us—nurses, doctors, or medics— had guns, so just how we were to defend ourselves was a mystery." Duckworth continued, "Word got back to our people still in Inchon that the 121st Evac had been annihilated, but the Chinese didn't see us and we were never attacked.[26]

"We went to Hungnam, near the Chosin Reservoir where the marines and the army were in an awful battle against the Chinese and North Koreans. We treated a lot of frostbite of hands and noses. We were watching all of these big American tanks going by our hospital, and heading south, but we didn't have orders to leave, so we stayed." Many American troops had been marching for days with little sleep, rest, or food. "They were tired, hungry, and cold," Duckworth remembered. "They died. They froze in their tracks."[27]

The 121st finally got orders to go to Hamhung on the Sea of Japan

*Sgt. Billy Gibson, Fifth Marine Division, USMC, visiting his sister, U.S. Army
Nurse Lt. Margaret Gibson, assigned to the 121st Evacuation Hospital
in Hamhung, North Korea, winter 1950.*

and board the USAT *Ainsworth*. "An LST took us out to the ship," Duckworth said. "I never had heard of a Jacob's Ladder. We were told we had
to climb up the rope ladder—several stories—to the deck. You didn't have
to know anything except to hold on to the ropes as tight as you could
and keep climbing. The crew on the LST [landing ship tank] told us to
keep climbing until we got to the top. 'If you slip,' they said, 'you'll end
up in the Sea of Japan!' When we got to the top, these navy men were
dressed in their blue suits, white shirts, and shined shoes, and we were in
fatigues and combat boots. We hadn't had a bath in at least forty days
because you didn't bathe in weather below forty degrees." Duckworth
smiled, "We must not have smelled too good because when we got to the
top, the navy men were supposed to help us climb onboard. They gave us
their hands but turned their heads away. We couldn't smell one another
because we all smelled the same. She looked serious. "It had gotten down
to sixty degrees below zero more than once while we were taking care of
patients at the 'Frozen Chosin.' I and a lot of other people nearly froze to
death.[28]

"We didn't have flush toilets in the middle of a combat zone. At least
we had moved up from a trench in a field to multiple-holers with seats.
One of our sergeants cut up his pile jacket and put the material around

the seat to make it a little more comfortable." She grinned and added, "It pays to have a good sergeant. Always take care of your sergeants and they will take care of you."[29]

Her smile disappeared and her eyes filled with tears that she wiped away with the back of her left hand. "The second-worst thing I experienced in Korea was the below-zero temperatures. The absolutely worst memory I have is of the marines and soldiers getting killed—they were getting killed all the time we were there. I don't like thinking about it, because it starts pictures of them back then, flowing through my mind—pictures that I'd rather not see." She took a deep breath and continued. "One of the good things I gained from my experiences in Korea is that I don't care about material things very much. I was told way back when I was a kid to be careful about what I owned because everything had a maintenance price attached to it. Every single thing! I don't want to pay that price anymore. It isn't worth the effort once you have learned what's really of value."[30]

She leaned forward again and her eyes seemed magnetic. "You may not agree with me, but I believe that all young people should be required to serve in the military for two years. Just as my father and brothers did, just as I did. We were taught that it was our responsibility. We did, and I'm glad I did."[31]

Congress and the president increased the authorized strength of the U.S. Army from 630,000 to 1,263,000 as of 31 December 1950. By the end of December 1950, there were 249 army nurses serving in Korea. By 1 January 1951, WAC strength stood at 8,674 with a goal set at 10,000. The number of recruiters for WACs rose from 90 to 240.

Flight nurses continued to face the added danger presented by old World War II planes used to evacuate wounded and ill soldiers and marines to Hawaii or the United States. On a flight carrying a planeload of marines from Korea to Hawaii, Navy LT Bobbie Hovis experienced the "joy" of flying in a plane that had seen its best days in the Second World War and the very busy days of the Berlin Airlift. Lieutenant Hovis remembered this particularly stressful flight. "On one flight from Korea to Hawaii an engine failed. We were about 100 miles out of Hickam [Field in Hawaii], when we lost the second engine," Hovis recalled. "There was a glaring possibility of losing a third engine. . . . The thought of ditching over water was always with us" on long med evac flights. This was especially true because these flights usually carried patients in heavy body casts, and getting them off the plane and into a lifeboat was no easy task. "Hickam dispatched two air-sea rescue aircraft and they took up station, one on our port and one on our starboard wing." Hovis knew that if the plane lost a third engine, they would have to ditch. When they reached Hickam, "there was a great sigh of relief when we received a direct emergency final approach clearance from the tower, and here we saw all types of rescue equipment—ambulances, cranes, foam trucks, and fire engines following us down the runway." Hovis continued, "When the aircraft rolled to a stop and the engines—all two of them—were shut down. Everyone onboard knew that our guardian angels were on duty that day."[32]

On 4 January 1951, the Communist Chinese recaptured Seoul in South Korea. In March and April 1951, General MacArthur warned of a stalemate unless his troops were allowed to attack Communist bases in Manchuria. Fearing an escalation of the war, President Truman relieved MacArthur of his UN Command on 11 April 1951, and Gen. Matthew Ridgway was appointed to take his place.

On 19 June 1951, Assistant Secretary of Defense Anna M. Rosenberg, who had witnessed the increase in the number of women in all branches of the armed forces and who believed that women "have a stake in this nation," convinced Congress to lift the 2 percent ceiling on the number of women in the military at least until 31 July 1954.[33]

Anna Rosenberg was born in Budapest, Hungary, in 1901. Her family relocated to America when Anna was ten years old. She became a naturalized citizen. Anna stood five feet three inches tall and weighed 110 pounds. In 1920, at age nineteen, Anna married rug merchant Julius Rosenberg.

In 1934, Anna served on the National Recovery Administration Board, and from 1936 to 1942, she served on the Social Security Board and as regional director of the Office of Defense. She was a member of the Manpower Commission and, by 1938, owned and ran her own public relations business, along with her son, Thomas J. Rosenberg. On 10 November 1950, Secretary of Defense George C. Marshall nominated Anna Rosenberg to be the assistant secretary of defense.

Later, when Rosenberg was accused of being a Communist, Senator Stuart Symington and Oveta Culp Hobby, along with Dwight D. Eisenhower, flocked to her defense. On 15 December 1950, the *New York Times* printed an article titled "Committee Clears Anna M. Rosenberg." The

McCarthy hearings that dominated the early 1950s had mistaken Anna Rosenberg for a different "Mrs. Rosenberg."[34]

In June 1951, the Navy Nurse Corps reached its peak strength for the Korean War of 3,238 nurses; they served in three hospital ships, *Consolation, Repose,* and *Haven,* rotated as station hospitals in Korean waters.

By 30 June 1951, it had been decided that the draft law needed to be changed, and once again the topic of drafting women came up. Col. Mary Hallaren and CAPT Mildred McAfee, the former WAVES director, favored drafting women for wartime and peacetime. The dean of Barnard College, Millicent Carey McIntosh, favored voluntary registration of women for the military. The former director of the SPARS, CAPT Dorothy Stratton, sided with compulsory registration of women. Those who were against the drafting of women included Dr. Harold Taylor, president of Sarah Lawrence College, who said that drafting women would put the integrity of America's social structure at risk. Vivien Kellems, an industrialist who lived in Connecticut, thought patriotism should be sufficient to get women to volunteer for military service and so no draft of women would be needed. The inconclusive discussion of this controversial issue did little to solve the problem of the need for "more hands" in the U.S. military.

On 10 July 1951, the *New York Times* published an article, "WACs Are Seeking 20,000 Volunteers," subheaded "Demands Five Times as Great as Supply; Lt. Haller Lists Advantages of Army Life." The article pointed out that despite peace talks in Korea, the WAC was building a peacetime force. On the same day, truce talks with Communist China began in Kaesong, Korea. Despite this brief gesture toward a settlement, the military nurse corps continued to recruit more nurses to fill their ranks.

At the Cornell Medical Center in New York, where Frances Shea worked as a nurse on the neonatal floor, articles about the military nurse corps needing women were posted on the hospital's bulletin boards. One day as Frances Shea stood reading the stories, she saw an article that said it was likely that nurses would be drafted in the very near future to help care for wounded and ill soldiers. Shea was twenty-one and she and a friend, June Armaly, another nurse, decided that they would not wait to be drafted.

"We didn't say the army, we didn't say the navy," ADM Frances Shea Buckley remembered. "So we took the subway down to Times Square where the recruiters were. And everybody was out to lunch except the marines. And we said to the marines, 'We want to join the military. We're nurses. What do we do?' " Buckley went on. "They told us, 'You go out this door here and you go over to the subway and you take it down to 123 Broadway. Take the escalator up to the third floor and ask to see the Navy nurse recruiter.' There was nothing about the army or the air force."[35]

The two young nurses did as they were told and found the navy nurse recruitment officer and told her that they wanted to join the navy, and the recruiter gave them papers to fill out. Frances Shea paused in filling in the information on the papers, looked up, and asked the navy nurse recruiter, " 'We'd like to ask you about some of the benefits of being a navy nurse.' The recruiter said, 'Listen, we need nurses so don't waste my time. Either you want to join or you don't.' " Shea and Armaly completed the papers without another question. "I didn't know how much money I was going to make. I didn't know that I wasn't going to wear my own nurse's cap. I knew absolutely nothing!" Shea remembered with a laugh.[36]

Shea and Armaly returned home and did their jobs until they received a letter telling them to report and be sworn in as navy nurses. "We still didn't know anything, so I asked the navy nurse who swore us in, 'Can you please tell me what are some of the benefits of being in the Navy Nurse Corps?' The navy nurse looked at me and said, 'Well, you can be buried in Arlington Cemetery.' "[37]

Shea's parents drove her to Portsmouth Naval Hospital in Virginia. She thought she had signed up for one year. When Shea went to her quarters, she found there were no private rooms; the nurses would sleep in an open bay. "I was welcomed by another navy nurse who had been there only a month or so and she said, 'Welcome aboard! You're here for two years!' The papers I had signed didn't stand; they didn't mean a thing!" Thus began the Navy Nurse Corps career of a navy nurse who would one day be director of the Navy Nurse Corps and who would be one of the first U.S. Navy women to attain the flag rank of rear admiral (upper half) [two stars].[38]

On 23 August 1951, the Chinese discontinued the peace talks. The same month, the Defense Advisory Committee on Women in the Services (DACOWITS) was formed. Fifty outstanding civilian women were invited to join DACOWITS; forty-four accepted appointments. The forty-four included the first three directors of the WAAC/WAC, WAVES, and USMCWR: Oveta Culp Hobby, Mildred H. McAfee, and

Ruth Cheney Streeter. Anna Rosenberg announced that the members of DACOWITS would help develop policies and standards for military women in areas such as recruiting, utilization of women, expanded career opportunities, housing, education, and recreation. On 18 September 1951, DACOWITS met for the first time and took on its first assignment: the development of a national, unified recruiting campaign.[39]

On 25 October 1951, peace talks resumed in Panmunjom and in a radio address on 11 November 1951, President Truman stressed how badly the U.S. Armed Forces needed women in its ranks.

In December 1951, Col. Mary Hallaren told news reporters that the reason there were no WACs in Korea was that the lack of the desired numbers of women volunteering for the armed services had forced them to postpone assignment of WACs to Korea for the foreseeable future.

In January 1952, Margaret A. Brewer joined the USMC. Margaret Brewer was born in Durand, Michigan, in 1930. She attended grade school in Michigan and graduated from Catholic High School in Baltimore, Maryland. In January 1952, Brewer received her bachelor's degree in geography from the University of Michigan at Ann Arbor. By March 1952, she was commissioned a second lieutenant in the USMC. Margaret Brewer would become the first Woman Marine to attain flag rank.

The Korean War dragged on for months and became unpopular on the U.S. home front. The truce talks had deadlocked in late 1951 and remained stalled for the better part of 1952 until they finally recessed for an indefinite period of time. In November 1952, General Eisenhower was running for president of the United States and made ending the Korean War a priority. With the peace talks reaching their two-year mark, Eisenhower arrived in Korea on 2 December for a four-day inspection.

On 25 January 1953, UN forces launched an attack against the Communist forces in Korea. Finally, on 27 July 1953, the armistice ending the Korean War was signed in Panmunjom. After thirty-seven months of fighting, the number of men in the military dropped from 3.7 million to 3 million. This was the highest number of active-duty forces ever during peacetime or during what came to be known as the Cold War. The women's branches fell quickly to their prewar strength and remained in that range for the remainder of the 1950s.

At the beginning of the Korean War, there were 22,000 women on active duty: 7,000 had line assignments in the WAC, WAVES, WAF, and

Women Marines; 15,000 were in the health field. By the end of the Korean War, between 500 and 600 U.S. Army Nurses had served in Korea in twenty-five medical facilities: field, mobile, train, station, and evacuation hospitals. At the end of that spring, there were 46,000 women on active duty: 13,000 WAFs, 10,000 WACs, 8,000 WAVES, 2,400 USMCWR, and an unknown number of health professionals.

Nineteen military women died during the Korean War, all by nonhostile causes. Seventeen of those women were military nurses.

Among the reasons for the low numbers of women in the military were the following:

1. Many of the women thought they were not needed or appreciated. Others felt they were placed in dead-end jobs and could not wait to be released in order to return to civilian life.
2. The civilian economy was strong and many who believed that they were unappreciated by the military felt they could do better in the civilian workforce or as housewives.
3. The women's branches did not offer enough opportunity in technical fields. This was particularly true of the navy.
4. During the Korean War, active-duty women were channeled into shrinking fields of clerical and administrative duties. In 1952, there were thirty-six ratings; in 1956, twenty-five ratings; in 1962, twenty-one ratings, a total loss of fifteen ratings.
5. Cost-of-living increases and salaries were much higher in civilian life.
6. In the aftermath of the Korean War, even the military was not clear on its needs for military women.
7. Most men in the military saw women as interlopers.
8. Women were now competing with men for positions, promotions, and ratings.
9. American society was firmly entrenched in the "elasticity theory" that said women were needed only in times of crisis and should return to their previous civilian employment when the emergency ended.
10. Society disapproved of women working outside the home and also disapproved of women serving in the military ranks.[40]

Added to these drawbacks was the fact that the military was inexperienced at recruiting women and did not go about it in a way that drew women into the service.

The fact that the military maintained few if any records on women during their wartime service and even fewer between wars seems to reflect the unimportance the military attached to women's service. When war or a crisis arose, the military had little or no idea how or where to contact former military women. No records were routinely kept of women's married names once they had left the military service, so it was very difficult to impossible to locate them when they were needed.

Women who might have chosen to remain in the military were most likely dissuaded by lack of military career opportunities, hostility from male service members, and the "last hired, first fired" attitude of the armed services regarding the service of women. One might assume that having to "re-create the wheel," or prove their abilities as if for the first time with every new war or crisis, did not encourage women to remain in or reenter military service. The tipping point for the realization of the need for, and efficiency of, women in the military would not become clear to the U.S. Armed Services for decades to come.

14

★

Women officers knew these inequities existed . . . nonetheless, many women did remain. The opportunities for promotion and advancement far surpassed those generally available to women in civilian life in the 1950s. The Army was a man's world, but so was civilian life.

—Bettie J. Morden,
The Women's Army Corps, 1945–1978

When the Korean War ended, the thirty-eighth parallel was again the demarcation line between North and South Korea, and the Cold War and the strategic posturing between the USSR and the United States had heated up considerably. No longer could the United States take comfort in its sole possession of the atomic and hydrogen bombs; the Soviet Union, with the help of a scientist who had worked on the Manhattan Project, and a husband-and-wife spy team, had exploded its first hydrogen bomb in August 1953. The monopoly that had provided America with the overrated security it had enjoyed for approximately eight years was gone forever. The Cold War had frozen its main adversaries into an arms race for perpetual military readiness and guaranteed mutual self-destruction.

In an America that had known a building boom of new homes for World War II veterans and their families, a new industry was about to take hold. That industry would be fueled by fear and a desire to survive the worst national catastrophe Americans could imagine. At the heart of that industry lay the insane idea that in an all-out atomic war, there would be winners and losers. That philosophy—that delusion—rested on ignorance, wishful thinking, and denial. As evidenced by atomic testing done by the United States, neither American government officials, the U.S. military, nor the American people had any accurate idea of the damage atomic weapons and radiation could inflict on human beings and on the environment in which they lived. Wishful thinking and denial took concrete form in bomb shelters built by federal and state governments and private companies and purchased by private individuals and families who hoped to be the survivors in cities and countries laid waste and uninhabitable by the very weapons they once saw as their guarantee of safety. The latitude and longitude of the country had not changed, yet the oceans that had once offered an expanse of invulnerability now seemed small and impotent to a nation living with the constant threat of annihilation. America could no longer afford the luxury of a demobilized military. The nation's industry that could afford to make plows, cars, and home appliances was now in the business of producing guns, tanks, and emergency supplies for government and air raid shelters for the private sector.

The nation's schools were no longer focused entirely on teaching children the knowledge and skills necessary to living a good and fulfilling life, but had added "how to" lessons in survival to school curricula. "Duck and cover" became as familiar to grade-school children as $2 \times 2 = 4$. Newsreels shown in movie theaters featured students ducking under their desks and covering their heads with their arms. The newsreels did not leave adults wanting. The films pointed out what to look for and remember about locating air raid shelters and how to use the emergency supplies prepackaged and stored in each location. The country's address was the same, but the nation was living in a new and scary place, a place where security and defense demanded a strong and well-prepared military. Ending the draft was no longer a viable option.

The U.S. Armed Forces would need a standing army, navy, and air force for the foreseeable future, and the voluntary military services of women offered a mitigating note to the demands that a standing army would place on America's men. The need for American women in the U.S. military placed the nation in a schizophrenic double bind. The nation and the armed forces wanted the benefits that the voluntary service of women could offer to the country but did not want to see the "normalcy" that had returned to it after World War II dislodged again. It was as if the nation had learned the words and internalized the messages of countless songs sung and listened to by soldiers in World War I, World War II, and Korea.

In World War I, the nation seemed to realize that a soldier's experience would change him and thereby change society. One popular song that reflected this worry in a lighthearted way was "How You Gonna Keep 'Em Down on the Farm After They've Seen Paree?" In World War II, questions were often posed in musical messages a soldier might send to his girl or a musical message that helped define his own unspoken worries. One such song, "When the Lights Go On Again," was popular in America and Great Britain. It spoke of a longing for peace and the return to things as they were before the war changed the nation.

America had been to war for the third time in the twentieth century and only a little more than half the century was passed. The fighting in Korea had stopped, but the Cold War was more alive than ever. The people who had survived one, two, or three of those wars were still determined to keep their country and their world as close as possible to what it had been before the wars began. At the end of each war, the resolution was clear: returning to normalcy meant returning to things in America just as they had been before men, and especially before women, left home to join the military or work in the country's factories, businesses, and professional offices. It seemed to many that with each war in which women served in the military or in the workforce on the home front, a few more women rebelled against the prewar status quo. And as the people back home and the soldiers who traveled to foreign battlefields in one or more of those bloody conflicts had wondered before them, people in the mid- and late 1950s questioned what would become of the nation they had left behind when they departed to defend their country and the nation's treasured values and beliefs. Maybe "Colored" people or unfeminine women wanted things to change, but the majority of Americans were more than pleased with the America they knew and loved before society was uprooted in order to confront yet another enemy.

Now, since the end of the Korean War, there was a new problem. Men were not volunteering for military service as quickly as they were needed, and women, who were once glad just to be allowed to join the armed forces, were asking for increases in benefits they would receive during and after each new tour of duty. How unfair it was for women who never faced the danger of combat to expect and ask for the same benefits and privileges of the "real" soldiers and sailors—the men who faced the dangers of combat and lived and worked in combat zones in order to provide the combat soldiers with the support they required.

There were situations, however, when military women were permitted to serve in places not usually open to them. In 1955, Woman Marine Pfc. Betty Sue Murray was assigned as the secretary to Maj. Gen. George F. Good. Since Women Marines were not permitted to serve in the Fleet

Marine Forces, Murray was unable to join the general to perform the secretarial duties to which she was assigned. After a few days, General Good could not find anything in his office and complained. Pfc. Betty Sue Murray received a waiver from the USMC and reported to General Good's office, where she began work as his private secretary.[1]

During the 1950s, the WAC, WAVES, WAF, and the USMCWR were restricted by law to 2 percent of the number of male members of the army, navy, air force, and marine corps. The Women Marines were further restricted by a decision of the marine corps itself to set its goal for Women Marines at 1 percent, though their numbers did not even rise to 1 percent. The WAC and the WAF had a gradual drop in the numbers of officers they could attract and/or retain. The WAF experimented with ROTC programs in a limited number of colleges. The army refused to use ROTC as a means to obtain women officers, and in the end, the WAF experiment failed and was discontinued. The WAVES, whose numbers had tripled to meet the demands of the Korean War, now were faced with slow promotions, fewer jobs in technical areas, and discouraging policies regarding marriage. Military careers were not attractive to American women after the Korean War for many reasons: inequities in benefits, male bias, restricted military occupational specialties, few career opportunities, and limited promotions. Rather than thriving, the women's branches were fortunate to merely survive.[2]

There were a few positive changes, however. On 6 October 1955, the U.S. Army Nurse Corps accepted its first male nurse. A nurse anesthetist, Edward Lyon, had applied and was accepted into the corps.

In June 1955, the *New York Times* published the article "Fort for Women Is Pastel-Tinted: Corps of 8,200 in Army Now Have Own Modern Center, Fort McClellan, Alabama." The article reported that the pastel-tinted barracks had thirty kitchens for cooking "a little something." The article went on to say that the women took physical exercises for added grace and poise, "instead of muscle-building. . . . Now and then, there's a cake baking contest."[3]

One must wonder about the number of women these new amenities dissuaded from joining the military. It seemed illogical to many women going through basic training at Fort McClellan that they were not permitted to pose or take photographs wearing army fatigues—uniforms necessary for much of their field training. It appeared to many that the army was perpetuating the life of the "double-bind": training women to respond

WACs in formation at the WAC Training Center, Fort McClellan, Alabama, 15 September 1956.

under combat conditions yet prohibiting them from being seen in photos or in public wearing helmets, combat boots, and fatigues. It was as if the public's "not knowing" would allow the training the public might object to—a perfect fit for a variation of the army's dictum in the twentieth and twenty-first centuries: "Don't show, don't tell," or "What they don't know won't hurt them."

In 1956, France withdrew its remaining troops from Vietnam. In a matter of months, the United States moved military advisers into Vietnam and began military training for South Vietnamese troops. The threat of Communism was constant and pervasive.

On 8 June 1956, Capt. Anna Mae McCabe was the head nurse of the emergency room at Walter Reed Army Medical Center in Washington, D.C., when the hospital's commander received word that President

Dwight D. Eisenhower was ill and was being admitted. "The chief nurse came into the emergency room and told me to put on a clean uniform and report to Ward 8, where the presidential suite was located. She had decided that the president, who was suffering from ileitis [an inflammation of the small intestine], should have special nursing care," Gen. Anna Mae McCabe Hays remembered. The chief nurse assigned Captain McCabe to "special" the president. "I started working on Ward 8 at 11:00 a.m. and continued working until 3:00 a.m. the next morning when the president was taken to the OR," General Hays remembered. The chief nurse told McCabe to go home, get some sleep, and be back on duty at 3:00 p.m. "I would have the 3:00 to 11:00 p.m. shift each day, and two other nurses selected by the chief nurse would work from 7:00 a.m. to 3:00 p.m., and 11:00 p.m. to 7:00 a.m. each day. It turned out that 3:00 p.m. to 11:00 p.m. were the hours when the president was most ill and in the most pain," General Hays recalled. As time went by, Eisenhower and McCabe became close. "One night, he said to me, 'May I call you "Miss" McCabe?' I was a captain and nurses were called by their rank. Eisenhower continued, 'When I was at West Point, we always called our nurses "Miss." I'd like to call you "miss," ' so after that I was always 'Miss McCabe' to him." One morning, McCabe's car broke down on her way to work. "When I got to his room, I mentioned the breakdown, and then went about taking care of him. He was in a lot of pain that day. The next day, his pain was worse. I was holding his hand and comforting him, and just when I thought he was finally asleep, he suddenly lifted his head and said, 'Did you get your car fixed?' "[4]

When President Eisenhower was discharged on 30 June 1956, Anna McCabe packed his home medical kit and Army Surgeon General Lt. Gen. Leonard D. Heaton, the president's personal physician, took the supplies to the Eisenhower home in Gettysburg, Pennsylvania. The Eisenhowers and McCabe remained close for years. "He and Mamie followed my career. Whenever I was promoted, President Eisenhower would send me flowers. When I was ill in the hospital, he sent me flowers. He would always know about me because General Heaton, who was our surgeon general, was very close to him," Hays said. "I'm sure it was he who told the president when I married and when my husband died."[5]

When asked if President Eisenhower ever transferred his authority to Vice President Richard M. Nixon, General Hays responded, "The president never relinquished his duties to the vice president." She continued, "The vice president often came to see him. I remember one time when he came to visit, the president was in great pain. The president said to me, 'Do you think I should see him?' I said, 'No. I don't think you should, Mr. President.' He said, 'Well, you go out and tell him that.' " General Hays went on, "And so I went out to the reception area, shook the vice president's hand, and told him that he couldn't see the president."[6]

In 1959, North Vietnam opened the Ho Chi Minh Trail. The trail ran from Laos through Cambodia and into North Vietnam. In the same year, the CIA began conducting covert operations in South Vietnam. Approximately one year later, the USSR strengthened its relations with India, Burma, and Indonesia. Months later, the USSR captured a U.S. spy plane in its territory. President Eisenhower denied that the U-2 plane was on a spy mission. When the Soviets produced the U-2's pilot, Francis Gary Powers, the United States was caught in a lie and the Soviets used the disclosure to support their contention that the United States was spying on the USSR. The Cold War tension between the two countries increased, and America became more determined to use South Vietnam as a base for covert operations designed to keep the Communists from taking over any additional territory in the Far East.

In 1961, the *Kodiak (Alaska) Mirror* published an article, "First WAVE Ice Observer? Commander Margaret Carver McGroarty, USN," explaining that Commander McGroarty, an experienced oceanographer and weather expert, had been planning an ice reconnaissance flight over the Bering Sea for more than a month. At the last minute, the scheduled ice observer, J. Serafion, AG2, was grounded due to an ear infection. CDR McGroarty, USN, was selected to fly the mission as ice observer and flight observer, a first for navy women.[7]

That same year also saw the return of Jacqueline Cochran as a spoiler to another program that promised great opportunities for women. In 1961, there were no military jet test pilots. There were, however, by 1960, more than 780 women pilots who held commercial pilot's licenses. The National Aeronautics and Space Administration's (NASA) Mercury astronaut program was also under development at that time, and the question arose regarding the involvement of American women. It was rumored that the USSR, now in a space race with the United States, was planning to send a woman into space. One of NASA's requirements for the astronaut

*CDR Margaret Carver McGroarty, USN, ops O,
FWC Kodiak, Alaska, on right, discusses weather and
ice situation with CDR E. E. Pierre, CO, VP-2.*

program was that an applicant must have experience as a test pilot on military jet planes. From 1959 to 1962, thirteen women pilots who did test fly military aircraft for the jet's manufacturers tried to convince NASA to admit women pilots into the astronaut program.

Two of the individuals who focused their attention on getting women admitted to the astronaut program were Jerrie Cobb, a female pilot from Oklahoma, and Dr. Randolph Lovelace, the owner of a clinic in Albuquerque, New Mexico, who tested male astronauts for NASA. When Dr. Lovelace expressed interest in testing women plots to determine if they could meet the physical and psychological requirements NASA had set for male applicants, Jerrie Cobb volunteered herself for testing and began getting in touch with other women pilots to get them to volunteer. Cobb was the first to be tested by Lovelace and did exceptionally well on every test administered to her. All of the women whom Cobb had contacted passed every test included in phase one of the tests Lovelace administered. All thirteen women were anxious to move on to the second and third phases of the testing series. When NASA stopped the testing of women applicants in 1961, Dr. Lovelace, who had started the tests without NASA's approval, had been counting on the support of the U.S. Navy, which had already told Lovelace it would back the testing of the thirteen women. Unfortunately, when NASA expressed its disapproval, the navy withdrew its support.

In 1962, Jerrie Cobb and Jane Hart, the former a woman tested by Dr. Lovelace and the latter the wife of Michigan's U.S. Senator Phil Hart, testified before the House of Representatives and had a private meeting with Vice President Lyndon B. Johnson. Their efforts were futile. "The reaction of the male establishment ranged from hostility to polite indifference to ridicule. LBJ summed it up when he scrawled on a memo, 'Let's stop this now.'"[8]

One of Cobb's most determined opponents was Jacqueline Cochran, the founder of the WASP in World War II. Cochran was undoubtedly an exceptional pilot and had the prizes and awards to underwrite her expertise. Unfortunately, Cochran had a history of trying to take over the leadership of any women pilots or any women's aviation programs supported by the military. Her first target during World War II was Nancy Love; her second target was Col. Geraldine P. May, the director of the WAF; and her new target was Jerrie Cobb, who had been appointed to lead the Mercury 13 women astronauts' program backed by the U.S. Navy and Dr. Randolph Lovelace. One might argue from past history that what Cochran could not take control of, she undermined. In a review of *The Mercury 13: The Untold Story of Thirteen American Women and the Dream of Space Flight,* by Martha Ackmann, Anne Bartlett of the *Miami Herald* wrote that "Ackmann portrays Cochran as less interested in promoting women's rights than in hogging the spotlight."[9]

Not long after Cochran tried and failed to take over the leadership in the training of the Mercury 13 women astronauts and failed to get Jerrie Cobb to back down, the program lost the support of the U.S. Navy and any hope they might have had with NASA. It is reasonable to suggest that Cochran's political connections and her husband's money gave her access and influence in many high places connected to the government, the military, and airplane contractors.[10]

The new year of 1962 brought the Cold War to a boiling point and the United States and the USSR within a hair's breadth of World War III. The

United States helped set up a military council in South Vietnam in the early months of 1962, but the events that dominated 1962 for military personnel and civilians alike was the Cuban Missile Crisis, which began on 22 October. The United States learned through satellite photos that the USSR had set up missile sites ninety miles off the southern tip of Florida. While President John F. Kennedy and his advisers in Washington, D.C., began to gather more information, analyze it, and decide the best possible response to the threat the USSR and Cuba now posed to the United States, military personnel were put on immediate alert and the defense posture of the nation was raised to DEFCON (Defense Readiness Condition) 3. In a matter of minutes, U.S. Armed Forces received orders that could bring them face-to-face with an old enemy in a brand-new world war. Ships, planes, and personnel responded to the emergency with disciplined obedience and moved into action without the briefest question. Years of training were paying off at a time when minutes might mean the difference between life and death.

Ships at anchor in Norfolk, Virginia, began immediately to get under way. They weighed anchor and moved south, leaving behind many of their crew members who were on shore leave. Sailors on leave made their way back to Norfolk and found that their ships had gone without them.

One ship already at sea, north of the Bahamas, was the USS *Truckee* (AO-147), an auxiliary oiler that moved to the rendezvous point for convoys taking part in a naval blockade of Cuba. "We were sitting in the middle of all these destroyers—two carrier groups," former LT John Neidel, USN, the ship's supply officer, remembered. "We were the only ship in the area with a helicopter onboard. When the weather was okay, the helicopter pilot—his call name was Scooter-9—would take off and buzz around looking for submarines. It was scary at the time. It was probably the scariest thing I ever did in my life. We were well aware that the *Truckee,* fully loaded, had a 38-foot draft—a bull's eye for a torpedo. You suddenly realized that you're the biggest target there—subs really wanted to hit oilers because if they sank the oilers, they could pretty much count on other ships having a limited number of days commission left before they ran out of fuel and became sitting ducks for subs and their torpedoes." Neidel continued, "I remember watching some of the enlisted men on deck—during a work break, one of them had a radio and had tuned it in to a Miami radio station. When they heard the news, my gosh, one guy after another went below and grabbed his life jacket and brought it up."[11]

It was the *Truckee's* job to resupply and refuel ships of the carrier groups. "We could refuel two ships at a time—one on our port and one on our starboard," recalled Carl Lockett, who was a young ensign then. "We spent some time the first few days getting sailors who had missed movement of their ships back onboard to fill out their crews. Ships coming out to the blockade would carry sailors onboard until they met up with the *Truckee,* then transfer the men to us, either by helicopter or highline. When we met up with ships in the convoys, we'd highline any of that ship's crew we had onboard back to their own ship." Lockett continued, "Nobody knew how long we'd be out there so they delivered our mail and Christmas packages to the *Truckee.*"[12]

The nuclear-powered USS *Enterprise* was one of the ships that the *Truckee* refueled. Quartermaster 2nd Class Patrick Joslyn, aboard the *Truckee,* remembered, "We worked day and night at our battle stations. From the bridge, I remember hearing the jets—which were fully armed—taking off and landing during the refueling process. No open flames, smoking, or even scratching metal was usually allowed because the JP-5, av-gas, was so flammable, and now, during refueling, these planes were continuing their activity. I knew that at any second, we could be at war." John Neidel recalled, "We carried both diesel and jet fuel so we could refuel carriers—then they could refuel ships in their carrier group—and they needed jet fuel to keep their planes in the air. Refueling was pretty tricky—especially at night. The lines had to be connected just so, and the ship's course and speed had to be matched with ours. Any turbulence could cause the lines to break or pull free, spilling highly flammable fuel on the ships and into the water." Neidel remembered, "As it turned out, we were in the blockade about fifty days and, during that time, we refueled 152 ships. We were busy."[13]

At the time the USS *Truckee* changed course and headed for the blockade, in the United States military personnel and equipment moved south by train, plane, and truck while military dependents were evacuated from the U.S. Navy Base at Guantánamo Bay, Cuba. Military hospitals began discharging all patients who could return to duty in an effort to clear bed space and surgical suites and make available supplies and equipment as well as free up the doctors, nurses, medics, and technicians for the thousands of casualties that might be expected should the crisis move into open combat.

At Walter Reed Army Medical Center, the miles and miles of hallways and tunnels that honeycombed the facility were strangely, eerily, deserted. Military personnel—men and women—and the health care givers and patients who remained seemed of one mind. Those who were able watched or listened to televisions placed at various locations on patient units. People were aware: quiet and waiting and ready to follow any military orders given to them. All those remaining at Walter Reed realized that they were sitting on a very likely target should the Cuban missiles be launched at the United States.

A visitor to Walter Reed would have been struck by the quiet and the absence of fear in every location where patients and/or staff were located. Patients were military, and the training and discipline they had known since basic or officer training took over without conscious effort. Patients who were ambulatory helped patients who were on bed rest or in wheelchairs. Their overriding objective, which though never given a voice was known, seen, and felt by every soldier under Walter Reed's roof, was "the Army takes care of its own," and the men and women housed in or near that historic medical center were determined to do just that. Army medics, men and women, would do it without a second thought: they would work "to conserve the fighting strength."

It was not uncommon for health care providers in the army to refer to Walter Reed Medical Center in private conversations affectionately as "Walter Wonderful," and each was determined to give the best possible care to their fellow soldiers. Each took pride in being part of a team the nation could count on, part of a U.S. Army that would offer no less than the best care to every wounded or ill soldier brought to them for help. The pride in country, in the U.S. Army, and in each other could be seen and felt everywhere. It was a privilege to serve in such an army and a privilege to serve at Walter Reed. Walter Reed Army Medical Center was simply the best in medical care that the United States and the army had to offer to any wounded or ill soldier—enlisted or officer—or to the president of the United States.

On the evening of 22 October 1962, President John F. Kennedy addressed the nation over television and radio. It was the first time the American people in general learned of the crisis facing the United States and the world. The address by the president informed Americans that "this government as promised has maintained the closest surveillance of the Soviet military buildup on the island of Cuba. Within the past week, unmistakable evidence has established the fact that a series of offensive missile sites was now in preparation on that imprisoned island. The purpose of these bases can be no other than to provide a nuclear site capability against the Western Hemisphere."[14]

The address went on to describe the two kinds of missile site installations: one that employed "medium-range ballistic missiles, capable of carrying a nuclear warhead more than 1,000 nautical miles," rendering them "capable of striking Washington, D.C., the Panama Canal, and Mexico City, or any other city in the southeastern part of the United States, in Central America, or in the Caribbean area." The other missile sites were not yet completed, but appeared to be for intermediate-range ballistic missiles able to travel over 2,000 miles and capable of hitting major cities in North, Central, and South America, "ranging as far north as Hudson Bay, Canada, and as far south as Lima, Peru."[15]

On 23 October 1962, an article in the *New York Times* stated that the White House had announced on the night of the twenty-second that President Kennedy and Vice President Johnson "would make no further political appearances in the congressional campaign because of the Cuban crisis." The White House saw this move as clear evidence that President Kennedy wanted to unify the country behind his decision to blockade Cuba and to keep the issue out of partisan politics.[16]

On 23 October 1962, Secretary of Defense Robert McNamara announced that the U.S. Navy would make contact with Russian ships within twenty-four hours. In addition, the secretary announced that the tours of duty of navy and marine corps personnel were extended until further notice and that the Guantanamo Naval Base in Cuba has been reinforced in preparation for an attack. On 26 October 1962, after trailing a Russian freighter throughout the night, a boarding party from a U.S. naval warship boarded, searched, and finding no offensive weapons, allowed the 10,657-ton *Marucla,* a U.S.-built liberty ship now registered in Lebanon, to proceed. One of the two destroyers taking part in the search of the *Marucla* was the *Joseph P. Kennedy Jr.,* named for President Kennedy's brother, a naval pilot killed in World War II.[17]

In addition to extending the tours of navy and marine personnel, Congress had authorized the call-up of 150,000 reserve personnel, 14,214 of whom were Air Force Reservists. These reservists were from twenty different states and would operate troop-carrier aircraft, moving military personnel from various states to their new duty stations. The army moved units into the southeastern United States, relocating artillery, airborne, aircraft, and personnel.[18]

On 28 October, Premier Nikita Khrushchev announced that construction on missile sites in Cuba had been stopped and that the sites would be dismantled and shipped back to the USSR. Photographs appeared in the *New York Times* with an article headlined "U.S. Finds Bases in Cuba Stripped, Missiles on Ships." The article made it clear that the U.S. Navy would confirm the removal of the missiles by alongside observations done with Soviet approval. The article also stated that some of the technicians and their dependents would accompany the missiles back to the Soviet Union. The Cuban Missile Crisis was at an end, but the Cold War had a long way to go.[19]

Days after 1963 began, Marge Hepler, a twenty-seven-year-old Pennsylvania native living in California, joined the WACs. Hepler's first acquaintance with the Women's Army Corps came through her sister, Sis, who was twelve years older and had joined the WAC in World War II. "I used to tease Sis about her having to wear GI underwear," Hepler said. "It was really funny to me that WACs had to wear khaki-colored underwear. I never thought I'd be joining up myself someday. When I graduated from high school, I moved out to San Diego to live with my younger sister. I got a job in a grocery store and a lot of navy wives came into the store to shop." She continued, "I used to hear them talking about the different places they had lived and about their husbands' deployments. And I thought, that sounds interesting. I think I'd like to travel like that. So when my sister got married, I decided to join the WACs. They offered women the most choices when it came to jobs and training. I asked for communications, and I got it. After training, I got to send messages all over the world." She smiled. "I had a top secret clearance."[20]

Marge Hepler was absolutely overjoyed when the WAC told her they were sending her to Germany. "I was transferred to Germany for a two-year tour—I extended a year so that I could accept it. I was stationed in Heidelberg and it was just beautiful." Her eyes seemed even more alive as she continued to speak. "I used to ride a bike up to the castle, where they had a great restaurant. I would sit at a table and drink coffee while I wrote letters home. The restaurant served you a small pewter pot of coffee and never ran you off, even if you nursed the coffee for two hours. It was wonderful." She smiled. "In the spring, I decided that I wanted to see the country outside of Heidelberg, so I started looking for a way to do that. I found out that an army laundry truck traveled a route, a big loop out

WAC Marjorie Hepler (on right) with a friend,
on the back of a laundry truck in Heidelberg,
Germany, 1965.

into the country, to deliver clean laundry and pick up the next bag of clothes to be laundered." She grinned. "The driver and the WAC sergeant said I could go if I wore fatigues." By that time, two friends wanted to go along. "The three of us dressed in fatigues and rode off on our new adventure." She laughed. "The first sergeant was sitting at a window watching us go, shaking her head. She couldn't imagine anyone asking to go on a laundry run." They got off the laundry truck, visited a post exchange, and looked around before the truck got back to pick them up for their trip back to their post.[21]

"For a while, I considered getting discharged in Heidelberg. I could have had the same job as a civilian if I agreed to stay. I decided to go back to the States and do more traveling to see my own country." She paused briefly, "I also got a job working in communications with the navy in San Diego. I worked with them for twelve years. I got thirty days of leave a year plus sick leave, so I also got to travel on my time off." She leaned back in her chair. "I will be forever grateful to the army. Not only did they train me in a job I could use in civilian life, they sent me to Germany and they gave me thirty days annual leave a year plus three-day passes." Marge Hepler smiled. "Joining the WAC is one of the best things I ever did in my life. I wouldn't have missed it for anything."[22]

Sheila Sutton, RN, joined the navy in 1963 and was stationed at Bethesda Naval Medical Center in Washington, D.C. Ensign Sutton had just arrived at the Bachelor Officers Quarters to get dressed for duty on the enlisted men's medical ward. As she changed her clothes, she heard the news that had been repeated again and again: President John F. Kennedy had been shot as he rode in his motorcade in Dallas, Texas. The president was later pronounced dead at Parkland Hospital, where he had been taken for treatment. "I remember going downstairs and seeing a group of my fellow navy nurses gathered around a TV watching and listening in silence as the moment that Kennedy was shot replayed again and again."[23]

As Ensign Sutton reported for her shift that afternoon, she was aware that the same tragedy that had gripped the nation also was closing its fist around Bethesda Naval Medical Center. Radios and TVs scattered around the hospital told the same story over and over, adding that Air Force One, carrying the president's body, was on its way back to Washington. At Bethesda, much of the Naval Medical Center was closed to the public as it prepared to receive and autopsy President Kennedy's body. "Much of the news on radio and TV over the next few days seemed unreal," Sheila Sutton Woosley remembered. "Every now and then I expected to wake up and find it had all been a nightmare." She paused, "But that didn't happen."[24]

Before 1963 came to an end, fifteen thousand U.S. military personnel were sent to Vietnam to train South Vietnamese troops to defend their country against North Vietnam and the Chinese forces becoming an ever more evident threat of another Cold War explosion that would be felt around the world. In December 1964, newspapers carried the story that U.S. military women were now being sent to Vietnam to act as advisers and training personnel for the South Vietnamese Women's Army Corps at their training center located in Saigon.

December 1964 also saw the new rule that said married women could now apply for the Army Nurse Corps. For anyone who was paying attention, it was obvious that the United States intended to take up arms once again in the warming Cold War and that it would make its stand in the country of Vietnam.

The year 1965 brought new and increased dangers to U.S. Armed Forces stationed in Vietnam. On 1 February, a story with the headline "Coup and Riot Liven Saigon Life for WACs" ran in the *New York Times*. The story said that WACs stationed in Vietnam had become veterans in the space of two weeks during which a coup d'état and anti-American riots rocked the city of Saigon. In March 1965, the U.S. Marines arrived in Da Nang.[25]

Halfway around the world and on America's doorstep, on 27 April 1965, the U.S. Marines invaded the Dominican Republic. Two days later, 2,200 paratroopers of the U.S. Army's Third Brigade of the 508th Para-chute Infantry Regiment and the Eighty-second Airborne Division descended on the Dominican Republic. President Johnson insisted that the invasion was to protect Americans living in or visiting the Dominican Republic. The real reason was the tension of the Cold War and the fact that the United States thought Fidel Castro might be thinking of inter-fering in the Dominican Republic. The United States was not willing to have a "second Cuba" in its own backyard. The Cuban Missile Crisis of 1962 had made the United States acutely aware of the aims of Commu-nism to establish a firm foothold in the Western Hemisphere and was determined that that would never happen.

A nationwide nursing shortage led the military to consider several long-delayed changes in order to meet the patient care demands created by yet another war. In August 1965, women in the U.S. Armed Forces could no longer claim marriage as a reason for discharge. On 25 August, the U.S. Navy commissioned the first male nurse, George M. Silver. By October 1965, there were approximately 150,000 American troops in Vietnam and in February 1966, 300 additional military nurses—army, navy, and air force—were sent to Vietnam.

U.S. Navy Nurses were serving in Vietnam aboard the hospital ship USS *Repose* (AH-16). The *Repose*, a veteran of World War II and Korea, had been recommissioned on 16 October 1965 after ten years of inactiv-ity. This ship had a 720-bed capacity and a helicopter platform on the stern. Frances Shea was among the twenty-nine Navy Nurse Corps offi-cers assigned to the *Repose*. "There was no special training before we went to Vietnam," ADM Frances Shea Buckley said. "We were anchored close into shore and the wounded would come out by helicopter; patients, the malaria cases were often brought out in small boats and loaded on the *Repose.* We were not permitted to pull into the harbor because we were combatants. There was a German hospital ship about one-third our size that was allowed to anchor in Da Nang Harbor. Germany was not a combatant, so it did not have to stay outside the harbor." Admiral Buckley paused briefly, "One good thing about the German hospital ship being allowed in the harbor was that when it left the harbor, it was because they knew when the area was about to be bombed or shelled. So we would pull out to sea, too, and return when things got quiet again. But even in the quiet times outside the harbor, we were always aware that the Communists could try to attach explosives to our anchor. Every once in a while, we could hear a couple of muffled explosions from under the ship. The crew would drop a couple of percussion grenades in order to keep enemy divers away from the ship."[26]

The *Repose,* a well-equipped, cutting-edge hospital of the era, lacked an amenity the nurses onboard missed several times a day, every day— locker space in the nurses' cabins to hang their freshly laundered uniforms. Those uniforms hung in the passageways between the nurses' cabins. The arrangement took some getting used to, when a nurse first reported for duty aboard the *Repose,* but after taking care of the ship's ample supply of casualties for a few days, the newcomer soon decided that uniforms hanging end-to-end in the nurses' passageway was a minor inconvenience that rated very low indeed, compared with the mission of their ship and the priority of the patients it carried. It did not take long for each new resident who would call the USS *Repose* "home" to realize that to each of her patients, who had slogged about in the heat in the snake- and bug-infested jungles of Vietnam seeking out the enemy and trying to stay alive, the *Repose,* with its clean decks and cool sheets, must look like a palace.

"The recovery room was the staging area for the operating rooms," Frances Shea Buckley remembered. "Triage was done right there. Some were recovering from surgery, and others were waiting for their turn to be taken into surgery. We had had so many patients at a time that we had them lined up in the passageway," Buckley continued. "Every third night, I'd work the OR. Someone was 'on call' for the OR every day. You had one day off a week, and you always had call the night before, and the night of your off day. You would work your call, and if you were up past midnight, you slept in the next morning. If you worked until 9:00 p.m., you reported for work the next morning. If the ship were in Da Nang Harbor on your day off, you could either go ashore to shop in Da Nang, or if you were sleepy, you could go to bed."[27]

Once in a blue moon, nurses could go to one of the beach parties the Seabees held on the beach they had fixed up for that purpose. "If you were a woman," Buckley said, "you had to be accompanied by a man. That was not a problem. The guys were really good about it. As nurses, we never trained with a .45-caliber automatic. The Geneva Conventions did not permit medical personnel to carry a weapon, so a man who was carrying a weapon accompanied the nurses."[28]

The tour of duty on the *Repose* was thirteen months. Every ninety days, the ship would pull into port in the Philippines for maintenance. Since the *Repose* carried its patients with it, the personnel had to work while there, but sometimes nurses could get a three-day pass and spend time ashore getting their hair done or getting a manicure or shopping. When the personnel of the *Repose* got a longer leave for R&R, rest and recuperation, since only married men were allowed to take R&R in Hawaii, the rest of the ship's personnel went elsewhere. Some corpsmen went to Australia; nurses usually went to Hong Kong or Thailand.[29]

In 1967, the number of army nurses in Vietnam doubled from the 300 assigned in 1966, and reached 640 army nurses located in combat zones within the country. One of the nurses included in that total was Maj. Connie Slewitzke. Major Slewitzke was appointed Chief Nurse of the Sixth Convalescent Center in Cam Ranh Bay. The center's patient census had grown to fifteen hundred and despite the fact that the army's table of organization allotted "zero" Army Nurse Corps officers to the center, ten had been assigned. They were part of the 7,600 Army Medical Service personnel (AMEDS) who were working in fifty-three individual units assigned inside the country of Vietnam.

Maj. Connie Slewitzke was born in Mosinee, Wisconsin, on 15 April 1931, and graduated with a diploma from St. Mary's Hospital in Wausau, Wisconsin, in 1952. She joined the Army Nurse Corps in October 1957. Slewitzke volunteered several times for Vietnam, without success. Finally, while her CO was out of state, Slewitzke, who was acting as chief in her CO's absence, phoned personnel and volunteered for service in Vietnam. She got her wish in June 1967 when she was transferred to the Thirty-sixth Evacuation Hospital in Vung Tau as assistant chief nurse. Six months later, she transferred to the Sixth Convalescent Hospital, just before the Tet Offensive of 1968. The number of patients and the acuity of their conditions far exceeded that usually seen in convalescent hospitals. Along with the wounds generally seen in combat zones, the number of malaria and hepatitis patients admitted was extremely high. Slewitzke had ten Army Nurse Corps officers and fewer than seventy corpsmen to serve a patient census that frequently hit fifteen hundred or more. Slewitzke placed a corpsman in charge of each Quonset hut that made up the Sixth Convalescent Center and assigned each of her ten nurses to supervise groups of huts. As the Tet Offensive increased in severity, Slewitzke spent hours each day making rounds and talking with nurses and corpsmen in an effort to raise morale in a system that offered few rewards or promotions, while still demanding hard work and long hours.[30]

Shortly after returning to the United States in the latter part of 1968, Slewitzke was promoted to lieutenant colonel and placed in charge of a walk-in clinic at Fort Myer, Virginia. The assignment was in answer to Slewitzke's request, in order that she might attend the University of Maryland and complete her bachelor of science degree in nursing and then

Thirty-six Evacuation Hospital at Vung Tau, Vietnam. Left to right: Majors Connie Slewitzke, ANC; John Del Grasso; Hannah S. Moynahan.

apply to the army for graduate work. While attending the University of Maryland, Slewitzke experienced some of the most emotional antiwar demonstrations to take place on college and university campuses.

"During Vietnam, I was so glad that when we were going to school at the University of Maryland, we didn't have to wear our uniforms," General Slewitzke said. "I think we would have been spit on, and God knows what." She took a deep breath. "It was terrible. The governor of Maryland had called out the National Guard to help keep the antiwar demonstrations peaceful. Some of the college kids would lie in the doorways to prevent you from going to class. Some of the students would say, 'I don't care if they close the school down—my parents are rich.' That made me angry. I told this guy that I cared because it was my opportunity to go to school." The general's face took on an even more serious expression. "Just as bad as the on-campus groups were . . . the people—Jane Fonda and the like— who would gather on the mall at lunchtime and yell at the demonstrators to get them more worked up than they already were. There was a group of these kids who would actually march through the classrooms while the professors were teaching. They'd yell all kinds of antiwar slogans. All of us military kids were very glad that we didn't have to wear our military uniforms, and that none of the students knew we were military." Slewitzke paused. "Things got rough at times. The demonstrators would throw tacks at people and use tear gas. It was a terrible time to be on any college campus. We military people stuck together and didn't tell anyone we were in the military. In nutrition class, students knew we were nurses, but no one guessed we were military." She shook her head. "It was a terrible time to be on campus."[31]

Connie Slewitzke graduated with a B.S. in nursing in 1971 and was assigned to the U.S. Army Command Headquarters in Heidelberg, Germany, as the chief of the administration branch of the nursing division. She returned to the United States in 1973 to attend the Command and General Staff College at Fort Leavenworth, Kansas. While enrolled in this program, Slewitzke's classmates elected her class president; she became the first woman and U.S. Army Nurse Corps officer to hold this position.

U.S. Army and Navy nurses stationed at hospitals in the United States did not find the fallout from Vietnam easy to deal with either. Military hospitals were receiving more wounded every day, and military health care providers were working long hours, six days a week.

Elizabeth "Bette" Davis joined the Navy Nurse Corps in 1966, was stationed at the Philadelphia Naval Hospital, and assigned to an orthopedic ward for enlisted patients. "The ward was large, forty beds with a corridor down the middle," Bette Davis Mitchell said. "There was another ward—just like it, next to that one, and a third, just like them—that was part of the three-ward grouping. All three were full of amputees from Vietnam. When these guys came in, they were usually withdrawn and very quiet. I think they were still trying to figure out what had happened to them. Yes, they were home finally; yes, they were out of an awful, awful hell. Almost all of them were in wheelchairs. And most of the new arrivals were moping around." Mitchell paused and the beginning of a smile turned the corners of her mouth up slightly. "The guys who had been on the ward for a while would not let the new guys feel sorry for themselves. They would pull their wheelchairs close by and say, 'OK, buster, buck up. Take a look around you. Look at Mike Taylor over there.' Mike was a triple amputee who was also blind in both eyes. He was one of my favorite patients." Mitchell continued, " 'There are guys here who have lost more than you and they're not moping. So stop feeling sorry for yourself.' Well, before you knew it, out came their personalities. It still gives me chills to remember how much they were transformed. They were teaching each other how to accept their wounds and live a full life." Mitchell shook her head. "They were something else!"[32]

"I can still see this guy, Douglas. He was a double amputee—below the knees. When he got his new prostheses, he walked the whole length of the ward without any assistance other than a cane. When he saw the tears on my cheeks, he said, 'Miss Davis, what's wrong?' I said, 'Not a thing, Douglas, I'm just very happy for you.' I really felt special to have the opportunity to help them get well. There's that bond between military people, between patient and nurse. I don't need one word—somehow, you just feel it. It's a very special thing when a military nurse first experiences it, but it's something she'll never forget."[33]

Of course, life as a military nurse is like life everywhere—it has ups and downs and Davis and her roommate got their share of the not-so-good days. Davis's roommate had been dating an enlisted man for months. He worked in prosthetics; that was where they met. They had already set their wedding date when she was called into the chief nurse's office and told that she would be leaving for Guantánamo Bay, Cuba, in one month. "She was really upset and said she wasn't going. They moved their wedding date up to the next week. When the time came for her to go to Gitmo, she was pregnant and received a discharge." Mitchell laughed, "That was great

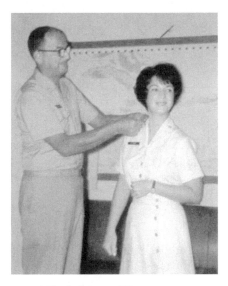

LT Elizabeth Davis, USNR, at promotion
to lieutenant, receiving her new bars from her
CO at Guantánamo Naval Base, Cuba,
on 1 January 1970.

until I was told that I was going to Gitmo in her place. They knew that I had dated an enlisted man in the past, so I was their second choice. I don't know who they thought nurses were going to date. You spent your life in the hospitals, and doctors and corpsmen were the only men you got to meet. The doctors were usually married, so that left the corpsmen." Mitchell smiled. "Anyway, I was very glad to get back to the States."[34]

In June 1969, the first military nurse killed by enemy action in Vietnam died in an enemy attack when a rocket scored a direct hit on her quarters. Lt. Sharon Lane was twenty-five years old; she was from Canton, Ohio. Lt. Lane's body was returned to a city and a nation that was about to go to war with itself. Americans were dividing themselves into two camps on the home front, and each saw the world, and the war, through very different windows. The first casualties to be shot dead on that battlefield had less than a year to live.

15

★

I knew the law would permit a woman to be selected for general, but I didn't think it would ever happen. There had been nothing in my experience and background to indicate they would ever get around to promoting a woman to general, and it was three years later when they finally did.
—Gen. Mildred Inez Bailey, AUS (Ret.)

Since the opening of the Ho Chi Minh Trail in 1959, Communists had made use of it to supply North Vietnamese forces fighting against South Vietnam and the American troops stationed there as advisers. The Communists set up strongholds in the Cambodian border areas known as the Fishhook and the Parrot's Beak. On an uneven border that ran approximately 620 miles between South Vietnam and Cambodia, the Parrot's Beak jutted into South Vietnam and placed the Communist enemy only thirty-five miles from Saigon. The majority of the Communist sanctuaries in Cambodia were located in the Fishhook and Parrot's Beak areas of the Cambodian borders, placing the Communist troops in an excellent strategic position to strike inside South Vietnam and to transport supplies to North Vietnam.

In March 1969, President Richard M. Nixon authorized the bombing of Cambodia, a neutral country, in complete disregard for the Geneva Accords and without informing the American people. In March 1970, with the help provided by U.S. Air Force B-52 bombers, General Lon Nol led a military coup against Prince Norodom Sihanouk, the ruler of Cambodia. The coup was successful and on 18 March 1970, General Lon Nol became Cambodia's new president. In early April, Lon Nol asked for help from the United States. In the last two weeks of April, the U.S. forces supported South Vietnamese troops who crossed the Cambodian border to rout the Communist forces using the sanctuaries as a staging area for their attacks into South Vietnam. On 1 May 1970, troops of the U.S. First Cavalry Division and the Twenty-fifth Infantry Division led South

Vietnamese troops into the Fishhook of Cambodia to kill or dislodge the Communists taking sanctuary there.

In the United States, the incursion of the U.S. forces into Cambodia was met with strong negative responses. The number of war protesters grew dramatically as fears spread that President Nixon was expanding the Vietnam War rather than disengaging from it. Protests over Cambodia had already ended in the deaths of four college students when the governor of Ohio called on the National Guard to contain war protestors at Kent State University demonstrating against the U.S. incursion into Cambodia. Retreating North Vietnamese troops who had captured large sections of northeastern Cambodia turned them over to a Communist group known as the Khmer Rouge. These actions strengthened the stand of the insurgency in Cambodia.

On 18 May 1970, Col. Mildred Bailey was working as the congressional liaison to the U.S. Senate. The legislation being debated was of little interest to Colonel Bailey, but she could not leave because she could not afford the risk that something of importance to the Women's Army Corps might be introduced in her absence. "I was kind of bored," General Bailey recalled, "when my counterpart with the Navy, a young WAVE officer, showed up. We had always helped each other, so when she leaned toward me and whispered in my ear, 'Come outside; there's something I want to tell you,' I got up and left." By agreement, they met at the place where they picked up papers and other supplies for their work. "She began by telling me that something very important was happening in the Senate—something that affected me and the entire army. She wouldn't say what it was, but instead directed me toward the office where I could track it down for myself." She paused briefly. "That guy in charge of the office said, 'Boy, do I have something I know you'll be interested in.' Well, that 'something' was the confirmation of the promotions of Colonel [Elizabeth P.] Hoisington and Colonel [Anna Mae] Hays to the rank of brigadier general. This was a great breakthrough in history, and the army was first! I was so thrilled that I immediately ran to a phone, called Colonel Hoisington's office, identified myself, and asked to speak with her. When she got on the phone, I identified myself to the colonel and said, 'Congratulations!' There was dead silence from the other end of the phone. Then Colonel Hoisington, in a deadly serious tone said, 'What do you mean, "Congratulations?" ' "[1]

Brig. Gen. Anna Mae McCabe Hays, Director of the U.S. Army Nurse Corps, the first woman in the U.S. Armed Forces to attain flag rank.

In Washington, D.C., on 11 June 1970, at a promotion ceremony, Col. Anna Mae Hays, U.S. Army Nurse Corps, and then Col. Elizabeth P. Hoisington, U.S. Women's Army Corps, were officially promoted to the rank of brigadier general. One of the civilian attendees at this historic occasion was former first lady Mamie Eisenhower, whose husband, President Dwight David Eisenhower, had died in 1969. Mrs. Eisenhower presented Anna Mae Hays with the first stars that had been pinned on her husband's shoulders when he was promoted from colonel to brigadier general. "I still have those stars," General Hays recalled. "I was very touched by Mrs. Eisenhower's kindness and generosity."[2]

For the first time in U.S. history, two American military women had attained flag rank. They were the first, but they would not be the last. An on-again, off-again debate had been taking place in Washington concerning ending the military draft and creating an all-volunteer force. If and when this happened, the U.S. Armed Forces would need tens of thousands more women in the army alone, not to mention the tens of thousands of women who would be needed in the other branches of military service.

The need for women in the all-volunteer military also would open doors for black women in the Army Nurse Corps. In 1970, Lt. Col. Margaret Bailey was the first black military nurse promoted to colonel. In 1964, Maj. Margaret Bailey had been the first black nurse in the U.S. military to be promoted to the rank of lieutenant colonel.

On Christmas Day 1970, thirty-eight-year-old physical therapist Maj. Aida Nancy Sanchez stepped off of a military plane and began one of the most unique tours of duty any military woman served while stationed in Vietnam.

Major Sanchez—Nancy, as she was known to her friends and colleagues in Santa Rosa, Puerto Rico—was born on 29 November 1932. Her father died when Nancy was twelve years old and family finances went from very comfortable, bordering on wealthy, to struggling to make ends meet in a family that consisted of her mother, two younger brothers, and Nancy. When Nancy was almost fifteen, she entered an essay contest conducted by the Sisters of Providence at Saint Mary-of-the-Woods College in Indiana. The top prize in the contest was a four-year college education at the school. The winner would be the high school student in Puerto Rico who wrote and submitted the best essay on logic. Nancy was declared the winner and had to decide, with her mother's help, if she would accept the scholarship and leave home for Indiana. " 'This is your opportunity—you go,' my mother told me. So here I was fourteen years old, alone, heading to [two years of high school then] college," Nancy Sanchez remembered.[3]

Major Sanchez was emphatic about the difference her education and the dedication of the Sisters of Providence made to the rest of her life. "I want to thank the Sisters of Providence. They did an incredible job with me—really made my life—how can I say—in molding me to a life that I would never have realized was going to be the way it was. And there was a tremendous amount of influence in my life, even in Vietnam, that came from my education from Saint Mary-of-the-Woods College. So I do want to thank the sisters. It was incredible!"[4]

Sanchez graduated from Saint Mary-of-the-Woods with a B.S. in biology and chemistry. Before graduation, Sanchez had spoken with her physical education teacher, Katherine Young, about her plans to become a physical therapist and was told about a program the U.S. Army had that would train college graduates with the appropriate courses in science to become physical therapists if they agreed to remain in the army for a prescribed period of time. Sanchez graduated from college in June 1952, joined the U.S. Army, and by September she was beginning physical therapy (PT) school at Brooke Army Medical Center in San Antonio, Texas. Sanchez's class had twenty students, and all of them had high grade-point averages in college. After completing the PT program and a one-year internship at Brooke Army Medical Center, Sanchez was stationed at Fitzsimmons Army Medical Center in Denver, Colorado.

One Saturday morning, while Sanchez was on duty, she and her fellow soldiers were surprised by a visit from President Dwight D. Eisenhower. Eisenhower had visited Sanchez's PT class at Brooke Army Medical Center years earlier and had spent time speaking with the students. Now, face to face with Eisenhower again, Sanchez was astounded when the president looked at her, "and he said, 'Oh, I know you! You are one of the

Maj. Aida Nancy Sanchez, Medical Specialist Corps, U.S. Army, at Ninety-fifth Evacuation Hospital, Da Nang, South Vietnam, 1970.

physical therapists from Fort Sam Houston, and you are from Puerto Rico, aren't you?' And I said, 'Yes, sir. Yes, sir.' I was so surprised. Can you imagine all that he had gone through—election campaigns, all of those things—imagine that! I never will forget that," Sanchez said. She went on to say that Eisenhower's mother-in-law lived in Denver, and he and Mamie visited every so often. "And what is so funny is that he used to cook a stew that he loved to make at his mother-in-law's house. 'I'm going to send you a pot of the stew, so you can taste it,' Eisenhower said. So, comes this secret [service] agent, a day or two later, it was a weekday, with a pot of stew." She paused. "The word went all over the physical therapy clinic that General Eisenhower—President Eisenhower—had actually cooked the stew, and I wanted to keep the pot, but my chief said, 'No, you're not the chief of this clinic. I am keeping the pot. You can taste it, but I am keeping the pot.' "[5]

Sanchez was discharged from the U.S. Army after serving several years and was working as the director of the children's rehabilitation program for the Department of Health in Puerto Rico when she received a letter from the Department of Defense, recalling her to active duty in the U.S. Army for service during the Vietnam War. The army sent Sanchez to the University of North Carolina at Chapel Hill. While there, she earned two master's degrees, one in physical therapy and one in psychology. Nancy Sanchez then went to work at Tripler Army Medical Center in Hawaii. After about one year on the job, Sanchez received a letter from the Department of Defense informing her that she would be departing for service in Vietnam before the year was out. "I said I would volunteer . . . but I did not expect it to be so fast," Sanchez said.[6]

Major Sanchez was assigned to the Ninety-fifth Evacuation Hospital in Da Nang. She was not there very long when Dr. Matterson, who had been the chief of physical therapy at Tripler Army Hospital when Sanchez was stationed there, wanted her to accept a special and top secret assignment.

The only thing Dr. Matterson could tell her was that the assignment involved traveling outside of Vietnam in civilian clothes, and the mission was top secret. "They never said where I would get the civilian clothes," Sanchez recalled. Once Sanchez accepted the assignment, she was given more information and taken to Saigon by helicopter to receive additional facts. Before leaving for Saigon, Sanchez had been told that her assignment would involve traveling to Phnom Penh, the capital of Cambodia, and treating Cambodia's president, Lon Nol, with physical therapy in order to help him recuperate from a serious stroke he had recently suffered. Dr. Matterson and Sanchez both had been at Tripler when Lon Nol had been admitted months earlier with another physical problem. The United States was backing President Lon Nol in hopes that he would help them prevent the incursion of Communists into Cambodia and away from the Ho Chi Minh Trail.

When the helicopter in which Sanchez was riding landed in Saigon, she was taken to a location where she met a U.S. Army general who told her that she would be given Lon Nol's medical records to read; that she could not take any notes or make any copies, but should read everything so she would understand President Lon Nol's medical history in order to treat him more effectively with physical therapy. " 'You're going to go to see President Lon Nol of Cambodia because he has suffered a stroke, and as you know, you know him,' the general told me. 'You sit there.' " Major Sanchez was enclosed in a glass room while she read. Later that day, a small plane transported Major Sanchez to Phnom Penh. She was then driven to the city's best hotel and escorted to her suite. "It was all very beautiful furniture with lots of food, even wine was put in there," Sanchez said.[7]

The next morning when Sanchez opened her door to go downstairs for breakfast, there were seven Cambodian men seated in aluminum lounge chairs. "I said, 'Why are you there?' They didn't speak English too well, but they spoke French . . . and this is what we spoke at home, French and Spanish . . . So [we spoke] a mixture between French and a little bit of English that they knew, we got along." Sanchez remembered, "They told me where we were, more or less. Then I went downstairs to breakfast, and there were two American men [seated at a table]. I didn't even bother to ask—and I don't know why they did not introduce themselves. . . . I noticed that they were there every day that I was there." She continued, "I finally went to them, and I said, 'Do you stay here?' And then they said, 'Major Sanchez, we are secret [U.S. Army Intelligence] agents. This is Colonel so-and-so, and I am Major so-and-so . . . '—I don't remember their names . . . 'We are protecting you. Anything you need please tell us.' [They immediately added], 'But you need to be quiet about it.' "[8]

Sanchez did not find out until later that the two army officers were assigned to her because there was so much Communist influence in the country that U.S. Army Intelligence was afraid she might be killed if the Communists found out who she was and why she was there. "They didn't actually know who they [Communists] were." Unfortunately, neither the American agents nor the seven Cambodians assigned to protect Major Sanchez were allowed inside the palace or even the palace compound. Inside these two places, Major Sanchez was on her own.[9]

After Sanchez had been working in the palace for several days, the colonel she had met briefly at breakfast in the hotel approached her to say that the U.S. ambassador to Cambodia wanted to speak with her and that the ambassador's car would pick her up at the hotel at 2:00 a.m. to take her to the U.S. Embassy. When she arrived at the embassy, the ambassador was seated with a group of other men and had large photos of Cambodians they wanted to show to Sanchez. " 'Look, you already went to the palace. You have already seen the president,' the U.S. ambassador said to me. 'Could you tell us if you have seen—just point at the pictures—at the people that you have seen there?' " Sanchez said she was taken by surprise. "But my God, I wasn't looking at all these people." She said the ambassador leaned forward and met her eyes. " 'Look, please look, Major Sanchez. You are the only one who can get in.' " His voice became even more emphatic. " 'You're the only one who can get in that palace, and we *really*—it's very—extremely important for our United States government to know if these people are there, and who they are—and you've *got to help us.*'"[10]

" 'Excuse me, please wait a minute,' " Major Sanchez said. " 'I was sent here to treat the president of Cambodia. Nobody ever told me that I was going to be sort of like a spy. I don't—I wasn't told.' " Sanchez continued. " '*Please,* it's just that you are *the only one* allowed there.' " The ambassador's voice sounded tense, his tone was pleading. " 'So *please,* this is *extremely important to our government.*'"[11]

Major Sanchez agreed to get the information for them, and when she went to the palace the next day, she managed to look at the faces of the people in the room without disturbing the rhythm of the exercises she was doing with President Lon Nol. At two o'clock the next morning, the ambassador's car picked Sanchez up and delivered her to the U.S. Embassy again. She did not waste any time in saying what she had found out. " 'Okay, I can tell you.' " She pointed at the large photos lined up on the conference table. " 'This one, he was here; he was there . . . that one, that one.' " She leaned back in her chair prepared to wait for the ambassador's reaction. Chairs were pushed back from the table as the men, almost in unison, got to their feet. The ambassador's voice fell into the room like an unexpected landslide. " 'Oh, my God! This is almost . . . ' " He stumbled over his words as he gathered up the photos and papers spread out on the table. " 'My God! Communist infiltration!' " He moved toward the door. "He said, 'We've got to start packing!' And I said, 'Wait a minute, you're not leaving me behind here.' I got to my feet. 'I'm going too.' "[12]

Five minutes later, Sanchez was seated in the ambassador's car and on her way back to her hotel. She continued working with President Lon Nol for more than a year. Before she left Cambodia for the last time, Sanchez taught Lon Nol how to walk with a cane. Obtaining a cane for the president turned into its own adventure. Sanchez told Lon Nol's private physician that she needed a cane so she could teach the president how to use it to get around. When she returned to the palace more than two weeks later, she was told that she could select the cane she found most suitable for President Lon Nol. President Lon Nol's doctor showed her a room where he had directed the canes to be placed as they arrived in Cambodia. When the door was opened, Sanchez could hardly believe her eyes. Hundreds of canes, of all styles, woods, decorations, and heights were suspended in rows from the ceiling by lengths of cord. She walked between the rows and finally settled on a cane from France. As it turned out, Lon Nol loved the cane, and its length was adjusted for his height before the walking lessons began.

In a matter of weeks, Sanchez decided that the president was ready to walk in the palace gardens and suggested an unplanned visit then and there. The president's doctor agreed and the three, along with several armed palace guards, walked out into the fragrance-filled air. As they made their way to the palace garden gate, Sanchez and the doctor walked on ᴇ ᴄh side, ready to steady or support the president whenever necessary. "In those one to three minutes that [it took and] don't ask me how—all of Cambodia was by the gate to see their president," Sanchez remembered. "I don't understand . . . [how it happened], but I had never seen the likes of that. It was a multitude . . . The soldiers were making shouting sounds . . . And here I am holding him up, and he was just going with his cane. . . . I had to grab, and the doctor did too . . . his cane was just going . . . and I'm saying to myself, how could this be? I [just] decided to take him into the garden and by that time, I'm telling you, you could hardly see. It was just a sea of people."[13]

It was not many weeks later that a dinner was given in the president's palace to honor Major Sanchez and General Robert Bernstein, the commanding officer of "all of us medical personnel in Vietnam [command surgeon in Vietnam] at the time. . . . It was a beautiful reception," Sanchez recalled.[14]

Major Sanchez returned to the Ninety-fifth Evacuation Hospital and, after extending her tour in Vietnam for an additional year, took up her regular duties with the hospital. The dangers she faced here were different from those that might have taken her life in Cambodia, but in many ways, the horrors of life in a combat zone and the horrors of war were even more vivid. Sanchez would assist the army nurses when the wounded were brought in, or when bombs and rockets fell in their area. She remembered one enemy attack in particular, but it was not unlike many others she experienced. They were triaging the people wounded from an enemy attack, and "I was [there giving] morphine to others [those badly hurt]," Sanchez said. "I had to count [several] heads and arms and put them together in the right numbers [in separate body bags]. . . . Some of them [the dead] were dead in pieces, and they were put in black body bags. " While the nurses were busy treating the living, "I and a couple of soldiers assigned to me, we had to take those body pieces . . . and put them in body bags so they were the same color, and there would not be two left feet, or two right hands. . . . We had [to match] light brown with light brown, dark brown with dark brown. . . . You see, some of the pieces came all on top or inside of a bag [all jumbled up]." They had to be sorted so the families did not feel they were just getting any pieces back instead of their loved one. "Part of my duty [was] to take those bodies out and place them . . ." Sanchez paused. "I'm sorry." Sanchez asked for the interview tape to be stopped for a time.[15]

"The nurses were the most incredible human beings anyone can e see in a combat scenario," Sanchez said. "Beth Tate, who was in charge of triage, and all of the nurses were incredible human beings." She went on to describe a Vietnamese soldier who was brought to the Ninety-fifth Evac with part of his brain outside of his skull. The neurosurgeon, Dr. Calvin Tsugio Tanabe, asked the nurse, Beth Tate, to get him some three-inch gauze and other supplies. "So . . . right in the middle of China Beach . . . with all the sunshine . . . the two sat there and they start cleaning this brain sticking out [of the soldier's cranium]. . . . They worked so quietly. Then [the doctor] shoves the brain back in [to the skull] and says, 'Let's take him to surgery.' " Sanchez's voice was stronger. "Do you know, he lived. And it was my turn then to rehabilitate him. He [finally] could walk with a cane and [ended up] helping me, as a translator, with South Vietnamese soldiers who were wounded and needed physical therapy. Amazing! Just amazing!"[16]

If one had to choose one word to describe the United States in the 1970s, "change" would definitely be high on the list of choices. The nation and the American people were squarely on a road that led away from the familiar illusion of security and homogeneity so aggressively sought in the post–World War II years of the 1940s and 1950s. The 1970s were a time when reality was becoming more visible and more difficult to ignore. Like an old and worn tapestry, the picture-perfect ideal of the American "natural and God-ordained society" that the majority of American people and their institutions so wanted to return to was showing the wear of time and the experience brought with it. The reality of an ever-changing society propelled into an uncertain future was harder to deny as the old threads that held it in place thinned, broke, and disappeared from the archetype still seen and longed for in so many hearts and organizations determined to hold it fast. World War II hung in America's past like a giant bell, tolling for a place in time that could never be recaptured and announcing changing currents, moving into a future that could not be stopped. The vibration from the sound of that historic bell was carried forward and would impact everything yet to come. Along with unwanted change came the darker, and even more dangerous, unwanted evolution. The eyes of generations had been opened and for every person willing to hold their eyes tightly shut, there were hundreds of individuals whose eyes would never close completely again. What they had seen, what they had experienced, could not be undone. Not even God could change the past, and not even America could un-ring the bell. Change was a living, breathing thing, and the paths it took might be slowed down, but they could never be stopped entirely.

One woman who had this fact brought home to her was ADM Faye

*Deputy Surgeon General RADM Faye G. Abdellah
(Ret.), first woman in the U.S. Public Health Service
to attain the rank of rear admiral (upper half or O-8).*

Abdellah, Ed.D., LL.D., RN, of the United States Public Health Service
(USPHS). On 1 November 1970, Dr. Abdellah had attained the rank of
Rear Admiral (lower half or O-7) and was appointed Assistant Surgeon
General of the U.S. Public Health Service. In 1974, Dr. Abdellah achieved
the rank of Rear Admiral (upper half or O-8) and thus became the first
woman in USPHS history to attain this rank, which is equivalent to the
rank of major general—two stars—in other branches of the U.S. Armed
Forces, and to be named Deputy Surgeon General of the USPHS.[17]

From the moment of her birth on 13 March 1919, Faye Abdellah
seemed destined to be a catalyst for change. As the daughter of a Scottish
mother and an Algerian father, she grew up in an atmosphere where even
the middle ground was too far left for her father and not far enough left
for a mother who wanted to see her daughter, as well as her son, educated
to whatever extent her intellect would allow.

When the German airship the *Hindenburg* exploded upon its arrival at
the Lakehurst Naval Air Station, New Jersey, on the evening of 6 May
1937, citizens from nearby towns rushed to the airfield to see if they could
help the victims. Among those people who arrived to help was eighteen-

year-old Faye G. Abdellah. "All I could see were people jumping out of the *Hindenburg*. The people were on fire," Abdellah remembered. "They were burning. I felt so helpless; I didn't know what to do. . . . It was then that I committed myself to nursing."[18]

Faye Abdellah had known since she was a child that if she wanted a college education, she would have to pay for it herself. Her father had adopted an Algerian view of a woman's place in society and made it clear that he would not pay for his daughter to attend any institution of higher learning. " 'In Algeria, women have no brains,' and my father thought that I should get married and have children and would not pay my tuition," Abdellah said. Faye received the emotional support of her mother, but paying for an education after high school was completely Faye's responsibility.[19]

Faye Abdellah attended the Fitkin Memorial Hospital School of Nursing (now the Ann May School of Nursing) in Neptune, New Jersey. She received a nursing diploma in 1942. Then, funded by a scholarship, she attended Douglas College, Rutgers University, in New Brunswick, New Jersey, where she studied chemistry and liberal arts courses in pursuit of a B.S. degree in nursing. Abdellah applied for admission to the Teachers College at Columbia University in New York City. Abdellah was accepted into Columbia's bachelor of science in nursing program and began classes. She remained at Columbia University, where she received a B.S. in nursing in 1945, a master of arts degree in 1947, and a doctor of education degree in education and psychology in 1955.

Between 1945 and 1948, Abdellah worked as an instructor in nursing arts, pharmacology, and medical nursing at Yale University School of Nursing in New Haven, Connecticut. While teaching at Yale, Abdellah experienced the first of what she calls her "beheadings." In 1948, Abdellah strongly objected to a 1937 textbook that was required for a graduate nursing course. Because the book was eleven years old, some notable scientific advances that had taken place since the book's publication were not covered. When Abdellah took her concerns to the dean of the graduate school, the dean informed her that the book was to continue as the required text for that particular course. Abdellah decided that she would take her objections to the court of public opinion and elicited the help of two colleagues to carry the aged textbooks to the Yale courtyard. Then her helpers quickly disappeared while Abdellah doused the books with gasoline and set them on fire. A very angry dean of nursing summoned Abdellah to her office the next day and informed her that she would be required to pay for every book she had burned and that her annual contract with Yale would not be renewed for the next year. "I ate peanut butter sandwiches for that year," Abdellah said. "To this day, I can't look peanut butter in the eye."[20]

In 1949, Abdellah joined the U.S. Public Health Service, a uniformed military service that in time of war or national emergency falls under the control and supervision of the U.S. Navy. Her first assignment was as a nursing consultant with the Western Interstate Commission for Higher Education (WICHE). Dr. Abdellah's second "beheading" occurred in 1957 when, as a senior consultant who managed multimillion-dollar research grant programs, she proposed the reorganization of the Nursing Research Center. The Nursing Research Center was then under the control of the division of nursing, and placing it under the care and oversight of the National Institutes of Health (NIH) would have permitted nursing to be recognized as a science and placed it under the NIH roof for research. Power once given is very difficult to take back, and those who would lose power in the reorganization fought extremely hard to have the attempted reorganization fail. The efforts for reorganization did fail, and Abdellah found herself receiving punishment for her progressive ideas. "The director of nursing was so upset, she put me on house arrest; I had no phone . . . I did some of my most extensive writing then," Abdellah remembered. "It took thirty years to get that research center for nursing at NIH."[21]

From 1974 to 1980, Captain Abdellah worked in the Office of Nursing Home Affairs (Office of Long-Term Care), Office of Assistant Secretary for Health and Human Services (DHHS). During a trip to San Diego, California, to inspect several nursing homes, Abdellah found herself with time to kill and decided to visit the San Diego Zoo before going to the next nursing home she had on her list for inspection. Later, she arrived at the next nursing home. She had learned through experience that violations of standards were not usually found on the first floor and, accordingly, insisted on inspecting the upper floors of the facility. She encountered such flagrant, substandard care that her anger had not subsided by the time she returned to Washington, D.C., that evening and decided to use the experience to motivate the members of the American Health Care Association, where she was scheduled to speak. She wanted to bring about the changes she knew had to be made to bring the care and environments of nursing homes up to, and, she hoped, higher than, the minimal standard for accreditation.

Dr. Abdellah began her address to the members of this accrediting body by telling them of using her extra time to visit one of the nation's best zoos. That done, she unleashed what she hoped would embarrass and anger those seated before her, so they would correct substandard care in the nursing homes they approved for accreditation. In a steady, cold, and measured voice, she spoke to the hundreds of people whose eyes were focused on her. "The animals in the zoo are better cared for than the patients in the nursing homes you approve." Abdellah recalled her words and her anger. Her eyes were alive with some of the energy she must have felt that day on that stage, in front of that audience whose members decided on a daily basis whether a nursing home had earned the right to be accredited. "It took two people to carry me off the stage and escort me to the door." The corners of her mouth moved slightly upward into the barest hint of a smile. "The next day, I received a phone call telling me to report to [Secretary of DHHS] Caspar Weinberger's office. The office took up an entire top floor. I thought I was about to be fired." She paused briefly, then continued. "He looked at me and said, 'Faye, whatever it is that you're doing, keep it up!' The lesson that I learned was that it was extremely important to have the support of your superiors." Her eyes were filled with energy again—this time, the energy was warm and complemented a broad smile. "I tried to temper my ways and be politically correct, but I'm afraid I'll always be a book-burner."[22]

Change was also what brought Capt. Karen I. O'Connor to work with NASA in its preparations for women astronauts on upcoming space shuttle flights. O'Connor graduated from Louisiana State University with a B.S. in nursing, joined the air force in 1970, and reported to Lackland Air Force Base in San Antonio, Texas. O'Connor had grown up in a family of four girls who had arrived in stair-step fashion. She had arrived on 29 December 1947 in New Orleans, Louisiana. Her father had served in the army during World War II, and she and her sisters heard many stories of life in the military, and they all had a positive theme. Her parents were devout Catholics, and all of their girls were pretty much sheltered from the "party" side of New Orleans. That sheltering extended to her college days, since Karen continued to live at home all through her years at LSU. "As a child, I would listen for hours to stories of my father's experiences in the military," O'Connor said. "I'm pretty sure that it was those stories and my father's view on military service that led me into joining the armed

Capt. Karen I. O'Connor, NC, USAF, 1970.

forces." O'Connor remembered, "Flight school was very interesting. I learned a great deal of things that I had not learned in LSU's program for my bachelor's degree in nursing." She paused. "In the oxygen deprivation chamber, there was an air force technician assigned to you. The tech watched you like a hawk, and when you got pale . . . the tech would put an oxygen mask on you. You won't be much help to patients being air-evaced if you can't recognize oxygen deprivation and fix it fast."[23]

Flight nurses also learn that for every 1,000 feet you gain in altitude, the outside temperature drops two degrees centigrade; that at 25,000 feet or more, humidity drops to 2 percent and that it is best to stay away from caffeine drinks and to drink a lot of water; that medical evacuation flights took a considerable amount of time on the ground because it took time to make sure that the correct patients were loaded or offloaded at each stop; that it was the flight nurse's responsibility to have the necessary equipment and supplies for each patient aboard; that the flight nurse "called the shots" and had the responsibility for each patient aboard.

The flight nurse also had to be familiar with the setup of the plane and the patient's status in transport, whether on a stretcher or seated. Burn cases usually flew on C-9s, which had equipment built into the plane such as oxygen and stretcher racks. Burn cases had to be well hydrated before they came onboard, and nothing invasive could be undertaken during the flight. "You couldn't hear blood pressures on noisy flights, so you had to palpate it," O'Connor recalled. "Of course, we carried all kinds of emergency drugs in case something out of the ordinary happened."[24]

O'Connor completed her active-duty time and was discharged. She was living in Atlanta when her reserve unit, which met at nearby Dobbins Air Force Base, was contacted to request volunteer flight nurses to take part in a temporary duty assignment to test equipment that would be onboard a future space shuttle flight. The testing would take place at Clear Lake, Texas, about twenty miles south of Houston. O'Connor had been doing private-duty nursing, was free at the time, volunteered, was accepted, and left for Clear Lake. "They knew the space shuttle would be flying soon and that it would have women onboard, so they needed to

have a bathroom that would accommodate women," O'Connor continued. "When I arrived in Houston, I learned that there had already been
some testing of equipment using flight nurses as volunteers, but that
because they were testing various types of equipment, the testing was done
in four- or five-week sessions."[25]

O'Connor and other flight nurses who had just arrived in Houston
were taken to Clear Lake and settled in the Bachelor Officers Quarters
(BOQ). The group of fourteen nurses would be testing equipment
onboard NASA's "Vomit Comet." They would work on weekdays; the
flights would be flown during the early morning hours, and each day's
flight would last approximately two hours. During those two hours, the
Vomit Comet would fly a parabola pattern that produced approximately
thirty seconds of weightlessness each time it was flown. The equipment
O'Connor and the other flight nurses would be testing was a commode
especially designed for women astronauts during flights of the space shuttle. The women would be using the commode during the period of
weightlessness. "These flights were pretty early in the morning because
they wanted you to wake up and *not* go to the bathroom at all. Get up,
get dressed, get a little food, and get into the plane," she said.[26]

The plane was not called the "Vomit Comet" for nothing. Weightlessness produced much the same sensation as most people have experienced
on an elevator or roller coaster, but the feeling could last for hours, even
days, in the weightlessness of space. In the Vomit Comet, it could last for
minutes, and then start again when the plane flew its next parabola. It
was the parabola that caused the weightlessness, and the weightlessness
that caused nausea and vomiting. The plane would climb to 24,000 feet
and from that altitude would begin a climb at a 45-degree angle, straight
up until it had reached a height of 36,000 feet. The pilot would then
announce to the crew and passengers that they were about to begin the
descent. The plane's nose would be pointed downward, begin its dive, and
quickly reach the point where microgravity, that is, weightlessness, was
reached and everything inside the plane that was not strapped down
would go into freefall—a state of weightlessness that would continue
approximately thirty seconds.

"The first flight, no one got any antinausea medication because some
people did not have a problem with nausea, they do not get sick." O'Connor paused briefly, then continued, "Well, I did, and I had my 'barf bag'
handy. . . . From then on, they gave us an atropine-based medication—

what they actually gave the astronauts while they were up in space. Once I started taking the medication every day, I was okay."[27]

The testing of the variously designed commodes for women astronauts was an adventure by itself. "I thought it was impossible to get up in the morning and *not* go to the bathroom, but you learn," O'Connor said. "I don't think anybody much older than thirty could do it." She smiled. "We were literally elbowing each other aside so we could be first." Before the plane started its 45-degree-angle climb, the woman who would do the testing got in place over the commode so she would be ready when weightlessness was reached on the downside of the parabola. "You got into a little stall, and there were cameras aimed only at the equipment to see if it worked—they weren't taking pictures of you," O'Connor said. "Actually, they showed us some film that had been taken before us." She remembered and laughed. "Some of those nurses had taken a marker and written something a little silly or dirty inside their thighs so it would show up on the film. Or they were flashing little signals. Anyway, you had to wait until the plane did its parabola and you were weightless before you peed." She leaned back in her chair. "If you weren't the one in the stall doing your thing, you were out there playing around.[28]

"There were regular crew members who were out there with you to make sure you were somewhere close to the floor when the plane came out of its parabola—so you didn't go slamming to the floor. It was fun, you played all kinds of games . . . someone would push you over, and you would go floating around. We'd try to drink some water, and it would float and splash down. It looked like mercury in little globules, floating around. We'd try to drink out of a cup, but it was really fun to see the water floating around. We tried to drink out of a bottle, but the water would pretty much stay in the bottle. We had a ball! You were weightless for about a minute, but it was a pattern—up forty-five degrees, down forty-five degrees—up, down, up, down. Like a roller coaster. The airspace had been cleared so the plane could fly in one direction, then turn around, and fly back doing the same thing. We would fly over the Gulf of Mexico. We were up there several hours because you had to wait until it was your turn to pee. There were twelve to fourteen flight nurses—people who were used to flying—people with a medical background so they could comment on how well things worked." She paused and took a drink from her glass. "Only one person could use the equipment at a time. For a few days, we would test one company's equipment, and then switch to another company's equipment. They knew it would take several four- to five-week sessions to complete all the tests. Some of the same nurses came back for another session; some didn't because they were working. Some came for all three sessions. I did two sessions."[29]

O'Connor continued, "They treated us really nice. We got a tour of NASA, went to the control rooms, and saw the underwater equipment. We had three or four rental cars for us to use. I had a friend who lived close by, and I spent my weekends there. We got our regular salary, plus per diem, plus flight pay. We wore a flight suit." The flight suit offered an additional challenge to using the commode. "In order to go to the bathroom, you had to take the whole suit down. In order to go to the bathroom, there were things on the sides of the commode to hold on to. Before these trials, they had not had special equipment for women. They had only had male astronauts before, and going to the bathroom was far less complicated for them. Women were in a sitting position and weightless. You didn't want the fluid to float up around you while you were weightless, so the device fit around you. I had never seen a female condom before. Some way, it fit up around you, flush up against your body. We never knew in advance which equipment we would be testing. I never had any trouble going, but some women did. There was a technician standing outside the little booth, and he'd say, 'Okay, we're ready to go on the down part. You'll be weightless in five seconds, so get ready.' Some people never could go."[30]

"The KC-135, better known as the 'Vomit Comet,' had three or four rows of seats. If passengers preferred, they could sit in a seat with their seatbelt fastened instead of floating around. I don't remember anyone choosing that option. It was too much fun floating around. Somebody brought a football onboard, and we played Vomit Comet football. That was a lot of fun. Oh, one more thing, the commode had suction—continuous suction. They tracked bowel movements too—if you could go." She smiled broadly. "The biggest thing I learned from the sessions was that I could go on command!" It might be justifiably argued that "you can't get more military than that"![31]

The year of 1978 proved to be a benchmark for the Women's Army Corps. The WAC had grown from 12,260 in 1972 to 52,900 in 1978. The office of the director, WAC, was discontinued on 26 April 1978, and on 29 October 1978, an act of Congress disestablished the WAC. After thirty-six years of serving America, the Women's Army Corps and the women who had served honorably in it and had proven their abilities and willingness time after time after time would no longer serve in a separate corps. Women were officially integrated into the U.S. Army. Women in the army and, by extension, women in the U.S. Armed Forces were once again asked to prove themselves capable of advancement. Instead of proceeding from the present into the future, women were expected to prove their worth to the military, despite thirty-six years of historic proof during World War I, World War II, Korea, and Vietnam, which the military, the nation, and history books evidenced an uncanny ability to ignore, forget, and leave for all intents and purposes undocumented in the history of the United States and the history of the U.S. Armed Forces. Women had been returned to the place where they had started—proving themselves in study after study, pilot program after pilot program, argument after argument. American men, who still had a monopoly on authority in the armed forces, were commanding women to begin again—and as in the board game of Monopoly, women were asked to "return to Go," but this time, starting again was euphemistically labeled "studies and pilot programs."

Changes in the regulations and in legislation during the 1970s continued throughout the decade. In 1971, the U.S. Air Force admitted women to its ROTC program, and the Joint Armed Forces Staff College admitted women for the first time. In 1971, the U.S. Army followed the air force and opened its ROTC program to women. The navy joined the trend when Chief of Naval Operations ADM Elmo Zumwalt issued Directive Z-116 which admitted a limited number of enlisted women into all enlisted ratings and opened fields including intelligence, public affairs, and cryptology to women. The navy also followed the air force and the army and opened its ROTC programs, chaplin corps, civil engineering, and its war college to women.

In 1973, the draft ended when the Selective Service Act expired. Based on needs of the military services, recruiting goals for women increased and continued to grow. In the same year, navy women became eligible for aviation jobs on noncombat aircraft, and the coast guard opened its ranks to women for regular active duty. In 1974, the army opened aviation duty on noncombat aircraft to women. The Coast Guard Academy admitted women in 1975. Progress continued into 1976 when Public Law 94-106 opened all federal military academies to women; the Supreme Court in *Crawford v. Cushman* ruled the discharge of pregnant female marines unconstitutional. The next year saw U.S. Air Force women eligible for aviation jobs on noncombat planes and U.S. Coast Guard women eligible for duty aboard ships. These changes and many more to come were in preparation of supporting the nation's all-volunteer force.

16

★

In his proposal to Congress, [President] Carter asked for the authority to register both men and women for a draft. Congress refused to allocate funds to register women, but did fund the registration of males.

Rostker v. Goldberg

On 1 July 1979, ADM Frances Shea was appointed the director of the Navy Nurse Corps. The young woman who had joined the Navy Nurse Corps twenty-eight years earlier, when army and air force recruiters stationed at Times Square were on a lunch break, would prove to be one of the most powerful catalysts for change to affect the future of the Navy Nurse Corps and navy medicine.

Along with responsibility for the U.S. Navy Nurse Corps, Shea was assigned responsibility for all the Naval Health Science Education Training Command (HSETC). Shea would manage and control every education program in the Navy Medical Department: residencies, medical school, cold weather programs, and a very large budget. When Shea took over, most of the money went to the Medical Department and very little to the Nurse Corps or Medical Specialist Corps. "Once they got somebody in there who was not a doc, that could change and it did," Admiral Shea Buckley said. The woman whose mother had asked her what she would be paid as a navy nurse and who responded, "I don't know . . ." was now in charge of a multimillion-dollar budget. "Some of the things the doctors had money for were ridiculous!" Shea Buckley continued. "The surgeon general agreed. I had total support all the way down the line, and the doctors came to respect it." She smiled. "They thought that I was going to close residency programs. I said, 'Hey, I'm a woman, and I'm a nurse, but I'm not stupid.' "[1]

Admiral Shea Buckley went on to say that things had changed tremendously since she had been a student nurse. "When the docs came to the desk, you got up and gave them your chair, and you made rounds with them." She paused. "There's much more camaraderie today. I see much better relationships among staff. Doctors are not so impressed with themselves."[2]

Shea knew that if women in the Navy Nurse Corps were going to advance in their careers, they needed to get out of the nurses' white ward uniforms. She also knew that the doctors would object to the change. "So I went to the Navy Medical Department and told them that the 'line' wanted the change; and I went to the 'line' and told them that Navy Medical wanted the change." She laughed. "I then went to the real mentors; I went to the Supply Corps—they've got money and the answers to everything. I went to the commander of the Supply Corps—an admiral from Brooklyn [Shea Buckley was from that area] and asked, 'Admiral, who has the responsibility to say what uniform the nurses can wear?' and he said, 'You got it.' 'Me? I have the authority?' And he said, and I quote, 'You bet your bippy, babe.'" Shea Buckley laughed again. "Anyway, we had to move with great caution. We had navy nurses who did not want to change. We chose four hospitals and asked them to wear the navy uniform-of-the-day, and not their white nurses' ward uniforms. All the chief nurses and their assistants had to change."[3]

When navy nurses complained, the director told them that they needed "to look like everyone else in the navy." The trial went on for one year, and then Admiral Shea met with the navy nurses who took part and asked if they voted for the uniform-of-the-day or to return to the white uniform and nurses' cap of the Navy Nurse Corps. "Every one of them voted for the change to go with the uniform-of-the-day," Shea Buckley remembered. "We had docs complaining—'How will we know that the nurses are clean if they are not in ward whites?' My response was, 'If that's what you're worried about, we have bigger worries than that.'"[4]

One of the things the navy nurses and Admiral Shea learned from the one-year study was "even if you were a captain or a commander and you were in a white ward uniform, you were 'Miss' Jones." Shea Buckley said, "Once you got into that navy uniform like everybody else, you were 'Commander' Jones." By October 1982, all navy nurses were required to wear the uniform-of-the-day—as all military women were—as a matter of course.[5]

Admiral Shea's next challenge regarding female navy nurses came with a request by U.S. Marines at Camp Pendleton, California. The Marines wanted a navy nurse to be assigned to their unit. Shea's first worry was that the marines would want only a male nurse. Since the marines did not have a billet [position] for a nurse, Admiral Shea was going to have to lend them a nurse. Shea informed the marines that a nurse would be lent to them. "So I said, 'Okay, I will give you the body, but it's got to be a woman.' And they said, 'Oh, no, no.' And I said, 'Okay, then you don't get anything. . . . That is your choice.' So they said to me, 'Well. Okay, we'll take her.' " Admiral Shea Buckley said, "So I sent this sharp nurse, this really sharp nurse . . . who knew her stuff—she used to teach in the ICU—so she went with the marines at Camp Pendleton." Some months later, Admiral Shea needed to talk with that nurse, so she called her at Camp Pendleton. "So I called her at the unit at Pendleton, and they said that she wasn't there. And I said, 'Well, where is she?' And they said, 'She's deployed with the troops to Okinawa.' We had won! Next phone call that I got was from [Camp] Lejeune [North Carolina]. 'Where's my nurse?' And that's when it started."[6]

The director dealt with assigning nurses to shipboard duty in the same manner. Her "fear" was that only male navy nurses would be assigned to the marines and ships, and that it would limit the promotional opportunities for women nurses. "They might as well get used to the idea. . . . And then we had nurses on carriers. I sent female nurses to places like Diego Garcia [an island in the Indian Ocean] and . . . to the Air Force Flight School. I would only send women. That was not against the men; it was not anti-male . . . now it doesn't matter—men and women—they go either way. But it did back then because they had no other women in Diego Garcia. A woman nurse was needed . . . to be there for women aboard ships that came in . . . they had to have a woman there for them." Shea Buckley recalled, "Once in a while, a hospital might run a nurse or two short, but in the long run—in the big picture—it was better for the corps and the navy and navy women. That's the way it should always have been."[7]

In his State of the Union Address in January 1980, President Jimmy Carter informed the nation that he intended to ask Congress to reinstate registration of all eighteen-year-olds for a draft, should a draft become necessary. The president did not say "all male eighteen-year-olds" needed to register. The president pointed out that his request for draft registration was directly linked to Russia's recent invasion of Afghanistan.

The question of registration for a draft gave birth to a debate on which was better for the country, a draft or an all-voluntary military. Those who favored the draft pointed out that the draft was a more equitable way of providing an armed defense for the country, since a draft would place the sons of the wealthy alongside the sons of the poor. Proponents argued that the mix of socioeconomic classes that the draft provided added strength to America's armed forces and gave rich and poor a feeling of responsibility for a country that had given them so much. Some proponents of the draft pointed out that the all-voluntary force, particularly the U.S. Army, had an increasing number of blacks and volunteers from lower socioeconomic groups. Others cited the contradiction of the citizens of a democracy or a democratic republic hiring a military force rather than participating in it themselves.

The proposed draft registration had already brought protesters to the streets in Washington, D.C. On 9 June 1979, Senator Sam Nunn of Georgia expressed his view of the all-volunteer military: "The all volunteer force structure cannot be sustained much longer, and we've got to do something about it." He said, "It is now on the ragged edge of viability, with mushrooming recruiting costs; unacceptable rates of attrition; severe shortages of critical skills, especially those of doctors; shortages of qualified recruits; and dangerously undermanned, lower quality reserves." Senator Nunn added that he did not feel the all-volunteer force would work in the future. The question, Senator Nunn explained, was whether the military was falling short of recruiting goals in the face of a shrinking supply of young men and women willing to sign up as volunteers.[8]

The article went on to point out that the military had already stated that if unemployment went down, as the administration said it would, the number of volunteers would decrease even further. Meanwhile, the Army Reserve and the National Guard would not attract as many people unless the alternative was the draft. Since the reserves are considered the first military replacement for casualties in the event of a war or crisis, thereby giving the military a chance to train and field new draftees, there would not be enough people in the reserves' ranks to fulfill the emergency needs that might present themselves. As for the National Guard, if they and their equipment were used as replacements for active-duty and reserve troops, who would remain to guard America's shores? Some proponents of registering eighteen-year-old women for the draft thought that women in the U.S. Armed Forces might be the perfect force to remain in the

United States to protect America in case of an invasion or attack on America itself.[9]

On 18 July 1980 in the case of *Rostker v. Goldberg*, the U.S. Supreme Court sided with the federal government; it upheld the statute requiring eighteen-year-old males to register for the draft while excluding eighteen-year-old females from draft registration, and said it was not unconstitutional. Speaking for the majority, Chief Justice William Rehnquist stated that the court was not competent in the area of military security and was deferring to Congress, which was charged by the Constitution with raising an army and a navy. This placed the decisions on which law to pass concerning the military squarely in the hands of Congress. The all-volunteer military would continue, and eighteen-year-old females would not be required to register for the draft beginning on 21 July 1980.[10]

Just weeks before the draft registration decision by the Supreme Court, the first women graduated from the nation's military academies. A total of 229 women were commissioned by their respective services: 55 from the U.S. Naval Academy at Annapolis, 98 from the Air Force Academy, 62 from the U.S. Military Academy at West Point, and 14 from the Coast Guard Academy. They represented 8 percent of the total graduates, approximately the same as the current male-to-female proportion in the military, and had an attrition rate slightly greater than that of their male classmates. These pioneering women of the Class of 1980 had survived strict discipline, hazing, weapons handling, physical challenges, and the scholastic rigors of academy life. Their five- to seven-year commitments to military service would play out in diverse geographical areas and in various military leadership positions in the evolving all-volunteer armed forces of the United States.[11]

History recorded the change in the makeup of the 1980 graduating classes of the U.S. military academies; newspapers, magazines, radio, and television marked the event. Many celebrated the accomplishments of these first female graduates and the trail they had blazed for women who would choose to follow them. Young girls still in high school or grade school had new role models and new choices in how they would live their lives; however, the military academies had alumni and students who did not view these historical developments in a positive way. These individuals were determined to rid the military academies of female cadets and the military of female troops in nontraditional roles. One of the most vocal of these men to speak against female cadets in the U.S. Naval Academy and women in the U.S. Armed Forces was James H. Webb, a 1968 graduate of Annapolis and a U.S. Marine Corps combat veteran of Vietnam. Mr. Webb, later Secretary of the Navy in President Ronald Reagan's administration and Democratic senator from Virginia during George W. Bush's second presidential term, wrote an article titled "Jim Webb: Women Can't Fight" that appeared in the *Washingtonian* in 1979. In that article, Webb states that the mission of the U.S. Armed Forces to fight was being corrupted by women in the military and that the corruption resulted in grave consequences to the national defense.[12]

The article begins by telling readers that while serving in Vietnam, Lieutenant Webb and his men went months without bathing; that when they bathed, they stood naked among one another near a village well, or in a stream, or even in the muddy water found in a bomb crater. Webb describes long marches with full field packs and weapons and carrying their wounded and the weapons their casualties could not carry as a result of their combat wounds. Webb then informs the reader how he and the other brave men under his command killed, suffered, bled, and died "in a way Washington society, which seems to view service in the combat arms as something akin to a commute to the Pentagon, will never comprehend." Webb goes on to describe their mission, "stripped of rhetoric," as "organized mayhem." Webb explains to the reader that what got him and his men through the "organized mayhem" was military organization, military leadership, "with an emphasis on interdependence, sometimes called camaraderie, that sustains a person through such a scarring experience as fighting a war."[13]

The article goes on to point out that America has "one of the highest rates of male-to-female violence in the world," that "rape increased 230 percent from 1967 to 1977," and that "wife beating is a problem that cuts across socioeconomic lines." After stating that he has no objections to women physicians, executives, or attorneys, Webb makes the clear and unambiguous statement, "But no benefit to anyone can come from women serving in combat."[14]

Webb then addresses the mission of the U.S. military academies as: "to prepare men for leadership positions where they may someday exercise that command which perpetuates violence on command." In Webb's own words, what the taxpayer is buying with a U.S. military academy education "are combat leaders, men with a sense of country who have developed such intangibles as force, clarity of thought, presence, and the ability to lead by example, who have lived under stress for years and are capable of functioning under intense pressure . . . combat leaders who can carry this country on their backs."[15]

The facts: Mr. Webb was either ignorant of the contributions of U.S. military women to America's victories in previous wars involving the United States, or he made a conscious decision to exclude that history from his 1979 article. The authors offered Senator Webb the opportunity to be interviewed in order to present his past and present positions on the issue of U.S. military women and to speak on where his stance has changed or remained the same and why. He declined to participate in an interview or to submit a written statement on those issues. In either case, the authors now offer these historical facts.

On 7 December 1941, when the Japanese attacked Pearl Harbor in Hawaii, U.S. Army and Navy Nurses were stationed there and in the Philippines, and U.S. Navy Nurses were stationed on Guam. Only fifteen minutes after Japanese planes bombed and strafed Pearl Harbor, Japanese aircraft bombed and strafed the U.S. Naval Base on Guam, one of the Mariana Islands. The five navy nurses stationed at the navy hospital withstood the attacks, which continued for two days, and cared for hundreds of wounded naval and marine corps personnel and civilians. When Japanese soldiers landed on Guam on 10 December 1941, house-to-house fighting began in the streets of Agana, Guam's capital city. When Agana and Guam fell, the five navy nurses were among the American military personnel taken prisoner by the Japanese armed forces. Those five nurses were later taken by ship to Japan and held as prisoners of war.

Hours later, U.S. Army and Navy Nurses cared for hundreds of wounded military and civilians while Japanese planes bombed and strafed Manila and its environs in the Philippine Islands. On 23 December 1941, the army nurses were told, along with other U.S. troops, to prepare for a withdrawal to Bataan. U.S. and Filipino soldiers would regroup and fight the enemy on the Bataan Peninsula while army nurses cared for the wounded and ill troops in hospitals set up along the beach and in the jungles of Bataan. The military nurses on Bataan withstood the same horrors and hardships of combat that afflicted U.S. military and Filipino forces designated as "combat troops," and the women suffered the same malaria, dengue fever, and hunger experienced by the troops they cared for in jungle hospitals bombed and strafed by the enemy. Army nurses, exhausted by sixteen- to eighteen-hour days, weakened by hunger, made ill from malaria and dengue fever, literally crawled from pallet to pallet on the jungle floor to care for hundreds of wounded and ill military personnel. Food and medical supplies were running out with no hope of resupply, and the Japanese army was drawing closer and closer every day. The hope that the United States would be able to come to the aid of the forces in the Philippines was soon shown to be wishful thinking.

On 22 February 1942, President Roosevelt advised Gen. Douglas MacArthur to leave the Philippines and make his way to Australia. Sixteen days later, on 11 March 1942, a U.S. Navy PT boat took MacArthur, along with his wife and son, to Mindanao, where they boarded a B-17 and were delivered safely to Australia where General MacArthur was to establish his new headquarters. It was patently clear that all who remained on Corregidor would either be killed by the Japanese or would become prisoners of war.

During the first week of April, it was decided that Bataan would be surrendered, and all but nontransportable wounded and ill troops along with the approximately one hundred army nurses and one navy nurse would be withdrawn across Manila Bay to the island of Corregidor. There the nurses would care for casualties in the underground hospital set up in Malinta Tunnel. The Japanese bombed and shelled the island day and night for weeks on end. When Corregidor was surrendered on 6 May 1942, U.S. military nurses, along with thousands of U.S. and Filipino troops, became prisoners of war. They remained POWs for the next thirty-seven months. During their imprisonment, the nurses cared for wounded and ill POWs and civilian internees despite constant hunger, malnutrition, beriberi, and face-to-face contact with the Japanese every day. They conducted themselves as U.S. Army and Navy officers despite the lack of food, medicine, and medical supplies and almost constant threats of death leveled by the Japanese on an all but daily basis. Liberation was delivered to Santo Tomas Internment Camp and the U.S. Army Nurses on 5 February 1945 and to Los Baños Internment Camp and the U.S. Navy Nurses on 23 February 1945. (The interested reader is referred to *All This Hell: U.S. Nurses Imprisoned by the Japanese,* by Evelyn M. Monahan and Rosemary Neidel-Greenlee and published by the University Press of Kentucky, 2000.)[16]

The Philippines were not the only location where U.S. military nurses faced the danger of becoming prisoners of war. On 8 November 1943, thirteen U.S. Army flight nurses and thirteen medical technical sergeants of the 807th Medical Air Evacuation Squadron (MAES), plus one young corporal who was catching a ride to his new base at the 802nd MAES, boarded a C-53 army aircraft at Catania Main Airfield in Sicily for a 260-mile trip to Bari, Italy, where they were to pick up wounded American troops and care for them as they were air-evaced to hospitals farther behind the front lines.

Their flight had been canceled twice in the previous two days due to winter storms in the area. A cold front was predicted for the Bari area, but the plane, her crew, and passengers were supposed to be on the ground long before any bad weather started. Unfortunately, when Lt. Charles B. Thrasher, the plane's pilot, radioed the airfield at Bari and requested landing instructions, he was unable to provide the password needed before such instructions were given. The weather deteriorated quickly and the plane was buffeted by strong winds and blown off course. At one point, the crew thought they saw an airfield and made an approach before realizing that the planes on the ground belonged to the Luftwaffe. As the pilot pulled up and headed away from the airfield, two German Messerschmitts pursued them and fired at the C-53 several times. A cloud bank helped the plane escape the German planes and, some time later, Lieutenant Thrasher crash-landed the plane in a field that came into view beneath the clouds. The crew chief was hurt in the landing and had to be helped from the aircraft.

As it turned out, the C-53 had landed in Albania, a country occupied by German troops and firmly behind German lines. Thus began a journey through enemy territory that would take the crew, the army nurses, and medics into Albanian partisan areas; they were bombed and strafed by German planes on several occasions, climbed up and over Albania's highest mountain peak in the dead of winter and at the height of a blizzard with snow on the ground waist high. Several donkeys, medics, and nurses slipped over a steep cliff and had to be rescued by the rest of their party. The only person riding a donkey at that time was the crew chief, who had injured his leg in the crash landing. Nurses walked through the snow wearing footwear not designed for such travel, holding fast to the tails of the donkeys in order not to lose their way in the white-out conditions the blizzard had created. Before they saw Italy again, the thirteen medics, thirteen army nurses, and the plane's crew walked approximately 850 miles through mountains, snow, and German-held territory in order to return to their own lines and to duty.[17]

The authors feel certain that the trek over more than eight hundred miles in Albania's worst winter can be counted right alongside the night marches traveled by Lt. James H. Webb and his men in Vietnam. The U.S. Army nurses not only marched out of Albania, they took care of several injured and ill men while they made the trip. America's military women have proven their strength, commitment, endurance, and courage a thousand times, yet somehow few, if any, of their accomplishments made it into U.S. history books or even into the military history of the U.S. Armed Forces in which they served.

In all, more than 350,000 women volunteered and served in the armed forces in World War II. Approximately 17,000 WACs served in combat areas overseas. Of the more the 59,000 U.S. Army Nurses who served during World War II, more than 30,000 served in combat zones and on the front lines of every major battlefield where the men in the U.S. Armed Forces fought or supported combat troops. Six U.S. Army Nurses were killed by enemy fire on Anzio Beachhead in Italy. Ten other U.S. military nurses were killed by enemy fire in other combat zones. More than 200 army nurses died while serving their country in World War II. More than 1,600 army nurses won combat and noncombat decorations, including Silver Stars, Purple Hearts, Bronze Stars, Air Medals, Legion of Merit Medals, Distinguished Service Medals, and other commendations. More than 550 WACs serving in the Pacific won combat decorations. U.S. Navy Nurses served in combat areas, in hospitals, on air-evacuation planes, and on hospital ships. Four thousand WAVES, 1,000 Women Marines, and 200 SPARS served in Hawaii during World War II. (See chapter 7 for the history of the Women Air Force Service Pilots [WASP].)

During the Korean War, more than 74,000 women served in the U.S. military. Six hundred army nurses served in Korea. Of those, 19 U.S. military women died. Of the approximately 250,000 women who served in the U.S. military during Vietnam, approximately 10,000 served *in* Vietnam. Eleven U.S. military women died while serving in Vietnam, one of them killed by enemy fire.

None of this information is stated or referred to in Mr. Webb's article titled "Jim Webb: Women Can't Fight." Perhaps the article should have been subtitled "U.S. Military Women May Not Shoot at the Enemy, But Can and May Be Fired Upon."

The authors are glad that neither Mr. Webb nor the men he led had to endure any time as prisoners of war; the authors are, however, disappointed that Mr. Webb did not present the facts that more than eighty-seven U.S. military nurses, after enduring the battles of Manila, Bataan, and Corregidor, and caring for thousands of wounded and ill soldiers, sailors, and marines, just as figuratively "carrying the country on their backs" as Webb and his classmates were "prepared" to do, went on "carrying" and caring for wounded and ill prisoners of war and civilian internees in Japanese prisoner-of-war/internment camps for thirty-seven additional months. It might be argued that a U.S. Marine Corps officer and graduate of Annapolis was obligated to present the facts as they are and not the "facts" as he sees them and to make clear that his personal opinions are just that—personal opinions—and not as manufactured "wishful facts" born out of prejudice, lack of academic scholarship, or what might be perceived as a deep and abiding unfairness and dishonesty where the contributions of U.S. military women in combat situations are concerned.[18]

Webb's opinions on U.S. military women in combat and the effects of military women on U.S. military culture vs. the facts: The intervening years between James H. Webb's 1979 article and the current-day wars in Iraq and Afghanistan are strong and irrefutable evidence that Webb's foresight is no better than his insight or his ability to take an objective stance on the topic of U.S. military women in combat. The authors, because of Senator Webb's refusal to grant an interview or supply any information on his current stands regarding the topics he addressed in his 1979 article in the *Washingtonian,* surveyed the literature—articles, interviews, newspapers, magazines, and electronic media—either authored by Mr. Webb, involving Mr. Webb, or written by an author addressing Mr. Webb's stands on the aforementioned topics. The authors admire and applaud Mr. Webb for his stand on and work concerning the new GI Bill, Post-9/11 Veterans Educational Assistance Act of 2008, and the amount of time—"dwell time"—a soldier or sailor is allowed to remain at home between deployments, an amendment to the 2008 Defense Authorization Act; however, they find his positions deplorable concerning women in the U.S. military, military women in combat, the military culture needed to produce military leaders, and the inability of "warriors" to control their sex drives and tendencies to violence beyond an eight-hour workday shift without giving those feelings physical or verbal expression.[19]

Mr. Webb's statements—"men fight better than women" and "men fight better without women present"—seem to be opinions based on belief rather than actual evidence. Mr. Webb's dismissal of the fact that women might be *needed* in the military and in combat in the future, are—to say the least—ill conceived, poorly reasoned, and indicative of a lack in the ability to plan or foresee the military needs that Senator Sam Nunn and others spoke about when an all-volunteer force was conceived, debated, and brought into existence. To understand the truth of this statement, one need only look at the factual history and current events involving U.S. military women in Iraq and Afghanistan.[20]

As of 31 May 2008, 97 U.S. military women have lost their lives in Operation Iraqi Freedom, and 13 U.S. military women have lost their lives in Afghanistan in Operation Enduring Freedom. Those lives were not more precious than the lives of the 3,979 men who lost their lives in Iraqi Freedom or the 495 men who lost their lives in Afghanistan in Operation Enduring Freedom; neither are the U.S. military women wounded in Iraq—all 585 of them—or the military women wounded while serving in Operation Enduring Freedom in Afghanistan worth one iota *more* than the 29,597 U.S. military men wounded in Iraq, or the 2,028 U.S. military men wounded in Afghanistan. However, neither is the military service nor the sacrifices these women made worth one iota *less* than the military service or sacrifices given by U.S. military men. These women *have earned* Purple Hearts, Silver Stars, Bronze Stars, Combat Action Badges, and other commendations. These women have served not only in combat zones, they have served on combat missions, for example, manning machine guns on Humvees while given the duty to protect other U.S. military or civilian personnel; they have taken part in searches for insurgents both in Iraqi homes, on the roads, in the streets, and at checkpoints where they are assigned to search Iraqi women for weapons and contraband.[21]

Anyone who heard President Bill Clinton's remark that whether he had sexual relations with Monica Lewinski depends on what the meaning of "is" is, will be interested to know that the definitions of "combat" subscribed to by the Department of Defense and by the U.S. Army are not in sync with each other. Both definitions are ambiguous enough to allow U.S. military women to be *used* on combat missions or in combat operations as long as the women are not officially *assigned* to a combat unit beneath the brigade level. U.S. military women cannot officially be sent to Iraq or Afghanistan to participate in direct combat; however, they can be to sent to Iraq for one particular reason, assigned to a noncombat unit, and then be "pulled" to take part in missions where the male soldiers involved are considered to be on combat missions. Sgt. Connie Rose Spinks was assigned to man the M249 Squad Automatic Weapon (SAW) on a Humvee, taking part in a "protection" mission when her Humvee was hit by a suicide car bomber, killing some and wounding her and others (see chapter 19).[22]

The young female marines "working in Falluja" at a checkpoint to search Iraqi women were not "assigned" to a combat unit when their truck was hit by a suicide car bomber, killing some and wounding others with second- and third-degree burns; nor were they considered "combat soldiers" when Iraqi insurgents fired on them while they lay on the road, taking care of each other and grabbing their rifles to fire at the enemy (see the Prologue).

Just as disturbing is the fact that for more than a century, American women have been volunteering to serve in the U.S. military in combat areas, have suffered wounds or been killed performing their duties, and yet were left out of U.S. history books and out of the history preserved and passed on by each branch of the U.S. Armed Forces. Ingratitude and injustice by the military, the Congress, historians, and even by relatives who leave women's military service out of family histories because no one cared enough to ask or thought that a woman just might have seen more "combat situations" than the men who never left the States, never heard an enemy bomb fall and explode or an enemy rocket attack, or heard an IED explode. The authors find Mr. Webb's opinions an insult of fairness to every American woman who has served in the U.S. Armed Forces of her country.

As far as Mr. Webb's comments in the remainder of his article are concerned, it is not possible to counter emotional, baseless, and patently sexist comments with logic. Mr. Webb's statements, including his description of Annapolis's Bancroft Hall as "a horny woman's dream," do not lend support to his conclusion that "these tendencies can be controlled in an eight-hour workday but cannot be suppressed in a twenty-four-hour, seven-days-a-week combat situation." Nor is Mr. Webb's following statement, "Introducing women into combat units would greatly confuse an already confusing environment and would lessen the aggressive tendencies of the units, as many aggressions would be directed inward, toward sex rather than outward toward violence. A close look at what has happened at the Naval Academy itself during the three years women have attended that institution is testimony to this," any more logical and fact-based than his previous sexist and illogical statements.[23]

The authors, who spent a combined fifty years working with military veterans and active-duty personnel, find it impossible to believe that U.S. men cannot control their "violent and sexual urges beyond an eight-hour workday," and consider Mr. Webb's statements in these matters illogical rationalizations for sexism and ignorance. Indeed, if Mr. Webb is correct about men not being able to control their "aggressive violent and sexual nature" for longer than an "eight-hour workday," it is a wonder that women are not being raped by men "who can't be expected to act against" what Mr. Webb considers "men's nature" on every street corner.[24]

On page 12 of Mr. Webb's article, he states, "Males in the society feel stripped, symbolically and actually. I wonder if that doesn't tie into the increase in rapes over the past decade. Rape is a crime of revenge, not passion. In any event, the real question isn't the women. The real question is this: Where in this country can someone go to find out if he is a man? And where can someone who knows he is a man go to celebrate his masculinity?" Success in war does not depend on masculinity or femininity or the celebration of either. Wars are won by citizens willing to put themselves in harm's way and die if necessary to protect their country.[25]

The U.S. Air Force was also busy creating new career paths for women. Another giant step along the path of change for military women was taken in October 1980, when Yvonne Morris began active duty and reported to Sheppard Air Force Base (AFB) in Wichita Falls, Texas, for three months of training on the Titan II Missile System. Morris's first close-up view of the Titan II missile came during a thirty-day deployment to McConnell AFB, Derby, Kansas, during the summer between her sophomore and junior years at the University of Virginia. Morris had enrolled in Air Force ROTC during her freshman year and the McConnell temporary duty was part of that program.

The thirty days at McConnell were filled with courses and instruction designed to see if the ROTC students were motivated and determined enough to succeed at challenges most had never faced before. Such courses in survival often end with an exercise to determine what the students learned. Usually, the students were left in a remote area without a supply of food or water. They would be on their own for several days and were to apply what they had been taught until they were collected by their instructors and debriefed.

Another challenge was learning to use a .38-caliber pistol. "I couldn't believe it," Yvonne Morris said. "My first time out of the box, I qualified as an expert marksman. I had never fired a handgun before. I think it had something to do with being very open to listening to what your instructor is telling you." She paused briefly. "I couldn't wait to tell my father and I called him on the weekend and told him, 'Dad, guess what I did.' I told him about my score with the .38 handgun and about eating grasshoppers for food on the survival test. His response was, 'Great!' And I could tell he was proud of me. I also got to tell him that I had graduated first in my flight."[26]

At the end of her thirty days at McConnell AFB, Morris returned to the University of Virginia (UVA) to prepare for her junior year. One of the decisions facing Morris was whether to interrupt her studies for a year in order to go to work and save enough money to get her through her next two years at UVA. Before the new academic year started, Morris was contacted by a recruiter from the air force, telling her that they would like to have her in the Titan II missile program after her graduation. Before Morris could say anything, the recruiter added that if she accepted the offer, the air force would pay all costs for her remaining two years at UVA. Morris accepted without hesitation and began her Titan training in the October following her graduation.

The classes and hands-on experience at Sheppard AFB included learning how the Titan II missile system worked and how the launchpad operated. The propellant fuel used in launch and during the flight of the Titan II was extremely toxic, and part of an officer's duty as a member of a Titan II missile crew was to transfer that fuel from a missile and replace it on a regular transfer schedule. One of the propellants, oxidizer nitrogen tetroxide, was poisonous when dissolved in water. The other propellant was an anticryogenic agent to prevent the oxidizer from freezing water when it mixed with water during the launch and flight to the target. Both substances were very toxic, so virulent that they could kill those exposed to them in a matter of minutes.[27]

The accidents causing the escape of propellant into a silo or onto a launchpad while Titan II crew members were working in the areas took the lives of several crew members during the twenty-one years of the Titan Missile Program—1963 to 1984. Investigation committees found that each of the accidents was caused by human error and not by faults within the Titan II Missile System. The accidents were discussed with students during the next stage of their training.[28]

When the three-month program ended, Morris and her flight were transferred to Vandenberg Air Force Base in California for several weeks of training on the classified aspects of a Titan II missile crew's job. "We learned how to use checklists; how to decipher coded [Emergency War Order Fast Reaction] messages that came in during an alert, and how SAC [the Strategic Air Command] does things." Crew members wore sidearms and were well instructed on when and why to use them. "Each of us knew that we would follow orders and procedures as we were charged to do our duty. I had no question at all that if the time came to push the button and launch those missiles, I would not hesitate." Instructors evaluated each student in the missile's procedure trainer. Morris said, "When you pass that evaluation, you have to give a classified briefing to the CO and this proves that you understand the classified responsibilities of your job. And it also proves that if you get orders to turn keys and launch missiles, that you will do that." Morris said that during alerts, checklist countdowns, and simulated launch, her thoughts were, "Please don't let me screw up, please don't let me screw up. I was so busy thinking that and following procedures that I never gave a thought to what would happen if I had to push the launch button."[29]

The responsibility of Titan II crew members for one another did not stop when they left the control room or the launch site. "Each of us knew that if we were to learn that a crew member was drinking to excess or just before reporting to a twenty-four-hour shift, we were to report that fact to our commander immediately," Morris recalled. "That also went for any domestic, romantic, or financial problems we learned about." Morris continued, "That kind of close contact frees the kind of knowledge we want to have about each other; it also makes a really strong bond; but for that to happen, you need to be on the same crew of nearly six months." Everyone in the program understood the importance of members of these crews staying focused on their mission.[30]

When training was completed at Vandenberg, Titan II crew members were transferred to their permanent duty stations. "We were all asked what our first choice of permanent station was. Mine was Davis-Monthan AFB in Arizona. Not many people chose the desert, so I got my first choice. At Vandenberg, we learned how the air force did things, and on our new permanent base, we would have six weeks of upgrade training to learn how the Strategic Air Command did things." At that point in the Titan system, the responsibilities of crews had been worked out. "Everything that we did with the Titan II system was done by a checklist that alleviates indecision—you don't have to depend on your memory—under stress, you can forget the color of your own eyes." The crew commanders were often junior officers. In Morris's early experience, she was a second lieutenant, the crew commander was a first lieutenant, and they had two enlisted men on their crew. Although Morris was the only woman on her crew, there were women on other crews at the missile site.[31]

After more than six months as a crew commander, Morris was selected for training as a Titan II missile commander. Each student completed the course work required, was tested, and had to go through a checklist with no mistakes. "When my partner and I were tested—my partner was a male officer who was senior to me and had much more experience than I—we reached the point where we had to do the math to figure out if our launch window was still open. Well, he got one answer and I got another. I thought I was right, but he was so much more experienced than I that I deferred to his figures and we launched the missile—in the test simulator." She paused, took a deep breath, and continued. "We were wrong. The instructors got up and came into the simulator control room. They weren't happy about what they had to do, and neither were we. My partner and I were out of the instructors' program, and we were each demoted on our jobs. I went back to line crew. I filled in for crew members who for one reason or another could not be on duty. The most time I spent with any crew at that time was two months. It was my job to see that they could pass their evaluations, so I couldn't develop strong ties with them. When my annual evaluation came up, I was selected for instructor training again and this time I passed. I became an instructor on upgrade training for crews for one year. Then I was promoted to senior deputy missile combat crew commander instructor; then I managed training for an entire wing."[32]

Morris described the one time in her air force career that she had been selected for something because she was a woman. "After I had been promoted to crew commander—about three months later, I developed terrible strep throat and the Flight Surgeon put me on medicine and cough syrup with codeine . . . and I was disqualified . . . from duty . . . because codeine is a narcotic, and I could not go on alert. I was home in my fuzzy pjs and slippers, watching TV and wondering, 'Oh, man, when is this going to be over?' " Morris paused. "The phone rang. It was my crew commander. 'I need you tomorrow.' I replied, 'The flight surgeon hasn't cleared me.' The commander asked, 'When was the last time you took your cough syrup?' " Morris told him that it was almost time to take it again. The commander replied, " 'Well, don't do that, lieutenant. I need you to go on alert.' " Morris agreed, got dressed, and went to the base hospital. Her physician conducted a blood test for codeine. The test was negative for narcotics, and he released Morris for duty, saying that she could go on alert the next day. "After I was finished and released by the surgeon, I found my squadron commander waiting in the hospital lobby," Morris said. The missile crews were evaluated annually by a unit whose job was to mobilize, fly to a wing, and that wing would have to show them all their records on operations. The inspection unit would select one crew to be evaluated in the missile trainer. Morris did not know at the time, because she had been ill and out of the loop, that the 390th was in the air and on their way to her wing. They would arrive the next morning and identify crews in that alert rotation to be pulled off for evaluation. Her squadron commander had it on good authority that the inspectors were looking for a good female crew commander. "I could barely talk. I had a sore throat," Morris remembered. Morris's commander told her again how much he,

1st Lt. Yvonne C. Morris, missile combat crew commander, Crew R-193, Launch Control Center, Titan II missile site 570–6, spring 1984.

her crew, and the wing needed her. He went on to say that he had every confidence that Morris could do very well. "We got a perfect score."[33]

In April 1983, Colonel Connie Slewitzke, Assistant Chief of the U.S. Army Nurse Corps, was appointed to a committee that was tasked with the mission of locating former POW nurses from World War II. Slewitzke suggested that the army and navy nurses who had served on Bataan and Corregidor and who were held prisoners of the Japanese be interviewed to preserve their history for future generations, both within and without the Army and Navy Nurse Corps. Slewitzke appointed twenty military people to do the interviews while the group was in Washington, D.C., for a recognition ceremony at the White House and a reunion. After thirty-eight years, these aging women were being recognized by the Veterans Administration and the Department of Defense.

Some of the former POW military nurses refused to be interviewed but after returning to their homes, changed their minds and called to say they were now willing to discuss some of their experiences. Colonel Slewitzke's staff located retired military people living close to the former POWs and assigned them to conduct the interviews, which are now included as part of the U.S. Army Nurse Corps Oral History Program.[34]

Another woman on the committee to honor former POW women was Dorothy L. Starbuck, the VA's Director of Veterans Benefits and former World War II WAC officer, who served in the European Theater of Operation. Together Slewitzke and Starbuck brought dedication, intelligence, and the authority to carry out their plans. The nation and the U.S. Armed Forces owe a debt of gratitude to these two women and the committee members who cared enough—and worked diligently—to present and preserve one of the nation's most valuable treasures for the American people and all the generations who will follow them.

September 1983 also saw the U.S. Army take several steps backward when it closed twenty-three military occupation specialties (MOS) that had previously been open to women, on the grounds that these army jobs were involved too closely with combat situations. Several months later, the army would be visiting their units in the United States, Japan, Korea, and Panama, asking women who had been forced to leave MOSs that were closed to them to reclassify for their previous specialties.[35]

One month later, U.S. troops were deployed in Operation Urgent Fury to restore stability in Grenada, a Caribbean country whose national leaders had been assassinated and where the presence of hostile foreign troops had been reported. There were more than a thousand Americans living on the island at the time. The army sent more than one hundred military women to Grenada to support the troops that landed there on 25 October 1983. These military women served in intelligence, military police, transportation, and communications. Once again, the U.S. Army was tangled up in its own ambivalence concerning the place of female soldiers in any hostile actions with a likelihood of combat taking place. An army officer in Grenada ordered four female MPs back to their duty station in North Carolina.[36]

When the four Eighty-second Airborne Division women reported at their post in North Carolina, senior officers ordered them back to Grenada to take part in the original mission to which they had been assigned. These actions and reactions, which took place between 2 November and 5 November 1983, were further evidence of the army's conflicted stand concerning assigning female soldiers to areas and with units likely to engage in combat. The words spoken by Representative Margaret Chase Smith more than forty-two years earlier when Congress and the U.S. Armed Forces were debating over the number of women to be permitted to serve in the military, which jobs should be open to women, where women should or should not be assigned were, "either you need these women, or you do not." Those words rang just as true and as clear in 1983 as they had in the Congress so many years before.[37]

In December 1983, the *Houston Post* carried an article, "Women GIs in Grenada," that described U.S. Army Lt. Katherine Henderson, dressed in her flight suit with a .45-caliber automatic strapped to her leg, piloting her military helicopter on night missions to seek holdout snipers in the hills. The article also mentioned Army Specialist Julie Escude, an MP assigned to guard the airport. Like all her brother and sister soldiers, she carried a weapon on or off duty. For Specialist Escude, that weapon was an M60 machine gun. More than two hundred army women took part in Operation Urgent Fury. These women received imminent danger pay while serving in Grenada.[38]

In September 1983, RADM Frances Shea and Brig. Gen. Hazel Johnson were honored by President Ronald Reagan at the White House. Admiral

Shea, now a rear admiral (upper half), the first two-star admiral in the U.S. Navy Nurse Corps, had postponed her retirement for three months in order to achieve a benchmark for her organization. "One of the reasons was that the Chief of Personnel asked several Flags [flag officers] to stay on for three months and I agreed. In addition, I was anxious to stay on because a bill had been passed . . . (through the efforts of other women Flag and General Officers) that would give us our second star . . . (from grade O-7 to grade O-8). . . . I was anxious to have that done, not so much for myself, because I would only have it for a couple of months, but because I wanted the precedent set . . . if we could get the precedent set that women had two stars . . . that would open the doors. . . . That's why I stayed on."[39]

Gen. Hazel W. Johnson, Director of the Army Nurse Corps, had been promoted to brigadier general on 1 September 1979. She was the first black American woman to achieve general officer status in all services of the U.S. Department of Defense. She also was the first Army Nurse Corps chief to earn a doctoral degree; she received her degree in education administration from Catholic University of America in Washington, D.C., in 1978. General Johnson retired on 31 August 1983 after twenty-eight years of service.[40]

RADM Frances Shea, NNC, USN; President Ronald Reagan;
and Brig. Gen. Hazel Johnson, ANC, AUS, 1983.

The year 1983 also saw the presidential appointment of CDRE Grace M. Hopper to the rank of rear admiral (lower half) O-7. This was another first for the woman the U.S. media had nicknamed "Amazing Grace." If ever a name suited an individual, it was seventy-seven-year-old Grace M. Hopper—the oldest officer on active duty.

This amazing woman was born Grace Brewster Murray on 9 December 1906 in New York City. Her parents, Mary and Roger F. Murray, were determined that their two daughters would have the same educational opportunities as their son. Grace's father encouraged both of his daughters not to follow the traditional roles or conventional paths assigned by society to women of that era. Grace followed her father's advice and pursued an education.

Grace received a B.A. in mathematics and physics from Vassar College in 1928; an M.A. in mathematics from Yale University in 1930; and a Ph.D. in mathematics from Yale in 1934. In 1930, Grace Murray married Vincent F. Hopper, an English instructor at New York University's School of Commerce. The couple separated in the early 1930s and divorced in 1945. Vincent F. Hopper was killed in World War II that same year. From 1931 to 1934, Grace Murray Hopper taught mathematics at her alma mater, Vassar College. After receiving her Ph.D., she continued to teach mathematics at Vassar but now as an associate professor.

In 1942, Grace left her teaching position at Vassar to accept a commission in the WAVES and served as a mathematician for the U.S. Navy's Bureau of Ordnance Computation Project at Harvard University, where she worked as a programmer on a calculation device known as the Mark 1, a forerunner of the electronic computer. In 1946, Grace M. Hopper left the WAVES and accepted a position in Harvard University's new Computational Laboratory. She continued to work on navy computers and maintained her naval commission in the U.S. Naval Reserve until 1966, when she retired. One year later, the navy recalled Commander Hopper to active duty and appointed her to oversee a project to standardize navy computer programs and

ADM Grace Murray Hopper, USN.

computer languages. In December 1983, Hopper was promoted to commodore.

Among the many awards that ADM Grace M. Hopper received in her long navy career was election as a Fellow of the Institute of Electrical and Electronic Engineers in 1962, and in 1969 Commander Hopper was selected by the Data Processing Management Association as its first Computer Sciences "Man of the Year." She created the computer language known as COBAL (common business-oriented language) and laid the foundations for the first practical compiler for today's computers—a program that translates written human instructions into codes that can be directly read by a computer. Chances are that the readers of this page have been impacted by one of Admiral Hopper's most lasting and widely used contributions to the world of computers and the English language. Admiral Hopper was the person who coined the phrase "There is a bug in the computer" back in 1945, when an actual moth caused a malfunction in the navy Mark 1 and was removed with tweezers.[41]

Among ADM Grace Hopper's most outstanding honors was her election—the first person from the United States and the first woman in history—to be made a Distinguished Fellow of the British Computer Society. She was also the first woman in history to earn a Ph.D. in mathematics from Yale University. The U.S. Navy paid her a fitting compliment by naming an Aegis destroyer (DDG 70) after Hopper—USS *Hopper*, aka *Amazing Grace.*

Admiral Hopper described herself as a "boat rocker," which the authors suspect is analogous to ADM Faye Abdellah's description of herself as a "book burner." Among the most complimentary words spoken about Amazing Grace Hopper were those of Secretary of the Navy John Lehman when he said, "She's challenged at every turn the dictates of mindless bureaucracy." And most certainly, the best advice Hopper gave to the groups of young people between the ages of seventeen and twenty years old who stood at the door to a future of discovery and meaningful contributions to human learning, knowledge, and the ability to change the world for good were "Go ahead and do it. You can apologize later."[42]

When Tracy A. Owens enlisted in the U.S. Navy in July 1988, she had completed one and a half years of a junior college program. Owens signed on with the navy hoping to be trained as a corpsman. There was a waiting list for corpsman training, and Owens faced a seventeen-month wait to attend that particular school. She made a decision and started her navy career as "undesignated," which put her in a category where the navy could assign her to whatever training was needed to fill jobs that were usually not the choice of volunteers, yet needed to be filled. After completing boot camp in Orlando, Florida, it was time to leave for the navy training that would prepare the "undesignated" for the job the navy had waiting for them. Owens described the selection process for the "undesignated." Those to be assigned for training stood in one large group. "A sailor stood in front of our group, pointed at a place roughly in the middle of the group, and said, 'This side of the room are seamen; this side are firemen.' . . . I was on the firemen side," Tracy Owens remembered. For the next five weeks, Owens would learn just what was expected of an undesignated fireman, an engineering rate. "I learned the tricks of the trade for electrician, boiler tech, and machinist mate—the very, very basic things." When her training was complete, Owens went home on leave, then flew into Norfolk, Virginia, and made her way to her new assignment, the USS *L. Y. Spear*, a submarine tender. "I was an undesignated fireman who did not have a job in the ship. . . . It was a long, long way from 'corpsman,' " Owens said.[43]

When Owens reported aboard the *L. Y. Spear*, it was Thanksgiving Day, so there was only a skeleton crew aboard. "The duty person said, 'What do you want to be—where do you want to work?' " Owens remembered. Owens chose electrician, "because I thought it would be cleaner," but she ended up assigned to the boiler room. "He [the duty officer] handed me a blanket and a pillow and said, 'We'll see you on Tuesday.' This was only Thursday." Owens was so unfamiliar with life aboard ship, that she mistakenly thought that she had to pay for meals, and she was short of cash. By the time another female sailor befriended her and she learned that "food was free," she had not eaten for several days.[44]

"I did go to the boiler room and I worked on boilers. I repaired them, cleaned them, and serviced them," Owens said. "There were no females down in the pit. They really didn't like me too well. It was rough. They didn't want women in the boiler room." Their attitude was that any woman down there was looking for a soft job, and they were not about to help her. "So they were mean," Owens remembered. "It took me five or six months to fit in. At first, I was the brunt of most of the jokes, and they only answered my questions when they felt like it," Owens continued.[45]

She finally got a break in the men's attitude toward her. "I remember one incident where there was a big valve behind the boiler; it's called a 'steam-stop.' My chief gave me a huge monkey wrench that was almost as big as me, and said, 'Go open the steam-stop.' I said, 'Okay.' I knew I couldn't open the valve, and no one had ever given me substantial help. I got to the valve, and when I looked up, there were some of the guys walking across the catwalk in my direction. They took the wrench and opened the valve for me. Then they handed the wrench back to me and said, 'Go tell the chief that you opened the valve.' That was my real break. Once they saw that I was going to work, they treated me like a little sister; I was part of the team." Owens wanted to change her rate (job) but was told that there were not enough people to replace her, so she would have to wait. "There weren't as many options as there are now," Owens said. "They just weren't available back then."[46]

Operation Just Cause, the military intervention in Panama, was launched on 20 December 1989. The goal of the operation was to arrest Manuel Noriega and bring him to the United States for trial. Noriega had taken control of Panama in 1983, when he became the head of the National Guard and used that position to widen and strengthen his power. Corruption grew in the government and Noriega became a key figure in drug trafficking. By 1987, Noriega was using his power to imprison or kill dissenters. Conditions worsened and reached a critical point on 15 December 1989, when the Panamanian legislature declared Noriega president and announced that a state of war existed between Panama and the United States. When Panamanians killed a U.S. Marine wearing civilian clothes, President George H. W. Bush ordered the implementation of Operation Just Cause—the largest U.S. military operation since Vietnam. Just Cause involved 25,000 troops. The operation achieved its goals when Noriega, who had taken sanctuary inside the Vatican Embassy, surrendered on 3 January 1990. Noriega was taken to the United States, tried on drug trafficking charges, convicted, sentenced to forty years in prison, and began serving his sentence in a federal prison in Miami, Florida.

Approximately 800 U.S. Army and Air Force women took part in Just Cause. Army women flew Black Hawk helicopters, carrying supplies and troops, doing their jobs—frequently under enemy fire. Air Force women flew cargo and refueling missions, again, frequently under enemy fire.

About 150 U.S. military women worked regularly in combat zones. Army and air force women worked in intelligence, special operations, finance, and the signal corps.

For a brief period of time in 1990, the name of one military woman serving in Operation Just Cause in Panama became a household word. On 20 December 1989 at approximately 1:30 a.m., Capt. Linda L. Bray of the 519th Military Police (MP) Battalion led a platoon of MPs in an operation to take and hold a military dog kennel near Panama City. When the platoon arrived, they received small-arms fire and realized that members of the Panamanian Defense Forces (PDF) were occupying the kennel building. Captain Bray gave an order to have the platoon's translator ask the PDF members to surrender. The only response was more gunfire from the kennel, and Bray's platoon returned fire until all enemy opposition ceased, and the platoon took possession of the kennel.

When Noriega surrendered and the story broke in newspapers in the United States, Capt. Linda L. Bray was celebrated as the first U.S. Army woman to lead a unit in combat. The Pentagon obviously decided to take advantage of the positive press about Captain Bray and her unit and released additional comments about the captain and the mission she had led.

On 4 January 1990, the *New York Times* published an article, "Noriega's Surrender: Army; For First Time, a Woman Leads GIs in Combat." Administration officials told the press that an army woman led an attack against Panamanian Defense Forces: "The first time a woman commanded American soldiers in battle." "Three P.D.F. men were killed . . . American troops could have been killed." Later the same day, White House spokesman Marlin Fitzwater told the press, "It was an important military operation. A woman led it, and she did an outstanding job." Pentagon officials added that women were barred from serving in direct combat roles, but were permitted to serve in military police units. The same officials were quick to add that "there was no hard and fast distinction between combat and military police roles in Panama." The spokesman also said that the force of thirty soldiers that Capt. Linda L. Bray led was composed of both men and women. "That official added that no one should draw a conclusion from Captain Bray's mission about the desirability of using women in such roles. . . . What has been demonstrated is the ability of women to lead, for men and women to work as a team without out distraction and for women to react in an aggressive manner."[47]

Captain Bray might well have been the answer to central casting's search for an unlikely woman to play the part of an American soldier leading thirty troops in an attack on an enemy position. Unlike the Amazons of old portrayed in a black-and-white movie, Bray stood five feet one inch tall and weighed slightly more than a hundred pounds. The company she commanded had 123 soldiers in it, men and women. The unit she led in the 20 December 1989 attack on a PDF facility was composed of men and women and, as it has always been in the U.S. Armed Forces, those men and women fought for the soldiers who fought with them. As Anna Quindlen discussed in her *New York Times* column of 7 January 1990, men in combat had already overcome the instinct of self-preservation in order to engage in combat, so why should they be overcome with an instinct to protect women? Quindlen quipped that such an assumption contradicted years of her own experience traveling on crosstown buses or elevators with men.[48]

The assumed instinct to protect women seems well controlled or non-existent among male firefighters working with female firefighters, or policemen working with policewomen. Finally, we come to the argument that men do not want to see women have to experience the horrors of war and combat. A review of the history of military women in World War I, World War II, Korea, Vietnam, Grenada, and Panama would reveal that the United States has sent female military nurses into combat zones and locations well within the range of enemy guns, planes, and bombs—in places like Bataan and Corregidor, Sicily and Anzio, nurses were just behind or on, and sometimes in front of, the front lines—in order to care for wounded GIs. When U.S. Army Nurses went in with the troops on D-Day in North Africa, American GIs and commanders called them ever forward to treat combat wounded, and on Bataan and Corregidor, they evacuated male soldiers—and General MacArthur's china and silverware—rather than allocate those women to all available space for evacuation.

There were no male military nurses in the military nurse corps until 1955 for the army, and 1965 for the navy; male military nurses are still in the minority. During the Battle of the Bulge in December 1944, women nurses were left behind to take care of male soldiers who needed their care. Unlike the horrors male soldiers experience in separate firefights, military nurses see the horrors of war—the decimated human bodies—every day, day in and day out. For military nurses, it is as if all the most horrible nightmares born of war are gathered up and brought to them—hour after hour, day after day. Women have never been spared the horrors of war, and anyone who thinks they have does not know their military history.

Anna Quindlen was right on target when she pointed out that the question of whether women should fight alongside men in combat goes to a deeply emotional level, tangled with what society expects, how society and men define themselves in contrast to the feminine. Are women frozen in place to preserve male gender roles? It must have been a shock for the Pentagon to realize that the publicity they gained from the dissemination of Capt. Linda L. Bray's story was affecting the public and the U.S. military in ways the Pentagon and Congress considered negative and potentially dangerous to the U.S. Armed Forces as they had known them and wanted them to remain.

There is a phenomenon in psychology called secondary gain, where an individual or institution is willing to accept something the person or the institution does not really want in order to gain something else it can acquire through the acceptance of the condition, that is, something derived from or consequent to a primary event or thing. It is very possible and probable that the U.S. Armed Forces, Congress, and the majority of our nation are willing to accept women in the military in exchange for the secondary gain of doing away with the draft and lulling themselves into the belief that America no longer needs a people willing to sacrifice and commit two or three years of service giving back to the country, or to accept an all-volunteer force no matter what the price, for the secondary gain of believing that the young men and women killed or wounded in war "knew what they were getting into when they volunteered."

The authors, who have spent a combined fifty years working with active-duty U.S. military, U.S. Armed Forces Reserves, and veterans from all of America's wars in the twentieth and twenty-first centuries to date, have heard too many Americans say in a callous or defensively angry tone of voice, "The people who are fighting volunteered. They didn't have to join the military," or "Wounded veterans get exactly the medical care and benefits they signed on for when they joined. It's always been like that." We have yet to meet the individual or institution that has not responded with denial and anger when they are told the facts that diminish the comfort provided by the secondary gain they would do just about anything to keep.

By the end of the first week in January 1990, the Pentagon and the Department of Defense were beginning to backpedal on their original statements concerning Captain Bray and the mission she led to secure the military dog kennel outside Panama City. The *New York Times* ran an article on 8 January 1990, "The U.S. and Panama: Combat; Report of Woman's Role Is Called into Question."[49]

The article quoted an army spokesman in Panama. "Col. James L. Swank said Captain Bray 'and all other female officers are currently unavailable for comment until authorized by the Secretary of the Army.' " The army seemed to be in full operational mode to "clarify, with newly acquired facts," the events that had propelled Captain Bray and her unit into the national spotlight and led to an allegedly exaggerated retelling of what Captain Bray and her unit had actually done during their mission to capture a PDF military guard-dog kennel. The army and government officials in Washington, D.C., and Panama were now disseminating information they hoped would quiet, if not end, the debate concerning using military women in direct combat roles. To slow down—if not completely stop—the debate, government officials were now telling a very different version of the events involving Captain Bray's unit's mission on 20 December 1989 and how that mission played out.[50]

For starters, the new "evidence" appears to have originated with the top commanders in the Panama-based Southern Command, which ran the entire operation. A spokesman for the Southern Command, Gen. Bill McClain, stated that Captain Bray never reported any PDF casualties, nor did the Defense Department's Panama-based Southern Command. General McClain told the press, "Your colleagues [in the press] must have reported that, from rumors." He added, "Bray was not even at the kennel when the shooting started. She was a half a mile away at a command post."[51]

In a follow-up article published by the *Los Angeles Times* on 11 January 1990, Lawrence J. Korb, former Assistant Secretary of Defense for Manpower, Installations, and Logistics during the first term of the Reagan administration and currently the director of public policy and education with the Brookings Institution, stated, "You can sit in a lab, or in a staff room in the Pentagon and say, 'This is more likely to be combat than that.' But everything becomes combat." Korb continued, "Panama is a turning point in the debate. People can no longer pretend that women are not going to be in danger."[52]

The article further states that women comprise roughly 11 percent of the United States' 2.1 million active-duty personnel and, according to the Pentagon, roughly 88 percent of all military job classifications are open to women. That boils down to approximately 56 percent of all actual military occupational specialties (MOS) since a large number of soldiers are assigned to combat-related jobs that continue to be barred to women. MOS positions open to women include transport pilot and missile silo officer. Yet, women are still barred from all army infantry, artillery, and armor; from navy submarines and all surface combat ships, and from flying air force fighters and bombers. The army cites gender distinctions in explaining why women who served in Panama will not be eligible to receive one of the army's most valued decorations, the Combat Infantryman Badge: because the units in which women serve are defined as "noncombat."

"The combat label and the combat definition have driven women crazy in the service for years," Gen. Evelyn Foote said. The article went on to site Northwestern University military sociologist Charles Moskos's statement that "If women are to be treated exactly like men in the military, then they have to be just as liable to be sent into combat as all men are."[53]

During the fall of 1989, the Defense Department Advisory Committee on Women in the Services (DACOWITS) recommended that women be allowed to enter all military fields, including combat, during a four-year test period. That test period was never established by the military, however, as an unbiased look at history already reveals; women have been "tested" again and again, without the results being tabulated, documented, and becoming part of the official record or even a part of the history written by America's historians during World War II, Korea, Vietnam, Grenada, or Panama. The Nigerian proverb that says "Until lions have their own historians, tales of the hunt shall always glorify the hunter" has proven to be true, generation after generation.

Meg Sternberg, the former vice chair of DACOWITS, said, "In the past when I've met with Congressmen, they've all said they're not going to deal with it until it becomes an issue they have to deal with." Sternberg added, "I've traveled all over the world and talked with thousands of women in the military, and at least seventy-five percent of them feel they ought to have the right to go into combat."[54]

Lawrence Korb, in 1990, hit the nail on the head again when he said, "Women are being put in danger, but denied the rewards that those in direct combat positions are entitled to in the service. Who gets promotions in the Air Force? The fighter pilot. The woman [who] is flying the tanker—she's in just as much danger, but she can't get the promotions."[55]

Gen. Evelyn Foote summed up the injustice faced by U.S. military women when she responded to a comment by Joseph Zengerle, a former Assistant Secretary of the Air Force: "We're not accustomed to seeing blinded women hobble off planes with amputated limbs, or women in prison camps threatened with rape or torture. Those prospects stir our emotions . . . in ways that have a bearing on our national sentiments and our national will. We haven't had to see that yet." General Foote's reply was a direct response to the myth that women have never been in harm's way, wounded, or killed, when she stated, "There were Navy women killed by terrorists in Naples. There were women on the flight that crashed in Gander. Nurses in Vietnam were killed and, during World War II, about eighty military nurses were captured by the Japanese and were prisoners of war for four years in the Philippines. They all survived and came home. But these facts continued to be brand-new news to so many people who never see women in this context. Women have been casualties in all wars—there's nothing new about that."[56]

17

★

Women in men-only jobs have proved their capabilities over and over—in outer space, on fire ladders, on the police beat and in the Persian Gulf. Their accomplishments proved the irrationality of the arguments marshaled against them. If questions remain about just how wide the door to combat roles should be opened, the only answers Americans should find acceptable must henceforth be founded in common sense.

New York Times editorial,
30 April 1993

On 2 August 1990, less than seven months after the official end of Operation Just Cause, Iraqi troops invaded Kuwait. Four days later, on 6 August 1990, President George H. W. Bush ordered the deployment of U.S. Armed Forces to defend Saudi Arabia in the opening volleys of Operation Desert Shield. Just eight days after Saddam Hussein's military marched into Kuwait, the U.S. Coast Guard began to take a major role in preparing America and the U.S. military for battles that were yet to come.

When the U.S. Navy asked the United States Coast Guard (USCG) to provide cutters and crews to aid in a naval blockade and inspection of the cargos of all ships sailing in the Iraq and Kuwait area, the marine safety officers of the coast guard became responsible for the establishment and supervision of post security detachments in the coastal ports of the United States. The port of Wilmington, North Carolina, was the jumping-off place for the majority of U.S. troops and equipment deploying to the Middle East. A young coast guard lieutenant, Jane Hartley, a native of Mount Dora, Florida, was stationed at the Port of Wilmington at the time and was aware of the major decisions being made in regard to port safety and how best to carry out the new mission of the coast guard in Operation Desert Shield. "The Navy asked for coast guard ships and crews, and was not happy when they looked at crew rosters," CAPT Jane Hartley remembered. "They wanted the coast guard to replace coast guard women who were in positions of leadership aboard those ships." Hartley went on

CAPT Jane Hartley, USCG (Ret.)

to explain that the coast guard trained and integrated women in 100 percent of the MOS categories available to coast guard men. The coast guard was a relatively small service compared to the army, navy, marines, and air force, and could not afford to squander the talents and skills of women or men in shaping the best possible organization to carry out the mission assigned to it. Lieutenant Hartley was living proof of that decision and resolve.[1]

In the early and mid-1970s, Hartley would have laughed at the thought of herself as a member of any U.S. Armed Forces military branch. "I'm a child of the sixties," Captain Hartley said. "The thought of going into the coast guard or any other military branch was about as far from my mind as it could get." She went on to explain that she was giving a dinner party, and her husband, a former navy corpsman, had invited his boss as one of the dinner guests that evening. "During dinner, my husband's boss started talking to me about how much the coast guard needed women," Hartley said. "I had graduated from the University of North Carolina at Chapel Hill with a master's degree in environmental biology, and North Carolina was not the best place for a woman to find a job in the environmental sciences." Hartley continued, "Anyway, I couldn't get this guy to shut up, and I needed to serve dessert, so I told him I would check out the coast guard in the very near future.[2]

"Fortunately, I had a father who encouraged his wife and daughter to explore possibilities not usually thought of as areas for women, so I did go to a recruiting station and talk to the recruiters. Six months later, I was in the Coast Guard Reserve. . . . After 'Knife and Fork School' [CG officer orientation], I reported to Oregon Inlet [on the Outer Banks], as a Coast Guard Reservist. I liked it right away, and I liked the people. From the beginning, and all through my career, I met people who blew me away . . . and on top of that, life in the coast guard was a lot of fun."[3] Hartley's voice sounded as enthusiastic as her words.

When Hartley was promoted to lieutenant junior grade, she took on new responsibilities. "I was appointed CO of my unit," Hartley said. "It was the first time in the Fifth District that a woman had been placed in charge of a unit of men, and the guys were wonderful. They respected and took care of me." Hartley went on to describe her first Fifth District inspection. She portrayed the officer doing the inspection as "the nicest man in the world," and quickly added, "but his inspections were ridiculous." Hartley recalled that day. "We were waiting for the inspecting officer to come by and get started. All thirty-five guys in the unit knew I was terrified. The chief was standing in front of me—everyone standing at attention—and he's giving me prompts so I would know what I was supposed to do at any particular moment." She took a deep breath. "Well, the inspecting officer gigged me for a sloppy salute. He said my little finger was down too far when I saluted." Hartley remembered that after the inspection ended, one of her men, a seaman third class who was a police officer in eastern North Carolina, was very angry because the inspector had gigged Hartley in front of her entire unit. "He wanted to tell this O-6 [captain] that one of his ribbons was on upside-down. And he wanted to tell the O-6 in private." Hartley chuckled. "I told him, 'Oh, no! Don't do that!' "[4]

Many of the men in Hartley's reserve unit worked as civilians at a nearby military base. One man in particular stood out in Hartley's mind for what she had learned about leadership while working with him. She was determined to have all of her unit receive training that would allow them to advance in grade. Her good intentions did not always have the effects she was hoping for. "This one guy—his name was 'Bubba'—and he was a seaman second class and couldn't care less about advancing in grade," Hartley recalled. "He belonged to one of the oldest families in Lizzie City [Elizabeth City]. He showed up. He did his reserve time and wasn't interested in promotions. When it came to carpentry, however, the man was a master magician. He could build or fix anything. One of the things he had made was a Steam Jenny that was used every year at Christmastime when the base held an oyster roast and invited all the brass from the district in Norfolk. Everyone would come. It was really a big deal." She paused, and then continued. "Well, Bubba hadn't been to school since Hector was a pup. He was as determined not to go to school as I was to have him go. I can remember the chief telling me, 'You really don't want to do this to Bubba, ma'am.' Well, yes, I did! Then the Steam Jenny broke, and it looked as if no one—Bubba—was going to fix it in time for the oyster roast. It was a major crisis because everybody and his brother were coming to this big yearly event, and there was no working Steam Jenny to roast the oysters on." She took a deep breath and exhaled slowly. "The chief is telling me, 'This is terrible. Bubba won't break easy!' Well, I lost. We got the Steam Jenny fixed and Bubba didn't go to school. I had to make a deal with him. I wasn't a kid when I went into the guard, and one of the things that I had learned through experience—and innately understood—was that you had to know when to hold them, and know when to fold them when you weren't going to win."[5]

That was the lesson the U.S. Navy learned about those coast guard vessels and crews that they needed for Operation Desert Shield. Hartley remembered, "The navy got its underwear in a bunch because we had ships going over [to Operation Desert Shield/Storm] with women as leaders in the theater and that was a real shakeup for them. They said, 'You can't do that!' And we said, 'Then you can't have the ships because you can't take the COs off the vessels.' "[6]

For some military women, their choice of the best way to arrive in the Persian Gulf had nothing to do with land or sea. Lt. Col. Nanette Gallant is one of those women. On 2 August 1990, when the U.S. Army's Eighty-second Airborne was put on alert for deployment to the Persian Gulf, Capt. Nanette Gallant volunteered and was selected as part of the advance party that would parachute into Saudi Arabia. She would ride in and jump from the first assault plane, and, for a period of time, she would be the only woman on the ground with nine hundred men of the Eighty-second Airborne. "When Kuwait was invaded, I got a call at home telling me to pack my bags because the division was alerted," Lieutenant Colonel Gallant remembered. "I went in to work and the colonel in charge of our unit . . . the Material Management Center, said, 'Well, who should be going on the first plane . . . to set up supply sources for the people going on the first infantry defense unit?' I said, 'Well, of course, it's me.' In the back of my mind, I didn't believe that they would let a woman do that. And he said, 'OK.' And I about fainted on the spot," Nanette Gallant said. "I was the first woman to ever go on the assault, which is the first plane, the assault command post with the Eighty-second, and I got in there and as far as I know . . . there was no other woman there when we first reached the ground. It was very strange. By the time all the planes landed it was me with nine hundred men, but nobody touched me, nobody bothered me. I felt like I was a regular teammate, so that was a pretty exciting thing—I'll always remember that."[7]

Nanette Gallant was born in Salt Lake City, Utah, in 1956. Her father had served as a medic during World War II and went to medical school when the war ended.

Gallant was taking university classes when she decided that she was out of shape and needed an early morning exercise class. "I saw a class for fitness that was offered at 6:00 a.m.—I had no idea that it was an ROTC class. I had been around the ROTC," Gallant said. "I joined the class, and could do, like, one push-up . . . and instead of laughing at me, they encouraged me, and I thought that was pretty neat . . . I became physically fit. They offered me a chance to go to camp, which I didn't know was basic training, so I did that."[8]

When Gallant completed airborne training, she was assigned to the Eighty-second Airborne Division and took every chance she could to jump. She attended jump master school; about 60 percent of the class washed out. She graduated and moved on to jump from a C-5, one of the largest planes the army flies. "It's so big that when you jump out and you look up, it's going over you and it seems like a lifetime," Gallant said. "It's just so huge. It can carry two tanks." Gallant continued, "As a master parachutist, you can do what is called chase jumps, and I made it my life to network to get parachute jumps. I would jump every Sunday. I would jump with every service—air force, navy, marine corps. I would try to jump as much as I could." Gallant paused. "You have to have sixty-five jumps to be a master parachutist and then a certain number of night jumps, a certain number of jumps with particular units called tactical and mass-tactical. I went out of my way to meet all the qualifications. It was kind of a badge of honor because, as a woman, if you don't have some of the things to be competitive, you're already fighting from the bottom up. Once they see that you have master wings at least you have one sign of recognition when you have to go into units with hard-core males."[9]

Captain Gallant's job on the ground in Saudi Arabia was crucial. "I was the acting Division Support Commander . . . and I was doing his job on his behalf, helping to locate where the tents go . . . where the supply areas would be, and we were waiting on the rest of our people to follow. Then I assumed my role as the General Supply Officer, and I worked with my NCOs to arrange for all the . . . food, fuel, all of those things."[10]

This would not be Nanette Gallant's last time in the Persian Gulf. Fifteen years later, she would return as Lt. Col. Nanette Gallant and again lead the Eighty-second Airborne troops in yet another war in the Persian Gulf.

One of the military women with the Eighty-second Airborne Division who arrived in the Middle East after Capt. Nanette Gallant was Army Chaplain Capt. Priscilla Mondt. Mondt, who was born in Des Moines, Iowa, on 15 October 1956, enrolled in ROTC while a student at the University of Tennessee at Chattanooga, where she majored in psychology and minored in education and Bible studies. Mondt attended the Assemblies of God Theological Seminary in Springfield, Massachusetts, and graduated in 1981. Mondt then served in the U.S. Army Reserves until she was called up for active duty in 1989. "I always knew I was going to end up being an army chaplain," Priscilla Mondt remembered. "I was always telling people that. No one told me that there was no such thing as a female army chaplain . . . it will never happen."[11]

After graduating from chaplaincy school at Fort Monmouth, New Jersey, Mondt was assigned to the Eighty-second Airborne and transferred to Fort Bragg, North Carolina, for jump training. "Well, I really didn't want to go to Airborne . . . A friend had given me a book about Airborne chaplains; I said, 'Lord, if this is really what you want me to do, then you're going to have to heal my knees,' because I had pretty strong knee problems, 'and get me to Fort Bragg where they jump.' So when they told me my first duty station was Fort Bragg, I was like, 'Oh, man!' My father had been Airborne . . . I didn't tell my father that I was in Airborne school. I wanted to call him on his birthday, the same day we were to graduate, but we got weathered out and had to wait until Monday," Mondt remembered. "I called him on his birthday, and he said, 'Where are you?' I told him I was at Fort Bragg, and he said, 'You're in Airborne school, aren't you?' I said, 'How did you know that?' He said, 'I knew that you were up to something . . .' " Mondt continued. "The men accepted me fine. There were a lot of women there. When it came to jump week, when I was doing my push-ups, I could see all these feet around me. When I got up, there were all these soldiers who were waiting on me, because they wanted prayer. The chaplains are sort of a good-luck charm. The CO told me that they'd never had a chaplain be the first out the door [of the aircraft] for the company. That was because they always sent the women first, so the women were not intimidated by the guys."[12]

After graduation, Captain Mondt reported to the Eighty-second Airborne Division, and in August 1990, she deployed with them to the Middle East. "When we rolled into Iraq, I wondered, 'Where are my role models?' I had nobody that had done this before, to ask questions of; that

Chaplain (Capt.) Priscilla A. Mondt,
headquarters, Division Support Command,
Eighty-second Airborne Division, March 1991,
with full gear ready to board C-130 to leave
Iraq going to Saudi Arabia for redeployment
back to the States.

was the first time that it dawned on me that I was a pioneer; I was the first female chaplain in the Eighty-second. That was the reason that they wanted me to be already qualified to be Airborne—they'd never had a woman chaplain before." Mondt recalled, "My first funeral that I did was a cremation. There was no body at the graveside. We were waiting for the family. There was a black sergeant major there who was in charge of the honor guard. We had been waiting an hour for these folks—they were late. We started chatting. He said to me, 'Ma'am, I've talked with you long enough. I want to tell you something. A couple of years back, we were talking with a chaplain, and we were betting on whether there would ever be a female in the Eighty-second,' and he said the chaplain said that there would be one, and the black man said that there would not be one. He said that it was hard enough for blacks to integrate; a woman [chaplain] will never come to the Eighty-second. He said, 'I lost that bet.' And he reached out his hand to shake mine and said, 'And I'm glad that I lost that bet. Welcome to the Eighty-second.' "[13]

Captain Mondt pointed out that ministering to the Eighty-second was easy. All of the men are on jump status and they considered the chaplain to be their good-luck charm and God's representative on the jump. "If the chaplain is with us, then God is with us, and we'll have a good jump," the soldiers would tell each other.

When Capt. Priscilla Mondt first arrived in Iraq, she was somewhat surprised to discover that some of the evangelical chaplains told the men that the end of the world was at hand, and they had better get saved. "They had been told *not* to question God," Mondt recalled. "I would sit with kids and they'd say, 'Well, this is oil that comes from fossils, and are dinosaurs in the Bible?' And my boss would get mad. I'd tell him that they were thinking and asking questions, and that meant they were actively thinking and searching."[14]

Mondt was emphatic concerning where the chaplains stood in regard to women. "I wasn't accepted by these chaplains because I'm a woman. Most of them were from evangelical backgrounds. I said, 'You all signed a statement that you can minister to any religion, any race, and both genders. Why don't you want me here?' One chaplain responded for all of the evangelical chaplains who were present. 'You sign that statement and then volunteer for the airborne where there are no women and then you came along and ruined it . . . ' The reason they could get away with that was that the general officer who was in charge of the Eighty-second at that time, General James Johnson, made it very clear; he openly said that he didn't want women in that division and that he was going to get rid of them by attrition. So it went from 1,500 or so with 300 women, and it went down to 150 women. He cut it in half and was working to reduce it more." Major Mondt continued, "Gen. Carl Steiner had sent me with his blessing—in fact he called while I was in airborne school and asked how I was. I thought people were lying when they said that he'd called. I said, 'Yeah, right!' He was a three-star general. He had me report to him when I got back from airborne school, when I got through. . . . And sent me down to the Eighty-second with the chaplain corps commander's blessing." Mondt paused. "When I got there, the two-star—the division commander—didn't have a choice; he had to accept me. And then, not only accepted me, but I ended up with a combat patch."[15]

Unfortunately, quite a few of the enemy that military women faced were American men dressed in the same uniform all American soldiers wore. Sexism was still alive and doing well despite the courage, patriotism, skills, and efficiency military women displayed every day.

On 22 August 1990, President George H. W. Bush authorized the call-up of members of the selective reserve to active duty in support of Operation Desert Shield. When U.S. Air Force Nurse Lt. Col. Patricia Wilson's reserve unit was called up for Operation Desert Shield, the reservists were flown to Scott Air Force Base in Illinois; most of its members were surprised that a medical unit, trained to backfill for an active-duty unit in the States, would be deploying to the Middle East in support of the coalition troops who would be fighting Iraqi forces to drive them back into Iraq. "We were very serious about our piece of the mission," Lieutenant Colonel Wilson remembered. "We had heard that we might deploy, and I had also heard stories about medical units deploying to areas where they were unprepared for the jobs that were assigned to them. We were a well-trained unit and I don't believe any of us considered ourselves unprepared to treat combat casualties." She paused. "What I and others did worry about was our lack of preparation for the field conditions we might face. We had never really been trained in the quick use of our gas masks in case of a chemical attack, but we had four days of field training ahead of us and going through the gas chamber was part of it. We also learned that all the physicians in our unit, except one, would be remaining at Scott Air Force Base. The only physician going with us from our group was our anesthesiologist.[16]

"Before leaving Robins AFB in Georgia, I had packed two bags. One with summer clothes in case we were sent to the desert, and one with winter clothes in case we stayed at Scott." In addition to going through the gas chamber, members of the reserve unit were issued M-16 rifles and taught how to aim, fire, and care of the weapon. Officers usually were equipped with a 9 mm, but the rifle had been issued to them instead. Wilson said that the one aspect of being deployed where they could have used more training was in the use of the gas mask in an emergency situation. "I spent some time sitting on my bed and timing myself, putting the mask on until I felt pretty confident that I could move fast and accurately," Wilson continued.[17]

"I heard that one unit landed twenty miles from the front and had no one with them who knew how to set up their tents. They had to live in foxholes and trenches until people who knew how to put the tents up and take care of their maintenance arrived." Lieutenant Colonel Wilson and her reservists felt lucky when they found themselves in an environment that, at first glance, did not appear to be close to anything. "When I got over my sleepiness, I took the time to look at a couple of maps and found out that our location wasn't even very close to the coastal city of Muscat [in Oman, on the Arabian Peninsula], which was the nearest city to us. In a few minutes, I realized that running into Saddam Hussein and his troops was not high on a list of probabilities. We were about six hundred miles from Kuwait and farther than that from Iraq."[18]

Lieutenant Colonel Wilson continued. "I had dreams before I left and after I got there . . . I felt so old. I should have been in a war back when I was twenty-two versus when I was forty-five because when I was forty-five, I kept dreaming about these young men who were in pain. And I had this syringe with morphine and I would just be running and I could hear these voices. I would be so tired because I couldn't get from one end down to the other end. I would wake up in a cold sweat thinking, they

Lt. Col. Patricia Wilson, NC, USAF (right) with fellow reservist,
Saudi Arabia, 1991, Operation Desert Storm.

don't need the forty-five-year-old Pat. They need the twenty-two-year-old Pat. And maybe I could keep up with this." Wilson said that she remembered all the long hours the nurses worked, and the intensity of that duty, during the Vietnam War. "I had a navy nurse friend . . . and they were fourteen hours on and then they'd have to get up again and go to work. I guess that's what I was envisioning and I thought that I just wouldn't be strong enough to do this. And then after I looked at the map again and thought that somebody would have to be a fool to come here and visit us! I didn't think it was going to happen. I felt so responsible. . . . I figured that I could man that darn gun. I was in pretty good shape at forty-five, but I wasn't sure that I could do the long hours and stay on top of my game."[19]

Wilson soon realized that the enemy they faced was boredom rather than the Iraqis. "We had no casualties and eight hundred people with little or nothing to do. When we first got there, we quickly learned that we'd have to make assignments to keep people doing something. Because we had a lot of people—450 were medical, the other were pilots, engineers, security police. From the medical standpoint, what were we going to do with these medical folks? There was nothing medical coming in here, so those of us who were educators went to work. You assigned them to where they were to work and assigned them mock casualties. We would mock up seventy people, then that got old." Wilson took a deep breath, then continued. "We decided to give them trauma courses because we had over fifty board-certified intensivists, several anesthesiologists, and ICU nurses, so we gave a mini-trauma course. We did a mini-ACLS [advanced cardiac life support] course. We did all these courses to keep them showing up, to keep them busy so that they had a schedule." Wilson went on, "It was hard to keep 450 people centered on a task and keep them motivated to show up for work and not looking for devious ways of not showing up. That was the hardest task. There also was the fact that there was a war coming to us."[20]

Wilson continued, "There was a canteen on the base, and you could have two beers in the evening, but there were some people who were having more than that. There was always a bar down there. There was a lot of stepping out of line. That's when I became very good friends with Greg. Greg was the nurse manager of the ICU at a Perry, Georgia, hospital. I said, 'Greg, let's make a deal here. I'm going down to the cantina. You and I are staying together, and you're walking back with me.' The atmosphere was not good. There were three guys—all MDs who were preying on the women. They were all high ranking—full colonels, active duty—and they were out of bounds." Lieutenant Colonel Wilson was outranked and in conflict with the situation she faced. "I felt real torn as to what to do. I can imagine people that are active duty on a deployment like that for a length of time. Fortunately, or unfortunately, I don't know, maybe I should have taken a stand. It was not good. It needed to be reported further up the chain." She paused. "I just took on a bodyguard. I have no idea what people may have been harassed, or beyond harassment, because there was a lot of that going on. Maybe I was just naïve, but I thought that the higher-ranking officers would try to control that kind of behavior [rather] than being the ringleaders. What kind of an example is this setting?"[21]

Getting used to the crowded conditions necessary in military situations was another challenge. Wilson met that challenge head-on. "There were six Porta-Potties in a line; the first week we were there, nobody would sit next to each other. The line was wrapped around . . . because you were waiting for people to get through, but nobody would sit next to each other. They would skip a potty. Whatever business you had to do, you had to do in front of everybody that was there." Pat Wilson smiled. "By the second week, there was no skipping the potties. You sat there and you had a conversation with your friend while you were going to the bathroom. . . . The showers were one big arena," Wilson said. "You had two minutes of water, so you had a patrol person who said, 'Your two minutes are up.' So you took all your stuff, and you lathered up. And then you rinsed yourself off. You didn't have much time. They had these funny little mirrors, like you get in a cheap purse, that really isn't a mirror, sort of a metal reflector. And you stand there and tried to do makeup for the first week, and then I thought, 'Naa . . . this isn't worth it.' And everybody is trying to get to the mirror, and brush their teeth—you get what you get," Wilson said. "It was harder for some people to take than other people. I adjusted to it OK, but some people, it offended the entire time we were there . . . that never got comfortable with it."[22]

Living arrangements in tents where cots were two feet apart and personal space nonexistent were a challenge. Wilson described the situation. "We had people who were middle-aged, because our tent had people who were majors and up. We had two full colonels, several lieutenant colonels, and a few majors; so we had some people who were very cold-natured, and some people who were very hot-natured and there was no one who wasn't vocal. . . . We had criers and we had 'stiff-upper-lip' folk, so at night when we would go to bed, we had two women who cried every night we were there. The one that was [between] them was as hard as hell." Wilson said, "Every night, we would go to bed with Sally and Theresa crying and this woman in between them, shouting at them to shut up. I stayed on my side of the tent. I thought that was a saving grace until we had a sandstorm and the tent fell down." Wilson went on. "They would lie down at night, and they hadn't had a hard day. . . . I could pretty much sleep through anything. The girl in the middle could not let that happen. She would say, 'What kind of an officer are you anyway? Let's hush, let's get some sleep . . . just suck it up.' Finally, I threw my boots at her one night. I said, 'Alicia! Leave them alone . . . they have got to get this out. They don't need to do this in front of the troops. This is their home and we are their family, so leave them alone!' So anyway, she didn't holler at them anymore."[23]

Crying tentmates were not the only thing living in the tents that could cause people to lose sleep. "We had these little flagpoles on the end of our cots because they scared us to death about these sucking scorpions and snakes—they showed us this movie before we went over there. So you had to shake out everything. And you had to put your boots up on these things so nothing would crawl into them."[24]

One of the most difficult times for deployed military was trying to talk on the telephone in a crowded tent. Pat Wilson found telephone duty particularly difficult. "We didn't have good communications and we weren't allowed to talk to anybody to let them know we were there. It was about a week; they wanted to be sure that everything was OK before we were allowed to make telephone calls," Wilson recalled. "They allowed us each to make one telephone call; the line wound all around . . . we had two minutes. Two weeks after that, we had a telephone tent. Officers had to take turns commanding it. We had about fifteen minutes. . . . We had to pay for it . . . but you had to take up the money for it and monitor booths, and when the fifteen minutes were up, the next person would come in because you had eight hundred people who were wanted to make calls home." Wilson said, "You would hear such horrible, horrible conversations."[25]

Each telephone booth had a door, but the top and the bottom were open, affording little privacy. "So you could hear . . . people who were running around on their spouse and telling them about it. Somebody who sold the house. 'Sorry, honey, I'm going off with Tommy. I sold the house and you're on your own.' So here's Tommy in the booth—this grown man crying in the booth. I say, 'Are you OK?' I got a real eye-opener. People would buy expensive things and tell their spouse, 'Hey, honey, guess what I did today? I bought all new living room furniture.' And here's the person on the other end who didn't have any input into what's going on. 'I sold the property at the lake today.' You're hearing all these transactions . . . it was just very sad what people do. I think the same thing happens, war after war after war." Wilson went on, "It gives people license to act out. It reminds me of people who drank too much alcohol, and say, 'That's why I did what I did. I don't want to hear it.' If there was a crack in the marriage or there was not a solid relationship, when deployment happened that happens. I did get to witness what happened to people that I did not even know, and it was a very sad part of deployment. I hated telephone duty, because you don't even know these people, so it was hard to provide some sort of support for them because they didn't feel comfortable; they were actually ashamed that you had heard their conversation; you were in a real privacy issue. 'Time's up.' You hated to interrupt what was going on. You pretended that you didn't hear it, but you heard it. And you could hear their end of the conversation and could just imagine the other end of the conversation. . . . It was very uncomfortable for all of us."[26]

The number of U.S. military women deployed to the theater during Desert Shield and Desert Storm was greater than that of U.S. female military deployed in any war before the First Gulf War. More than 40,780 military women served in theater and in all military occupational specialties other than those considered direct combat specialties. When the First Gulf War began, U.S. military women comprised 11 percent of the total armed forces.

As if for the first time, the American press discovered that U.S. military women were facing the same dangers as U.S. military men. As if for the first time, national media brought pictures of military women deploying and serving with their units, wearing battle dress uniforms (BDUs), Kevlar helmets, combat boots, and carrying M-16s and 9 mm sidearms. And as if for the first time, national media asked if America was ready to see her daughters return home in body bags, as amputees, blinded, or suffering from post-traumatic stress disorder (PTSD). When it was announced in February 1991 that one of two army soldiers missing in Saudi Arabia near the Kuwait border was Specialist 4th Class Melissa Rathbun-Nealy, the twenty-year-old daughter of Leo and Joan Rathbun of Newaygo, Michigan, the press posed the question, "How will the American public respond to seeing women taken prisoner of war, knowing that they could be raped and/or tortured?"

The question was truly more rhetorical than information-seeking, since the press needed only to search media archives from World War II to learn how America had reacted to the Japanese capture of more than eighty-five U.S. military nurses when first Guam, then Bataan, and finally Corregidor fell in the Philippines in 1942. Those U.S. military women had remained in Japanese internment camps for more than three years before America and her Allies liberated the Philippines and set their brothers and their sisters free. Yet despite these facts, NBC News, researchers, and Bryant Gumbel, host of the *Today Show* at that time, went on the air and spoke about America's "first" two female POWs, Melissa Rathbun-Nealy and Rhonda Cornum, and asked how Americans would react to seeing their women as POWs or returning home in body bags. If anyone ever wondered how long the memory of the American people or the American media was, they had a large part of their answer.

The American public had historically reacted to the news of the capture, wounding, or deaths of their daughters in the armed forces just as they had responded to their sons' suffering those fates. It was not the American public alone that had created the myth that only its sons in the military went into harm's way. The American public had had the help of the U.S. Congress, the U.S. military, the U.S. media, and the historians who chronicled America's history and wars in creating and continuing that illusion; soon it was firmly established as myth and delusion in the American mind by repetition, tradition, and exclusion of military women from U.S. and military history books that filled American libraries—public and private.

American female soldiers, sailors, aviators, marines, and coast guardsmen were facing combat wounds and death while serving in an American war, yet the written history of that service remained like a reflection in a funhouse mirror, where reality is the last thing those who look upon the reflection see. No one who looks honestly at the history of U.S. military women by examining their deeds can possibly doubt their commitment, their courage, their patriotism, their endurance, or their determination to shoulder the full responsibilities of U.S. citizenship, despite the fact that the rewards of doing so are unjustly denied to them by the very Constitution and nation they protect.

For the female military personnel serving in the First Gulf War, the lack of equality and fairness they experienced in the theater and in some of the media back in the States was difficult to ignore. The reactions of their male comrades-in-arms varied. For one navy nurse, LT Betty Carr, who served in Dhahran, Saudi Arabia, where an Iraqi Scud missile killed twenty-eight American soldiers, the respect of her male military comrades was a source of pride and camaraderie. "There was one small tent with a TV in it where we were, and when we were off-duty, we'd all run over to it to catch the news." Lieutenant Carr continued, "There were over a thousand men and women in my group, and if a reporter made the mistake of mentioning only 'the men' serving here, there would be boos from both the women and the men. The men were totally supportive. They'd say, 'We want people to know it's the men and women of the U.S. military.' The pride I felt was overwhelming."[27]

For other soldiers serving in the theater, the challenge of winning the respect they were entitled to from the male soldiers serving beside them was more difficult to acquire than zeroing in on an Iraqi Scud missile. One of the African American female officers who helped redefine the roles of women in the U.S. military was army Lt. Phoebe Jeter. Lieutenant Jeter was one of the thousands of African American women who were faced with discrimination not only as a woman but also as a woman of color. Jeter led an all-male platoon of a Patriot missile battery. "I was in charge of the van that was the engagement control center—where we fire [the Patriot missiles] from. I was in charge of everything that happened inside that van. It was *my* responsibility."[28]

On a January night in Riyadh, Saudi Arabia, a Scud missile alert was sounded. Iraqi Scud missiles had been fired and were on their way to target the military base Jeter was assigned to protect. During her three years in the U.S. Army since graduating from ROTC, Jeter had been through many exercises where she acquired, targeted, and shot down incoming enemy missiles. This time was different because this time was for *real.* If she choked or missed her targets, there would be very real casualties on her military base. "Those Scuds could be carrying chemical warheads, and even if they weren't . . ." they could do tremendous damage on the base. Lieutenant Jeter ordered the launching of thirteen Patriot missiles and destroyed at least two Iraqi Scuds headed for the U.S. military base.[29]

Of the almost 41,000 women who were deployed to the Persian Gulf Theater, it is estimated that 40 percent were black. Like all the women soldiers serving in the "Sandbox," black women faced the primitive conditions of desert life: no electricity, no running water, no bathrooms, and all of it came wrapped in heat in the sumer that reached 120 degrees or higher, day in and day out.

Several of the black women faced dual discrimination from male GIs who made it only too clear that they felt that "war was a man's job" and women had no business in it. Add to that the discrimination that was directed at their skin color, and it is not difficult to understand that the war was by no means the only challenge black women and all women faced in theater. Nor did the frustration end with the sexism and racism in the Gulf. While Senior Airman Theresa Collier, twenty-three, was serving in the Gulf, someone on the naval base back in the States, where her husband was a sonar technician, scratched the letters 'KKK' into the hood of her car. Lieutenant Jeter had a few words of advice for military women. "If you're a woman, *whatever* you are doing, believe in yourself, because there are a lot of people out there who don't care about you or what you're doing." Lt. Carla Reed summed it up pretty well when she said, "No matter how significant or insignificant our contributions were, they couldn't have done it without us."[30]

What Lt. Carla Reed said was true; however, when the formal cease-fire was signed on 11 April 1991, and the troops came home, the debate about whether to permit female military personnel into direct combat assignments was starting all over again and the Joint Chiefs of Staff were divided on the issue. The arguments of the chiefs of the marine corps and the army were not any more logical than they had ever been, but they were just as emotional and patently discriminatory as those heard in and before Congress for the previous seventy-seven years. Despite the fact that in May 1991 the House of Representatives, in acknowledgment of the contributions made by U.S. military women to the Allied victory over Iraq, had voted to repeal the bans against women flying navy, air force, and marine corps war planes in combat, the army and marine corps argued that the ban must remain in place. The emergency in the Gulf was over, and so was the military's need for women in everything but "direct combat"—the definition of which seemed to grow more and more narrow with war and to expand again when the peace returned.

Despite all arguments to the contrary, in 1991 the law, 10 USC 8548, banning women from serving aboard combat aircraft engaged in combat missions, was repealed when the Kennedy-Roth Amendment was attached to the Defense Authorization Act of fiscal year 1992–93.

In the same year, the President's Commission on the Assignment of

Women in the Armed Forces was convened. Arguably, the commission was stacked with right-wing conservatives who had already made up their minds not only to bar women from *direct* combat, but to overturn the Kennedy-Roth Amendment that repealed 10 USC 8548. An article in the *New York Times,* "Panel Is Against Letting Women Fly in Combat," stated that the recommendation came in an eight-to-seven vote. There was a point where the conservative members of the fifteen-member commission walked out, stating that the opposition was not giving them a sufficient opportunity to voice their stand against women in combat in a report on the commission's recommendations. One panel member, Brig. Gen. Thomas V. Draude of the Marine Corps, asserted that conservative members were engaging in blackmail to get their way.[31]

The head of the presidential commission, Robert T. Herres, a retired air force general and former vice chairman of the Joint Chiefs of Staff, told the panel that there was no compelling reason to ban women from flying combat planes. The article went on to say that in a debate that often seemed "to turn on social policy rather than military considerations, conservative panel members argued that it was wrong to allow women to kill. Joining forces with other members of the panel, they tipped the balance against allowing women to fly in combat."[32]

The article concluded with, "Sarah F. White, a master sergeant in the Air Force Reserve, who sponsored a measure to bar women from flying combat missions, complained that there were 'women who were willing to kill or be killed to promote equal opportunity.' "[33]

In 1993, Secretary of Defense Les Aspin directed all services to open combat aviation to women. He further directed the navy to draft legislation to repeal the combat ship exclusion found in 10 USC 6015. The secretary also directed the army and marine corps to study opening more assignments to women. More than one thousand military women were deployed in military operations in Somalia between 1992 and 1994.

The military risk rule, which closed many supporting units in ground combat operations to women, was rescinded by the Department of Defense in 1994. This action opened more than 32,000 army jobs and approximately 48,000 marine corps jobs to women. In the same year, Congress repealed 10 USC 6015, opening most navy combat ships to women, excluding submarines and several smaller-class ships.

One of the first women to benefit from this change was Tracy Owens. Owens, who had begun her U.S. Navy career in 1980 as a twenty-two-year-old enlisted woman working in the boiler room of the USS *LY Spear,* became so dissatisfied that she made up her mind to leave the navy unless she could receive further training and be assigned a new MOS. The warrant officer with whom she was speaking asked her which navy job she thought she would like to pursue. "Legalman," Owens responded without hesitation. The warrant officer told her to apply for that school.[34]

In the years that followed, Owens attended several training programs, and in 1994 she was commissioned. Despite the fact that the warrant officer who had told Owens to apply for legalman training had retired, he attended Owens's commissioning ceremony and pinned on her first bars. (Owens later served on a combat ship, the USS *Carl Vinson,* as a legalman.)

Another woman directly affected by the repeal of legislation that excluded women from serving on combat ships was Deborah Davis.

After completing a one-year internship at Portsmouth Naval Hospital, navy physician LT Deborah Davis was assigned to the destroyer tender (AD-38) USS *Puget Sound,* which was scheduled to be decommissioned in six months, on 27 January 1996. The ship had a crew of 1,500, of whom 500 were women. Lieutenant Davis, the only physician aboard,

LTJG Tracy Owens, USN, aboard the USS Carl Vinson, *2005.*

had a physician's assistant and seventeen corpsmen under her command. The ship was well equipped with radiology and a laboratory and a technician to man each. "It was the last thing I thought I would ever be doing," Davis remembered. "I was surprised to find out that the ship was scheduled to be decommissioned, but I did get out to sea a number of times, once during Hurricane Felix. It was enough to get my toes wet."[35]

By the time LT Deborah Davis reported aboard, the *Puget Sound* already had women assigned. "Destroyer tenders were unique because they were some of the first navy ships to have women assigned to them, so it wasn't as much of a transition as aboard some other ships." Davis paused briefly. "There wasn't any major issue about women being accepted on destroyer tenders when I went aboard the *Puget Sound*." Deborah Davis was the ship's first woman doctor, but the other officers soon realized that a female physician might be a blessing on the ship.[36]

"As a department head, I got to attend management meetings with the EX-O [executive officer], commanders, and lieutenant commander department heads, and I learned a lot about management. When the EX-O would say a woman had to leave the ship to have a complete physical or just a Pap smear, I would tell them, 'She doesn't have to go anywhere. I can do the whole thing right aboard ship.' " Davis chuckled. "It seems that every ship has its share of men and women who are looking to get out of work, or better yet, to have to leave the ship for a particular kind of care the male physician and executive officers weren't willing to question." She laughed. "Well, I let them know that I could do everything needed without them having to go off the ship. And I think they were glad that I was firm and I wasn't a pushover."[37]

Quarters for women aboard the ship allowed for privacy without a lot of crowding. "I had my own cabin and it was a decent amount of space. We had our own lavatory . . . and I had a sink in my cabin. We had shared showers just down the way."[38]

Lieutenant Davis was a good observer of human nature and management techniques and was open to learning from what she observed. When asked about sexual harassment on the ship, she was quick to reply, "I think there was a lot less sexual harassment on a ship than in civilian life, and I think that's due to several things. One is that there are strict rules on a ship—everyone is under a microscope. If they mess up, they'll face punishment. In civilian life, if someone gets sexually harassed, their only option is often to take legal action. The military has strict rules and procedures for infractions." She paused for a second or two. "I also believe that sexual harassment is more prevalent among enlisted people than among officers."[39]

When the *Puget Sound* was decommissioned, Lieutenant Davis was transferred to a new position with the command amphibious group 2 (CAG2), which was located on the navy base. "I was the medical officer there. The CAG2 was the overseer of multiple ships. That's where I got to see how they were retrofitting some of these ships for women. Remodeling a ship was kind of like getting your house remodeled," Davis said. "It was dusty for a while, but it was usually a matter of putting a few separations in place, partitioning an area or two off from the male crews' quarters, and making sure people could still get to where they needed to go in the ship."[40]

It was at this assignment that Lieutenant Davis experienced the only incident of her navy career that occurred because of her gender. "I can remember only one occasion when I thought that someone was treating me differently because I was a woman. I was at a department heads' meeting and we were seated around a conference table—there were everybody from the commanders to the chaplain, all sitting around the table, waiting for the admiral to show up. There was a large plate of freshly baked cookies on the table because the admiral loved cookies." She took a breath and continued. "I was about five months pregnant at the time—I planned it that way, so that I'd have left the ship. I took a cookie from the plate, just like everyone else, and this commander looked at me and said, 'That's not good for your health.' I was the only female in the room except the [enlisted] girl who was doing the slides. I said, 'Frankly, sir, it's none of your business.' He put me on the spot. He didn't say that it was bad for the health of the overweight chaplain who was sitting across the table from me . . . nor did I say in return to him that smoking was bad for his health—which I knew that he did." Davis laughed. "There was dead silence in the room and I'm not sure that anyone finished their cookie. . . . And that was the first and last time any such comment was ever made to me."[41]

Lieutenant Davis had joined the navy in 1991

ENS Deborah Davis, MC, USNR, 1991.

during her first year of medical education. "I figured it was easier to owe the navy time than to owe some bank a lot of money. And as it turned out, I really liked the navy life. It was interesting, challenging, and fun. I remember being invited by the Seabees to drive a huge Humvee during a training exercise up at Fort Story. I'd go up there to supervise the corpsmen or do some physicals. I was six months pregnant at the time, and I drove that Humvee through the water and up over the sand on the beach. It was great fun!" Her tone of voice was just as convincing as her words. "I couldn't wait to get home and tell my husband, 'John, guess what I got to do today!' That was some of the fun I had in the military."[42]

On 22 March 1996, Sgt. Heather Lynn Johnson became the first woman to earn the silver Tomb Guard ID Badge—Third U.S. Infantry. She was the first woman to earn a place in the Old Guard and guard the Tomb of the Unknown Soldier at Arlington National Cemetery.

An article in the *New York Times,* "Role of Women in the Military Is Again Bringing Debate," stated that increasing reports of rape, sexual assault, and harassment involving drill sergeants at army training bases had renewed a debate as to how far the armed forces should go in integrating women into its male-dominated culture. Blaming the victim and tolerating the aggressors still appeared to be the military's preferred technique in addressing male misconduct and criminal assaults. Will an organization that chastises its male soldiers by comparing them—in derogatory terms to women—ever strive to reach a place where women are respected as soldiers, and men who commit felonies will be punished and discharged from the military? The possibility seems unlikely in a country that depends on bringing volunteers into the military with the promise of cash bonuses, and a failure of leadership that tolerates felons within its ranks rather than institute a draft or universal service, which politicians are fairly certain will alienate voters who are happy with the secondary gains they receive from tolerating an all-volunteer military they do not have to deal with in their civilian lives.[43]

The Women in Military Service for America Memorial (WIMSA), located at the entrance to Arlington National Cemetery, was dedicated on 18 October 1997. The driving force behind the memorial was Brig.

Brig. Gen. Wilma Vaught with dedication crowd at the women's memorial, 1997.

Gen. Wilma Vaught, USAF (Ret.). General Vaught was born on 15 March 1930 in Pontiac, Michigan, and raised on a farm in Scotland, Illinois. After graduating from the University of Illinois, Vaught attended the University of Alabama at Tuscaloosa, and earned a master's degree in business.

In 1957, Vaught joined the air force and was later the first female graduate of the U.S. Armed Forces Industrial College at Fort McNair in Washington, D.C. Vaught held comptroller positions at various air force bases around the world. In 1966, she was the first woman to deploy with a Strategic Air Command Bombardment Wing on an operational deployment. In 1980, Vaught was promoted to brigadier general. She served on DACOWITS (Defense Department Advisory Committee on Women in the Services) from 1982 to 1985 and also held a collateral position as Chair of NATO Women in the Allied Forces Committee. She retired from active duty in 1985.[44]

These women created their own pioneering tradition and what they accomplished would serve America well in its next war, which was only months away.

18

★

It was such an evil day, that terrorists could do something so bad. But, in spite of the evil, there was so much goodness, too. People responded with tremendous goodness. That was reassuring.

—Col. Jonathan C. Fruendt, MD
Deputy Assistant Surgeon General for Force Projection

At 8:45 a.m., on 11 September 2001, American Airlines Flight 11, with ninety-two people onboard, smashed into the North Tower of the World Trade Center. Television and radio programming was interrupted with the news that a plane had crashed into the North Tower. Several of the announcements were followed by a rhetorical question of how any plane flying on a not-a-cloud-in-the-sky day could run into anything as large and as tall as either of the Twin Towers. Less than twenty minutes later, at 9:03 a.m., United Flight 175, with sixty-five people onboard, slammed into the South Tower of the World Trade Center. Any notion that these planes hit the Twin Towers by accident would arguably have required the suspension of reason to maintain.

When American Airlines Flight 77, with sixty-four people onboard, stabbed its way into the west side of the Pentagon at 9:40 a.m., Americans knew that their country was under enemy attack. At 10:07 a.m., United Flight 93, with forty-four people onboard, dived into a corn field in Shanksville, Pennsylvania, exploding on impact.

When ADM Faye G. Abdellah learned that a plane had hit the Pentagon, she immediately took steps to help the hundreds of injured. "I felt that I was prepared for *this* emergency," Abdellah said. "I had come full circle. At Lakehurst, they had put out calls for help. The blimp [German airship *Hindenburg*] had just circled our house. My brother had said, 'Maybe there's something we can do. Let's go!' "[1]

In between the explosion of the *Hindenburg* and the terrorist attack on the United States, ADM Faye Abdellah could claim numerous extraordinary accomplishments. Abdellah's untiring work included her being one of the founders of USUHS (Uniformed Services University of Health Sciences) on the grounds of the National Naval Medical Center at Bethesda, Maryland. This university provides medical and nursing education for members of the U.S. Armed Forces; Abdellah then went on to develop the graduate program, which awards a master's degree in nursing at USUHS.

ADM Faye Abdellah moved quickly to help the victims of the attack on the Pentagon. "At the Pentagon, there were horrible burn cases. At least half or more of the casualties had been sprayed with jet fuel . . . and flames." Abdellah leaned forward in her chair. "This time I could do something. I arranged for our military nurses who were in the master's program at USUHS to go to the Pentagon to help the injured."[2]

As medical military personnel started for the Pentagon from Walter Reed Army Medical Center and other military bases in the area, the staff of the DiLorenzo Tricare Health Clinic in the Pentagon had already sprung into action. In minutes, employees injured in the collision or in the explosion of the plane's almost full 11,406-gallon fuel tank began arriving at the clinic. Maj. Lorie A. Brown, chief nurse of the Pentagon's clinic, described what she saw. "Horrible burns, singes, and head wounds," Brown recalled. "Hundreds of people began pouring out of the corridor because the crash site on the west side of the building was such that we were . . . opposite. We were clear, a clear avenue for people to escape. People then [began] bringing patients up our way, knowing where we were. And that was it." Brown said, "As soon as I saw two or three patients coming our way, we called the MASCAL [mass casualties event], started galvanizing all of our assets, and put our plan in action, the plan that we've been practicing for the year that we've been here. That made a huge difference, having practiced our roles and worked our pieces." She continued, "My role that day was to manage the scene. [The clinic commander] was not here. He was at Walter Reed and wasn't able to get here . . . with the traffic being stopped."[3]

For the Deputy Assistant Surgeon General, Col. Jonathan C. Fruendt, MD, the explosion of the Boeing 757 in the west wall of the Pentagon did not go undetected. "It was not loud in our office, but it was very clearly the sound of an explosion." Colonel Fruendt hurried into the corridor by his office to determine what was happening. He had not gone far when he heard a commotion behind him and turned to see people running in his direction and smoke drifting down the corridor. Fruendt hurried in the direction from which the crowd was coming and went out into the central courtyard. People were streaming out of the building. Fruendt headed for the health clinic. "I went into the health clinic and I found Major . . . Brown. . . . She was clearly in charge; she was talking with someone, very calm, incredibly organized, and after she had finished talking, she turned to me, and I said, 'I'm a physician, what can I do to help?' " Fruendt said, "She thought for just a moment, and she said, 'Go to the courtyard. We're setting up triage there.' " Colonel Fruendt went on, "The first person I saw was a female army lieutenant colonel who was having difficulty breathing. It looked like she may have had an inhalation injury. . . . We started some oxygen, and I also got an IV started. People had been exposed to a heavy dose of jet fuel in the air and on their clothes and skin."[4]

American flags began appearing on every street and country road and not just one or two. An individual could stand on a corner and see American flags flying in front of houses up and down the block. Those who did not own a flag went and got one to the sound of Kate Smith singing "God Bless America." Other Americans—men and women who wear the uniform—were already preparing to carry that flag to Al-Qaeda in Afghanistan. Thousands more would soon follow.

When the Fifteenth Marine Expeditionary Force (MEF) landed undercover in Afghanistan in November 2001, navy LT Tracy Bilski was one of the three navy women who deployed with them. Once again, the myth that female military personnel were not deployed on combat missions in support of combat teams was in stark contrast to reality. Marine Special Forces were deployed on one of the first assault missions against al-Qaeda in Afghanistan, and the medical team accompanying them to a forward base they would establish in a bombed-out, deserted town near Kandahar depended on LT Tracy Bilski for any critical trauma surgery that might be needed by the marines of the Fifteenth MEF. The mission of the marines was to stage an assault over four hundred miles into the landlocked country of Afghanistan. They were to establish America's first forward operating base, Camp Rhino, ninety miles southwest of Kandahar.

Marines of the Fifteenth MEF who were wounded were brought back to Lieutenant Bilski and the other members of a team who were there for one reason: to give the wounded their best chance for survival from combat wounds and injuries. Bilski remembered those times. "Thankfully, we only had two major incidents where we took a lot of casualties, and well, we used everything. We used our drinking water, we used everything for that, and we were able to get them off the base quickly. . . . We didn't have the resources to keep them."[5]

LT Tracy Bilski and the other two military women who deployed to Afghanistan with the Fifteenth MEF would not be the last U.S. military women in Afghanistan. Those still to arrive would follow in their footprints—or they would pilot military helicopters and planes through the skies above them. Either way, they would leave their mark for other female patriots to follow.

One year and one day after the 9/11 attacks on the United States, President George W. Bush encouraged the United Nations to act on imposing its resolutions against Iraq. Bush pointed out that if the UN failed to do so, the United States would have no choice but to act on its own. On 11 October 2002, the Congress voted to give Bush the authority to attack Iraq.

On 21 December 2002, President Bush authorized the deployment of American troops to the Gulf region, and the United States began a buildup of military personnel that reached more than 200,000 in March 2003. Between 24 February and 14 March 2003, all diplomatic efforts by the United States stopped. Bush gave an ultimatum to Saddam Hussein—either he leave Iraq in the next twenty-four hours or face an attack by the "coalition of the willing," which included the United States, Britain, Spain, and Bulgaria.

President Bush declared war on Iraq on 19 March 2003, and the war began with the second round of air attacks on Iraq in a much-publicized media event the U.S. Department of Defense had dubbed "Shock and Awe." U.S. troops crossed into Iraq in force, streaming into southern Iraq over the Kuwait border. By 24 March 2003, troops were within sixty miles of Baghdad and encountered the strongest resistance they had faced so far by Iraqi forces in the cities of Nasiriyah and Basra.

The American people and the world watched the live and repeated coverage of the war on CNN and other twenty-four-hour news networks, or on network evening news shows—the repeated and persistent view of long lines of military convoys of Humvees, tanks, and other military vehicles rolling across the desert with a sense of inevitability. In many ways, the "roll to Baghdad" resembled an adventure program one might see on the

History Channel or National Geographic Channel: organized, hot, dry, and professional, with the exception of large numbers of Humvees rather than Land Rovers, with large caliber guns instead of cameras mounted on their roofs, and with soldiers rather than archeologists—wearing Kevlar instead of an Indiana Jones hat. And best of all, no American or coalition soldiers' body parts strewn across beachheads like breadcrumbs, announcing in vivid color, "This Way to War."

For generations of Americans who had never served in the military, let alone served in wartime, war must not have looked too bad, especially to a majority of Americans who never had to worry about being drafted into the armed forces, let alone a war. There must have been millions of young Americans and their families, consciously or unconsciously thanking God and Washington for an all-volunteer force that had stepped forward with informed consent—professional warriors—and each had "signed on by their own choice." Not bad. Not bad at all.

News stations and print media announced on 2 April 2003 that Special Operations Forces had rescued Pfc. Jessica Lynch from an Iraqi hospital in Nasiriyah. She had been wounded, then captured with twelve other soldiers from her unit, 507th Ordnance Maintenance Company, after their supply convoy was attacked on 23 March. Stories of a heroic stand at the attack site swept across America as television stations played and replayed video footage of the twelve remaining troops in Iraqi hands being interviewed by their Iraqi captors.

In the following days, U.S. tanks entered Baghdad and engaged an enemy who put up less resistance than the United States had forecast previously. Two days later, British troops captured Basra, Iraq's second-largest city.

When Baghdad fell on 9 April 2003, U.S. and coalition troops took control of the city. While U.S. soldiers helped crowds of Iraqis tear down a large statue of Saddam Hussein that stood in a city square, television cameras carried live-action coverage and replays of the historic event. Many Iraqis danced and cheered in the streets. Two days later, the same news channels were showing hundreds of Iraqis carrying looted merchandise out of public buildings, ammunition dumps, and national museums, loading them in the back of pickup trucks, and driving away, while American soldiers were either nowhere in sight or shown on camera standing with M-16s in hand, not making a move to restore order in a situation clearly out of control. Two days later, Secretary of Defense Donald Rumsfeld stood before television cameras in the United States and reminded the American public that "stuff happens" and that "freedom is untidy." Clearly, the new freedom being celebrated by thousands of Iraqis lived up to Secretary Rumsfeld's words.

On 13 April 2003, U.S. forces liberated the remaining twelve POWs being held by the Iraqis. One of those released was Spc. Shoshanna Johnson, another U.S. Army woman present when the members of the 507th were attacked and thirteen of its troops taken prisoner, along with two pilots who had been captured after their planes had been shot down by Iraqi gun crews near the city of Karbala.

The Department of Defense announced on 16 April 2003 that "major fighting in Iraq is over." On the same day, Bush signed a $79 billion supplemental spending bill for Iraq. On 1 May 2003, President Bush flew out to sea to meet the returning aircraft carrier, USS *Abraham Lincoln*. Television captured the commander in chief as he exited the plane and walked across the deck, flight helmet at his side. Later, he appeared before the same cameras, and beneath a large, printed banner that read "Mission Accomplished," as he declared that "major combat operations in Iraq were ended." Millions of Americans who had followed the war on television, radio, and in the print media celebrated the end of a brief, relatively inexpensive war and what was, for the great majority of Americans, a reasonably priced exercise in the flexing of America's muscles.[6]

One of the first military women to arrive in Iraq after President Bush's address under the Mission Accomplished banner was forty-two-year-old Marine Corps MGySgt Rosemarie Weber. "It's hard to explain," Master Gunnery Sargeant Weber said. "First of all, when you come in to land, you can see your first sight of bomb damage, wreckage, planes blown up on the runway, and also that Stephen King–like quality where everything is just dead." Sargeant Weber continued. "You could see the civilian portion of the airport, you could see how it should have been—but nothing. No movement. It was extremely eerie. Then you get out and you're hit with 145-degree heat. And it's at that point that you're putting on your helmet, your flak vest, all your protective gear." She paused. "So, outside, it's 135 degrees. Inside, your body temperature under that flak vest feels like 150 degrees."[7]

Weber and her group grabbed their gear and got on a military bus for the ride to Saddam Hussein's Republican Palace in a compound that had been dubbed the Green Zone. Weber was again aware of eerie quiet in the deserted streets. "We get to this palace compound, which is kind of like a gated community. And now, all of a sudden, it's busy like a bee-hive . . . with our forces everywhere. But again, it's hot, it's dirty, and they had just started setting up."[8]

Four-man trailers, often seen on construction sites, were being set up. A few were ready and even fewer were inhabited. Weber described the living conditions. "Two-sided, two rooms with a bathroom—a shared bathroom in the middle—two people in each room. So eventually, they were up and running and that was very posh. It's the only time that you go from a palace to a trailer, and you've actually gone up a notch in the social hierarchy. But when we first got there, we slept on the palace floor, any nook or cranny. There were just people camped out everywhere."[9]

When they first arrived in Iraq, Weber's party consisted of four people: two lieutenant colonels, one colonel, and Weber herself. It was their job to get the place up and running. In time, additional personnel were added to the group, but the core staff never reached more than twelve or thirteen people to get the entire Ministry of Defense for the Coalition Provisional Authority up and operating. It was the job of Weber's advance group to set up everything that would be needed: offices, computers, furniture—whatever would be necessary for the Ministry of Defense to do their job of standing up an Iraqi Army. "We also set up all the office procedures in connection with our people," Weber said. "Anything office people would take for granted, we had to set up from scratch."[10]

The terrible heat and humidity made every challenge just a little more difficult to deal with day in and day out. There were no showers at first; the only food was meals ready to eat (MRE). It was impossible to get a really cold drink of anything. Added to this was a degree of organizational confusion. "Please understand that what I am about to say is Weber's opinion rather than an official take on the situation." Weber continued, "Here we had a military operation being run by a civilian organization. You could sometimes see the power play between General [Ricardo] Sanchez and his civilian counterpart in *how* we should be doing things, and *what* we [military] should be doing. It caused confusion.[11]

"The incident that made me catch my breath the most, I think was one day we went out . . . we had gotten some intelligence that there were some people burning some records. And those records were vital because it told us . . . how much ammo, how many weapons were being stored. So we could account for things and figure out what else was still floating around out there in the country," Weber said. "So we get there just a few minutes too late, and we can see that the stuff is already on fire. So you jump out in formation, shadowing . . . to make sure everybody is covered and taking care of each other. But meanwhile, this is one of those times . . . times where they're . . . serious. 'I'm shooting at you, not towards you.' And they were shooting back because they realized they were caught . . . red-handed. And so that got a little hairy.[12]

"But the scariest part about that incident was there was a young marine in our group and our job at this point, Coalition Provisional Corps, is not a combat unit. We're not out there to shoot people dead. We're out there to regain this, without doing that. We're not a combat unit. So it's not a face-off with the enemy like it would be in a combat unit. And yet, there's this one young marine who I happened to see out of the corner of my eye drop down on one knee and actually started to take aim like you would on the rifle range at this one young Iraqi that was running. . . . They were done at this point—shooting at us—at least we thought so," Weber said. "And it scared me to death that this guy was seriously considering shooting someone who, at this point, was no threat to us, but was ready to drop him just like that, when they were already on their way, leaving the area. And it wasn't our mission to bring them in dead or alive. . . . It wasn't our mission to bring them in at all. It was our mission to get this intelligence."[13]

Weber paused and then went on. "The scariest thing was to see regular men and women like myself who had not ever . . . had no personal reason to hate these people, were not in a unit that had actually been fired upon . . . to see how easily and to feel it in myself, how easily that beast within you comes to the surface. And you turn into some kind of an animal yourself. And you really have to pay attention to that and check that, and you have to watch each other, and kind of keep that in check. Or the next thing you know, you're doing things that you know are not morally right, but somehow, that's okay." Weber paused. "It's okay because why? Because you're in a war zone? No, that doesn't make it okay, unless it's your mission and you're in a combat unit and you have things to do and there's reason to retaliate in those kinds of ways and whatever, that's fine. But we were not." She took a deep breath. "And so seeing . . . it happened to the civilians that were with us—civilian security details. . . . That's frightening. It's very frightening. . . . We live in America. We don't have . . . cause to behave like that and it really goes to show you that human beings are just another kind of animal, and if you're not careful and you don't use the brains that God gave you, you just get wrapped up in that and start doing really stupid, crazy things," Weber continued. "They stopped it right there at the time, and then there was a little ugly altercation right there, but in the end, everybody had his chance to breathe, take another look, and then you don't do that again. But it's frightening when it happens."[14]

As Weber's deployment drew to an end, she realized she was *ready* to go home. "The definitive experience that told me that it was time for me to come home is I started to get jumpy and paranoid as things started to escalate. First of all, I had done my job. I had done what I was sent there for, so the rest was just . . . to do what someone else, anybody else, needed help with." When MGySgt Rosemarie Weber's tour was up in October 2003, she returned to the United States.[15]

With the declaration that major combat operations had ended in Iraq, America experienced the highs of victory celebrations and the feelings of invulnerability that, more often than not, accompany the celebrations of "easy victories." The American death toll in Operation Iraqi Freedom stood at 139, a number many Americans who had watched the Iraq War on television and followed U.S. victories in the print media thought was very small and very reasonable. The United States, now considered the world's only superpower, was strutting about like a teenage drunk, convinced of his own invulnerability.

America's intoxication with victory and its equating of "victory" and "minimal casualties" with "war" was destined for a shorter stay with soldiers and their families than with those who had never served in the military, had no family or friends in the military, and who, because the draft had been replaced with the all-voluntary military, were in no danger of finding themselves in a combat zone in the Middle East unless they decided to work there as civilian contractors at many times the salary of GIs.

Before 2003 ended, however, that feeling of intoxication was replaced by a post–Mission Accomplished hangover, with increasing numbers of Americans seeing an escalation in violence in Iraq's cities and by the numbers of killed and wounded still growing.

19

★

This is how the war planners wanted it. . . . No new taxes, no draft, no photos of coffins, no inconveniences that might compel voters to ask tough questions. This strategy would have worked if the war had been the promised cakewalk. But now it has backfired. A home front that has not been asked to invest directly in a war, that has subcontracted it to a relatively small group of volunteers, can hardly be expected to feel it has a stake in the outcome five stalemated years on.
—Frank Rich, *New York Times*

Patricia D. Libengood was twenty years old when she enlisted in the U.S. Marine Corps Reserve on 5 August 1999. Her reserve unit was in Ebensburg, Pennsylvania. Corporal Libengood was part of an advance party of her unit that arrived in Iraq on 5 August 2004.

The advance party was to work at Base Operations at Unit Movement Control Center (UMCC). "I was an E-3/corporal, and I was taking over for a lieutenant and a staff sergeant," Patricia Libengood Dean remembered. "I was nervous about that. I was taking on a billet way beyond my grade. The purpose of it [my job] was to ensure safety of convoys that were either leaving our base or coming to our base. It entailed checking route safety, keeping track of the number of vehicles and personnel, and then tracking them by satellite as they traveled."[1]

The marine corps had assigned Libengood to the billet after evaluating her civilian work experience with computers and her military occupational specialty in transportation. "It was really tough," Libengood Dean said. "You were dealing with hundreds of lives, and if you make one tiny mistake, it could cause someone to get hurt or even killed. I coordinated over three to four hundred convoys and we had no losses. I was relieved."[2]

Convoys of supplies and personnel were among the insurgents' favorite targets. Car bombs and improvised explosive devices (IEDs), followed by small-arms fire, were among the favorite methods of insurgents for attacking convoys, killing the personnel, and destroying or stealing the supplies carried in the convoys. The chief ways of avoiding such incidents were to vary the routes convoys took between two points, to provide adequate security vehicles to protect the convoy, and to make sure that the trucks and other vehicles in the convoy were sufficiently armored in case of enemy attack.

Many soldiers and veterans heard Secretary of Defense Donald Rumsfeld's response to a question concerning "up-armored" vehicles and how to provide the soldiers in Iraq the best possible "up-armoring" for the vehicles they rode in every day. "You go to war with the army you have. They're not the army you might want or wish to have at a later time," was considered by many veterans and armed forces personnel to be less than inadequate and coldly insensitive to the men and women whose lives were on the line when the army sent them to war with inadequate armor on Humvees, Bradley fighting vehicles, tanks, and trucks.[3]

An article in the *New York Times* in September 2004, "For 1000 Troops, There Is No Going Home," provided some sobering facts for a nation still suffering from a post–Mission Accomplished hangover. Among the facts provided in reference to the first thousand warriors to die in Iraq were these: more than 70 percent of the dead were soldiers in the army; more than 20 percent were marines; more than half were in lowest-paid enlisted ranks; approximately 12 percent were officers; 75 percent of the troops died in hostile incidents, most often from IEDs, small-arms fire, or rocket attacks; 25 percent died of illness or accidents, truck and helicopter crashes, or gun discharges. The average age of soldiers who died was about twenty-six. The youngest was eighteen, the oldest, fifty-nine. Approximately half were married. By September 2004, at least twenty-four female service members had died in Iraq.[4]

When Connie Rose Spinks was seventeen years old, she asked her parents for an unusual birthday present: She wanted their signatures on a military document that would allow her to join the U.S. Army Reserve. Her mother accepted her youngest daughter's wishes, but her father presented what seemed like an immovable obstacle to her plans to enlist. It was not as if her father disliked the military; he had nothing against the armed forces as a whole. He very definitely had objections, however, to his baby daughter being involved with any organization that might decide one day to send her off to war. There were family members who had served in the military in the past, and two male cousins who were currently on active duty with the army; however, they were men, and Connie—she was his youngest daughter.

After three months of determined and all but perpetual begging from his youngest girl, Mr. Spinks signed the forms, and Connie's path into the army reserves was wide open. On 13 October 2000, Connie Rose Spinks began basic training at Fort Jackson, South Carolina.

"They called it 'Relaxin' Jackson.' They were strict, and they taught you military discipline and things like that, but they weren't 'dropping' [the military practice of 'Drop and give me fifty push-ups'] you all the time," Spinks recalled. "They were pretty relaxed there." Spinks paused. "I was in for a reality check when I went to Fort Bragg, North Carolina, to do my AIT—advanced individual training. When I got to Fort Bragg—that was *real* training. They were hard on us; they were *real* hard—physically, mentally—in every kind of way. They had us pushing . . . if we weren't working as a team, if we thought we had individuals instead of being a team effort, then everyone got 'dropped.' They were trying to teach us to have that camaraderie straight-up. That's where you get your training, so you're in classes part of the day, as well, to learn your job. They're strict on you to study during study hall time. . . . They're very strict.[5]

"Mom was diagnosed with MS, which is multiple sclerosis, approximately three months after I got to Fort Bragg. By this time, we were learning how to become a team, and as soon as I found out . . . everyone came to me, and we started a prayer circle, and they said, 'We're gonna be here for you.' They asked if I needed to take time off to go home or whatever. My mom told me to just stay out there, and she'd keep me updated. That was my fondest memory," Spinks said.[6]

"Before my deployment, we got thirty days of FTA [Field Training Activity] at Fort McCoy in Wisconsin. There, we learned how to do tactics as far as where we head out on convoys with our military vehicles—Humvees. We learned weapons training with the M-249, which is the Squad Automatic Weapon, or the SAW gun. We learned about the .50 cal. We learned about different weapons and different tactics and things we were going to be using, so we did a thirty-day field training exercise," Spinks recalled. "After Fort McCoy, that's when I went back to Fort Bragg to actually go overseas. I was at Fort Bragg for approximately three weeks before shipment to Kuwait, and then later to Iraq."[7]

Spinks then turned her attention to her unit's deployment to Iraq. "I was activated for the Homeland Security in 2001. I did that for approximately five, six months. Then I was activated again in 2002 to go over to Iraq, but at that time, my entire unit wasn't being deployed. It was this particular team. So I didn't have to go, because they didn't choose my team to go over at that time. So at the end of 2003 was when we found out that in 2004, we were going overseas." Spinks continued, "So, we had approximately eight months to prepare, and for six of the eight months, I was doing language training." For the next six months, Connie Spinks studied Arabic and Kurdish. When the program ended, she had two months to relax with friends and family before actually deploying for Iraq by way of Kuwait. Spinks arrived in Kuwait on 8 September 2004. As Sergeant Spinks stepped off the plane, the first thing to make an impression on her was the heat. "It was 120 degrees! And you have all of your armor, as far as your IBA, which is your initial body armor, you have your weapon, you have your Kevlar, you have your 'ruck,' you have tons of water . . . so in 120 degrees, it's hot. It's killer-hot, and you have all this extra weight, so you really—it's not comfortable to walk around, to move around. So it took awhile. We were there for two weeks, and then bodies could get acclimated to the temperature, and I adjusted well. After the first week, I was adjusted to the temperature. . . . I thought, okay, I can deal with it," Spinks remembered.[8]

The next and permanent deployment location for Spinks and her unit, the 426th Civil Affairs (CA) Battalion out of Upland, California, was Mosul, Iraq, approximately 225 miles north of Baghdad. "And when I got there, it was actually cooler in Iraq; it was like 100 degrees—instead of 120. I was like, oh, it's cool here. The wind would blow—we had trees there—it wasn't just all sand and dirt. . . . it was okay."[9]

In Iraq, Spinks's 426th Civil Affairs Battalion team was integrated into a regular schedule for assignments. "My schedule that I was on, I would have gate guard, which is . . . for the initial gates. People would say, 'I want to come onto the base' and have to go through. We were there for our Civil Affairs with our interpreter." Spinks continued. "Then we'd have tower guard [duty] which is outside the perimeter . . . you guard the perimeter. I would get that once a week. . . . The days I didn't have those duties . . . I would be doing CA missions, going outside the wire, working with interpreters or the national populace. I stayed . . . until about seven, and that was pretty late. I felt pretty good. I was getting a lot of things accomplished, and our teams completed missions successfully, and we were making a difference. We were starting to have an impact in-country, and I enjoyed it."[10]

Spinks recalled that guard duty in the towers could be especially stressful. "While I was there, there were about three attacks, and then there was a mortar that had failed to . . . it was about 300 or so feet from us. So that was scary. To hear it, and to feel the vibration, and hear the siren go off, yeah, that was really scary."[11]

The authors must once again disagree with Senator Jim Webb's thoughts and beliefs expressed in his 1979 article titled "Jim Webb: Women Can't Fight." Mr. Webb's assertions that men cannot control their sex drives beyond an eight-hour workday are just as ridiculous in the twenty-first century as they were in the twentieth century. The facts speak for themselves. Sexual assault and sexual harassment of military women by U.S. troops were a problem, and it was growing in direct proportion to the army's lower standard for admission and the number of waivers the army issued for felony convictions that normally would have kept those individuals out of the military. Their presence, and the environment their presence condoned, led to a variety of problems and crimes among military personnel.[12]

Sadly, and perhaps criminally, the army did not act to stop the sexual assault and harassment by their men and others—who were made eligible by drastically lowering the standards for admission—on female soldiers in particular, and all troops who *did not* require such waivers to enlist and serve. Necessity, in the absence of a draft, had placed the U.S. Army in a dangerous double-bind. Even the "all-volunteer backdoor draft" of Stop Loss was unable to ensure the army the numbers of troops it continued to need for wars in Afghanistan and Iraq and to fulfill the army's commitments elsewhere in the world and at home. So a once-proud U.S. Army was taking just about any male applicant in order to field enough troops in Operation Enduring Freedom and Operation Iraqi Freedom. Sexual assault, harassment, and a demoralized environment for all soldiers were part of the results the army was accepting as it exchanged numbers for integrity and the rule of law.

Sgt. Connie Rose Spinks and other female soldiers in Iraq frequently stood double guard duty because there were not enough women to maintain a regular schedule; a new program that paired "Battle Buddies" required a man and woman to serve in pairs. "I didn't receive any sexual harassment while I was over there," Sgt. Spinks said. "There was an incident . . . [and] they changed things for us. Because [in] the unit we replaced, there was an actual rape at one of the towers." Spinks explained that the female who had been raped was on guard duty with only an Iraqi interpreter and that the Battle Buddy system had been implemented by the time her unit had arrived. "That's why, a lot of times, our unit would have to do more duty because we had [so few] females, that if your battle buddy had guard duty, you had it. So, we had it twice as often as the guys would. But there weren't any [further] incidents that I know of."[13]

Sgt. Connie Rose Spinks was relieved to find that Iraqi men did not express the same lack of respect for female U.S. soldiers as they did for their own Iraqi women. "Before I left and [when I arrived] . . . I already had the [idea] that they would just treat us awful because they don't respect women, so I was like, okay, I'm gonna have to deal with some men that are just not gonna like me because of my skin color; they're not gonna like me because of my sex. I was prepared; but when I got over there, the Iraqis that I worked with, they were very respectful. When I was there they were very friendly. They were teaching me more about their language and their culture. They were very helpful. And they treated me so respect-fully. I couldn't even say anything about it though. I know how they treat their women, but as far as being a U.S. soldier, as far as being a female sol-dier, being an African-American female soldier, I was not treated badly by them at all. Nope. It surprised me, too; it really did. I wasn't ready for that, but I accepted it—okay, that's good."[14]

On 13 October 2004, the day after Spinks's twenty-second birthday, her team left on a mission that involved traveling to several locations, tak-ing pictures, and returning to their base. The 426th Civil Affairs Battal-ion Team received a briefing concerning that mission. "We had different teams that were gonna go out, and they told us that we would . . . that I specifically would need to be doing security. . . . I was gonna be a SAW gunner in the middle vehicle. That day I got up, we didn't leave out until . . . it was late morning," Spinks said. "The first thing I did was pre-pare the weapon, got everything loaded up, went out to Ninawa [several miles northeast of Mosul], which was a marketplace that we were rebuild-ing . . . to take some pictures. . . . We did that successfully.[15]

"Now the incident occurred when we were heading back to camp. It was comfortable, I would say high nineties, as far as the temperature out-side, and it was a clear day," Spinks said. "There was a lot of traffic, though, on the road, especially on the left side. And, as so far as the mid-dle vehicle, which was the position that I had, I was doing left-to-right security. So at the particular time of the incident, I had my weapon posi-tioned to the left, because that was the heavy flow of traffic. I noticed we were coming up to a ramp . . . where a vehicle was trying to get into our direction," the sergeant recalled. "Whenever you're in a convoy, you're not supposed to let anyone get in between your vehicles. So this vehicle was speeding up to get in between the first vehicle and my vehicle, and . . . I position my weapon to the right, and I said in Arabic, '*Oga ter erami,*' which means to stop, and then the vehicle slowed down, but he didn't completely stop. So I said, '*Obs ter erami,*' which is 'Stop or I'm gonna shoot.' And at that time, he floored it. He hit the gas so hard [that] before I even had a chance to pull the trigger . . . he had run into my vehicle, and that's when it exploded." Spinks paused for several seconds.[16]

"When it exploded, I was ejected from the turret. I sustained burns to my face and my hands. I had broken my femur, shattered my right ankle, fractured my left ankle, broke two fingers in my left hand, had perforated eardrums. I had a lot of injuries. There were some other people that were ejected as well. One had a broken jaw; the other had a broken foot and a broken rib." Despite her serious injuries, Spinks remained conscious throughout much of the trip to, and treatment in, the receiving center of the hospital. She retained the memory of much that followed in that first "golden hour" when getting to a trauma team at a hospital can mean the difference between life and death. "I was conscious. I could smell flesh burning. I could hear small-arms fire, 'cause it was an ambush. There was firing coming from the left side after the explosion on the right. So we were set up. And all I could remember was hearing our first vehicle lay suppressive fire, and people coming to rescue me and those two other gentlemen, the two lieutenants that were injured as well. I can remember hearing the machine guns laying down all these rounds, just laying down all these rounds, and I can remember feeling pain. I felt this for just a brief second, and then I didn't feel any pain. All I can remember was yelling, 'Help.' I yelled 'Help' one time, and by that time two people from the third—the last—vehicle came, and they dragged me and they threw me and the two lieutenants on the vehicle, so we were about six or seven people piled up in this one vehicle, and we headed off to the hospital. My face was bleeding, and they just kept saying, 'Spinks, you're gonna be okay. Spinks, you're gonna be okay.' Lieutenant . . . he had a broken jaw, but I can remember his face was *so* swollen. He was trying to talk to me. Everybody was just sitting there; they were just trying to reassure us."[17]

Sgt. Connie Rose Spinks had suffered another wound not so easily recognized by most observers. In some respects, the scars of that wound needed as much or more attention as those to her physical body. "My greatest regret is not pulling the trigger. Because . . . I saw that man. . . . I looked at him dead in the face. He was driving . . . a little bitty ol' Toyota pickup. . . . He did not look like he wanted to kill—like a homicide or suicide bomber. . . . They would be . . . clenching the wheel, looking like they're on some death mission. This gentleman was just driving. He had both hands on the steering wheel; he didn't have any passengers. . . . He looked me right in the face . . . right in my eyes . . . and that was it, I thought he was gonna obey me. *I did not know* that he was out on this mission. I did not know that he was gonna attack us, or that he hated Americans, or that he hated the military. He looked like a normal Iraqi—and over there . . . they don't know how to drive; they don't obey the signs, so I'm like, okay, I'm gonna give him the warning. I'm gonna put my weapon over there, no big deal."[18]

On the day of Spinks's discharge from the hospital, Lieutenant Perry, who was in charge of the family readiness office and support group assigned to Spinks's unit, arrived from California.

During her hospitalization, Spinks had asked about the others in her unit who had been injured and had been told, in general, that they were "doing fine." Lieutenant Perry was there with Sergeant Spinks's mother. "My mom of course was here, 'cause she was here through the entire ordeal with me, through all my surgeries and everything. . . . They came to me and they brought a chaplain in . . . and I knew something was up. I said, 'Mom, why did y'all bring the chaplain? I'm getting out of the hospital.' She said, 'Well, sweetie, we have something to tell you.' Lieutenant Perry said, 'Spinks, I need to tell you something. I'm going to tell you now, because I think you're strong enough to handle it.' I said, 'Sir, what is it?' He said 'Lieutenant Colonel Phelan and Major Saltee—they didn't survive the incident.' I remember saying, 'No. No!' and I started crying. I remember saying, 'I should have shot that guy.' I asked exactly what killed them. Why didn't they make it? They said that the side of the vehicle was crushed. Then all of the shrapnel and . . . the vehicle was on fire. They reassured me [that] they didn't feel it. They said as soon as the truck hit the Humvee, they were already gone. So they didn't make it. I asked about the families, how their wives and children were doing. They said, 'Everybody's doing fine. Everybody's just concerned about you and the others.' It was hard. I had a lot of guilt, and I had a lot of anger about the situation. It took about four days for me to come out of that."[19]

The car bomber had struck Sgt. Connie Spinks's convoy on 13 October 2004. On 17 October 2004, she arrived at Brooke Army Medical Center in San Antonio, Texas. She remembered awakening briefly on the seventeenth and awakening more fully on the next day. "I remember that when I awakened, my mom and dad were there by my bed. My dad was in the room for like one minute, and I just looked at him, and then he left the room. I turned to my mom and I said, 'Why did he leave?' She said, 'Oh, he just went to get something to eat.' Later on, she told me that [it was] because he was crying. That was it. She said that was the first time she'd ever seen him cry. Even when my grandfather was killed, he didn't even cry at the funeral. Then when I was in the hospital, he cried. He cried over me." Spinks continued, "It was very emotional because I kept asking my mom, 'How do I look?' My hands were bandaged. Everything was just bandaged on me. Both of my legs were casted. So I'm like, 'Mom, what does my *face* look like? Is it okay?' Because they would put cream on it, they would be doing all these things to my face, and I'm like, 'Do I look really bad?' She said, 'No, baby girl, you're still beautiful.' . . . For two weeks when I was in the hospital, they didn't let me see myself." Spinks paused. "No one would bring a mirror. No one took pictures. . . . I knew something was up, but I didn't know exactly what it was. So one night I had the little TV in front of me . . . and I turned the TV off, so it was just a black screen, and on the black screen, I could see my reflection. When I first looked at it, I thought, Well, that is light. I was expecting something different. It was so white. I thought, This can't be right." When Sergeant Spinks's mother came into her hospital room the next morning, Spinks asked her mother for a mirror. "When I looked at it, it was light, and it was blistered. On one side it was blistered up, and I was like, oh, my goodness. My doctor said, 'You're gonna be perfect.' "[20]

The doctors and nurses assured Connie that her pigmentation would start to return. It would take a while, and it would take extra protein; they told her to eat meat and drink Ensure. "They told me all the things I needed to do to get healthy," Spinks said. "And how to take care of my burns. That's why they were putting cream on my face so much, and they continued to do that until I could use my hands for myself."[21]

Sgt. Connie Rose Spinks had joined, or been drafted into, a very exclusive club—U.S. military women who have won the Purple Heart for wounds inflicted by the enemy during war.

When LCDR Colleen Glaser-Allen, age thirty-four, reported for duty aboard the USS *Carl Vinson* (CVN 70), she would be the ship's first woman department head in the Legal and Security Division, Command

Judge Advocate. Colleen had grown up in a family that was aware and proud of a military tradition for its men. Her father had served as a marine during the Vietnam era, and her grandfather had served in a minesweeper in World War II. Colleen had heard a few of their stories growing up and had seen her share of movies where the U.S. Navy and Marine Corps fought their way to the aid or rescue of their fellow sailor or Leathernecks, not to mention the army or the air force.

During her second year of law school at the University of Illinois Law School in 1993, Colleen applied to the U.S. Navy and was commissioned in September 1993. After graduating and passing the Illinois bar exam, Colleen completed the navy's Judge Advocate General (JAG) School in Newport, Rhode Island, in December 1995. Colleen was assigned to the U.S. Naval Base in Norfolk, Virginia, where she worked in litigation until 1998 when she was transferred to Rota, Spain. She returned to the U.S. in 2001 and was stationed in Everett, Washington, where she served as a JAG officer on the admiral's staff. In the summer of 2004, LCDR Colleen Glaser-Allen was assigned as head of the JAG department aboard the USS *Carl Vinson,* at its home port at Bremerton, Washington. Lieutenant Commander Glaser-Allen would be the first female JAG officer to serve as head of the JAG department on the *Vinson.*

Several of the women on the crew had already cracked the brass ceiling aboard the *Vinson,* as testified to by the fact that when Glaser-Allen joined the ship, there were two other female heads of departments, one the

chief engineer and the other a dentist with the rank of captain. In addition to these three highly placed female navy officers, the chief petty officer was a female, and there were other navy enlisted women who held advanced ranks. Lieutenant Commander Glaser-Allen would also begin her shipboard duty with a new skipper for the *Vinson,* CAPT Kevin Donegan, whom Glaser-Allen would remember as "the only person who expected more out of me than I did out of myself. And he's the one."[22]

As the USS *Carl Vinson* prepared for its seventh deployment—Global Combat Deployment—which would begin in Janu-

LCDR Colleen Glaser-Allen, JAGC, USN, 2005.

ary 2005, the skipper, Captain Donegan, wasted no time in conveying to his crew exactly what he expected from them and exactly the behaviors he would not tolerate from his officers or the enlisted personnel. "The captain made it very clear that his officers were responsible for the actions or omissions of the personnel directly under their supervision."[23]

LCDR Colleen Glaser-Allen had approximately one hundred people who answered to her and those individuals operated not only the legal system of the *Vinson* but also its brig, its sheriff, and its guards. "We didn't have gender issues aboard the *Vinson,*" Glaser-Allen said. "If anything, I think they went out of their way not to have gender issues. They saw me as 'the judge' first, and as a girl second. I don't think it was any different for me than it was for the guy I replaced, or for the guy who replaced me." Glaser-Allen paused. "I never had to go to the dentist, the female captain, and say, 'I'm not being treated well.' " She gave another example. "When the Wing—aviators and their crews—came aboard, they liked to give me a hard time, but they were like big brothers; if anyone outside our group disrespected me—oh, forget about it. They were all over them. I don't doubt that there was sexual harassment somewhere in the ship," Glaser-Allen said, "but I never saw it, or heard about it. And I was accessible to the crew."[24]

Lieutenant Commander Glaser-Allen spoke of CAPT Kevin Donegan with undisguised respect. "Within the first month the skipper came onboard, he put out his policy. It was 'page 13' that all of us had to sign: sexual harassment, fraternization guidelines. And he basically told everyone, 'I'm the new skipper. I'm not going to mess with this. We're getting ready for deployment in January and I'm not going to tolerate it [sexual harassment, fraternization]. *I will not tolerate it.*' " Glaser-Allen paused. "He told the kids, 'You need to understand that I'm not playing. We'll look at every case on a case-by-case basis. I have a female lawyer.'[25]

"It was interesting because the legal department was unique. I am a female; my number two was a female. My LCPO—lead chief petty officer—was a female, and she was a master-at-arms on top of it. All the leadership in my legal department just happened to be female. The only JAG guy who wasn't was in the sheriff's department. The sheriff was this huge guy. It was kind of funny because we used to laugh about how he couldn't get a word in edgewise. Our special agent onboard won't even mess with the guy. It was kind of an interesting dynamic. I don't remember any sexual harassment cases at all." She took a deep breath. "We did have some fraternization cases, probably about five—maybe six officers and enlisted, and enlisted and enlisted, where they didn't respect the chain of command. The skipper would get on the site TV thing—we had TV throughout the ship—and he would do a port brief. He would talk about safety in the port, what to look out for."[26]

Lieutenant Commander Glaser-Allen discussed the issue of waivers for felons, which the army exercised in efforts to meet recruitment quotas. The navy appeared to have an entirely different view regarding the handing out waivers to prospective applicants. And the navy was just as anxious to get rid of the "bad apples" as the army was eager to grant a waiver and accept them. "We were kicking people out for drugs at Newport News [Virginia] and those kids were getting in the army. I couldn't believe it! Some of those little punks would come in and say, 'Well you can go ahead and discharge me, but I'll be in the army next week.' And I'd say, 'Wow!' It is my understanding that when you get kicked out of the navy with a drug case or something like that, you got an RE4 code, you can't reenlist in the navy. Apparently, the army is bending the rules and letting some of these kids in."[27]

Lieutenant Commander Glaser-Allen also addressed the importance of adhering to the Geneva Conventions. Unlike many in the Bush administration, many in the U.S. Navy did *not* consider the Geneva Conventions "quaint." "Aviators take Geneva Conventions very seriously. Legally, I don't understand the whole thing. . . . My skipper made sure that the several people we had as 'guests' in *my brig*—some for a few days, some for a week or so—were well treated. How do I treat these people? Follow the Geneva Conventions. We did everything we could do to accommodate: medical care, special meals, prayer rugs. . . . How do you *not* follow the Geneva Conventions? My guys were responsible for their care and feeding. The captain said, 'I am not going to have an Abu Ghraib on my ship.' And, it would not happen on *my* watch." Glaser-Allen paused and then continued. "I got videotape of the whole thing so I can prove how they were treated. Some of those guys [prisoners] were sick when we got them, and it was hard to understand what was wrong with them. Every one of them left healthier than when we got them. It wasn't that they were abused—they were sick when we got them. We had enough kids onboard who could speak languages enough to find out what they wanted to eat— can they eat meat? My job was simply to transport. I don't know what happened to them—don't think I want to know."[28]

For 99.44 percent of the men and women serving in today's military, and for the veterans who served before them, the Geneva Conventions are taken very seriously. The overwhelming majority of active, reserve, and National Guard troops and the veterans of the U.S. Armed Forces with whom the authors spoke since the start of Operation Iraqi Freedom were saddened or angered by the Bush administration's stand on their relevance of the Geneva Conventions to today's world. For the men and women who are in combat zones, and their families and friends, the Geneva Conventions are tremendously important, not only for what they say in loud, clear tones about the individuals they protect, but for what they say about the American people who believe living by them is essential to hold on to humanity in an endeavor as inhumane as war.

"We were in places where we knew that if the people had half a chance, they were going to kill us," Col. Carolyn Carroll remembered about her tour of duty in Afghanistan. After more than twenty-five years of active duty with the U.S. Army, Colonel Carroll knew as much, if not more, than the majority of career army officers about life over, on, in front of, and behind that most mystical of all U.S. military concepts concerning the front lines of combat in the War on Terror. She lived on those amorphous front lines in Afghanistan, and still saw the front lines in the First Gulf War, where they had embedded themselves forever in her memory.[29]

Col. Carolyn A. Carroll had been filling roles in the military and civilian world since the mid-seventies and had succeeded in both worlds, with a definite emphasis on the military. "Military" and "army" were interchangeable terms for the colonel and had been ever since she decided to make the army a career. For a single mother, that decision came with special challenges not an ordinary part of a soldier's life. The army did not permit single mothers with underage children to enlist in the service at the time Carroll was a nineteen-year-old divorced mother, responsible for the support and care of her child. An army recruiter Carroll knew suggested that she enlist in the National Guard and, after serving there for a month or two, switch to the U.S. Army Reserve as a single mother with prior service, and eventually go active duty if she wanted to do that.

When Carroll found out that the army recruiter had not filed all of the paperwork he had had her complete and had failed to document her army test scores and submit them for processing, she realized that the recruiter was trying to get her to go to bed with him and she decided to stay in the National Guard. Carroll found out that she could enlist in the Civilian Acquired Skills Program, go to basic training for two or three weeks, and return to her guard unit as an E-3 with two years of college or two years of work experience in her military occupation specialty (MOS). Further, she learned that if she did six months of on-the-job training in her MOS, she could receive an automatic promotion to E-4. Carroll successfully followed that path.

In 1976, for the first time, women could attend the State National Guard Noncommissioned Officer Academy, referred to as BNOC—Basic Leadership Training for NCOs. BNOC was a three-week summer course and there were more than two hundred people attending it. Carroll, a tomboy growing up, did well physically, academically, and in leadership evaluations. She also won a land navigation competition. Carroll was nominated as distinguished graduate by her peers and the faculty, but the sergeant major of the academy told Carroll, "We will not have a woman as a distinguished graduate." She appealed to the state adjutant general. The only other woman in the class, who just happened to be the secretary to the State Adjutant General, called him on the phone and explained what had transpired. Carroll was vindicated and went through the closing ceremony as the distinguished graduate.[30]

The battalion personnel section where Carroll worked had never had a female NCO. Despite the fact that Carroll had had E-5 stripes pinned on her at BNOC graduation, when she returned to her unit, she was told she would be a specialist and not a sergeant. "I said, 'Oh, no, I earned my stripes.' It was like, 'We can't let a female [be in charge]. You look good; you're smart; you've got it, but you're still a woman.' I was a feisty young kid. I was like—in your face. I said, 'You're not going to take my stripes away!' " Carroll got to keep her stripes.[31]

In the next two years, Carroll applied for officer candidate school (OCS) at Fort Benning, Georgia, and for active duty. Again, a general officer who felt the infantry had no need for female officers denied her admission. It took Carroll ten months to negotiate the bureaucracy, and she was finally admitted to the course. In July 1981, Carolyn Carroll graduated from OCS, and in January 1982 she went on active duty with the U.S. Army. Lt. Carolyn Carroll next applied for flight training for helicopters. Since personnel in supply division were not admitted to flight training, Lieutenant Carroll transferred to the Transportation Corps and was accepted for flight training on helicopters. When she graduated, Carroll was rated to fly front seat in the Cobra, and although not rated for the Kiowa OH-58, she knew how to fly, and did fly, the OH-58. She was soon rated for and transitioned into flying Black Hawks. About eight years later, she also qualified on the Soviet helicopter the Hip. She ended up with a rating for three aircraft: HU-1 or Huey, Black Hawk, and the Hip. She flew the Hip and took the part of "the enemy" in war games on various occasions.

In 1988, Captain Carroll requested a year to finish work on her bachelor's degree and was sent to the University of Kansas to complete her undergraduate courses. When Captain Carroll was three-fourths of the way through her final year at college, she went to speak with the brigade commanding officer about her upcoming command. The first words out of the commanding officer's mouth were, " 'I understand you're a single parent with six kids.' Those were his very first words to me. And then he proceeded to tell me all of the issues they had with single parents—now they were males. . . . I personally think that single males were not so good at juggling it all. I think that not just in the military, but in society as a whole, when a man is a single parent, they'll . . . pat him on the back and say, 'You know, you're a hell of a man for taking on those kids, being a

Capt. Carolyn Carroll after being rated in the Russian Mi-17, Hip—then the only female aviator in the U.S. Army to be so rated—standing with her boss, Col. Bob Harmon, AUS.

good father, and holding down a job.' Well, you know, they don't say that to women! So, after I got to listen for an hour to him, he said, 'Well, when you come here, you're going to be an assistant to somebody.' I said, 'Sir, when I leave here, I'm going to call Branch [headquarters personnel for the command] and I'm going to request *not* to be assigned here when I graduate. I'm coming here to take command—a company command—because I already had one officer who doesn't like women and who discriminated against me and kept me from getting a command. So HRC [Human Resources Command] has told me . . . they assigned me here because this is a division, and I am a senior captain, and I'm not going be anybody's assistant! So, very nice meeting you; you're going to lose a good officer because I know how to manage my six kids. I wouldn't be here today if I didn't know how to take care of my family and be successful in my career. So, I don't need somebody telling me all the rules [about] taking time off work. I will find a job somewhere else.' " Colonel Carroll paused. "I lived twenty-five miles from the airfield. By the time I got home, my oldest daughter's calling, 'Mom, somebody's been calling three or four times saying you need to call them before you call Branch.' So I called the brigade adjutant and he said, 'Colonel So-and-so was so impressed with you, he said that if you decide . . . He doesn't want you to call Branch; in fact he's already called Branch and told them he doesn't want to lose you. And he's going to make you the executive officer in one of the aviation companies.' "[32]

In August 1990, Major Carroll deployed to Operations Desert Shield and Desert Storm. On the day that U.S. and Coalition troops started moving across the desert in the direction of Baghdad, Major Carroll flew her Cobra helicopter above and in front of advancing American and Coalition troops. She looked down at the ground and saw a sight she would never forget. "I was in Desert Storm in the First Infantry Division. They led the attack across the burn. I think one of the most exciting things that I did was I actually flew missions the day of the ground attack. It was like a World War II movie because you had tanks and ammo carriers, big tracks, refuelers moving across the desert on line, and it was like the whole world was rumbling." Colonel Carroll paused. "It was interesting . . . while flying with male pilots, sometimes they didn't have the confidence, initially, if they didn't know me, and because I was a female. That was a little challenging, but in my normal, headstrong way, I fixed that off the front."[33]

Colonel Carroll continued. "The unit I was in . . . except a few of our contact teams, didn't come into direct contact with the enemy," Colonel Carroll remembered. "I did not have any life-and-death situations, although I did fly and land at a location that had a Scud missile attack and I didn't have my mask with me. I was actually sitting on the pot and thought, Oh my God! They'll tell my family, 'She left her mask in the aircraft and died on the shitter! She didn't take her mask with her.' " Colonel Carroll chuckled.[34]

"I think that my experience in Desert Storm was a very positive experience." Colonel Carroll took a deep breath. "I felt like as executive officer—we had a big company with attachments that we had right at three hundred people—I think I was able to mentor a lot of soldiers, male and female. You have lots of time out in the desert when you're not moving around a lot. You get very close. Some of those young kids, I saw as senior NCOs who are officers now, you still have kind of a special bond. . . . When you're in situations where you could die—we did have one soldier who lost his wife in an aircraft accident—another crew chief . . . all those sorts of things do bring people together. Overall, it was a very positive experience because, not only did I have the opportunity to meet wonderful people and feel like I was doing some good, I felt like . . . we had a mission and we did the mission well. And that all our kids came back home—alive and safe. I had a good experience as far as how you move things in a battle. We were there when we were getting attacked a lot. Although we did not get hurt . . . [we learned] how we handled things under stress. At that time in that company, we had forty to fifty females—a large percentage of females—and we had no problems. Part of that could have been that they had a female officer in leadership. I was a very people person, always moving around, finding out what was going on."[35]

Lt. Col. Carolyn Carroll, AUS, on duty in Afghanistan, 2006, serving as executive officer of a NATO unit, Canadian Army.

Lieutenant Colonel Carroll was deployed to Afghanistan in 2005. She worked closely with American soldiers and Special Forces, and she learned a lot about the kind of memories these soldiers brought home with them and about the ways that the Taliban used lies and fear to provide themselves with a limitless supply of young people who, because they never learned to read, depended on Taliban and al-Qaeda members to teach them about the Koran and exactly what God required of them if they were to live as good and pious Muslims and be taken immediately to heaven when they gave their lives in jihad. Colonel Carroll remembered the sacrifices of American soldiers and the terrible memories that embedded themselves deep within their minds, their hearts, and their souls. Years later, the pictures, the sounds, the odors, and the screams would return to haunt them with guilt and the deeply abiding conviction that they had failed their fellow soldiers and themselves. Colonel Carroll had heard the horror stories often enough, had seen more than enough on her own, and knew only too well that those sights and sounds were permanent. They might be dimmed, choked, or silenced for periods of time, but they would never be far from consciousness.

"One of the jobs I had the last six months there, I did tour the country and we did go to locations where you knew the people would kill you if they had half a chance; that was a little bit different. In working with the soldiers who were actually out with units—male and female—in Afghanistan, I don't know if we had the same issues as we have now in Iraq where you have such a high death rate and such a high incidence and chance that every time you go out, there's a chance that you might not come back. I think the whole atmosphere is a little different in Afghanistan. The mission is different there. . . . I think we should be there for a generation, but I think that it's a good thing that we're there. If we left, I think the Taliban would come in and all these madrassas—military schools—they don't read, but they teach them the Koran, but not necessarily an accurate version. Because they are illiterate and can't read for themselves, like children growing up who know only what they hear." Colonel Carroll paused. "I actually witnessed that in a village in one of the most violent areas of Afghanistan. We were doing a bridge dedication where we had built a bridge. I was executive officer for a general officer. His interpreter was telling me that what the [village] interpreter was saying to the people there was not true. They are like lambs being led to the slaughter. They are like children who believe what's being told to them and they don't even teach them right."[36]

20

★

Following the 9/11 terrorist attacks, the White House team has pushed hard to expand its powers, sometimes pushing the limits of constitutional restraints and the rules of civilized nations, and the best example is the twisted logic behind allowing the rough treatment of prisoners.

—"Torture of the Law,"
San Francisco Chronicle, 24 April 2008

The men and women who comprise America's armed forces today stand in a place unknown to U.S. military forces at any time in America's past. The authors are convinced that in order for our readers to understand the uniqueness of that place, it is necessary to understand the why and how of the decisions that brought us to this particular moment.

Without a doubt, the wars in Iraq and Afghanistan are unique not only in U.S. military history, but in American history as well. The composition of America's armed forces; the conditions in which U.S. military men and women train, live, and fight; and the American home front to which the veterans of these wars return are without precedent in the history of the United States. You, and we, the American people, are entitled to know how and why these conditions exist, and how and why they continue. Never before has so much been demanded of so few, at so great an individual and family cost, with so few benefits devolving to those who bore the battle or to their loved ones.

On 13 January 2004, Spc. Joseph Darby, a military police officer (MP) at Abu Ghraib Prison, some twenty miles west of Baghdad in Anbar Province, gave a compact disk containing photos of abuse of Iraqi detainees—men and women—to the army's Criminal Investigation Division (CID). Just two days later, Lt. Gen. Bantz J. Craddock, senior military adviser to Secretary of Defense Donald Rumsfeld, and VADM Timothy Keating, director of the Joint Staff of the Joint Chiefs of Staff, received an e-mail that summarized the abuses captured on camera and downloaded to the CD handed over by MP Joseph Darby. The e-mail described abuses including forcing female detainees to expose themselves to the guards; having male detainees pose nude while female guards pointed at their genitals; forcing detainees to perform indecent acts with each other; and guards physically assaulting detainees by striking them and/or dragging them by means of a lead attached to choke chains or collars around their necks. In addition, there were photos of hooded detainees with wires attached to them for the purpose of delivering electric shocks; male detainees being threatened by police dogs in the care of military guards; and male detainees made to wear women's underwear on their heads. The CD contained approximately one hundred photos documenting detainee abuse, and the videotape was not included in the collection of photos on the disc.

This was not the army's or the Department of Defense's first clue that something was seriously amiss at its military prisons for detainees outside the borders of the United States. On 23 July 2003, Amnesty International reported that it had received complaints of torture of detainees by U.S. forces in Iraq. Approximately five weeks later, Brig. Gen. Geoffrey Miller, commander of the military prison for terror suspects at Guantanamo Bay, Cuba, conducted an inquiry on interrogation and detention procedures in Iraq. The investigation was conducted between 31 August and 9 September 2003. General Miller's report suggested that prison guards at Abu Ghraib could be used to help set conditions for the interrogation of prisoners at military prisons in Iraq. The famous Abu Ghraib military prison was guarded by the 800th Military Police Brigade, which was commanded by Brig. Gen. Janis Karpinski. The 800th was a reserve brigade and had had minimal training, if any, in procedures for guarding military prisons. Abu Ghraib is Iraq's largest military prison and was overcrowded with approximately 7,000 detainees and understaffed with approximately 90 poorly trained military police guards to supervise the seven thousand inmates in their care.

During October 2003, the Red Cross conducted a "no notice" inspection of Abu Ghraib Prison, and later submitted a report to U.S. military authorities in Iraq detailing the abuses they found. The Red Cross later expanded its report to include serious violations it found at Abu Ghraib between March and November 2003.

Between 13 October and 6 November 2003, Maj. Gen. Donald Ryder, provost marshal of the army, investigated conditions at U.S. military prisons in Iraq and later submitted his findings to military authorities. His reports included findings that problems with abuse of detainees were present throughout Iraq's U.S. military prisons; that guards were poorly trained for the jobs assigned to them; and that *military police guards should not be tasked with assisting interrogators* by making the prisoners more pliable to interrogation, since it is the job of the military police *to keep the prisoners safe.*

In the last week of November 2003, the CIA Inspector General began investigating the deaths of two Iraqi prisoners who died during interrogation. One of these prisoners died at Abu Ghraib, the other at an unspecified location.

On 14 January 2004, the army launched a criminal investigation of prisoner abuse at Abu Ghraib. On 14 or 15 January 2004, Gen. John Abizaid, Chief of Central Command, informed Gen. Richard Myers, Chairman of the Joint Chiefs, about the investigation and told General Myers that the investigation was "a big deal."

On 16 January 2004, Central Command issued a one-paragraph news brief notifying the public that the army was investigating "incidents of detainee abuse" at unnamed U.S. military prisons in Iraq. Three days later, Gen. Ricardo Sanchez ordered a separate administrative investigation of the 800th Military Police Brigade. On 31 January, Sanchez appointed Maj. Gen. Antonio Taguba to conduct that investigation. Just days later, Secretary of Defense Rumsfeld and Vice Chairman of the Joint Chiefs of Staff Gen. Peter Pace briefed President Bush on the prisoner abuse investigations and the circumstances that triggered the inquiry. Clearly, top officials in the White House and the Pentagon were aware of what occurred to warrant such investigations.

On 2 February 2004, General Taguba and his staff of twenty-three military personnel arrived at Abu Ghraib and began interviews. On 26 February, General Sanchez announced the suspension of seventeen military personnel. Sanchez gave no details.

On 12 March 2004, Gen. Antonio Taguba presented his report to his commanders. Among other things, he and his investigators found widespread abuse of detainees at Abu Ghraib by military police and military intelligence. He underscored the findings of Major General Ryder that military guards *should not play any role* in the interrogation of prisoners. Just eight days later, the army announced the possibility of courts-martial for six U.S. soldiers accused of prisoner abuse at Abu Ghraib. On 4 April, an internal army review of prison management recommended administrative action against unnamed commanders in Iraq.

On 6 April 2004, Third Army Commander Lt. Gen. David D. McKiernan approved General Taguba's report. Six days later, the Pentagon received a phone call from CBS *60 Minutes II* informing them that they intended to broadcast photos of the Abu Ghraib Prison abuse within one week. On 14 April 2004, General Myers called CBS News anchor Dan Rather and asked for a delay of one week on the basis that broadcasting the photos could incite Iraqi violence against American troops and endanger the lives of ninety Western hostages being held by Iraqi insurgents. CBS agreed to the delay. Myers called again on 21 April 2004 and requested another delay. That delay, too, was granted. One week later on 28 April 2004, *60 Minutes II* broadcast the photos and the story. Americans and people around the globe were appalled and angry at the graphic abuse of detainees by U.S. soldiers.

In spite of having been informed many times, and having the photos and the soldiers available to them for at least three and a half months, Bush, Rumsfeld, and Myers each claimed that the *60 Minutes II* broadcast was the first time they had seen the photos. If what the three men were saying is true, one must wonder at the lack of judgment and irresponsibility that led them *not* to request the photos, in order to be completely cognizant of the problems and conditions at Abu Ghraib Prison. In view of the fact that CBS and Dan Rather had spoken with the Pentagon and General Myers directly, it stretches belief to the breaking point to accept that anyone with a sound mind would *not* ask for and look over the photos carefully in order to be better prepared for public reaction as soon as the photos aired on television. One would hope that men entrusted with the safety and care of the nation would have the good sense to prepare for the reaction of the American public more accurately and thoroughly than they had prepared for the reaction of the Shiite, Sunni, and Kurdish people of Iraq and of Iraq's neighbors after the U.S. and Coalition invasion on 19 March 2003. In time, the American people would learn that Bush, Rumsfeld, and Myers, along with others in the Bush administration, had more to worry about than the people's reaction to what they had seen and learned from the CBS *60 Minutes II* broadcast of 28 April 2004.

On 1 May 2004, General Sanchez approved the report submitted by General Taguba. Two days later, Bush instructed Rumsfeld to make sure that each and every soldier responsible for the shameful and appalling acts committed at Abu Ghraib be punished. Meanwhile, Rumsfeld's aides were telling the press that Rumsfeld had not as yet read the Taguba report, but had been kept updated concerning it, and that Rumsfeld would find time to read the actual report prior to the date of his scheduled appearance before Congress to address and answer questions about prisoner abuse at Abu Ghraib in Iraq and Guantánamo Bay, Cuba.

On 6 May 2004, the day before Rumsfeld's testimony before Congress, Bush apologized to the Iraqi people for the abuse at Abu Ghraib and announced that Rumsfeld would remain in his cabinet. The latter part of the announcement was most likely aimed at the thousands of Americans calling for Rumsfeld's resignation.

On 7 May 2004, Rumsfeld appeared before a joint committee of the Senate and House and issued two apologies, one for the abuse at Abu Ghraib and the other for laxity in informing the president and Congress. He also proposed compensation for the victims at Abu Ghraib and forming a panel to review the U.S. military prison system.

One army general watching the Rumsfeld testimony was Maj. Gen. Antonio M. Taguba. Although Taguba's name was on the report, he was not scheduled to appear before the committee. Taguba listened and watched intently and, a little more than three years later, remembered being appalled by Rumsfeld's testimony. Taguba told journalist Seymour M. Hersh during interviews for an article that appeared in the *New Yorker*'s 25 June 2007 edition that he believed that Rumsfeld's testimony was simply not true. He expanded on this when he told Hersh that he knew that Rumsfeld had a mind like a "steel trap" and was by no means suffering from CRS ("can't remember shit"). "Photographs were available to him—if he wanted to see them." Taguba went on to say that Rumsfeld and his aides had abused their offices and had no idea of the level of honesty and integrity the American people expected of them. It saddened Taguba to see that Rumsfeld and his aides had dragged a lot of military officers down with them.[1]

General Taguba also accused the Bush administration of spinning on the cause of the abuses at Abu Ghraib, saying it was the result of the decisions of enlisted personnel who took it upon themselves to pull "college-boy pranks" on the detainees at Abu Ghraib. Taguba believed exactly what military veterans know the world over—enlisted personnel do not take the initiative to start new programs, let alone to turn a cell block into an X-rated reality TV program where offenders take snapshots and videos of their unlawful, immoral actions. Plausible denial loses its luster as it piles one ridiculous statement upon another in an attempt to build a defense out of lies, spin, intimidation, and the well-worn dodge of executive privilege.[2]

The Abu Ghraib scandal had reached a point where officers and Bush administration officials were no longer trying simply to save face with evidence mounting against them; they were saying and doing whatever it took to save their asses from war crime indictments that might result in years of imprisonment. Taguba believed what the majority of military veterans had known from the start: that the enlisted were receiving guidance from officers, contractors, and government officials who had duped those under their command into breaking national and international law. In fact, Taguba told Seymour Hersh that he had been given orders to investigate *only* the military police and *not* to investigate those above them in the chain of command. Taguba made it clear that he was legally prevented from investigating anyone in higher authority.[3]

After General Taguba's report was made public, he was in Kuwait where Gen. John Abizaid was visiting. In the backseat of Abizaid's chauffeur-driven Mercedes sedan, with Abizaid's interpreter seated in the front, Abizaid turned to General Taguba and told him that he and his report would be investigated. Taguba was disappointed rather than angry. Taguba remembered thinking that he had been in the army for thirty-two years and Abizaid's was the only remark that made him feel like he was in the Mafia.

During the investigation at Abu Ghraib, Taguba became convinced that intelligence personnel were exploiting MPs who had never been given the procedures that were standard in guarding prisoners. Intelligence personnel would tell MPs to "loosen a guy up for interrogation" or to "make sure he has a bad night." Taguba was also convinced that General Sanchez knew exactly what was going on at Abu Ghraib, and records indicated that Abizaid had been in the prison many times and had "sat in" on an interrogation.[4]

General Taguba was summoned to appear at a closed meeting of the Senate Armed Services Committee on 11 May 2004. At that meeting, Under-Secretary of Defense Stephen Cambone testified that he had not known of the specifics of the Abu Ghraib abuse until he saw Taguba's report. Senator Jack Reed of Rhode Island asked Taguba if he had read Miller's report stating a major recommendation to use MP guards to aid in conditioning detainees for interrogations. Taguba answered that he did consider the use of MPs to assist in conditioning detainees for interrogations, a recommendation made by General Miller. Taguba also confirmed that he had concluded that after Miller's visit and recommendations, Military Intelligence took control of the MPs.

General Taguba was scheduled to return to Third Army for duty when his work with the Abu Ghraib report was finished. Instead, General Taguba was stationed at the Pentagon to work in the Office of the Undersecretary of Defense for Reserve Affairs. The assignment was a lateral move. Later, a retired four-star army general told Taguba that he, Taguba, had been placed in his current assignment so the Pentagon could keep an eye on him.

In the daylight hours of 12 March 2006, six American GIs assigned to a traffic checkpoint outside the town of Mahmudiyah, Iraq, changed out of their American army uniforms, dressed in black clothing—complete with masks—and made their way toward an Iraqi house within sight of their checkpoint with the intention of carrying out a plan each had agreed to many days earlier. The author of the plan, Pfc. Steven D. Green, twenty-four, had introduced the idea one evening while the group was playing cards and drinking Iraqi moonshine. The soldiers decided to adopt Green's idea: They would go to the house, which could be seen from their checkpoint, a house whose residents they had seen and watched many times through binoculars and discussed many times over the past weeks.

It was a fourteen-year-old girl who interested the soldiers. In fact, they had spoken to her many times, flirted with her, and had made indecent remarks and gestures to her even when one or more of her family members was present. The youngster, the oldest girl in the family of six, lived with her parents, two brothers who attended school in Mahmudiyah, and a younger sister, age five years. The soldiers knew that the only male in the home would be the father, Qasim Hamza Raheem, a forty-five-year-old farmer. The mother, thirty-four-year-old Fakhriyah Taha Muhasen, would be at home, along with fourteen-year-old Abeer and her five-year-old sister, Hadeel. The couple's sons would be at school for most of the day, as usual. The family would be no match for five young American GIs, trained in combat, carrying weapons, and armed with a plan they had studied and talked about for days.

On the morning of 12 March 2005, the six American soldiers drank Iraqi moonshine mixed with an energy drink and hit golf balls aimlessly as they went over the plan for the last time. When the six were dressed in the black clothing they had secured for their crime, one soldier, Sgt. Anthony W. Yribe, remained behind to man the traffic checkpoint. When the other five GIs arrived at the house, Pfc. Bryan L. Howard separated from the other four and, armed with a two-way radio, stood guard for the purpose of warning his buddies should anyone approach the house while his four friends were still inside or on the grounds.

When the four reached the house, they found the parents and their two daughters outside. The four GIs followed the plan, and while Pfc. Steven D. Green took the parents and their five-year-old daughter into a bedroom of the house, the remaining three soldiers, Sgt. Paul E. Cortez, Spc. James T. Barker, and Pfc. Jesse V. Spielman, took the older daughter into the living room, where Sgt. Cortez pushed the fourteen-year-old to the floor, lifted her dress, tore off her underwear, and raped her. When Cortez finished, the other men began to take their turns raping the young girl.

Several gunshots rang out from the bedroom, and Pfc. Steven D. Green walked into the room. "I just killed them. All are dead," he announced. Without further conversation, Green put down the AK-47 he was carrying and claimed his turn to rape Abeer while Sergeant Cortez held the young girl down in order to make Green's intentions less difficult to accomplish. When Green finished, he picked up his AK-47 and shot the fourteen-year-old once in the face, waited several seconds, and fired two more rounds into the youngster's body.[5]

The four GIs decided to destroy any evidence that might connect the murder to them. Barker poured the fuel from a kerosene lamp over the lower portion of Abeer's body. As Barker finished emptying the kerosene over Abeer's torso down to and including her feet, Green reentered the living room and told the three men that he had opened a propane tank, and they needed to leave the house and the area before the tank exploded and set fire to the house. All five GIs returned to their traffic checkpoint, changed back into their uniforms, and gave their black clothes to Yribe to burn. Green also gave the AK-47 used in the slayings to Yribe, with instructions to throw it into the nearby canal.

The propane in the tank that Green had opened did what he had intended—set fire to the house. Neighbors saw the smoke and went to investigate. When they found the bodies of Abeer, her parents, and her five-year-old sister, they went to a checkpoint manned by Iraqi soldiers and reported the crime.

While Iraqi soldiers made their way through the carnage at the crime scene, Barker was grilling chicken wings for himself and his buddies. They were sitting together eating and talking when Iraqi soldiers arrived at the American checkpoint, reported the grizzly murders, and asked that an

American soldier go with them to investigate the scene. Barker accompanied the Iraqi soldiers to the house where, just hours before, he and his buddies had raped and killed fourteen-year-old Abeer and murdered her family. The Iraqi military and police determined that the crimes in Mahmudiyah on 12 March 2006 had been committed by unknown insurgents.

In late March 2006, Private 1st Class Green was given his second appointment with the army's Combat Stress Team. As an investigation by the Associated Press would reveal months later, this was not the first time Green had turned to the army for help. On 21 December 2005, Green had been treated by the Combat Stress Team for persistent ideation concerning homicide and rage over the deaths of eight men in his unit. Green reported at the time that he "wanted to kill lots of Iraqis" as payback for his buddies who had been killed by them. As media investigations would reveal in mid-2006 and 2007, the 12 March 2006 crimes committed by Green and four other soldiers in his unit was not Green's first encounter with law-breaking.[6]

In fact, given a childhood replete with troublemaking in school and at home, and a record that included three arrests and jail time served, Green would never have been accepted into the army prior to the severe shortages of recruits and troops available to deploy to Iraq and Afghanistan. The army knew what they were getting when, days after his release from jail, Green enlisted and was given a moral waiver for criminal history in order to make accepting him possible. That "moral waiver" changed the lives of Green and the soldiers who served with him at the traffic checkpoint outside of Mahmudiyah and helped end the lives of an Iraqi father and mother and their two daughters.[7]

In short, the damage done by these moral waivers—more of which are being granted than ever before in order to obtain enough troops to prevent the complete collapse of the U.S. Army—may have been less recognizable to the American public than having few or no troops volunteering for the army. But in many ways the moral waivers were—and are—doing more damage than the gross shortage of troops could ever have accomplished. The moral waivers, granted by an administration that preached moral values, were allowing *people who would have been soundly rejected by an army not on the brink of collapse* to be welcomed and greeted as heroes and presented to the American people as "America's best and brightest," altruistically stepping forward to volunteer to protect America from terrorists.[8]

In a very real sense, the Bush administration used moral waivers to build a Trojan army out of recruits who would not have been accepted in the army without ignoring how low army standards had fallen and how insidious, pervasive, and costly the problems these Trojan soldiers brought with them would be or how much damage the problems would inflict on the U.S. Army, the Army Reserves, the National Guard, and on America itself.

In April, Pfc. Steven Green was returned to Fort Campbell, Kentucky, to be evaluated for combat stress. In May 2006, just eleven months after his enlistment in the army, Private 1st Class Green received an honorable discharge with a diagnosis of "personality disorder."[9]

In June, Pfc. Justin Watt, twenty-three, a member of the same unit, called his father with a question. "If you knew something bad about your brothers, would you come forward?" His father told Justin that if what the "brothers" had done was very bad, then he would have to make a very difficult decision. Later that month, Private 1st Class Watt told his counselor the story he had been told by Spc. James T. Barker. The counselor made it known to the company commander, and within days actions had been initiated to charge the men connected with the gang rape and murder of fourteen-year-old Abeer and the slayings of her parents and five-year-old sister. Since Green had been discharged from the army approximately a month earlier, the army contacted civilian authorities in North Carolina, and on 30 June 2006, Steven D. Green was arrested and charged with rape, murder, and lesser crimes such as breaking and entering and arson.[10]

Since Steven D. Green was a civilian, he would be tried in a federal court. Each of the soldiers charged would face a general court-martial at Fort Campbell. Barker was the first to plead guilty, and on 15 November 2006, he was sentenced to life confinement with the possibility of parole in twenty years. Sgt. Paul Cortez pled guilty, and on 22 February 2007 was sentenced to one hundred years of confinement with the possibility of parole after ten years. Pfc. Bryan L. Howard pled guilty, and on 21 March 2007 was sentenced to twenty-seven months' confinement. Pfc. Jesse Spielman pled not guilty, and on 4 August 2007 was sentenced to 110 years of confinement with no possibility of parole. Sgt. Anthony W. Yribe was charged with dereliction of duty for not reporting the crimes. After agreeing to testify against the others charged in the case, he received a less than honorable discharge from the U.S. Army. On 27 April 2009, a jury in Paducah, Kentucky, found Steven D. Green guilty. On 22 May 2009, Green was sentenced to life in prison without parole.[11]

News of the rapes, murders, and the men who committed them appeared all around the world. When news of the charges against the American soldiers reached the Iraqi people, a group of Iraqis kidnapped, tortured, mutilated, and killed two soldiers from Green's old squad while they stood guard at the same traffic checkpoint where Green, Cortez, Barker, Spielman, Howard, and Yribe plotted their crimes and to which they returned to grill and eat chicken wings once the crimes had been completed. In order to make clear that the two soldiers were killed in retaliation for the rape and murders of 12 March 2006, Iraqis took a video of the mutilated soldiers and made the video and commentary available to the public and to the U.S. Army troops stationed in Iraq.

Despite the fact that the authors are convinced that no circumstance, including war, can justify the heinous crimes committed by these American soldiers on the afternoon of 12 March 2006, they also believe that the blame and guilt for these atrocities do not end with these enlisted men. Enlisted soldiers are expected to carry out the plans and orders of all officers and officials appointed over them. Enlisted soldiers live and work in the environment and with the rules—written and spoken—that come down to them through the chain of command. Where they fight, which equipment and supplies they use, the rules of engagement, and the military cultures in which they live, eat, sleep, and interact are provided to them and for them through the military chain of command.

From a soldier's first day in basic training, that chain of command is outlined and made ever present in the recruit's mind and heart. Military order depends on military discipline; military discipline depends on the Uniform Code of Military Justice and the officers and noncommissioned officers who interpret the laws, rules, customs, and traditions to be followed by each soldier, from four-star generals to first-day recruits.

The Department of Defense and the Department of the Army have never been shy about making clear that the U.S. military and, so, the U.S. Army, is governed by a hierarchy of officers and civilian officials appointed or elected to plan, execute, and carry out military missions in accordance with the Uniform Code of Military Justice and the lawfully appointed or elected superiors in the Pentagon and in the field charged with delivering those orders to the soldiers. If any soldier wonders who is in charge, he or she needs only to look at the insignia of rank—worn or spelled out in writing—for the purpose of making the chain of command visible and present in all situations: in peace, in war, at one's duty station, in transit, or in the barracks. And if any president of the United States has ever made it clear that he sits at the top of that chain of command, it was George W. Bush, commander in chief and, in his own words, "the decider."

Just as the buck once stopped at the desk of President Harry S Truman, the "military buck" stops at the desk of the commander in chief. A phrase that expresses the arrangement very well in the military is "Loyalty Up, Loyalty Down." Loyalty and responsibility run both ways, up and down, in the military command hierarchy. It is that military hierarchy that sets the tone for all military situations and environments. The structure of that hierarchy has been in existence more than two hundred years, and for many of those years two of its main supports have been the Uniform Code of Military Justice and the Geneva Conventions.

For many Americans with a military background and a good dose of common sense, the first signs that all might not be well with our planning for the invasion and occupation of Iraq came with the first television pictures of Iraqis looting public and government buildings in Iraq and hauling off anything they could carry to the back of pickup trucks and driving away with looted merchandise either while an American soldier stood by and watched or without an American soldier in sight.

For many who had served in the U.S. Armed Forces, knew their military history, and had friends and relatives in uniform, one of the first questions that sprang to mind was: Where are the troops who should be stopping the looting and imposing the rule of law? And when they heard stories of breaking into ammunition bunkers and the threat of those weapons being carried off by Iraqis, the question, Where are the American and Coalition troops to stop this and to restore order? sounded in voices much louder than the theft of lamps, furniture, and office equipment.

The authors remember well the camera shots when Secretary of Defense Donald Rumsfeld commented that "stuff happens" and said he was tired of seeing images of the same man carrying the same lamp out of the same building played over and over again. However, as news reports continued to be broadcast of widespread looting, Rumsfeld's explanation of "stuff happens" and "television playing the same shots of the same man, with the same lamp" were no longer even minimally satisfactory. In the days and weeks that followed, reports of major looting made their way to the news and into American homes.

As weeks rolled into months, and months led into summer, and summer into fall, other questions were being asked: Where are the WMD? Where are the mobile chemical labs, the stores of nuclear materials for nuclear weapons? And finally, How could our intelligence have been so wrong? Why were female soldiers being wounded, killed, and taken prisoner, when they were not technically in combat? Why were female soldiers in safe jobs, like supply, some of the hardest hit? What percentage of the U.S. forces in Iraq and Afghanistan was made up of female soldiers? The answers drifted in slowly, and with them, additional questions and doubts.

One of the issues that continued to be addressed by women serving in the military in Iraq, Afghanistan, and Kuwait had to do with sexual assaults perpetrated on U.S. female soldiers by U.S. male soldiers. In an environment replete with combat stress and described by Lt. Gen. Ricardo S. Sanchez as "a 360-degree combat zone," soldiers redeployed to the United States were increasingly reporting symptoms compatible with posttraumatic stress disorder (PTSD). As tours in Iraq became extended and redeployment became the rule, the number of soldiers and veterans reporting PTSD continued to climb. Living conditions, food, and a "360-degree combat zone" placed GIs under constant combat stress that for many became more difficult to handle after each successive redeployment to Iraq and Afghanistan.[12]

For the majority of U.S. soldiers, time spent off duty with fellow soldiers offered some relaxation with friends who shared the dangers as well as a place of relative safety, free of worry for a time, knowing that there were no enemies hiding in their group, that they were in the company of people who wished them only good things. Sad to say, however, there were GIs in groups who were denied this comfort and consequently suffered the additional stress of knowing that not all their comrades wished them well and that some had already done them harm, and would again if circumstances permitted. For Orlinda Marquez, a U.S. Army officer in the 1980s, officer training prior to that time was not supportive of women who had been sexually assaulted. During a PBS *NewsHour* segment, "Rape in the Ranks," Marquez described what happened after a woman reported a sexual assault. "Your peers begin to turn against you. Your command turns its back on you. This business that 'we take care of [our] own,' once you're the victim, you're no longer 'their own' that they take care of. They persecute the victim while they protect the offender."[13]

That group of fellow soldiers shared two things in common: they were females, and they lived with the extra stress of knowing that there were male soldiers who saw them as a means of sexual gratification, even if it had to be attained through violence and rape. In a 360-degree combat zone, women in the military faced all the hardships, dangers, and enemies that confronted their brothers-in-arms and, in addition, faced one even more insidious than insurgents or Al-Qaeda: the men of the U.S. military who had in the past raped or would in the future attempt to rape their female comrades-in-arms. It was a hostile environment brought about by the perfect storm of circumstances that created the impression that "anything goes"; that Iraq was a "no rules zone" where as long as a man showed up at his post to perform his mission, he could *take* whatever he needed to keep himself fit for combat.

As the years went by in Iraq, the number of sexual assaults on U.S. military women increased, as did the number of murders and suicides following the rapes. In 2004, there were 1,700 reported sexual assaults against U.S. military women. Of those assaults, only 329 ended in charges brought against men who perpetrated the crimes. That year, 2004, also saw a halfhearted effort of the Department of Defense to address the cases of sexual assaults, rapes, and sexual harassment of U.S. female soldiers by U.S. male soldiers, which had become commonplace in the U.S. military, especially in Iraq, Afghanistan, and Kuwait. The numbers had risen so high that the Department of Defense and the nation were forced to address the issue. Finally, the Department of Defense published the "Task Force Report on Care for Victims of Sexual Assaults, Overview Briefing, May 13, 2004."

The findings and recommendations of the Task Force Report were as follows:

FINDINGS, BROADLY CHARACTERIZED:

- DoD policies and standards need to focus on sexual assault.
- Services' stovepipe policies need to be integrated for effective prevention and response.
- Commanders need guidance, resources, and emphasis on prevention and response.
- Victim response capabilities need more resources and uniform guidance.
- Efforts to hold offenders accountable need to be made more transparent.

RECOMMENDATIONS:

- Establish a single point of accountability for addressing sexual assault matters.

- Discuss leadership responsibilities at May Combatant Commanders Conference.
- Fill gaps in sexual assault information through DoD-wide communication outlets.
- Convene a summit to develop strategic courses of action on critical, unresolved issues.
- Develop DoD policies for prevention, reporting, response, and accountability.
- Establish an Armed Forces Sexual Assault Advisory Council.
- Provide manpower and fiscal resources to implement required policies and standards.
- Develop an integrated strategy for sexual assault data collection.
- Establish program evaluation, quality improvement, and oversight mechanisms.[14]

Unfortunately for the victims, the U.S. military, and the nation, the next four years would show clearly that the commander in chief, the secretary of defense, and the military branches had not followed up on their own recommendations. Like the armor that U.S. troops needed in Iraq and Afghanistan, another need brought to the attention of the chain of command and to the Secretary of Defense, Donald Rumsfeld, the recommendations to address the issues of sexual assaults, rapes, and sexual harassment would be addressed even more slowly than was the DoD's response to the lack of adequate armor in the war zones.

During the last week of July 2008 and the first week of August 2008, it was learned that three years had passed since the DoD was to name fifteen people to a civilian task force to investigate allegations of sexual assault of military personnel; they were not appointed until early 2008 and as of August 2008, not one meeting of that task force had been held. It strains credulity to believe that the DoD and its agents had any real intention of following up on their own 2004 recommendations, when four years later, they had not even had the first meeting of the proposed task force.

During congressional hearings in July and August 2008, it was learned that the Principal Deputy Undersecretary of Defense, Michael Dominguez, had ordered Dr. Kaye Whitley, chief of the Sexual Assault Prevention and Response Office (SAPRO), to refuse to comply with the subpoena issued by the U.S. House of Representatives' subcommittee of National Security and Foreign Affairs to address the problem of sexual assault, rape, and sexual harassment, and to refuse to discuss why—after more than four years—that task force still had not held its first meeting.[15]

As the authors know from their own military service and frequent contact with senior military officers and enlisted over more than a decade, the U.S. military is not a democratic organization and the chain of command is taken very seriously. We have been told by senior female and male military officers that if the military wanted to fix the problem, they could do it quickly and decisively by holding commanding officers accountable for the criminal actions of their troops and bringing the aggressors before a court-martial for their crimes. These facts are addressed by the army's Lt. Gen. Claudia J. Kennedy in her book, *Generally Speaking*, and by the air force's Maj. Gen. Jeanne Holm in her book, *Women in the Military*, as well as in our interviews and conversations with Chaplain Maj. Priscilla Mondt, Col. Carolyn Carroll, and CAPT John Miller, USNR (Ret.). The statistics also bear this out.[16]

In 2005, the number of sexual assaults against women in the military increased to 2,374. In 2006, the Department of Defense changed its reporting perimeters for sexual assaults from a calendar year to a fiscal year, making comparisons difficult. The 2006 statistic was reported as 2,947, or a 24 percent increase from 2005 and a 73 percent increase from 2004. Sixty percent of the 2,688 sexual assaults reported in 2007 were rapes.[17]

Other changes regarding the manner in which sexual assaults against women were seen began in 1993 when the UN General Assembly passed a Declaration on the Elimination of Violence Against Women. In 2002, the International Criminal Court declared that it would now consider rape to be a war crime.[18]

Rape is no stranger to war, and never has been. Yet for anyone who had studied military history, it was clear that the wars in Iraq and Afghanistan had produced very different patterns of rape and murder than had appeared in previous wars. This was especially true when considering the rape, and even murder, of U.S. female soldiers by U.S. male soldiers. The statistics in this regard were staggering. One of every three women in the U.S. military was now the victim of sexual assault, including rape.

In addition to tragedies of sexual assault, rape, and murder, the commander in chief, the Pentagon, and the army chain of command must be held accountable for the deaths of female soldiers who died of dehydration, which was the direct result of the fear female soldiers felt regarding the very real possibility of being raped by their brothers-in-uniform. The soldiers were living and working in temperatures that reached more than 115 degrees every day where all military personnel wore battle dress uniforms complete with body armor to help protect them from their designated enemies. Many of the female soldiers decided that the best way to avoid becoming a victim of sexual assault, rape, and even murder was not to go to the women's latrine area at night. In order to be able to make it through the night without a trip to the latrine, some women stopped drinking liquids at 3:00 p.m.—not a good idea but a decision that reflects how deep the fear of sexual assault was for female soldiers who had to live in an environment where rape and sexual assault were epidemic and neither the chain of command nor the commanding officers of individual units used their authority to hold the sexual predators responsible or to make the area safe for female soldiers serving with these units. Even the simple act of adding more lighting to areas like the women's latrines might have had some positive effect, and it is reasonable to ask why such actions were not taken.[19]

During the third week in January 2006, Col. Janis Karpinski testified before a panel of judges at the Commission of Inquiry for Crimes against Humanity Committed by the Bush Administration, that the deaths of at least three female soldiers in Iraq were caused by dehydration and that the army covered up the cause of death. "Under orders from [Lt. Gen. Ricardo S.] Sanchez, he [Maj. Gen. Walter Wojdakowski, Sanchez's top deputy in Iraq] directed that the cause of death be no longer listed [on the death certificate or other documents that were likely to be seen by the media and the public]. Women were dying because the U.S. Army did nothing substantive to lower the risks of sexual assault and rape. Here we have three deaths of military women, and still no orders to prevent future crimes in those categories were taken. This is just one more crime compounded by a cover-up, in an environment of hostility and misogyny."[20]

The authors have chosen to present three of the rape cases in order to acquaint the reader with the lawless conditions that have been and are permitted to exist in Iraq, Afghanistan, and Kuwait. That lawlessness exists because the entire chain of command—from Mr. Bush, the commander in chief in the White House, to the commanding officers of military bases on which the crimes occur—chose not to correct the lawless environments and attitudes that permit, tolerate, and thereby encourage such war crimes to continue. The authors have spoken with scores of senior officers and have been told, "If the military wanted to fix the problem, it would already be fixed." As retired navy pilot CAPT John Miller said, "It's leadership . . . leadership can change it [sexual harassment/assault]. . . . It's all about what a CO will put up with, and what he will not tolerate. . . . As you know, a CO has a tremendous amount of discretion."[21]

In July 2005, nineteen-year-old Pvt. LaVena Johnson was found dead on a military base in Balad, Iraq. Despite strong evidence that Private Johnson had been murdered, the U.S. Army ruled her death as suicide by a self-inflicted M-16 rifle shot to the head. From the time Private Johnson's body was returned to her parents in St. Louis, Missouri, Dr. John Johnson and his wife, Linda, had discounted the idea that their daughter committed suicide. Dr. Johnson examined his daughter's body carefully and found that bruising was evident on and about her face, that uniform white gloves had been glued to LaVena Johnson's hands, and that her right hand had been burned badly before the gloves were applied. In addition, Dr. and Mrs. Johnson had talked to LaVena every day for periods of an hour or longer. Private Johnson was assigned to a communication facility and calling home was easy for her. Mrs. Johnson stated that LaVena evidenced no signs of depression or suicidal ideation. These facts were underscored by a note written to the Johnsons by LaVena's commanding officer, Capt. David Woods. Woods included the words, "LaVena was clearly happy, and seemed in good health, both physically and emotionally."[22]

For approximately two and a half years, Dr. and Mrs. Johnson, along with family and friends, pursued, with unwavering effort, the truth of how and why their daughter died and why the U.S. Army had done such a poor job of investigating her death. The Johnsons used the Freedom of Information Act and the help of congressional offices to obtain the official documents connected to their daughter's death. The documents requested came in slowly, yet with each new document came answers and questions that led to additional requests through the Freedom of Information Act.[23]

A drawing of the criminal investigation scene showed the M-16 laying perfectly parallel to Johnson's body. The drawing also showed that Johnson's body had been found under a wooden bench, inside a burning tent. The witness who found the body stated that he had heard a gunshot and went to investigate. That is when he found the burning tent and Johnson's body. The army's official investigation report made no mention of anyone's finding a burning tent, or the fact that parts of Johnson's body were also burned.

After two years of document requests, the army finally provided a set of papers that included a photocopy of a CD. Dr. Johnson then requested a copy of the CD itself. With some coaxing from a congressional office, the army eventually complied and sent a copy of the CD. Dr. Johnson was surprised to find photos of his daughter's body at the crime scene, along with photos of his daughter's naked body taken during the investigation.

The photos revealed that LaVena Johnson had been struck in the face with a blunt object, possibly the stock of an M-16 rifle. The blow had broken her nose and knocked her teeth backward. The back of her clothing had debris all over it, suggesting that Johnson had been dragged from one location to another. There was a distinct blood trail from outside a contractor tent into the tent in which her body had been found. It also indicated that the right side of her body and her right hand had been burned, and one of her elbows was distended. The photos of Johnson's nude body also showed bruises, scratches, and teeth marks on her upper body. The photographs of her genital area revealed massive bruising and lacerations. Also, a corrosive liquid had been poured into her genital area—most likely to destroy DNA evidence of a sexual assault. Despite the multiple traumas to her body, Johnson was found fully clothed, suggesting that she had been attacked outside the tent, then dragged inside the tent and the tent set on fire.[24]

The army investigation first came to the conclusion that LaVena Johnson's death was a homicide, but later, and with no additional evidence, changed its original finding to "non-combat wound—self-inflicted—suicide." Despite many requests for LaVena Johnson's case to be reopened, the army has refused and insisted that its original investigation was complete and fully thorough.[25]

Another death that the army ruled a suicide is that of twenty-year-old Pfc. Tina Priest, Fifth Support Battalion, First Brigade Combat Team, Fourth Infantry Division, Fort Hood, Texas. Priest had been raped by a U.S. soldier in February 2006 at Camp Taji, Iraq. Pfc. Tina Priest's body was found in her room on 1 March 2006 with—by army determination—a self-inflicted M-16 wound to her chest, eleven days after she was raped. The army's findings are disputed by Private First Class Priest's mother. Mrs. Priest stated that she spoke to her daughter after the rape and, although upset, her daughter was not suicidal. Mrs. Priest continued to ask the question, How could her petite five-foot-tall daughter with a short arm-length have held and fired the M-16 at the angle the bullet entered her body? The army's continued attempts to answer Mrs. Priest's question have been repeatedly debunked by the question itself, and by the eight hundred pages of evidence the army compiled and submitted.[26]

Murder charges against the soldier whose sperm was found on Priest's sleeping bag were dropped several weeks after Priest's death. The soldier was found guilty of disobeying an order and fined $714 for two months, given thirty days' restriction to the base and forty-five days of extra duty.[27]

One week later, on 8 March 2006, nineteen-year-old Pfc. Amy Duerkson, Fourth Combat Support Battalion, First Brigade, Fourth Infantry Division, also in Fort Hood, Texas, suffered a gunshot wound. Three days later, on 11 March 2006, Private First Class Duerksen died of her wound, which the U.S. Army listed as "self-inflicted." Duerksen's diary was found open to a page where she had written about being raped while in training, after unknowingly consuming a drink laced with a date-rape drug.[28]

The individual Pfc. Duerksen had listed as her rapist was arrested by the army and charged with rape. Despite the fact that no one who had known Amy believed her gunshot wound was the result of a suicide, the army, as far as can be determined, never investigated the shooting as a possible homicide.[29]

It is ironic that one of the arguments used again and again by the military, the Congress, far-right religious leaders, and by individual male soldiers to bar U.S. female military personnel from combat was the innate response of U.S. male soldiers to protect women and men's desire never to put them in a position where they might be captured by the enemy, sexually abused, and raped. The fear that females might be raped if captured made for tense scenes in American western movies, where the cowboy always saved a bullet to kill the woman if it looked as if their position might be overrun by savage Indians or equally savage Mexican bandits. As the authors look back on those movies, they cannot keep from wondering why none of those "damsels in distress" ever objected to the idea of being shot for their own good.

Then came World War II movies and Veronica Lake willingly blowing herself up with a hand grenade after distracting a platoon of Japanese soldiers, so Claudette Colbert and the other U.S. Army nurses could escape being captured and raped by a brutal and savage enemy. It made for a tense and interesting scene in the 1940s movie *So Proudly We Hail,* but it bore no true relation to what actually happened to a group of U.S. Army and Navy Nurses captured by the Japanese in 1942, when Bataan and Corregidor fell and General MacArthur was on his way from the Philippines to Australia with his top male military officers, his wife and son, and their china and silverware. Sixty-eight U.S. Army Nurses (and eleven U.S. Navy Nurses in Manila) were left behind with the certain knowledge that they would either be killed or captured by the Japanese who had taken Bataan and would soon capture the island of Corregidor.

In real life, as the authors related in *All This Hell: U.S. Nurses Imprisoned by the Japanese,* U.S. Army and Navy Nurses spent thirty-seven and forty-one months, respectively, as Japanese prisoners of war, with the idea of rape being one of the lesser tragedies that might befall them. Each of the army nurses did carry a lethal dose of morphine—hidden in her hair. Should she ever face a situation where the very real horrors of war she faced every day made choosing to live less attractive than death, she could make her decision and have the means to carry that decision out. These were the same military nurses who had withstood the bombing and shelling of Manila, Bataan, and Corregidor; the same women who had cared for wounded GIs with little food, medicine, or surgical supplies while Japanese soldiers moved ever closer to the jungle hospitals on Bataan. They were the same women who had withstood the Battle of Bataan and cared for wounded GIs and enemy soldiers in the hot, dank hospital of Malinta Tunnel while Japanese bombs and artillery shells fell on the island day and night. *So Proudly We Hail* did not do these American heroines justice. The truth is much more astounding than any Hollywood producer could possibly have imagined.[30]

Veronica Lake and Claudette Colbert in the movie So Proudly We Hail.

During Desert Storm when army physician Maj. Rhonda Cornum, whose helicopter crashed on a medical evacuation flight to pick up wounded, was captured by Iraqis along with other members of the helicopter crew, the White House, President George H. W. Bush, and the Pentagon were quick to point out that they expected Major Cornum, Spc. Melissa Rathbun-Nealy, and all POWs held by the Iraqis to be treated with the respect the Geneva Conventions and civilized nations had agreed upon. Major Cornum did report, after the First Gulf War ended and she and the other POWs were released, that an Iraqi soldier had groped her breast, but that she was not raped or otherwise sexually abused. Specialist Rathbun-Nealy and the male soldiers held prisoner also reported that they had not been abused by the enemy. It was obvious that Iraq had acted in accordance with the Geneva Conventions. Once again, the most frequently voiced fear for barring military women from combat did not come to fruition. The Geneva Conventions and international law had once more proved their value in protecting American and Allied forces.

More than five years after "major combat operations ended in Iraq," the men and women of the U.S. military who were told they would be greeted in Iraq as liberators would be engaged in bloody combat in such cities as Falluja, Sadr City, Basra, and Mosul. The casualty numbers that stood at 139 when Bush posed beneath the Mission Accomplished banner and declared that "U.S. forces and their allies had been victorious in Iraq" had not yet climbed to more than 4,000 dead and 30,004 wounded. The American people had been struck by the loss of civil rights and habeus corpus; stunned at the Bush administration's declaration that the Geneva Conventions were now "quaint" and did not apply to anyone declared by Mr. Bush to be an "unlawful enemy combatant"; shocked by the evidence that U.S. military forces had mistreated, tortured, raped, and caused the deaths of detainees in their care; rocked by the rapes, murders, and suspicious deaths of Iraqi and U.S. military women by U.S. military men; shaken by the revelation that America had set up a system of secret prisons where it sent those declared "enemy combatants" to be tortured in order to force confessions and information from victims no valid court in a democracy would consider legal and uncoerced according to the standards set by international law.[31]

It is horror enough that officials of the Bush administration met in the

White House to decide on which methods of torture could, and would, be used on detainees declared by President George W. Bush to be "unlawful enemy combatants" and beyond the protections of the Geneva Conventions and standards set by international law; however, there is a special horror that accompanies the knowledge that U.S. military women who volunteered to serve in their country's armed forces have been raped and killed by U.S. military men and that the U.S. Army and Department of Defense have not only failed to stop the attacks, but have created an environment where rape, torture, sexual assault, and murder are no longer aberrations in a military that enables such a culture of lawlessness and misogyny to exist and thrive.

If you think that is an unreasonable statement, consider the fact that the DoD did not have a policy concerning sexual assault—or even a definition of sexual assault—until 2005. This, despite the fact that as early as 1992, women in Congress were calling on the military to address and punish military personnel guilty of rape and/or sexual assault. Rep. Carolyn Maloney of New York said, "Eighteen studies have been done in the past sixteen years, investigating the problem of sexual assault in the military," and yet the sexual assault of U.S. military women continues.[32]

Just as CAPT Kevin Donegan, skipper of the USS *Carl Vinson,* held each man serving in his ship accountable for sexual harassment and/or sexual assault and had a ship where such crimes were the exception, not the rule, every commanding officer in the U.S. Armed Forces has the power to stop such crimes in the populations of the military personnel under their command. Should those commanders need a nudge to do so, the Secretary of Defense has it in his power to order those officers to start enforcing the laws against such behaviors. And if the Secretary of Defense needed encouragement to have given such an order, the U.S. Congress and the commander in chief, President George W. Bush, could have given such an order from the top down. Failing this, the U.S. Congress has the authority and responsibility to hold the commander in chief, George W. Bush, responsible for dereliction of duty. It was not the *lack of authority* that prevented such orders but, rather, the *lack of will* in a lawless environment created and nourished by a president, White House officials, and a Congress that did not take such crimes seriously or did not know how serious the crimes were and did all they could to hide the damage until "their watch" was ended and the crimes became the problem of another president and another Congress.

21

⭐

Some scholars have noted that since the draft was abolished in 1973, the country has begun developing what could be called a warrior class or caste, often perpetuating itself from father or uncle to son or niece, whose political and cultural attitudes do not reflect the diversity found in civilian society—potentially foreshadowing a social schism between those who fight and those who ask them to.

> —David M. Halbfinger and Steve A. Holmes,
> "A Nation at War," *New York Times*
> 30 March 2003

Unfortunately for the American people, problems do not resolve themselves by ignoring, denying, hiding, or spinning them. If any one or combination of these methods could solve the problems facing the U.S. military or the assaults brought to bear on the Constitution and the Bill of Rights, the Bush administration would long ago have rendered the United States problem-free. Instead, the country stands in a vulnerable position, militarily and constitutionally. Americans are suffering from delusions of adequacy concerning the ability and readiness of our armed forces to meet our military commitments and to provide our men and women in the military with adequate and equitable military justice and the right to equal protection under the law.

This failure of our military and political leaders to provide a nonhostile and equitable environment for our military personnel is staggering. Female soldiers not only face an uphill battle in avoiding sexual assault, rape, and murder perpetrated on them by male soldiers and officers in their own units, they are punished by the military and the men with whom they serve for reporting the sexual predators who prey upon them. Sgt. Jennifer Hogg of Iraq Veterans Against the War put it very well when she said that "women in the military are regarded as second-class citizens, ripe for abuse." Hogg also pointed out that female soldiers in Iraq and

Afghanistan are put in a double bind when they are denied the training given to male soldiers in the infantry because of the rules that bar women from serving in the infantry, and yet are exposed to combat conditions every day. Women are assigned as gunners on Humvees, but serve without the combat infantry training provided to the men who serve beside them. It is staggering to realize that female soldiers go on assignments and are exposed to combat conditions on a daily basis, but denied the infantry training that would better prepare them for their military duties in Iraq and Afghanistan combat zones.[1]

In his book, *Wiser in Battle: A Soldier's Story,* Lt. Gen. Ricardo S. Sanchez, former senior military leader in Iraq, addresses the positions the Bush administration had placed the military in with its inadequate planning for Operation Iraqi Freedom, and the bad choices the White House made while micromanaging the Iraq War. When Lieutenant General Sanchez was removed from his command after the scandal of detainee abuse at Abu Ghraib and put in command of training the V Corps in Germany for deployment to Iraq, he was determined that these troops would be trained properly and fully for their deployment despite the fact that he would not deploy with them.[2]

Sanchez had inherited that job when Maj. Gen. John Batiste abruptly resigned from the U.S. Army because of his disgust with the Bush administration. Batiste was not happy with the administration since it had forced Gen. Eric Shinseki to retire in 2003 for bucking the Bush administration, and Secretary of Defense Donald Rumsfeld in particular, concerning the number of troops that would be needed to take and occupy Iraq. Rumsfeld was determined to take and occupy Iraq with a fraction of the number of troops General Shinseki told him he would need. (Major General Batiste later testified before the U.S. Congress concerning Rumsfeld's inadequate leadership and gross mishandling of the war.)

During training, it became even clearer to Sanchez that the wars in Iraq and Afghanistan had cost the army's combat proficiency training dearly. Combat troops were trained for specific missions rather than for high-intensity combat, which required many more skill sets. Sanchez made up his mind to make sure that none of the troops he was responsible for training would be deployed to Iraq or Afghanistan without successfully completing all required training in high-intensity fighting skills. Those skills were the soldiers' edge in winning battles and keeping themselves and their buddies alive.

During the summer of 2005, Sanchez was contacted by Maj. Gen. Doug Robinson, who had been placed in command of the First Armored Division, which Sanchez was training. Robinson told Sanchez that the division had received orders to deploy immediately to Iraq. Robinson went on to say that he realized the First Armored could not be certified as fully trained at that point, but if Sanchez would order the division to deploy, they could complete their training in Kuwait. Sanchez refused. He told Robinson that if the Bush administration wanted the division deployed before they completed their training, Robinson "would have to find a four-star general to order him in writing to do so." With this gauntlet thrown down, the division remained in Germany and completed their training *before* they were deployed to combat in Iraq.[3]

One of the big advantages Bush and his officials had going for them in selling the fear and the need for military action against Iraq was an American public who could not at that time conceive of their president and their government lying to them in order to build momentum for a preemptive war. Unfortunately, the words of Secretary of State Colin Powell in the United Nations, as he presented the "evidence" that Saddam Hussein had weapons of mass destruction and was an imminent danger to the security of the United States, were accepted totally by the majority of the American people, in part because this was one of the generals who had led U.S. and allied troops to victory in expelling Saddam and his army out of Kuwait and liberating the Kuwaiti people in the First Gulf War. In the eyes of most Americans, Gen. Colin Powell was a straight-talking American patriot who cared about his troops and would not send men and women into combat in Iraq without hard evidence that such a preemptive war was necessary.

Even when no weapons of mass destruction (WMD) were found in Iraq, there was an effort on the part of the administration to convince Americans that WMD would eventually be found. More than five bloody years later, WMD have not been found in Iraq. However, Iraq has been transformed into a training ground, a boot camp, for terrorists who poured across Iraq's unprotected borders—unprotected thanks to the insufficient number of American and Coalition troops to cut off the well-worn routes and stop the terrorists at the borders.

It must have been painful and infuriating for Lieutenant General Sanchez and other senior officers in the military to realize that invading Iraq would have to be one of the worst—*if not the worst*—decisions ever made by an American president and his administration. General Sanchez verbalized those feelings when he said, "None of it [Bush's stated reasons for invading Iraq] was true. Iraq had no links with al Qaeda. No nuclear weapons program and no stashes of chemical or biological weapons. I was on the ground in Iraq and I know. We never found anything."[4]

WMDs or not, U.S. and Coalition troops were in Iraq, and despite the declaration of Mission Accomplished, more and more U.S. and Coalition forces and innocent Iraqis were being wounded or killed with each passing week and more and more Americans were accepting the fact that they had been lied and fear mongered into an unnecessary war where American military men and women were not liberators, but rather an occupation force that was the target of Iraqi insurgents whose numbers grew larger with every passing week.

The Bush administration now had another problem—how to recruit enough volunteers to maintain troop levels in Iraq, while still fighting a war against Al-Qaeda in Afghanistan.

The U.S. Army and Marine Corps were already recruiting increasing numbers of men who had been charged with crimes that would have disqualified them from military service in America's previous wars. The military began offering sign-up bonuses for men and women who enlisted in the U.S. Army. Those bonuses were extremely enticing to the unemployed and young men and women who hoped they could earn enough GI benefits to attend college when their contracts had expired. The bonuses, an "economic draft" as they might rightly have been called, were helped along by the U.S. Army's lowering its enlistment and retention standards.

The military had entered a downward spiral, and, as it descended, it became more and more obvious that the very culture of service in the U.S. Army was changing, and not for the better. The recruits coming into basic training were younger, less educated, and predominately from blue-collar families, with little to offer to the private employment market. One sergeant confided that the new recruits were "mainly interested in what type of wire wheels they could buy once they could buy a car."

Since bonuses were not paid until a soldier had spent a required length of time in the service, money needed by recruits during basic training was often hard to come by. In addition, actually receiving the bonus the army offered frequently required much individual effort, and sometimes outside help, before the soldiers actually received the money. It was not unusual for older recruits to provide the money needed to buy cleaning supplies for the barracks. (No, you have not read that incorrectly. The army was requiring recruits to buy their own cleaning supplies to keep the barracks clean and ready for inspection.)

When the authors attended a graduation ceremony for recruits successfully completing basic training, they were surprised to find high school juniors in the ranks. The high school students were members of a delayed-entry program that put students who had completed their junior year of high school through basic training in the summer. The student would return to high school to complete his senior year and upon graduation would be accepted directly into the army. We are speaking here of seventeen-year-olds with little life experience to enable them to understand what they were committing to when they signed on to an army that would soon find itself at war.

As the war in Iraq escalated, the number of recruits decreased. To counter the downward turn, the army offered larger bonuses and increased the number of moral waivers it issued to would-be recruits. Along with the larger number of moral waivers, the army, which now needed troops desperately, relaxed traditional military discipline even further to keep the soldiers it had been able to attract.

In order to avoid the need for a draft as long as possible, the Bush administration activated the reserves and the National Guard. Men and women from their late thirties to early and mid-fifties were brought into the wars in Iraq and Afghanistan. Some retired military men and women expected the reserve and the guard to be used to "backfill" at military posts in the States while regular army troops did the combat tours in America's two wars. They were wrong. Reserve troops and the National Guard continued to deploy to both Iraq and Afghanistan.

In 2006, the new secretary of defense, Robert M. Gates, ordered that the tours of duty for army personnel be extended from twelve months to fifteen months and, in addition, issued Stop Loss orders to prevent individuals whose contracts with the army had been fulfilled from leaving military service. Stop Loss was, and is, equivalent to a backdoor draft, since it *forces* soldiers to remain in the army beyond their agreed-upon contracts.

In another effort to avoid reinstating the draft, the army began redeploying its troops for multiple tours in Iraq and Afghanistan. Soon the time at home between deployments was shortened, and army men and women were serving their third or fourth deployment to Iraq and Afghanistan. Between 2002 and May 2008, 58,000 U.S. Army men and women were forced to remain on active duty after they had fulfilled their contracts with the army.[5]

U.S. Army Maj. Priscilla Mondt, chaplain with the Eighty-second Airborne Division, described how soldiers felt about their unexpected changes in tours of duty: "They didn't like it; some were very angry. There was one guy who had retirement orders approved, and he was told to go to Iraq. Another guy with his retirement orders approved, I recommended that he escort a psychiatric case back [to the United States] because he was the senior guy, and once he got back to Fort Hood, he was allowed to retire. But they were just so mad. When you already can't figure out why you are there, and then you're told you have to do it longer, it is very difficult."[6]

Multiple redeployments of army men and women to Iraq increased by at least 50 percent the chance of these troops developing post-traumatic stress disorder (PTSD). Along with increasing numbers of returning and redeployed troops with symptoms of PTSD, and increasing numbers of wounded troops being discharged from the military, several unpleasant, callous, negligent, and illegal actions were visited on ill and wounded troops in Iraq and the United States; they also affected Iraq and Afghanistan veterans applying to the Department of Veterans Affairs for benefits for medical and psychological conditions that they acquired while serving in Operation Iraqi Freedom and Operation Enduring Freedom. The VA received so many requests for medical and psychological help that, by 2008, it had a backlog of 400,000 cases waiting to be evaluated for service-connected disabilities.[7]

Despite the long waits for appointments at VA medical centers, regional offices, and clinics, the Bush administration cut the funding to the Department of Veterans Affairs and refused to back a new GI Bill that would give veterans benefits similar to those provided to World War II veterans when they returned home. Not only did the Bush administration refuse to support the new GI Bill introduced by Senator Jim Webb, but, in addition, President George W. Bush threatened to veto the new GI Bill if it passed Congress and arrived on his desk for signature. This, from a president and an administration who labeled anyone who disagreed with their policies as "unpatriotic" and accused dissenters of not supporting U.S. troops.

While the VA had a backlog of 400,000 cases waiting for appointments, and Congress was trying to pass a new GI Bill, the U.S. Army was busy trying to get as many soldiers as possible to Afghanistan and Iraq, even if that meant going to despicable lengths to put "living bodies" in place in America's two combat zones.

On 10 February 2008, the article "Fort Carson Forcibly Removed Soldier from Mental Hospital and Deployed Him to Iraq War" appeared in the *Denver Post*. The Fort Carson soldier in treatment for bipolar disorder and alcohol abuse at Cedar Springs Hospital was released from the hospital at the insistence of the U.S. Army at Fort Carson and deployed to the Middle East with the Third Brigade Combat Team. After spending thirty-one days in Kuwait, the entry point for soldiers assigned to Iraq, the twenty-eight-year-old soldier was diagnosed as suffering from bipolar disorder, paranoia, and possible homicidal tendencies by the military mental health professionals at a Kuwait base.[8]

Upon further inquiry, the *Denver Post*'s reporter learned that the soldier had checked himself in to Cedar Springs Hospital during the second week of November after a failed suicide attempt while under the influence of alcohol. The soldier's treatment program was scheduled to continue until 10 December. On 29 November, the soldier's commanding officer appeared at the hospital and ordered the soldier to leave the hospital so that he could be deployed with his Third Combat Team to Operation Iraqi Freedom. This soldier had served in the army for three years and had already completed one tour in Iraq. The article went on to say that in late 2007, Fort Carson had sent seventy-nine soldiers who were medical "no-goes" to light duty in Iraq. In order to make sure that the twenty-eight-year-old soldier deployed with his team on 1 December 2007, he was placed under a special watch to make sure he did not desert before his deployment was in progress.[9]

Apparently the army was incapable of learning from its mistakes or was under such pressure from Washington to field "living bodies" for deployment to Iraq that it continued its deployment and redeployment practices despite the articles that appeared in the *Denver Post*. On 8 April 2008, another article appeared: "Deployed for Third Time with Both PTSD and TBI, a Fort Carson Soldier Died of Drug Overdose in Iraq." The article reported that Staff Sgt. Chad Barrett, thirty-five, was undergoing a medical evaluation for post-traumatic stress disorder and traumatic brain injury (TBI) resulting from his previous two deployments in Iraq. Staff Sergeant Barrett had already been assigned a "permanent profile," indicating that his diagnoses disqualified him for retention in the army. Supposedly, Barrett requested that the medical board evaluation be stopped in order that he could deploy with the Third Brigade Combat Team to Iraq. Clearly, if by any chance Barrett actually made such a request, the U.S. Army at Fort Carson was legally bound to stop his deployment.[10]

In Iraq on this third deployment, Barrett worked as a radio operator from 6:00 p.m. to 6:00 a.m. He was taking four prescribed medications: Klonopin for anxiety, Pamelor for severe migraines, and Lunesta and Ambien to help him sleep.[11]

Shelby Barrett, Chad Barrett's widow, reported the circumstances she had learned from military reports: Staff Sergeant Barrett was sent to Iraq and given an M-16, but was not allowed to have ammunition for the weapon. His military occupational specialty was gunner, but because of his medical condition, he was placed on night duty in the radio shack. Working at night interfered with his established medication schedule and isolated him from his fellow soldiers in the Third Brigade Combat Team. "There was no way in hell he should have been deployed. The army saw him as just another set of boots on the ground," Shelby Barrett said. "Three deployments is two too many. The army took my husband from me. The army destroyed my husband."[12]

On 8 April 2008, the Center for American Progress reported in an article, "Veterans' Mental Health by the Numbers," that the U.S. Army had listed 121 suicides in 2007. This was a 20 percent increase in the number of suicides since 2006. The army also listed 2,100 attempted suicides and self-inflicted injuries in 2007. This was an increase of 600 over the figure of 1,500 listed for 2006; and an increase of 1,600 over the figure of 500 listed for 2002.[13]

On 23 April 2008, an article in the McClatchy newspapers carried a story that reported that the Veterans Administration had lied about the number of veterans who have attempted suicide. The VA had reported that veteran suicide attempts in 2007 numbered fewer than 800, and an interoffice e-mail revealed that the numbers for that year had reached 12,000. Senator Patty Murray of Washington State stated that the VA's mental health programs were overwhelmed by the number of veterans from Iraq and Afghanistan seeking psychological help, while the VA simultaneously downplayed the facts to the American people and Congress.[14]

The existence of a memo written by Dr. Ira Katz, the chief of the VA's Mental Health Program, bore the title "Not for the CBS News Interview Request." The memo was addressed to Ev Chasen, director of the VA's Department of Communication. Its first line read "Shhh!" and went on to state that the VA's suicide prevention coordinators were reporting approximately 1,000 suicide attempts per month among the veterans the VA was currently treating in their facilities. The memo ended with the question, "Is this something we should (carefully) address ourselves in some sort of release before someone stumbles on it?"[15]

The Bush administration was successful in keeping the wars in Iraq and Afghanistan as far from public view as possible. The VA e-mail labeled "Shhh!" is simply the tip of the iceberg of the human cost of a war that affects fewer than 1 percent of Americans. The administration had ordered that no photos of the caskets of deceased military men and women be taken or displayed in the national media. Neither were photos to be taken of wounded troops disembarking from medical evacuation planes or hospital ships. The Bush administration did all it could to keep the realities of war and the American public separated from each other. Unfortunately, many Americans were doing more than they knew to help the government achieve that goal.

We Americans are a very fortunate people. We need only look at the conditions in which people live under totalitarian governments and in third world countries. When the Founding Fathers risked everything to give this nation the gift of a democratic republic, they knew that the cost of keeping that democratic republic and the rule of law, which is its life's blood, is eternal vigilance. In fact, the costly gift of freedom comes with an extremely high price—a price so high that no amount of money or influence could buy that gift or keep it from being taken from us.

The price the American people pay for the blessings of a democratic republic has always been, is, and will always be *eternal vigilance*. In the United States, one of the means we have always employed is to make sure we are on watch against anything and anyone that would tear our freedom from our hands, or even more stealthily take it from us so slowly that we will not feel it going, until it is gone. The former danger has always been easier to see, and easier to defend against. We have the world's most powerful military to protect us on this front, and they have a history of doing their job so well that the gift the Founding Fathers gave to this nation is still within our keeping.

The greater danger to our democratic republic is not from attempted theft but rather from complicit loss. It is much easier to recognize and defend against a foreign enemy than to remain vigilant enough to recognize and defend against those in our own country who would talk us into giving up the gift of freedom—our democratic republic and the rule of law that keeps it alive—either unknowingly, law by law, right by right, bit by bit, until we awaken and find that freedom is gone, or by handing it over law by law, right by right, to people or a government that promises us security and safety in return for our most precious gift.

Some of us may think that can never happen, yet history shows us that freedom has been surrendered exactly in that way in the past. What it took then, and what it would take now, is for a people to unknowingly relax vigilance for the more comfortable position of blind and uncritical trust in a great leader who demands only the unquestioning loyalty of the people he protects from all foreign enemies.

As if that were not enough, this leader will protect the American public, and individual privacy, by not allowing a free flow of information that might "confuse" and "worry" the public unnecessarily. In a way, one might say that this leader is wise enough to protect us from worry about things that are "not as bad as they look" or that are necessary sacrifices in order to keep our nation secure and us safe. What a deal! Freedom for free!

Or, if after some thought, we come to the conclusion that freedom is *not* free, we might consider creating a mandatory program of universal national service. It might offer us, men and women who are required to serve the nation for two years, the option of choosing military service or civilian service through government programs such as rebuilding the U.S. infrastructure, working in public health or with a government agency, etc. For those who choose the military, we might provide education benefits or guaranteed loans for a home or a business. The details could be worked out. Universal national service could also provide a window between the ages of eighteen and twenty-eight to fulfill the obligation. Universal national service could provide this country with something it has not had in almost forty years—the feeling that the country and the nation confer more than rights, that they confer *responsibility* and require *eternal vigilance*.

Universal national service just might be what our country needs to get citizens back to being "owners" of this nation and not just uninvolved "renters." Or, we, the people, can wait until a military draft is an absolute necessity. It's really up to us. However, the authors are convinced that the U.S. military of today, which depends on bonuses and low standards to attract its recruits, is not working well. It is, in fact, a danger to the continued existence of America, to the ability of our nation to restore the Constitution, the rule of law, and the balance of power to the three branches of our federal government so critically wounded and disfigured by two terms of an administration that ruled as a self-appointed monar-

Pfc. Patty Libengood, USMC, while serving in Iraq, August 2004–February 2005.

chy rather than led as the democratic republic this country has been since it was founded more than two hundred years ago.

Thomas Jefferson spoke words that need to be placed center stage in our nation's consciousness today, for they speak a basic truth, which, if ignored, neglected, surrendered, or stolen by force or stealth, places our nation and therefore our country on a road that will lead to loss of freedom and to dictatorship. Jefferson's insight must be engraved on the hearts and minds of an American people—an American electorate—that has been stampeded by lies, half-truths, callous and calculated spinning, into a state of fear that has turned American values upside down. Jefferson's words call us back to the sense and equilibrium that produced a "bright city on a hill" and "the Greatest Generation." Our nation still has the strength and the opportunity to find its way again—if only it hears and remembers Thomas Jefferson's voice: "If a nation expects to be ignorant and free . . . it expects what never was and never will be."

Hopefully, the American people will choose to accept the *responsibilities* that go along with the *rights* this nation bestows on its citizens and will realize that making a few personal sacrifices may just prevent our nation from losing everything.

ACKNOWLEDGMENTS

We want to thank our editor, Victoria Wilson, and her assistant, Carmen Johnson, for their encouragement and support. Thank you, as well, to production editor Victoria Pearson, whose patience we appreciated as we worked collaboratively toward publication.

We are most appreciative of the women and men who were kind enough to be interviewed and who generously gave their time and provided the information that was invaluable to writing this history.

We extend a special thank-you to Brig. Gen. Wilma Vaught and her staff at the Women in Military Service to America (WIMSA) for their continued encouragement and research assistance.

ABBREVIATIONS

AAA   Antiaircraft Artillery
AAF   Army Air Forces
ACLS   Advanced Cardiac Life Support
AFB   Air Force Base
AFHQ   Allied Forces Headquarters
AGF   Army Ground Forces
AH-1   Huey Cobra helicopter
AH-64   Apache helicopter
AMEDS   Army Medical Service
ANC   Army Nurse Corps
ASF   Army Service Forces
ATA   Air Transport Auxiliary (British)
AWS   Aircraft Warning System
BDU   Battle Dress Uniform
CA   Civil Affairs
CDR   Commander (Navy)
CH-53   Sea Stallion Sikorsky helicopter
CIA   Central Intelligence Agency
CID   Criminal Investigation Division
CO   Commanding Officer
DACOWITS   Defense Department Advisory Committee on Women in the Services
DEFCON   Defense Readiness Condition
DHHS   Department of Health and Human Services
DNA   Deoxyribonucleic acid
DoD   Department of Defense
E-3   Enlisted-Three pay grade
ETO   European Theater of Operations
ETUSA   European Theater of Operations United States Army
EX-O   Executive Officer
FTA   Field Training Activity
FWC   Fleet Weather Reconnaissance
GOP   Grand Old Party, the Republican Party
HIP   Russian-made Mi-8 Hip helicopter
HMMWV   Humvee
HSETC   (Naval) Health Science Education Training Command
HU-1   Huey helicopter
IBA   Initial Body Armor
ICU   Intensive Care Unit

ID   Identification
ID   Infantry Division
IED   Improvised Explosive Device
JAG   Judge Advocate General
LCDR   Lieutenant Commander (Navy)
LCPO   Lead Chief Petty Officer (Navy)
LCT   Landing Craft, Tank
LST   Landing Ship Tank
LTJG   Lieutenant Junior Grade (Navy)
MASH   Mobile Army Surgical Hospital
MEU   Marine Expeditionary Unit
MISLS Military Intelligence Service Language School
MOS   Military Occupation Specialty
MP   Military Police
MRE   Meals Ready to Eat
MTO   Mediterranean Theater of Operations
NAACP National Association for the Advancement of Colored People
NAS   Naval Air Station
NATO   North Atlantic Treaty Organization
NATRON8 Navy Air Transport Squadron 8
NCI   Navy Criminal Investigator
NCO   Noncommissioned Officer
NNC   Navy Nurse Corps
O-1   Naval ensign, army 2nd lieutenant
OCS   Officers Candidate School
OH-58 U.S. Army Kiowa Warrior helicopter
OEF   Operation Enduring Freedom
OIF   Operation Iraqi Freedom
PL   Public Law
PT   Physical Therapy
PT   Physical Training
RAF   Royal Air Force (British)
ROTC   Reserve Officer Training Corps
R&R   Rest and Recuperation
RET.   Retired
RSRS   Readjusted Service Rating System
SAC   Strategic Air Command
SAW   Squad Automatic Weapon; an M-249
SHAFE Supreme Headquarters Allied Forces Europe
SPARS U.S. Coast Guard Women's Reserve (contraction of the Coast Guard's motto
           Semper Paratus, Always Ready)
SWPA   South West Pacific Area
TDY   Temporary Duty
UH-1   Huey helicopter
UH-60 Black Hawk helicopter
UMCC   Unit Movement Control Center
USAF   United States Air Force
USAFF United States Army Forces Far East

USAID United States Agency for International Development
USC United States Code
USMCWR United States Marine Corps Women's Reserve
USN United States Navy
USNR United States Naval Reserve
USPHS United States Public Health Service
USSR Union of Soviet Socialist Republics
USUHS Uniformed Services University of the Health Sciences
VA Veterans Administration/Department of Veterans Affairs
VP Patrol Squadron (Navy)
WAAC Women's Army Auxiliary Corps
WAC Women's Army Corps
WAF Women's Air Force
WASP Women's Auxiliary Service Pilots
WAVES Women Accepted for Volunteer Emergency Service
WFTD Women's Ferry Training Detachment
WIMSA Women in Military Service to America
WPAC West Pacific

GLOSSARY

CAPTAIN'S MAST: A nonjudicial hearing or case review by the captain of a ship for the purpose of dismissing the case, meting out a punishment, or sending the case forward to a court-martial.

COURT-MARTIAL: A military court that is appointed by the commanding officer to try a military member for an offense against military law.

DROPPING: The military practice of "Drop and give me fifty push-ups."

FIFTY CAL.: .50-caliber machine gun.

FLIGHT: A military formation of three to six airplanes.

GIGGED: Given a military demerit.

GROUP: A unit of three squadrons.

HIGH-LINE: Transferring materials or people between two ships at sea by a series of ropes, pulleys, and a platform or seat.

LIBERTY: Naval term for permission given to an enlisted sailor to leave the ship for a short period of time such as overnight.

MADRASSA: An Islamic religious school.

RATE: The grade of a sailor.

RUCK OR RUCKSACK: Backpack/pack for carrying items.

SQUADRON: A military unit of three flights.

STOP LOSS: A military policy put into effect during Operation Iraqi Freedom/Operation Enduring Freedom in which military members who are within ninety days of deployment or who are currently deployed are prohibited from retiring or from leaving the army when their contracts are completed. National Guard and reservists are barred from leaving the service after their units have been alerted for mobilization.

TRIAGE: The process of initial sorting of patients or wounded to determine their needs and move them to appropriate medical intervention.

UNIFORMED SERVICES UNIVERSITY OF THE HEALTH SCIENCES (USUHS): The military university in which the students are active-duty officers of the U.S. Armed Forces who are being educated in dealing with wartime casualties, infectious diseases, disasters, and public health emergencies.

WING: A unit consisting of two groups.

NOTES

INTRODUCTION

1. David E. Jones, *Women Warriors* (Washington, D.C.: Brassey's, 2000), p. 15.

PROLOGUE

1. Michael Moss, "Fatally Exposed: Ambush in Falluja; Hard Look at Mission That Ended in Inferno for 3 Women," *New York Times,* 20 December 2005.

CHAPTER 1

1. Fredrick N. Rassmussen, "Last Female WWI Veteran Dies," *Baltimore Sun,* 29 March 2007, www.baltimoresun.com
2. "Christoffers Was a Daring Young Woman . . . ," *Franklin County (FL) News,* 24 January 1985, p. 10.
3. Rassmussen, "Last Female WWI Veteran Dies."
4. "WAVES Won't Go to Sea," *Springfield (MA) Sunday Union and Republican,* 13 September 1942.
5. Col. Robert Piemonte, ANC, USAR, *Highlights of the History of the Army Nurse Corps* (Washington, D.C.: U.S. Army Center of Military History, 1987), p. 7.
6. Ibid., p. 8.
7. Ibid., p. 9.
8. Ibid., p. 10.
9. Capt. Doris M. Sterner, USN (Ret.), *In and Out of Harm's Way: A History of the Navy Nurse Corps* (Seattle, WA: Peanut Butter Publishing, 1997), p. 19.
10. Ibid., p. 39.
11. "Woman's Suffrage Amendment Valid: Supreme Court, in a Unanimous Decision Read by Brandeis, Holds It Constitutional," *New York Times,* 28 February 1922.

CHAPTER 2

1. "Rogers' Election," *Time,* 13 July 1925, http://time.com/time/magazine/article/0,9171,720460,00.html
2. Mattie E. Treadwell, *U.S. Army in World War II: Special Studies, The Women's Army Corps* (Washington, D.C.: Office of the Chief of Military History, Dept. of the Army, 1954), p. 8.
3. "Woman's Hospital Unit for France," *New York Times,* 7 October 1917.
4. Treadwell, *U.S. Army in World War II,* p. 10.

5. Ibid., p. 12.
6. Ibid., p. 25.
7. Lt. Col. William E. Dyess, *The Dyess Story* (New York: G. P. Putnam's Sons, 1944), p. 47.
8. "Defense Crushed: Stimson Reveals Defeat Followed Failure to Get In More Food, Corregidor Is Held," *New York Times,* 10 April 1942, p. 1.
9. "Senate Sends Back New Bill for WAAC," *New York Times,* 26 April 1942.
10. Helen Cassiani Nestor, U.S. Army Nurse Corps Oral History Project, interviewed by Department of Defense, Washington, D.C., 9 April 1983, p. 11.
11. "Hobby's Army," *Time,* 17 January 1944, pp. 57–62; Oveta Culp Hobby, fact sheet, WAC Museum, Fort McClellan, Alabama, WWII files, 1990.
12. Maj. Gen Guy V. Henry, letter to Col. Mary L. M. Rasmuson, Director WAC, 20 January 1965, archives, WAC Museum, Fort McClellan, Alabama, WWII files.
13. Lynn Pyne, "Very First WAAC That Ever Wuz," *Phoenix News-Sun,* 20 May 1977, p. 9.
14. Billie Davis Voigt, letter to authors, 7 September 1992, authors' archives, Atlanta, Georgia.
15. Stella D. Therault, questionnaire, 1989, authors' archives, Atlanta, Georgia.
16. Brig. Gen. Elizabeth Hoisington, AUS (Ret.), interview and questionnaire, 1989, authors' archives, Atlanta, Georgia.
17. Vicky Chiboucas Sarandis, interview and questionnaire, 1989, authors' archives, Atlanta, Georgia.
18. Ibid.
19. Bettie J. Morden, interview and questionnaire, September 1989, authors' archives, Atlanta, Georgia.
20. Maj. Gen. Jeanne Holm, USAF (Ret.), interview, 14 November 2004, Washington, D.C., authors' archives, Atlanta, Georgia.
21. Ibid.
22. Billie Davis Voigt, letter to authors, 24 October 1992, authors' archives, Atlanta, Georgia.
23. Mary Ellen Rogers Grayson, questionnaire, 1989, authors' archives, Atlanta, Georgia.
24. Kathleen Branson, questionnaire, 1989, authors' archives, Atlanta, Georgia.
25. Treadwell, *U.S. Army in World War II,* p. 77.
26. Ammora Kelledy Koetting, questionnaire, 1989, authors' archives, Atlanta, Georgia.
27. Gwendolyn Clymer Niemi, interview and questionnaire, 11 August 1989, authors' archives, Atlanta, Georgia.
28. Rena Lampman Anderson, questionnaire, 1989, authors' archives, Atlanta, Georgia.
29. Lynn Ashley, Ph.D., interview with authors, 18 January 2007, Atlanta, Georgia.

CHAPTER 3

1. CAPT Joy Bright Hancock, USN (Ret.), *Lady in the Navy, A Personal Reminiscence* (Annapolis: Naval Institute Press, 1972), pp. 50–51.
2. Virginia Crocheron Gildersleeve, *Many a Good Crusade* (New York: Macmillan, 1954), p. 267.
3. Hancock, *Lady in the Navy,* p. 54.
4. Ibid., p. 55.
5. Ibid.

6. "Ad Brings Story of 3 Women in Marines in 1918," *New York Herald Tribune,* 13 February 1943.

7. "Senate Approves Women for Navy," *New York Times,* 3 July 1942.

8. "Woman Navy Corps Blocked in House," *New York Times,* 6 July 1942.

9. "Hits Lipstick in Navy," *New York Times,* 7 July 1942.

10. Hancock, *Lady in the Navy,* p. 56.

11. Ibid.

12. "Hits Lipstick in Navy."

13. "House Completes Women's Navy Bill," *New York Times,* 22 July 1942.

14. Ibid.

15. "Women's Navy Bill Signed by Roosevelt," *Montgomery (AL) Journal and Times,* 31 July 1942.

16. "Smith College Chosen as Training Place for Women's Naval Auxiliary," *Daily Hampshire Gazette,* 31 July 1942.

17. "Dr. McAfee Able Leader with Sense of Humor," *New York Herald Tribune,* 4 August 1942.

18. "Wellesley President Slated for Women's Naval Reserve," *Christian Science Monitor,* 31 July 1942.

19. "Dr. Meta Glass, Educator, Dead," *New York Times,* 22 March 1967.

20. "Smith College Chosen as Training Place."

21. "Mainbocher Adds Waves to Clients," *New York Times,* 15 August 1942.

22. "You'll Be Wearing," *New York Times,* 10 January 1943.

23. "Director Says 'WAVES' to Wear Enough Make-up to Be Human," *Trenton (NJ) Gazette,* 4 August 1942.

24. WAVES National, *Navy Women, A Pictorial History 1908–1988* (n.p., April 1990), pp. 126–27.

25. Elinore Johnson Folk, questionnaire, 1989, authors' archives, Atlanta, Georgia.

26. Bergstrom Brugger, questionnaire, 1989, authors' archives, Atlanta, Georgia.

27. Joyce Courtney Rode, questionnaire, 1989, authors' archives, Atlanta, Georgia.

28. "Women's World," *Pathfinder,* 27 February 1943.

29. "Marines to Enlist 19,000 Women Aides," *New York Times,* 13 February 1943.

30. "Marines Proud Its Women Aides Lack Nickname," *New York Herald Tribune,* 21 February 1943.

31. "Marine Reserve Swears in First 14 Women Here," *New York Herald Tribune,* 20 February 1943.

32. "Lady Marine," *Daily Hampshire Gazette,* February 1943.

33. Martha Jane Williams Hylton, questionnaire, 1989, authors' archives, Atlanta, Georgia.

34. Mary G. Simons Winters, questionnaire, 1989, authors' archives, Atlanta, Georgia.

35. Dorothy Adams White Pifer, questionnaire, 1989, authors' archives, Atlanta, Georgia.

36. Josette Dermody Wingo, *Mother Was a Gunner's Mate: World War II in the WAVES* (Annapolis: Naval Institute Press, 2000), p. 15.

37. Elizabeth Hundley Clark, questionnaire, 1989, authors' archives, Atlanta, Georgia.

38. "The Most Rewarding Work," *New York Times,* 15 August 1943.

39. Ibid.

40. "U.S. Nurses Escape Hit Hospital Ship," *New York Times,* 28 September 1943; Evelyn M. Monahan and Rosemary Neidel-Greenlee, *And If I Perish: Frontline U.S. Army Nurses in World War II* (New York: Alfred A. Knopf, 2003), p. 261.

41. Theresa Karas Yianilos, *Woman Marine* (La Jolla, CA: La Jolla Book Publishing Company, 1994), p. 31.
42. Virginia Shepherd Alred, questionnaire, 1989, authors' archives, Atlanta, Georgia.
43. Barbara Johnson Owens, questionnaire, 1989, authors' archives, Atlanta, Georgia.
44. Alice Julian Herman, questionnaire, 1989, authors' archives, Atlanta, Georgia.
45. Betty Margaret Rickord Farrell, questionnaire, 1989, authors' archives, Atlanta, Georgia.

CHAPTER 4

1. Captain Alene Dresmal, "Girls Showed Courage as Torpedo Hit Ship, Writes Captain Alene, a WAAC," article from WAC Museum, Fort McClellan, Alabama, WWII file, 1990.
2. Georgia B. Watson, *World War II in a Khaki Skirt* (Moore Haven, FL: Rainbow Books/Betty Wright, 1985), pp. 29–43.
3. Charity Adams Early, *One Woman's Army: A Black Officer Remembers the WAC* (College Station: Texas A&M Press, 1989), pp. 15–16.
4. Ibid., pp. 18–20.
5. Ibid., p. 62.
6. Ibid.
7. Ibid., p. 63.
8. Mattie E. Treadwell, *U.S. Army in World War II: Special Studies, The Women's Army Corps* (Washington, D.C.: Office of the Chief of Military History, Dept. of the Army, 1954), p. 106.
9. Ibid., p. 118.
10. Ibid., p. 119.
11. Ibid., p. 120.
12. Evelyn M. Monahan and Rosemary Neidel-Greenlee, *And If I Perish: Frontline U.S. Army Nurses in World War II* (New York: Alfred A. Knopf, 2003), p. 77.
13. Ibid., p. 83.
14. Gertrude Margarite Bertram, questionnaire, 1989, authors' archives, Atlanta, Georgia.

CHAPTER 5

1. Dorothy Louise Nims Klutz, letter, 27 May 1989, authors' archives, Atlanta, Georgia.
2. "First WAVE Ensign Goes to Navy Yard," *New York Times,* 16 February 1943.
3. "First Lady Hails Women in Service," *New York Times,* 20 February 1943.
4. Mabel Duncan O'Neill, questionnaire, September 1989, authors' archives, Atlanta, Georgia.
5. "WAVES Show Skill with Gas Masks: Drills at Northampton Produce Plenty of Tears as They Uncover in Shack," *New York Times,* 10 March 1943.
6. "Seven Women Doctors Await Navy's Call When Commissioning Bill Is Signed," *New York Times,* 14 April 1943.
7. "WAVES Too Delicate to Witness War," *Christian Science Monitor,* 24 April 1943.
8. Margaret A. Hightower Griffin, questionnaire, 1989, authors' archives, Atlanta, Georgia.

9. Jean K. Deckman Snow, questionnaire, September 1989, authors' archives, Atlanta, Georgia.

10. Ibid.

11. Betty McCartney Dore, questionnaire, 26 August 1989, authors' archives, Atlanta, Georgia.

12. "Mme. Chiang Visits School for Waves," *New York Times,* 10 June 1943.

13. "Walsh Opposes WAVES Overseas," *New York Times,* 16 June 1943.

14. "Knox Plans to Use Waves 'Anywhere;' He Says He Will Ask Congress to Permit Services Abroad at the Points of Need," *New York Times,* 28 July 1943.

15. "WAVES Cut a Cake on First Birthday," *New York Times,* 2 August 1943.

16. Mary C. Lyne and Kay Arthur, *Three Years Behind the Mast: The Story of the United States Coast Guard SPARS* (n.p.; n.d.), p. 115.

17. Ibid., 115–17.

18. Ibid.

19. Theresa Karas Yianilos, *Woman Marine: A Memoir of a Woman Who Joined the U.S. Marine Corps in World War II to "Free a Marine to Fight"* (La Jolla: La Jolla Book Publishing Company, 1994), p. 116.

20. Mary V. Stremlow, "Free a Man to Fight: Women Marines in World War II," p. 27. http://www.nps.gov/rchive/wapa/indepth/extContent/usmc/pcn-190-003129-00/sec5.htm.

21. Ibid., 4.

22. Ibid.

23. Yianilos, *Woman Marine,* 226.

24. "Major Hurst to Command Women Marines, Arrives," *Hampshire Gazette,* 12 March 1943.

25. "New Marine Recruiting Station Opened in Times Square," *New York Times,* 8 August 1943.

26. Alice H. Bennett, questionnaire, 1989, authors' archives, Atlanta, Georgia.

27. Vera Cooper Sullivan, questionnaire, 3 October 1989, authors' archives, Atlanta, Georgia.

28. Katherine M. McIntyre Foley, questionnaire, 11 August 1989, authors' archives, Atlanta, Georgia.

29. "October Draft of Fathers Held to Non-War Workers," *New York Times,* 20 October 1943.

CHAPTER 6

1. Mattie E. Treadwell, *U.S. Army in World War II: Special Studies, The Women's Army Corps* (Washington, D.C.: Office of the Chief of Military History, Dept. of the Army, 1954), p. 192.

2. "Green Denounces War Service Bill," *New York Times,* 18 March 1943; "Draft for Women? National War Service Bill Fails to Win Endorsement of Women in Congress," *New York Times,* 30 April 1943.

3. Treadwell, *U.S. Army in World War II,* p. 199.

4. Ibid., p. 200.

5. Ibid., p. 203.

6. Ibid.

7. Ibid., p. 204.

8. Ibid., p. 205.
9. Ibid.
10. "Supplemental Report on Rumors," War Department, Armed Service Forces Report, Public Relations Branch, 9 July 1943, National Archives, Washington, D.C., RG 160, pp. 1–3.
11. Treadwell, *U.S. Army in World War II*, p. 176.
12. Ibid., p. 177.
13. Charlotte E. Hertle, questionnaire, September 1989, authors' archives, Atlanta, Georgia.
14. Treadwell, *U.S. Army in World War II*, p. 179.
15. "5,000,000 Workers McNutt's 1943 Goal," *New York Times,* 26 April 1943.
16. Laura Branton Bamford, letter to authors, January 23, 2007; Hannah Moore Branton, interview, 1998, authors' archives, Atlanta, Georgia.
17. Lynn Ashley, Ph.D., interview, January, 18, 2007, authors' archives, Atlanta, Georgia.
18. "Our Manpower Mobilized: Figures for the Armed Forces, the Farms and the Industries of the Country," *New York Times,* 11 July 1943.
19. Ibid.
20. "WAC Lacks 85,000 in Reaching Goal Set for Enlistments," *Radio Digest,* 28 July 1943.
21. Ibid.
22. "Women Must Take Million More Jobs," *New York Times,* 3 September 1943.

CHAPTER 7

1. Leslie Haynsworth and David Toomey, *Amelia Earhart's Daughters: The Wild and Glorious Story of American Women Aviators from World War II to the Dawn of the Space Age* (New York: William Morrow, 1998), p. 30.
2. "American Women to Ferry Planes," *New York Times,* 24 January 1942.
3. Haynsworth and Toomey, *Amelia Earhart's Daughters,* p. 30.
4. "Women Will Form a Ferry Command," *New York Times,* 11 September 1942. On 9 March 1942 the U.S. Army reorganized, and the Army Air Forces was established under the command of Lt. Gen. Henry H. Arnold. Mary H. Williams, *U.S. Army in World War II, Chronology 1941–1945* (Washington, D.C.: Center for Military History, United States Army, 1994), p. 28.
5. "Women Air Force Service Pilots Killed in Service," part 1, p. 3, http://www.wwii-womenpilots.org./wasp-kia/38kia.html.
6. Edna H. Bishop, questionnaire, September 1989, authors' archives, Atlanta, Georgia.
7. Haynesworth and Toomey, *Amelia Earhart's Daughters,* pp. 74–75.
8. "Women Airforce Service Pilots Killed in Service," p. 3.
9. Marjorie M. Gray, questionnaire, August 25, 1990, authors' archives, Atlanta, Georgia.
10. Ibid.
11. Dorothy Eppstein, questionnaire, 1989, authors' archives, Atlanta, Georgia.
12. Lizbeth Ann Morgan Hazzard, questionnaire, 17 November 1989, authors' archives, Atlanta, Georgia.
13. Doris Brinker Tanner, letter to authors, authors' archives, Atlanta, Georgia.
14. "Women Air Force Service Pilots Killed in Service," pp. 4–5.
15. Haynesworth and Toomey, *Amelia Earhart's Daughters,* p. 129.
16. "Women Air Force Service Pilots Killed in Service," p. 6.

17. Elizabeth M. Lewis, letter to authors, 19 September 1989, authors' archives, Atlanta, Georgia.
18. "American Merchant Mariners Struggle for Veteran Status," www.usmm.org/struggle vetstatus.html.
19. Elizabeth M. Lewis, questionnaire, 19 September 1989, authors' archives, Atlanta, Georgia; "Young Woman Tells of Wreck of Sailing Ship Off Carolina," *Norfolk Virginian Pilot*, 30 November 1942.
20. Lewis, questionnaire.

CHAPTER 8

1. Mattie E. Treadwell, *U.S. Army in World War II: Special Studies, The Women's Army Corps* (Washington, D.C.: Office of the Chief of Military History, Dept. of the Army, 1954), p. 221.
2. Ruth Cohen, "WACs, Deportment Commendable, Report Declares," *Houston Post*, 11 July 1943.
3. Ibid.
4. Jeanne Davis Nixon, questionnaire, 24 July 1989, authors' archives, Atlanta, Georgia.
5. Ibid.
6. Martha "Marty" McQuan, questionnaire, 1989, authors' archives, Atlanta, Georgia.
7. Sara W. Meenson, questionnaire, 1990, authors' archives, Atlanta, Georgia.
8. Anna M. Palmares, questionnaire, 1989, authors' archives, Atlanta, Georgia.
9. Ibid.
10. Rita Geibel, interview, 27 July 1989, authors' archives, Atlanta, Georgia.
11. Ibid.
12. Ibid.
13. Ibid.
14. Ibid.
15. Katherine "Kitty" Huling, questionnaire, August 1989, authors' archives, Atlanta, Georgia.
16. Geibel interview.
17. "Summary of Investigation of Conditions in the Third WAC Training Center, Fort Oglethorpe, Georgia," U.S. War Department, Office of the Inspector General, Washington, D.C., 29 July 1944, National Archives, Washington, D.C., RG 158.8, 333.9, Fort Oglethorpe Investigation, Exhibit A, 1.
18. Ibid.
19. "Consultation Request and Report," Memorandum WDSIG-333.9, 3d WAC Training Center, Ft. Oglethorpe, GA, Subject: Investigation of conditions in the 3d WAC Training Center, Fort Oglethorpe, GA, 29 July 1944, Exhibit A, Incl. 1, 2.
20. "Plasma Alone Not Sufficient," *New York Times,* 23 August 1943.
21. "Summary of Investigation of Conditions," 30.
22. Elizabeth Petrarca Natzke, interview, 16 June 1989, authors' archives, Atlanta, Georgia.
23. Ibid.
24. "World Pistol Marks to Quantico Marines," *New York Times,* 4 September 1944.
25. Kathryn Pribram, interview, 12 June 1989, authors' archives, Atlanta, Georgia.
26. Natzke interview.
27. Ibid.

28. Julia Harris Isaac, questionnaire, 1989, authors' archives, Atlanta, Georgia.
29. Natzke interview.
30. Treadwell, *U.S. Army in World War II,* pp. 433–35.
31. Ibid., pp. 437–38.

CHAPTER 9

1. Dorothy L. Starbuck, interview, March 1989, authors' archives, Atlanta, Georgia.
2. Ibid.
3. Mary Ellen Graydon Rogers, questionnaire and correspondence, 30 August 1989, authors' archives, Atlanta, Georgia.
4. Ibid.
5. Ibid.
6. Ibid.
7. Frances Lillo Walt O'Shea, questionnaire and interview, July 1989.
8. Frances Lillo Walt O'Shea, unpublished essay.
9. Ibid. and O'Shea interview and questionnaire.
10. Betty Magnuson, questionnaire and correspondence, 10 July 1989, authors' archives, Atlanta, Georgia.
11. Starbuck interview.
12. Mildred Glendenning, questionnaire and correspondence, August–September 1989, authors' archives, Atlanta, Georgia.
13. Capt. Anne Grey, USN (Ret.), interview, 13 June 1989, authors' archives, Atlanta, Georgia.
14. Ibid.
15. "Solving the Enigma—History of the Cryptoanalytic Bomb," www.msa.gov/publications/publi00016.cform.
16. Ibid.
17. Ibid.
18. Ibid.
19. Col. Margaret E. Bailey, ANC (Ret.), *The Challenge, Autobiography of Colonel Margaret E. Bailey* (Lisle, IL: Tucker Publications, 1999), p. 25; Col. Margaret Bailey, ANC (Ret.), interview, 14 November 2004, Washington, D.C., authors' archives, Atlanta, Georgia.
20. Charity Adams Early, *One Woman's Army, A Black Officer Remembers the WAC* (College Station: Texas A&M University Press, 1989).
21. Gurthalee Clark, questionnaire and correspondence, July 1989, authors' archives, Atlanta, Georgia.
22. Margaret F. Barbour, questionnaire and correspondence, June 1989, authors' archives, Atlanta, Georgia.
23. Alice McKoy Ishmael, questionnaire, June 1989, authors' archives, Atlanta, Georgia.
24. Ibid.
25. Georgia Reynolds, questionnaire and correspondence, July 1992, authors' archives, Atlanta, Georgia.
26. Ibid.
27. Beatrice Rivers Gallagher, questionnaire, 6 October 1989, authors' archives, Atlanta, Georgia; Emory A. Massman, *Hospital Ships of World War II* (Jefferson, NC: McFarland & Company, 1999), p. 307.

28. Ruth Lewis Reynolds, questionnaire and correspondence, 10 October 1989, authors' archives, Atlanta, Georgia.

29. Bella Abramowitz Fisher, questionnaire and correspondence, interview, 7 October 1989, authors' archives, Atlanta, Georgia.

30. Gerald W. Thomas, *Suicide Tactics: The Kamikaze During World War II,* p. 10. www.airgroup4.com./kamikaze.htm.

31. Ruth Blanton Chaney, questionnaire and correspondence, 28 September 1989, authors' archives, Atlanta, Georgia.

32. "Paris Celebrates in Carnival Spirit," *New York Times,* 8 May 1945.

33. Starbuck, interview.

34. "War News Summarized," *New York Times,* 7 May 1945; "Churchill to Talk to Empire Today," *New York Times,* 8 May 1945.

35. "Wounded Direct Glance to Pacific," *New York Times,* 8 May 1945.

36. "Germany Surrenders, Wild Crowds Greet News in City While Others Pray," *New York Times,* 8 May 1945.

CHAPTER 10

1. *WAVES Newsletter,* NAVPERS, Washington, D.C., July 1945, p. 4.

2. *WAVES Newsletter,* NAVPERS, Washington, D.C., August 1945, p. 8.

3. Lillie Peterson Homuth, interview with authors, September 2000, Florence, Kentucky, authors' archives, Atlanta, Georgia; Evelyn M. Monahan and Rosemary Neidel-Greenlee, *And If I Perish* (New York: Alfred A. Knopf, 2003), p. 454.

4. "General's Burial," *Time,* 20 August 1945.

5. "End of Okinawa," *Time,* 2 July 1945.

6. "How Effective Is 2%?" *Time,* 16 July 1945.

7. "Army Wide Critical Scores Set for Release of Officers," War Department, Bureau of Public Relations, Washington, D.C., dated 6 September 1945.

8. "War Department Demobilization Plan," War Department, Bureau of Public Relations, Press Branch, Washington, D.C., 2 August 1945.

9. "Discharge Policy for Women in Service Whose Husbands Return from Overseas," War Department, Bureau of Public Relations, Press Branch, 26 June 1945.

10. Maj. Gen. Jeanne Holm, USAF (Ret.), interview, 14 November 2004, Washington, D.C., authors' archives, Atlanta, Georgia.

11. Mattie E. Treadwell, *U.S. Army in World War II: Special Studies, The Women's Army Corps* (Washington, D.C.: Office of the Chief of Military History, Dept. of the Army, 1954), pp. 404–9.

12. "Post-War Education Plans of WAC Enlisted Personnel," Summary, 6 July 1945, Information and Education Division, Report No. B-158.

13. Jane S. Wilson and Charlotte Serber, eds., *Standing by and Making Do: Women of Wartime Los Alamos* (Los Alamos, NM: Los Alamos Historical Society, 1988), p. 24.

14. Ibid., p. 62.

15. Iris Bell, *Los Alamos WAAC/WACs: World War II 1943–1946* (Sarasota, FL: Coastal Printing, 1993), pp. 20–21.

16. Ibid., p. 21.

17. Vera Lindsey McDaniel, questionnaire, September 1989, authors' archives, Atlanta, Georgia.

18. F. G. Gosling, *The Manhattan Project: The Making of the Atomic Bomb* (Washington, D.C.: U.S. Department of Energy, October 2001), p. 50.

19. Grace E. Gosnell, ANC, questionnaire, 1989, authors' archives, Atlanta, Georgia.
20. Evelyn M. Monahan and Rosemary Neidel-Greenlee, *All This Hell: U.S. Nurses Imprisoned by the Japanese* (Lexington: University Press of Kentucky, 2000), pp. 136–37.
21. Gosnell questionnaire.

CHAPTER 11

1. Yaiye Furutani Herman, interview, 14 June 1989, authors' archives, Atlanta, Georgia.
2. Ibid.
3. Ibid.
4. Ibid.
5. Joseph Gollomb, "Japanese Black Dragons—Our Truly Hellish Arch Enemy," *San Antonio Light,* 11 January 1942, pp. 13–15.
6. "An Invasion of U.S. Termed Tokyo Aim," *New York Times,* 12 January 1942.
7. "'Black Dragon' Acts Shown on Coast," *New York Times,* 1 April 1942; "Indictment Names 'Black Dragon' Ilk," *New York Times,* 28 January 1943.
8. "Toyama of Japan Terrorist Leader," *New York Times,* 6 October 1944.
9. "Araki and Kuzuu Put in Tokyo Jail," *New York Times,* 23 November 1945.
10. "Women Again Appeal Veterans Preference," *New York Times,* 8 February 1945.
11. "Special College Routine for Women War Veterans," *New York Times,* 3 June 1945.
12. "Aid for Women Veterans—Club Federation Offers Help and Counsel in Finding Jobs," *New York Times,* 24 September 1945.
13. Betty J. Morden, *The Women's Army Corps, 1945–1978* (Washington, D.C.: Center of Military History, U.S. Army 1990), p. 30.
14. Ibid.
15. "Bradley Asks Best for Disabled Men," *New York Times,* 21 October 1945.
16. "Most of the Girls Are Glad to Be Out," *Christian Science Monitor,* November 1945.
17. Frances A. Miernicke Plenert, interview, July 2001, authors' archives, Atlanta, Georgia.
18. "The Girls Come Home," *Evening Bulletin,* 8 November 1945.
19. "Changes Women Veterans Need to Make," *Glamour,* January 1946.
20. "Crowded Colleges Reject Veterans: Hundreds Turned Away Daily in City, Legion Post Finds, O'Dwyer Plans Study," *New York Times,* 31 December 1945.
21. Benjamin Fine, "Colleges Warned Not to Bar Women," *New York Times,* 8 May 1946.
22. "Girls Study Rights Debate on Forum: Asking Them to Stay Away from College to Aid Veterans Is Defended and Decried," *New York Times,* 22 May 1945.
23. Ibid.
24. "The Woman Veteran," Research Service Office of Coordination and Planning, Veterans Administration, Washington, D.C., 31 August 1946.

CHAPTER 12

1. *The WAVES Newsletter,* NAVPERS, Washington, D.C., January 1946, p. 2.
2. Col. Mary V. Stremlow, USMCR, *A History of the Women Marines, 1946–1977* (Washington, D.C.: History and Museums Division Headquarters, U.S. Marine Corps, 1986), p. 15.
3. Ibid.
4. "Women Ex-Marines Meet: 200 Celebrate 4th Anniversary of Formation of Unit," *New York Times,* 14 February 1947.

5. House of Representatives Subcommittee No. 9, Committee on Armed Services, Eightieth Congress, First Session; Col. Mary T. Sarnecky, ANC, *A History of the U.S. Army Nurse Corps* (Philadelphia: University of Pennsylvania Press, 1999), p. 291.

6. Bettie J. Morden, *The Women's Army Corps, 1945–1978* (Washington, D.C.: Center of Military History, U.S. Army, 1990), p. 46.

7. Ibid.

8. Maj. Gen. Jeanne Holm, *Women in the Military: An Unfinished Revolution* (Novato, CA: Presidio Press, 1982), pp. 114–15.

9. Morden, *The Women's Army Corps, 1945–1978*, p. 48.

10. Ibid., p. 50.

11. Ibid.

12. Ibid., pp. 51–52.

13. Margaret Chase Smith, *Congressional Record*, 23 March 1948, 7338; Morden, *The Women's Army Corps, 1945–1978*, p. 52.

14. Morden, *The Women's Army Corps, 1945–1978*, p. 53.

15. "Congress Prodded on Military Bill," *New York Times,* 29 March 1948.

16. Morden, *The Women's Army Corps, 1945–1978*, p. 53.

17. Ibid.

18. "Women in Military Service Now Have Regular Status," *New York Times,* 27 June 1948.

19. *Women in the Military: Where They Stand,* 5th ed. (Washington, D.C.: Women's Research and Education Institution, 2005), p. 4.

20. Jeanne Holm, interview, 16 November 2004, Washington, D.C., authors' archives, Atlanta, Georgia.

21. Ibid.

22. Ibid.

23. Ibid.

24. Ibid.

25. "First Wave Officer in Europe Has Duty with Berlin Airlift," *Naval Aviation News,* November 1949; "Back Home, 2nd Tour Here for Wave CDR," *The Carrier* 20, no. 9 (7 March 1958), Naval Air Station, Alameda, CA.

26. CDR Margaret Carver Smith McGroarty, USN (Ret.), questionnaire, 23 October 1989, authors' archives, Atlanta, Georgia.

CHAPTER 13

1. Lt. Col. Carolyn M. Feller, ANC, USAR, and Maj. Constance J. Moore, ANC, eds., *Highlights in the History of the Army Nurse Corps* (Washington, D.C.: U.S. Army Center of Military History, 1996), p. 23.

2. Ibid., p. 23; Don Lawson, *The United States in the Korean War* (New York: Abelard Schuman, 1964), pp. 25–26.

3. Betty J. Morden, *The Women's Army Corps, 1945–1978* (Washington, D.C.: Center of Military History, U.S. Army, 1990), pp. 97–99.

4. Mattie E. Treadwell, *U.S. Army in World War II: Special Studies, The Women's Army Corps* (Washington, D.C.: Office of the Chief of Military History, Dept. of the Army, 1954), p. 93.

5. "Army Issues Call for 1,644 Women," *New York Times,* 26 September 1950.

6. Martha J. Briley, questionnaire, September 1989, authors' archives, Atlanta, Georgia.

7. Ruth Marschall, letter to authors, 14 August 1989, authors' archives, Atlanta, Georgia.
8. Marie L. D'Elia, questionnaire and letter to authors, 7 September 1989; "Veterans Council Presents Awards for Service, Heroism," *Daily Local News* (West Chester, PA), 9 February 1989, authors' archives, Atlanta, Georgia.
9. LCDR Ruth Margaret Sullivan, USNR (Ret.), questionnaire and letter to authors, 23 October 1989, authors' archives, Atlanta, Georgia.
10. Margaret Driscoll, 1989 questionnaire, authors' archives, Atlanta, Georgia.
11. Morden, *The Women's Army Corps, 1945–1978,* p. 97.
12. Winifred "Parky" Parker Ralston, questionnaire and letter, 23 August 1989, authors' archives, Atlanta, Georgia.
13. Sgt. Haruo Sasaki, AUS, Testimony, Report of Aircraft Accident, 6 October 1950, USAF Haneda Air Base, Japan.
14. Sgt. Haruo Sasaki, AUS, Inclusion #12, Report of Aircraft Accident, 6 October 1950, USAF Haneda Air Base, Japan.
15. LCDR Bobbie Hovis, NC, USN (Ret.), "Korean War Flight Nurse," *Navy Medicine,* January–February 2001, p. 19.
16. CAPT Doris Sterner, NC, USN (Ret.), *In and Out of Harm's Way* (Seattle, WA: Peanut Butter Publishing, 1997), p. 234; Emory A. Massman, *Hospital Ships of World War II* (Jefferson, NC: McFarland & Company, 1999), pp. 431–32.
17. Sterner, *In and Out of Harm's Way,* p. 232.
18. Ibid., p. 233.
19. Ibid., pp. 233–34.
20. Hovis, "Korean War Flight Nurse," p. 20.
21. Brig. Gen. Anna Mae McCabe Hays, ANC (Ret.), interview, 16 November 2004, Arlington, Virginia, authors' archives, Atlanta, Georgia.
22. Ibid.
23. Capt. Katherine Jump, ANC, chief nurse, Fourth Field Hospital, interview, 12 April 1986, Alexandria, Virginia, WIMSA, Oral History Project, Arlington, Virginia.
24. U.S. Army Air Forces Report of Major Accident, No. 9-26-8, 27 October 1950, Ashiya Air Base APO 75, U.S. Army Air Forces.
25. Col. Margaret Gibson Duckworth, ANC, AUSR (Ret.), interview, 25 July 2006, Austell, Georgia, authors' archives, Atlanta, Georgia.
26. Ibid.
27. Ibid.
28. Ibid.
29. Ibid.
30. Ibid.
31. Ibid.
32. Hovis, "Korean War Flight Nurse," pp. 22–23.
33. Public Law 51, Eighty-second U.S. Congress, First Session; Morden, *The Women's Army Corps, 1945–1978,* p. 100.
34. "Committee Clears Anna M. Rosenberg," *New York Times,* 15 December 1950.
35. RADM Frances Shea Buckley, interview, 15 March 2007, authors' archives, Atlanta, Georgia.
36. Ibid.
37. Ibid.
38. Ibid.
39. Morden, *The Women's Army Corps, 1945–1978,* p. 72.

40. Linda Witt, Judith Bella Faire, Britta Granrud, and Mary Jo Binker, *"A Defense Weapon Known to Be of Value: Servicewomen of the Korean War Era* (Hanover and London: University Press of New England, 2005), pp. 249–251; Maj. Gen. Jeanne Holm, *Women in the Military: An Unfinished Revolution* (Novato, CA: Presidio Press, 1982), p. 157.

CHAPTER 14

1. Col. Mary V. Stremlow, *A History of the Women Marines, 1946–1977* (Washington, D.C.: History and Museums Division, Headquarters, U.S. Marine Corps, 1986), p. 68.
2. Ibid., p. 62; Betty J. Morden, *The Women's Army Corps, 1945–1978* (Washington, D.C.: Center of Military History, U.S. Army, 1990), p. 134; Jean Ebbert and Marie-Beth Hall, *Crossed Currents, Navy Women from WWI to Tailhook* (New York: Brassey's, 1993), pp. 133, 135.
3. "Fort for Women Is Pastel-Tinted: Corps of 8,200 in Army Now Have Own Modern Center, Fort McClellan, Alabama," *New York Times,* 5 June 1955.
4. Brig. Gen. Anna Mae McCabe Hays, interview by Dr. John F. McHugh, Lehigh County Historical Society Oral History Program, 27 December 1990, pp. 16–18.
5. Ibid., 19–20.
6. Ibid.
7. "The First WAVE Ice Observer?" *Kodiak (Alaska) Mirror,* 1 December 1961.
8. Anne Bartlett, "Aspiring Astronauts," *Atlanta Journal Constitution,* 6 July 2003, p. C-4.
9. Ibid.
10. Leslie Haynsworth and David Toomey, *Amelia Earhart's Daughters: The Wild and Glorious Story of American Women Aviators from World War II to the Dawn of the Space Age* (New York: William Morrow, 1998), pp. 236–37.
11. John A. Neidel, interview, 15 March 2008, authors' archives, Atlanta, Georgia.
12. Carl Lockett, interview, 18 March 2008, authors' archives, Atlanta, Georgia.
13. Patrick R. Joslyn interview, 25 August 2009, authors' archives, Atlanta, Georgia; Neidel interview.
14. John F. Kennedy, "Cuban Missile Crisis Address," October 1962, americanrhetoric.com, p. 22.
15. Ibid.
16. Cabell Phillips, "Kennedy Cancels Campaign Talks," *New York Times,* 23 October 1962.
17. Jack Raymond, "Vessels Spotted," *New York Times,* 24 October 1962; Morden, *The Women's Army Corps, 1945–1978,* p. 189; Jack Raymond, "Navy Boards a Freighter, Lets Her Continue to Cuba," *New York Times,* 27 October 1962.
18. Jack Raymond, "Airmen Called Up," *New York Times,* 28 October 1962; Morden, *The Women's Army Corps, 1945–1978,* p. 189.
19. Max Frankel, "U.S. Finds Bases in Cuba Stripped, Missiles on Ships," *New York Times,* 9 November 1962.
20. Marge Hepler Turo, interview, 26 October 2007, authors' archives, Atlanta, Georgia.
21. Ibid.
22. Ibid.
23. Sheila Sutton Woosley, interview, 6 October 2006, authors' archives, Atlanta, Georgia.
24. Ibid.
25. "Coup and Riot Liven Saigon Life for WACs," *New York Times,* 1 February, 1965.

26. RADM Frances Shea Buckley, USN (Ret.), interview, 15 March 2007, authors' archives, Atlanta, Georgia.
27. Ibid.
28. Ibid.
29. Ibid.
30. Gen. Connie Slewitzke, ANC (Ret.), interview, 14 November 2004, Arlington, Virginia, authors' archives, Atlanta, Georgia.
31. Ibid.
32. Elizabeth Davis Mitchell, interview, 8 March 2007, Atlanta, Georgia, authors' archives, Atlanta, Georgia.
33. Ibid.
34. Ibid.

CHAPTER 15

1. Gen. Mildred Bailey, interview, 16 November 2004, Arlington, Virginia, authors' archives, Atlanta, Georgia.
2. Brig. Gen. Anna Mae Hays, ANC (Ret.), interview, 16 November 2004, Arlington, Virginia, authors' archives, Atlanta, Georgia.
3. Lt. Col. Aida Nancy Sanchez, AMSC, AUS (Ret.), interviewed by Kate Scott at WIMSA, Oral History Project, Arlington, Virginia, 29 June 2004, pp. 2–3.
4. Ibid., p. 4.
5. Ibid., p. 7.
6. Ibid., p. 10.
7. Ibid., p. 12.
8. Ibid., p. 13.
9. Ibid.
10. Ibid.
11. Ibid.
12. Ibid., p. 14.
13. Ibid.
14. Ibid., p. 15.
15. Ibid., p. 19.
16. Ibid., p. 20.
17. "Faye Abdellah First Woman to Reach Top Public Health Service Rank," *HEW Newsletter,* 16 December 1974, p. 3.
18. RADM Faye Abdellah, USPHS (Ret.), interview, 17 November 2004, Annandale, Virginia, authors' archives, Atlanta, Georgia.
19. Ibid.
20. Ibid.
21. Ibid.
22. Ibid.
23. Karen I. O'Connor, interview, 18 April 2006, Atlanta, Georgia, authors' archives, Atlanta, Georgia.
24. Ibid.
25. Ibid.
26. Ibid.
27. Ibid.

28. Ibid.
29. Ibid.
30. Ibid.
31. Ibid.

CHAPTER 16

1. RADM Frances Shea Buckley, USN (Ret.), interview, 15 March 2007, Atlanta, Georgia, authors' archives, Atlanta, Georgia.
2. Ibid.
3. Ibid.
4. Ibid.
5. Ibid.
6. Ibid.
7. Ibid.
8. Bernard Weinraub, "Debate over Volunteer Military Fueled by Registration Proposals," *New York Times,* 10 June 1979.
9. Ibid.
10. *Rostker v. Goldberg,* 453 U.S. 57 (1981).
11. James Feron, "First Battle Over, Women Leave Academies for Careers in Military," *New York Times,* 25 May 1980.
12. James Webb, "Jim Webb: Women Can't Fight," *Washingtonian,* November 1979.
13. Ibid., p. 1.
14. Ibid., p. 2.
15. Ibid.
16. Evelyn M. Monahan and Rosemary Neidel-Greenlee, *All This Hell: U.S. Nurses Imprisoned by the Japanese* (Lexington: University Press of Kentucky, 2000).
17. Evelyn M. Monahan, Rosemary Neidel-Greenlee, and Agnes Jensen Mangerich, *Albanian Escape: The True Story of U.S. Army Nurses Behind Enemy Lines* (Lexington: University Press of Kentucky, 1999).
18. Webb, "Jim Webb: Women Can't Fight," p. 2.
19. Rick Maze, "Webb Confident 1-to-1 Dwell Time Plan Will Pass," *Army Times,* 24 September 2007, p. 26.
20. Webb, "Jim Webb: Women Can't Fight."
21. Defenselink Casualty Report 2008, Department of Defense, www.defenselink.mil/news/casualty.pdf, 31 May 2008.
22. Margaret C. Harwell, et al., *Assessing the Assignment Policy for Army Women* (Arlington, VA: RAND National Defense Research Institute, 2007).
23. Webb, "Jim Webb: Women Can't Fight," pp. 4–5, 9.
24. Ibid., pp. 4–5.
25. Ibid., p. 12.
26. Yvonne Morris, interview, 1 August 2006, authors' archives, Atlanta, Georgia.
27. David K. Stumpf, *Titan II: A History of a Cold War Missile Program* (Fayetteville: University of Arkansas Press, 2000), p. 32.
28. Ibid., pp. 215–51; Morris interview.
29. Morris interview.
30. Ibid.
31. Ibid.

32. Ibid.
33. Ibid.
34. Brig. Gen. Connie Slewitzke, ANC, AUS (Ret.), interview, 14 November 2004, Arlington, Virginia, authors' archives, Atlanta, GA; oral histories of some of the POW navy nurses are included the archives of the Navy Medical Department, Washington, D.C.
35. Larry Carney, "Women Asked to Return to Reopened MOSs," *Army Times,* 28 November 1983.
36. "Grenada Collective Action: A Quick Reference Aid on U.S. Foreign Relations," *GIST,* Bureau of Public Affairs, U.S. Department of State, Washington, D.C., January 1984.
37. "Army Women Upset over Non-combat Role in Grenada Invasion," *Stars and Stripes* (European Edition), 14 December 1983.
38. "Women GIs in Grenada," *Houston Post,* 8 December 1983.
39. CAPT Doris M. Sterner, NC, USN (Ret.), *In and Out of Harm's Way: A History of the Navy Nurse Corps* (Seattle, WA: Peanut Butter Publishing, 1997); Buckley interview, 15 March 2007.
40. Brig. Gen. Dorothy B. Pockington, AUS (Ret.), ed., *Heritage of Leadership: Army Nurse Corps Biographies* (Ellicott City, MD: ALDOT Publishing House, 2004), pp. 97–101.
41. "Admiral Grace Murray Hopper: Pioneer Computer Scientist," San Diego Super Computer Center, n.d., www.sdsc.edu/ScienceWomen/hopper.html.
42. "Amazing Grace: The Unforgettable Grace Hopper," *A Different Point of View: Newsletter of the National Women's History Museum* 9, no. 2 (Spring 2007).
43. LTJG Tracy Owens, USN, interview, 17 October 2006, Atlanta, Georgia, authors' archives, Atlanta, Georgia.
44. Ibid.
45. Ibid.
46. Ibid.
47. Michael R. Gordon, "Noriega's Surrender: Army; for First Time, a Woman Leads GIs in Combat." *New York Times,* 4 January 1990.
48. Anna Quindlen, "Public and Private; March Forward," *New York Times,* 7 January 1990.
49. Philip Shabecoff, "The U.S. and Panama: Combat; Report of Woman's Role Is Called into Question," *New York Times,* 8 January 1990.
50. Ibid.
51. Ibid.; John M. Broder, "Female's War Exploits Overblown, Army Says; Panama: No Enemy Soldiers Were Killed, and the Firefight Lasted Only 10 Minutes, Officials Disclose," *Los Angeles Times,* 6 January 1990.
52. Marlene Cimons, "Women in Combat: Panama Stirs Debate," *Los Angeles Times,* 11 January 1990.
53. Ibid.
54. Ibid.
55. Ibid.
56. Ibid.

CHAPTER 17

1. CAPT Jane Hartley, USCG (Ret.), interview, 20 June 2007, Atlanta, Georgia, authors' archives, Atlanta, Georgia.

2. Ibid.

3. Ibid.

4. Ibid.

5. Ibid.

6. Ibid.

7. Lt. Col. Nanette Gallant, USA, Eighty-second Airborne, interview, 21 January 2005, by Kate Scott, Fort Bragg, North Carolina, WIMSA, Oral History Project, Arlington, Virginia.

8. Ibid., pp. 6–7.

9. Ibid., p. 3.

10. Ibid.

11. Maj. Priscilla Mondt, USAR (Ret.), interview, 14 May 2007, Atlanta, Georgia, authors' archives, Atlanta, Georgia.

12. Ibid.

13. Ibid.

14. Ibid.

15. Ibid.

16. Col. Patricia Wilson, USAF (Ret.), interview, 18 April 2006, Atlanta, Georgia, authors' archives, Atlanta, Georgia.

17. Ibid.

18. Ibid.

19. Ibid.

20. Ibid.

21. Ibid.

22. Ibid.

23. Ibid.

24. Ibid.

25. Ibid.

26. Ibid.

27. Drew Jubera, "America's Women of War," *Atlanta Journal Constitution,* 27 May 1991.

28. Laura B. Randolph, "The Untold Story of Black Women in the Gulf War," *Ebony,* September 1991.

29. Ibid.

30. Ibid.

31. Michael R. Gordon, "Panel Is Against Letting Women Fly in Combat," *New York Times,* 4 November 1992.

32. Ibid.

33. Ibid.

34. LTJG Tracy Owens, USN, interview, 17 October 2006, Atlanta, Georgia, authors' archives, Atlanta, Georgia.

35. Deborah K. Davis, MD, interview, 14 August 2006, Atlanta, Georgia, authors' archives, Atlanta, Georgia.

36. Ibid.

37. Ibid.

38. Ibid.

39. Ibid.

40. Ibid.

41. Ibid.

42. Ibid.

452   Notes

43. "Role of Women in the Military Is Again Bringing Debate," *New York Times,* 29 December 1996.

44. Brig. Gen. Wilma Vaught, USAF (Ret.), interview, 16 November 2004, Arlington, Virginia, authors' archives, Atlanta, Georgia.

CHAPTER 18

1. RADM Faye Abdellah, USPHS (Ret.), interview, 17 November 2004, Annandale, Virginia, authors' archives, Atlanta, Georgia.

2. Ibid.

3. Maj. Lorie Brown, USA, "Chief Nurse Describes 9/11 Response," interview, 27 September 2001, Office of Medical History, Office of the U.S. Army Surgeon General, http://history.amedd.army.mil/booksdocs/opnoblegle/.

4. Col. Jonathan C. Fruendt, MD, USA, "Doctor Describes 9/11 Response," 25 September 2001, Office of Medical History, Office of the U.S. Army Surgeon General, http://history.amedd.army.mil/booksdocs/opnoblegle/.

5. LCDR Tracy Bilski, MC, USN, interview by Judy Bellafaire, 13 April 2006, WIMSA, Oral History Project, Arlington, Virginia, p. 12.

6. "President Bush Announces Major Combat Operations in Iraq Have Ended," http://www.cnnnews.com, 1 May 2003.

7. Master Gunnery Sergeant Rosemarie Weber, USMC, Oral History Transcript, interview by Kate Scott and Lee Ann Ghajar, 27 January 2006, WIMSA, Oral Hisory Project, Arlington, Virginia, pp. 10–11.

8. Ibid, p. 11.

9. Ibid., pp. 11–12.

10. Ibid.

11. Ibid., p. 15.

12. Ibid., pp. 20–21

13. Ibid., p. 23.

14. Ibid., pp. 23–24.

15. Ibid., p. 25.

CHAPTER 19

1. Patricia Libengood Dean, questionnaire, 16 March 2006, authors' archives, Atlanta, Georgia.

2. Ibid.

3. Thomas E. Ricks, "Rumsfeld Gets Earful from Troops," *Washington Post,* 9 December 2004.

4. Monica Davey, "For 1,000 Troops, There Is No Going Home," *New York Times,* 9 September 2004.

5. Sgt. Connie Rose Spinks, USAR, interview by Kate Scott, WIMSA Oral History Project, 26 January 2006, Arlington, Virginia, p. 3.

6. Ibid.

7. Ibid., p. 4.

8. Ibid., pp. 4, 8.

9. Ibid., p. 6.

10. Ibid.

11. Ibid., p. 7.

12. James Webb, "Jim Webb: Women Can't Fight," *Washingtonian,* November 1979.
13. Spinks, interview.
14. Ibid, p. 8.
15. Ibid.
16. Ibid.
17. Ibid, pp. 8–9.
18. Ibid., p. 9.
19. Ibid., p. 10.
20. Ibid., p. 11.
21. Ibid.
22. LCDR Colleen Glaser-Allen, USN, interview, 2 September 2006, Atlanta, Georgia, authors' archives, Atlanta, Georgia.
23. Ibid.
24. Ibid.
25. Ibid.
26. Ibid.
27. Ibid.
28. Ibid.
29. Col. Carolyn Carroll, AUS, interview, 11 April 2007, Atlanta, Georgia, authors' archives, Atlanta, Georgia.
30. Ibid.
31. Ibid.
32. Ibid.
33. Ibid.
34. Ibid.
35. Ibid.
36. Ibid.

CHAPTER 20

1. Seymour Hersh, "The General's Report: How Antonio M. Taguba Who Investigated the Abu Ghraib Scandal Became One of Its Casualties," *New Yorker,* 25 June 2007.
2. "Limbaugh Substitute Host: Rush Was Right on Prison Abuse—'This is like college; this is like fraternities,' " *Media Matters for America,* 18 May 2004, http://mediamatters.org/items/200405180001; "Limbaugh Returned to Downplaying Abu Ghraib Prisoner Abuse as 'Hazing' and 'An Out-of-Control Fraternity Prank,' " *Media Matters for America,* 31 August 2004, http://mediamatters.org/items/200408310002.
3. Hersh, "The General's Report."
4. Ibid.
5. David S. Cloud and Kirk Semple, "Ex-GI Held in 4 Slayings and Rape in Iraq," *New York Times,* 4 July 2006.
6. Gregg Zoroya, "Soldier Describes Anguish in Revealing Murder Allegations," *USA Today,* 13 September 2006.
7. Robert F. Worth and Carolyn Marshall, "GI Crime Photos May Be Evidence," *New York Times,* 5 August 2006; Sandy Leon Vest, "A War over Nothing," *Marin County's News Monthly,* September 2006.
8. "U.S. Army Increases Use of Moral Waivers to Meet Demand for Troops," Guardian.co.uk, 21 April 2008.
9. Jonathan Finer and Joshua Partlow, "Four More GIs Charged with Rape, Murder,

Fifth Soldier in Iraq Accused of Dereliction of Duty for Failing to Report Incident," *Washington Post,* 10 July 2006.

10. Zoroya, "Soldier Describes Anguish in Revealing Murder Allegations."

11. Vicky Taylor, "Spielman Being Held in the U.S: Summary of the Mahmudiya Massacre," *Chambersburg Public Opinion* and *USA Today,* 13 September 2006; James Dao, "Ex-Soldier Gets Life Sentence for Iraq Murders," *New York Times,* 22 May 2009.

12. Lt. Gen. Ricardo Sanchez with Donald T. Phillips, *Wiser in Battle: A Soldier's Story* (New York: HarperCollins e-books, Kindle Edition, 6314-176340-44, 2008).

13. Betty Ann Bower, "Rape in the Ranks," Online NewsHour, PBS News, www.pbs.org/newshour/bb/military/jan-june04/bab_04-26.html, 26 April 2004.

14. "Task Force Report on Care for Victims of Sexual Assault, Overview Briefing, May 13, 2004," U.S. Department of Defense report, http://www.dod/gov/reports.

15. Ann Wright, "Editorial Column: Sexual Assault in Military: A DoD Cover-Up?" http://www.veteransforcommonsense.org/ArticleID/10821, 4 August 2008; "Sexual Assault in Military 'Jaw Dropping,' Lawmaker Says," *CNN,* 4 August 2008, http://www.veteransforcommonsense.org/ArticleID/10817.

16. Lt. Gen. Claudia J. Kennedy, AUS (Ret.), *Generally Speaking: A Memoir by the First Woman Promoted to Three-Star General in the United States Army* (New York: Warner Books, 2001); Maj. Gen. Jeanne Holm, USAF (Ret.), *Women in the Military: An Unfinished Revolution* (Novato, CA: Presidio Press, 1982); Col. Carolyn Carroll, AUS, interview, 11 April 2007, Atlanta, Georgia, authors' archives, Atlanta, Georgia; Maj. Priscilla Mondt, USAR (Ret.), interview, 14 May 2007, Atlanta, Georgia, authors' archives, Atlanta, Georgia; CAPT John Miller, USNR (Ret.), interview, 26 February 2006, Scottsdale, Arizona, authors' archives, Atlanta, Georgia.

17. Jessica Pupovac, "Silenced in the Barracks," *In These Times,* 3 March 2008; "Sexual Assaults Up 40% in 2005," *Army Times,* 27 March 2005.

18. "Declaration on the Elimination of Violence Against Women," *News Center,* 13 July 2006.

19. Marjorie Cohn, "The Fear That Kills," www.alternet.org, 31 January 2006.

20. Ibid.

21. CAPT John Miller, interview.

22. Ann Wright, "Is There an Army Cover-Up of Rape and Murder of Women Soldiers?" *Common Dreams News Center,* 28 April 2008; Daniel R. Brown, "Family Lays to Rest Pvt. LaVena Johnson," *St. Louis American,* 27 July 2005.

23. Ibid.

24. Ibid.

25. Ibid.

26. Ibid.; "USA Pfc. Tina M. Priest," www.nooniefortin.com, 1 March 2006.

27. Wright, "Is There an Army Cover-Up of Rape and Murder of Women Soldiers?"

28. Ibid; Kasey Jones, "Fort Hood–Based Soldier 'Loved People, and They Knew It,' " Associated Press, *Temple Daily Telegram,* Temple, Texas, 21 March 2006.

29. Ibid.

30. Evelyn M. Monahan and Rosemary Neidel-Greenlee, *All This Hell: U.S. Nurses Imprisoned by the Japanese* (Lexington: University Press of Kentucky, 2000).

31. "DoD Personnel and Procurement Statistics," U.S. Department of Defense, 2003 to 2008; "Casualties in Iraq: U.S. Military Deaths in Bush's Iraq Quagmire," http://www.ac.wwu.edu/~stepan/USfatalities.html.

32. Jane McHugh, "Congresswomen Urge Punishment for Sexual Assaults," *Army Times,* 12 April 2004.

CHAPTER 21

1. Nancy Van Ness, " 'Dykes, Whores or Bitches': One in Three Military Women Experience Sexual Abuse," http://www.alternet.org/story/85099/.
2. Lt. Gen. Ricardo Sanchez with Donald T. Phillips, *Wiser in Battle: A Soldier's Story* (New York: HarperCollins e-books, Kindle Edition, 6314-176340-44, 2008), Part IV, p. 23.
3. Ibid.
4. Ibid.
5. Julian E. Barnes, "U.S. Army's 'Stop-Loss' Orders up Dramatically over Last Year," *Los Angeles Times,* 9 May 2008.
6. Capt. Priscilla Mondt, USAR (Ret.), interview, 14 May 2007, Atlanta, Georgia, authors' archives, Atlanta, Georgia.
7. Paul Sullivan, executive director, Veterans for Common Sense, "February 4, 2008: VCS Testimony—President Bush Slashes VA Spending as VA Expects 333,000 New Iraq and Afghanistan War Veteran Patients to Flood into VA Hospitals," http://www.veteransforcommonsense.org, 7 February 2008.
8. Erin Emery, "Fort Carson Forcibly Removed Soldier from Mental Hospital and Deployed Him to Iraq War," *Denver Post,* 10 February 2008.
9. Ibid.
10. Erin Emery, "Deployed for Third Time with Both PTSD and TBI, a Fort Carson Soldier Died of Drug Overdose in Iraq," *Denver Post,* 8 April 2008.
11. Ibid.
12. Ibid.
13. "Veterans' Mental Health by the Numbers," Center for American Progress, www.veteransforcommonsense.org, 8 April 2008.
14. Les Blumenthal, "Senator: VA Lying About Number of Veteran Suicides," McClatchy Newspapers, 23 April 2008.
15. Ibid.

INDEX

Page numbers in *italics* refer to illustrations.

ALSO BY EVELYN M. MONAHAN AND ROSEMARY NEIDEL-GREENLEE

AND IF I PERISH

In World War II, 59,000 women voluntarily risked their lives for their country as U.S. Army nurses. When the war began, some of them had so little idea of what to expect that they packed party dresses. The reality of service quickly caught up with them, whether they waded through the water on the historic landings on North African and Normandy beaches, or worked around the clock in hospital tents on the Italian front as bombs fell all around them. For more than half a century these women's experiences remained untold, almost without reference in books, historical societies, or military archives. After years of research and hundreds of hours of interviews, Evelyn M. Monahan and Rosemary Neidel-Greenlee have created a dramatic narrative that at last brings to light the critical role that women played throughout the war. From the North African and Italian campaigns to the liberation of France and the conquest of Germany, U.S. Army nurses rose to the demands of war on the frontlines with grit, humor and great heroism. A long overdue work of history, *And If I Perish* is also a powerful tribute to these women and their inspiring legacy.

History/Women's Studies/978-1-4000-3129-0

ANCHOR BOOKS
Available at your local bookstore, or visit
www.randomhouse.com